SUMMONED TO JERUSALEM

Books by Joan Dash

SUMMONED TO JERUSALEM:
The Life of Henrietta Szold

A LIFE OF ONE'S OWN:
Three Gifted Women and the Men They Married

SUMMONED TO

JERUSALEM

The Life of Henrietta Szold

By JOAN DASH

Wipf and Stock Publishers
EUGENE, OREGON

Grateful acknowledgment is made to Hadassah, The Women's Zionist Organization of America, Inc., for photographs 1, 2, 3, 4, 6, 7, 8, 10, 11, 19, 20, 21, 22, 23, 26, 27, 28, and 29.

Grateful acknowledgment is made to the Zionist Archives and Library for photographs 9, 13, 14, 15, 16, 17, 18, and 25.

Keren Hayesod, Jerusalem, is the source of photograph 24. Photograph 5 is reproduced with the kind permission of Eli Ginzberg.

Portions of this work originally appeared in *Hadassah Magazine*.

Wipf and Stock Publishers
199 West 8th Avenue, Suite 3
Eugene, Oregon 97401

Summoned to Jerusalem
The Life of Henrietta Szold
By Dash, Joan and
Copyright©1979 by Dash, Joan
ISBN: 9781592443055
Print date: 7/28/2003
Previously published by Harper & Row, Publishers, 1979

to my father
Samuel Zeiger
of blessed memory

Contents

Illustrations follow pages 116 and 244.

Acknowledgments

I am indebted to a great many individuals and institutions here and in Israel both for research material and for help in making use of it: to the staff of the Central Zionist Archives, Jerusalem, especially Michael Heymann, their director, with whom I had several illuminating conversations on Zionist history, and Rachel Ever-Hadani, who supervises the Henrietta Szold Archive; to the staff of the Zionist Archives and Library, New York; the Jewish Collection of the New York Public Library; the Seattle Public Library; the staff of Suzallo Library, University of Washington, particularly the resourceful Tom Bolling; the library of the Jewish Theological Seminary, New York; the Archives of the American Jewish Joint Distribution Committee, under the direction of Rose Klepfisz, and finally Hadassah, who were cordial and helpful from start to finish of this long project. Their files and archives were invaluable, as was the cooperation of Selma Zack.

I am most grateful to Marie Syrkin for a critical reading of the manuscript and important insights into Zionist history, as well as her encouragement at several stages; to Michael Heymann for finding the time to read and comment so perceptively on the manuscript; to Judith Epstein of Hadassah, who read and patiently analyzed the manuscript with me by mail and telephone; to Dr. George Allison for a discussion of the psychoanalytic implications of Miss Szold's childhood; to Laureen Nussbaum and Marianne Klein for translation from German; to Sue Nessel and Ora Ashdit for research in New York and Jerusalem respectively; to Leila Charbonneau for editorial help; to Patricia Myrer of McIntosh and Otis for early encouragement of the book and loyal support throughout; to Ann Harris of Harper & Row for the sympathetic, patient and wonderfully discerning editing that helped me thread my way through masses of material when they seemed to have lost their shape, and to my husband for believing it was possible that I might do a creditable job.

People who have allowed me to interview them or have shared their recollections of Miss Szold through letters include: Eva Stern-Michaelis, who brought the drama of Youth Aliyah vividly to life; Dr. Michael Bluestone, who recreated Palestine in the mid-twenties; Alexandra Lee Levin, a candid, charming and hospitable informant, and Emma Ehrlich, who was never too busy to talk about Miss Szold.

Also: Raymond Rubinow, Sarah K. Stein, Rose Halprin, Recha Freier, Shalhevet Freier, Hanan Schechter, Rabbi and Mrs. Mordecai Kaplan, Alexander Dushkin, Sylva Gelber, Reuben and Bathsheba Katznelson, Dr. Helena Kagan, Jonathan and Chava Magnes, Shulamit Cantor, Rebecca Shwarz, Dr. Arieh Feigenbaum, Ilse Bickart, Lotte Steigbügl, Lotte Beyth, Zena Herman, Leah Becker, Moshe Medzini, Chanoch Rinott (Hanoch Reinhold), Carl Frankenstein, Zipporah Bloch, Robert and Zip Szold, Mrs. Friedrich Ollendorff, Arieh Lifshutz, Yehuda Yaari, Edwin Samuel, Irma Lindheim, Marian Greenberg, Tamar de Sola Pool, Chaim Japhet, Adele Ginzberg, Eli Ginzberg, Sarah Levin Cooper, Rabbi Arthur Lagawier, Franz Ollendorff, Sara and Benjamin Levin, Margaret Doniger, Marlin Levin, Max Cohen, Jacob Tsur, Ernst Simon, Jastrow Levin and many others.

SUMMONED TO JERUSALEM

Prologue

February 1943: a crowded railway station in Haifa, Palestine. Classes of school-children with their teachers, workingmen in heavy boots, British soldiers, rabbis, journalists and photographers wait for a train to pull in. They have been expecting it for months. All through a winter of death and anguish the Jews of Palestine have waited for this train.

There are wildflowers on the hillsides now and the children on the platform carry great bouquets of them. Others have chocolates or fruit; among the crowd is a sprinkling of Arabs holding sacks of oranges. Everyone strains to catch sight of the train, and when they see it they see that the windows have been flung open so that hundreds of little hands wave blue-and-white flags in the sunlight. The train is packed with Jewish children who have been traveling since the fall of Poland in 1939. Palestine is their journey's end.

In front of the crowd and somewhat apart from it stands a delegation with an official appearance headed by an old woman. Past eighty, not quite five feet tall, she carries a large purse by the straps and seems unaffected by the almost hysterical expectation that surrounds her.

The train comes to a halt in the station, the doors open and children swarm out. Dark-haired, dark-eyed, sallow-skinned, dressed in clothes that are new but ill-fitting, they are too small for their clothes, almost too small for their own bones. Little boys wear military sweaters and big pith helmets given them by British soldiers in India, their hair beneath the helmets cropped so short it must have been shaved. Older children carry infants on their backs. Girls of fourteen and fifteen clutch the hands of younger ones as if to prevent their being wrenched away. The people on the platform, a few at first, then dozens, then almost everyone, begin to sing "Hatikvah"—"The Hope"—the Zionist anthem.

Someone shouts out the name of a town in Poland. Others follow with other towns. Some of the children shout back. The two groups surge toward

1

each other. A father sees a son he had believed to be dead. A girl on the platform recognizes a boy who lived next door to her in Poland and asks after his parents but he breaks into wild sobs and cannot answer.

A man has walked off the train to stand before the old woman and grasp her hand. He is her colleague and partner, who went to Suez to escort the children home. He introduces her to several of the *madrichim*, the youth leaders who cared for the children during part of their wanderings. This is Miss Szold, he says; everyone already knows the name.

In the midst of the introductions Miss Szold examines the faces of the children. She has a tightness in her chest, the start of some respiratory ailment she will ignore as long as possible because the fate of these hundreds of children must be settled. Their journey is ended, yes, but their future will be shaped by bitter political rivalries. Telegrams from all over the world have been flying at her telling her what side to take. From within the country rabbis and politicians and the leaders of workingmen's delegations pelt her with advice, requests, commands. Beneath the apparent calm she is taut and apprehensive. She dislikes being told what to do and wants no advice from America, South Africa or Palestine.

She sees also that the children are not what she had expected. That they would be bone thin, undersized, covered with scars and sores from having lived like animals in the Russian forests, Miss Szold knew beforehand. What she was not prepared for are their faces, in which she can find no trace of childhood—no mischief, no laughter, only cold suspicion. How will she deal with such children?

There is the pile of telegrams on her desk; there are a half dozen men with whom she must somehow work although she does not trust them or the political parties they represent; there is the pain in her chest—and now this: children who are unlike any she has ever seen although she has dealt with thousands. She climbs up the steps of one of the buses that will take her and the children to the British quarantine station; sitting in the front, she places her purse on her lap before her as if to shield her from what lies ahead.

I

BALTIMORE

1

When Rabbi Benjamin Szold and his bride left Hungary for America in 1859 both families felt they were out of their minds to do it. The decision was sudden and rash, and prompted by a job that fell into the rabbi's lap by default. A congregation in Stockholm had invited him to give three trial sermons. Deciding in the end that he was too Orthodox for them they chose another, older rabbi, who received at the same time an urgent summons from a German-speaking congregation in Baltimore, to which he reacted with understandable reluctance—why uproot himself and his family to travel to a vast and semisavage land? He wrote to Szold saying, I will accept the Stockholm post, see if the Americans will take you in my place.

Szold wrote to America, then rushed off to consult the girl he loved. Sophie was willing; the Americans were willing. They married in August and set out for Baltimore one month later—Benjamin Szold, aged thirty, and his twenty-year-old bride, bringing with them Sophie's young brother and a cousin of the rabbi's. Within five or six years all expected to be back in Cziffer, for America was an adventure, a fling, while Hungary was home.

But in America they stayed. Perhaps Szold was ready after all to put audacity behind him, to send out roots, to grow comfortably bald and domestic. His youth in a German-speaking village of Austro-Hungary had had a sadly makeshift quality. His mother died when he was five; his father remarried but he too died, in a sudden, horrible accident by scalding, four years later. The child was sent to live with a succession of uncles. Studying at yeshiva in order to become a rabbi, he was often hungry, more often achingly lonely. At eighteen he went to Vienna to drink up German culture and was caught in the revolution of 1848, a slim, dark-skinned, dark-haired boy of quick and sudden enthusiasms, banished with his fellow students when the revolution failed.

He returned to the town of Pressburg then, close to the village where he was born, and worked as a freelance tutor in the countryside. There he

met a prosperous, competent Jewish widow who managed a brewery, the mother
of a large family including several daughters. He fell in love with Frau Schaar
and all her daughters. Later he settled on the next to youngest, and when
she became engaged to someone else he learned to love the youngest, Sophie.

One day Frau Schaar offered to send Szold, along with two of her boys,
to Breslau to study. There he attended the secular university, also the theological
seminary, hearing at night the lessons of the little boys and living in two worlds
at once: the Gentile world of Homer and Horace, Schiller, Goethe and Lessing,
and the Talmud, the "sea of Talmud," vast, rich, trackless, into which the
student was supposed to be flung, sink or swim. He learned long portions of
Homer by heart, and the Hebrew Bible, entire. A friend of his Breslau days
remembered Szold as typically Hungarian in appearance, the skin yellowish
dark brown, the eyes black and fiery, the hair dense above a fierce little black
beard; "his facial muscles were extraordinarily vital." He was full of fire and
flame in those days, also full of Hebrew and Talmud, but in his innermost
nature a dreamer.

In America he had in his charge a young wife who was hardly more than
a girl, away from home and a large, close family for the first time. Also the
two young relations. Also the entire congregation Oheb Shalom, Lover of Peace.
And even these were not the sum of his new responsibilities, for the new
land made its own pressing demands: the unknown language; the culture; the
strangeness of everything political; the blacks, whom he saw for the first time
in his life; the war that was brewing, in which he put himself on the abolitionist
side in a city technically belonging to the North but in spirit defiantly Southern.
In Baltimore the Hungarian fires were banked until they became a benign
and tender warmth.

Baltimore was a charming city, the third largest in the Northern states
and full of Germans, Jews and Gentiles, who clustered together in clubs, athletic,
musical, literary, political; there were German bookstores and newspapers, even
a theatrical stock company, and over all an air of German *Gemütlichkeit*—
easygoing kindliness and good nature, cozy, comfortable, tolerant.

Baltimore was known for beautiful women, for exquisite parks and abundant
woodlands just beyond the town, for heaped-up market stalls glowing with
fruit, fish, flowers. Sophie was the daughter of a formidable housekeeper, and
now that she was a wife and rebbitzin she would become her mother's equal.
Determination was a mark of her character, as was a craving for excellence.
She would learn English. Bits of paper were scattered all over the house on
which Sophie scribbled English words and their meanings, or copied passages
from books; she would educate herself, not from any particular pleasure in
education, but because she knew it was right that one read classic literature.

She would become a splendid cook, she would sew and embroider and fill the house with plants and flowers, for which she had an actual vocation. Baltimore had many small, narrow houses, several stories high, and the Szolds lived in one on South Eutaw Street, not far from the congregation in the German section. It was a modest house, for the members of Oheb Shalom were mostly peddlers and shopkeepers of Germanic thrift with a Germanic resolve to get ahead.

Sophie kept them at a distance. Because she was married to a man of refinement and education she preferred not to be at the beck and call of those who happened to pay his salary. She wanted to be herself, and that self had a richly earthy quality, an almost peasant practicality and heartiness as well as a capacity for sudden angers. "The Schaars can have no pleasure," it was said of her childhood family, "they can't even mourn; they can only get angry." She missed them painfully. For years Sophie was to feel she was leading an alien existence among materialistic, money-grubbing people who were her spiritual inferiors, and her children grew up with the phrase *"bei uns zu Hause"*—with us, at home—meaning this is how things were in Hungary, this is how we ate, dressed, spoke, behaved. There were two styles in everything, the American style and the finer style "at home."

It was a happy marriage. The rabbi craved love and tenderness and doted on his wife, his Sophietchkam, and she loved him in return, perhaps less dotingly. She was too energetic to dote; there was no dreaminess in her. They were a well-matched pair, the rabbi gentle, generous, large-minded, and Sophie eager to take charge of daily life, daily decisions, the money, the house, the future. He would think and she would do.

By spring she was pregnant. Their first child was born in December 1860, a girl whom the rabbi named Henrietta after Henrietta Herz, a Berlin Jew who had established a well-known nineteenth-century literary salon and studied Sanskrit, Malay, Turkish. Four months later America went to war with itself.

When the baby was two years old Sophie wrote to her mother: "Henrietta speaks daily of the dear Grandmother. Here we are all right, thank God, except that the cruel war which has raged so long has made living so expensive. Paper money is devaluated, and food prices are three times higher than when we arrived." It was a cruel war in many ways; one Reform rabbi in Baltimore was forced to flee the city because of his abolitionist sentiments.

A second daughter was born that year, but she died within months. When Henrietta was four there was a third infant, also a girl, who lived less than a year. A few months later Sophie was pregnant again, and a fourth daughter, Rachel, arrived only weeks before Henrietta's fifth birthday. So her first five years were lived out against the distant noises of civil war and the daily mysteries of birth and sickness and death, and her young mother, who bore it all stoically, was shared with the phantom babies around whom one had to tiptoe while they hovered between worlds.

Henrietta was skinny, dark-haired and sallow like her father. She came to believe that she must be a stepchild because her mother was so fair and blue-eyed, with rosy cheeks and an air of freshness; she admired her mother, but from a distance. It was her father she loved and turned to and followed about. He was her own special person. He warmed to her; endlessly patient, incapable of anger, he chose her as his companion and apprentice. Perhaps he too suffered in some degree from his wife's preoccupation with sick babies.

The child was on her own a good deal of the time during those early years, not only because her mother was in the nursery but because she was a compulsive housekeeper. She wanted to look well in the eyes of the congregation; the same people for whom she felt a vague contempt were not to be given the chance of criticizing her as a slipshod housewife. Sophie had maids, but she was impatient and quick-tempered, a perfectionist who had to oversee every household operation. Her small daughter spent much of her free time in a tiny rocking chair in the rabbi's study, leafing through big books on the lower shelves. Father and daughter were company for each other.

Rachel was the first of Henrietta's sisters to survive the first year, and as Henrietta was her father's child so Rachel became her mother's. She was domestic, softly feminine, musical.

Henrietta surrounded herself with pets, dogs, cats and baby chicks whom she once hugged to death. She picked up pine shavings and fastened them to her hair like ringlets and admired herself extravagantly. She said whatever came into her head; she once offered to show a visiting member of the congregation a picture of himself, then fetched one of her books and pointed to a picture of a parrot. But when she was five or six years old a new trait developed, one that was to remain with her for the rest of her life. She became hideously self-conscious; most of the daring and mischief drained away and she weighed each word she said. Her age of innocence had ended mysteriously and abruptly and with it all she ever knew of carefree childhood. A photograph taken when Henrietta was six shows her frowning into the camera, awkward, intense, fiercely unattractive.

Once the war was over life became normal again, and the congregation began to grow in numbers and prosperity. Talk in the Szold household often centered on the battle between Orthodox and Reform Judaism—Orthodoxy unchanging and rigid, Reform eager to shed the heavy baggage of centuries. Even the rabbi wavered. Reform was rational and it tempted him, yet its followers tended to throw the baby out with the bath water. In the end he took a position between the two schools of thought. The congregation resisted, but for a time at least the rabbi led and they followed. Henrietta's childhood reverberated with the sounds of this struggle.

Just as the rabbi stood up to his congregation, so did he stand up to the community at large. He was determined to do what he believed was right, Jewishly right, in the sense that the Talmud declares the overriding importance of fair dealing between man and man. In postwar Baltimore the idea that newly emancipated slaves required an education was considered laughable, but Szold joined the Baltimore Association for the Education and Moral Improvement of the Colored People, serving as one of its leaders.

The child Henrietta became his aide, his secretary, literally his right hand, for the rabbi suffered from rheumatism and arthritis and his handwriting was cramped, difficult to read. His older daughter, who went to school at the ungraded classes of the congregation, grew indispensable to him, as he was to her. He became a refuge from the self-consciousness that afflicted her. At the age of eight she read Goethe's *Hermann und Dorothea* with him; a few years later she read proofs of the German portions of the Hebrew-German prayer book he prepared. From infancy on she spoke German as readily as English, but she learned Hebrew during long hours in her father's study, the only one of his children to do so. Whatever was precious to him he transmitted to Henrietta; Jewish literature and history, Jewish jokes, the weaknesses of the Jews as well as their grandeur always held for her the glamor of her father's presence.

Two more babies were born, first Sadie, then Johanna who became Henrietta's special charge. Now the house on Eutaw Street was seen to be shabby as well as overcrowded, even though the young relatives had left. It was clear the Szolds would never return to Europe; in America a father of daughters "can look more peacefully . . . into the future than he can in Europe," Sophie wrote to her mother. "The only thing necessary for girls here is a good education. Nobody talks about dowry." Sophie still missed her family and longed for them and hoped to visit soon, but in the meanwhile they would move to a larger house in an uptown neighborhood—she was pregnant again.

This was how they came to Lombard Street, thirteen-year-old Henrietta and her sisters Rachel, Sadie, Johanna and the baby Bertha, who was born on Henrietta's birthday. On Lombard Street the family lived out a succession of golden years that were to be forever strung together in Henrietta's memory as radiant with innocence and love. Although she stood on the brink of adolescence now, there was no turmoil, no rebellion, only the orderly march of weekday to weekday to Sabbath, blessed Sabbath, when Sophie was queen and the rabbi was king, and a just God ordered the universe, a God as merciful, gentle and wise as Rabbi Szold, whom he surely resembled.

America was expanding, rushing from country to city, building railroads and factories, tearing down forests. People went west, land-grant colleges sprang up in raw wilderness. Young girls by the thousands left home and went to work in textile mills. Great fortunes were made by men of iron will; money, getting and spending, was the spirit of the age.

But in the best neighborhoods of Baltimore the old South still rode in broughams and victorias behind liveried servants. On Lombard Street, Jews and Gentiles lived side by side, some tremendously rich, others only comfortable. The Szolds' house was one of the plainest, red brick, three stories high, with white marble front steps on which Henrietta sat with the younger ones, leaning against the iron railing, reading, watching. Organ-grinders passed with their monkeys. Scissors grinders, umbrellas-to-mend men and ancient blacks carrying in each hand a two-gallon bucket of oysters called out to housewives. There were great baskets of crabs and the cry "Crabbie, crabbie, crabbie," and women hung out of windows to call down their orders from the Gentile houses, for oysters and crabs were not eaten in Jewish homes. Baltimore beauties with bunches of violets took the air, some still in hoop skirts with tightly corseted waists, but the hoop was on its way out and skirts were veering backwards, ruffling, draping, looping, ready to burst into bustles. Factories learned to make fringe, and clothing became increasingly elaborate, every margin quivering with fringe or gleaming with passementerie. Henrietta wore high-buttoned shoes and short schoolgirl skirts and was conscious of having pretty ankles, but in three or four years her skirts would descend to the ground and she too would be a young lady. Never a fashionable one, she promised herself. There was a Quaker meeting house not far from her home, and whenever one of the Quaker women went by in plain gray clothes and poke bonnet framing a face serene, calm, almost passionless, Henrietta thought, When I grow up that's how I will look.

The house on Lombard Street was crowded. The rooms were narrow, the girls noisy and active, there were two Gentile servant girls as well as the two adults and a constant flow of congregational callers. They came to the formal parlor or the rabbi's study next door to it, lined floor to ceiling with books, German, Hebrew, Hungarian, French, English. Dark heavy draperies at the windows, transparent curtains behind them, a clutter of pictures on all the walls and fringe on everything.

The upstairs belonged to the girls. In a sitting room with sunny windows facing south they had their square rosewood piano, where they played duets by the hour, Strauss waltzes, arrangements of Beethoven symphonies, counting out loud and laughing at themselves. No one but Rachel was truly musical, certainly not Henrietta, who practiced laboriously. They gathered there with their friends after school and worked at sewing or lessons, gossiped, giggled and when they were older talked about boys. There was a good deal of poking fun at people, for several of the girls were talented mimics. Henrietta specialized in the pretentious manners of dignitaries of the congregation. She imitated the way they took snuff, the way they walked to the platform when called up to read from the Torah. Good and dutiful to an extravagant degree, a tiny flame of mischief flickered somewhere inside her, a spark of antagonism that mocked the powerful.

The center of the household, the "family altar," according to the rabbi, was the dining room, long and narrow and papered to look like walnut. There the table was opened to its fullest length, always, and the Szolds gathered around it three times a day. That their father was present at each meal, that he worked at home while every other father they knew went away to work, was for the girls a mark of their difference from others. They were superior, perhaps, but they were different, and they saw the proof at every meal. The parents sat at the ends of the table, with Henrietta next to her father. He talked about foreign affairs, national affairs, Jewish conditions in America and abroad. Crime, corruption, railway accidents were brought forth from two daily newspapers, one German, one English. A trial would be analyzed; according to Talmudic law, he would say, this man is innocent and for the following reasons. Then came the whole, rich, point-by-point dissection of human motive and divine intent. Whatever went wrong with the world was due to man's greed and lack of public spirit, which are not new, and he would reach into the teeming depths of Talmud to prove it, fishing up fresh treasures each time and garnishing them with Jewish anecdotes, folk tales and sayings. He had a sly, gentle wit.

It was a peculiarity of this life around the dining table that most of the rabbi's talk was addressed to Henrietta. The mother came and went between kitchen and dining room, but Henrietta stuck to her father's side, attending to the babies—Johanna, whom she had taken over entirely, and Bertha, who was adorable and self-absorbed and still an infant—buttering their bread, mopping their faces. She attended to the older girls as well, by repeating fragments of her father's conversation in words Rachel and Sadie could understand. So that all the impact of the rabbi's personality and intellect filtered through Henrietta to the younger children. She spoke fluent German, the youngest knew hardly a word of it; those in between knew varying amounts. It was the same with Jewish learning and Hebrew and the rabbi's profound belief in the perfectability of man. What they acquired of his philosophy and values they got from their eldest sister.

He had made her his heir. Everyone in the family knew it. Partly it was because he was a gifted teacher in need of a pupil, partly because of his own frustration with his American role: in America rabbis had no time for scholarship, for all their time was consumed by congregational duties. He yearned for a life of Jewish scholarship, and since it was denied to him the next best thing would be to set his daughter's feet on that path. She had the temperament for it. She learned quickly; she was docile, capable of being led. There was an exquisite bit of a flower garden behind the house and alongside the house a narrow, brick-paved strip where the little girls played with their dolls. Here Henrietta came early each summer morning dragging her books: the world history in German, the dictionaries, English, German, Hebrew and French. Also Dickens, whom she devoured, and every single issue of *St. Nicholas* magazine. The younger ones remembered her as always wreathed with books. She had passed the examination to enter high school and was now the only Jewish girl at Western Female High.

There she got on well with her classmates and even made friends with some, but her intimate friends were always Jews. In the seventies, there was little antisemitism in Baltimore or anywhere else in America, but there was just enough so that a girl as self-conscious as Henrietta could feel it imperative to announce her Jewishness wherever she went—subtly, to forestall rejection. If she had not announced it no one might have known, for she looked like the rest of her classmates. She moved and sat like a proper Victorian girl, stiff-backed, with no crossing of the arms or legs, no lounging in the chair. She wore her long dark wavy hair—lovely hair, which she brushed a hundred strokes each morning and was proud of—tied back with a bow. Her dresses were homemade, of good material and meant to last; for state occasions she had a pair of gold button earrings. Barely five feet tall, heavier than she should have been, Henrietta was plain. Except for Rachel they were all remarkably plain.

When Henrietta was fifteen her sister Johanna died of scarlet fever. Sophie endured this death with her usual fortitude—she had four healthy girls and she was pregnant again—but to Henrietta it was a wrenching blow. She shared a room with Rachel and the two grew closer as they grew older, but Johanna had been like her own child. For some time afterward she suffered from St. Vitus's dance, a nervous disorder for which fresh air, tonics and iron were prescribed. But the best medicine was the new baby, again a girl, whom they named Adele. Henrietta adopted her in Johanna's place.

Here is Henrietta in her teens, expressing good wishes for the Jewish New Year to her parents:

> If you only knew how ashamed I feel of myself when I transgress against you even in the smallest way, what remorse I feel on such occasions, then you would see how sincerely all my resolutions are meant, and how I appreciate all you bestow upon me so willingly. It is made clear to me day by day that the Almighty has blessed me and my sisters with solicitous and kindly parents, who foster and nourish both our minds and our bodies with great care. I constantly find reasons to admire your loving attention, your unselfishness and your noble devotion.
>
> I wonder what I can do to requite you for everything—no, everything is impossible, but at least how to make a beginning. I can only reiterate the old promise that I have already made so often, that is: to do my duty untiringly and cheerfully, to be extraordinarily diligent, to obey you painstakingly, and to love you with all the gratitude and filial emotion at my command . . .
>
> Your fervently loving daughter,
> Henrietta Szold

The letter is written in German, a language that lends itself to the high-flown. Clearly it had been worked and reworked. Indeed Henrietta was never able to dash off letters or to delegate their writing to others; her father taught her that every word must be written *aus der Fülle*, out of the abundance of the heart, so that for the rest of her long life she was to be burdened by the need to write abundantly, personally and in profound detail even to people she had never seen.

But this letter is more than Germanic and heartfelt. Its spirit is that of one who demands too much of herself. Her dutiful parents, one of the younger girls used to say, were pagan hedonists compared with Henrietta. Somehow she had transmuted her mother's aloofness—the sense of being an exile in an alien land, of being apart from the congregation and above them, as well as the healthy contempt for their materialism—into a rigid code. She was different, she felt it in her bones; she longed to be like everyone else and was aware that she would never be. She must earn the love of those about her by hewing to a certain line, by forcing herself to perform every atom of her duty to both parents and all four sisters, and by loving them unfailingly. Her mother called her *"Kamelchen,"* the little camel, the burden bearer.

At seventeen, among forty-eight young ladies in dresses of virginal white, Henrietta graduated from Western Female High School as the top student. What would come next? The girls had whispered in the hallways at school about Vassar, a distant dream, especially for Henrietta, whose family was not rich; her mother scrimped to pay for piano and painting lessons. In any case Vassar was far away, as were the few other colleges that took women: Wellesley, Cornell, Oberlin.

One year before her graduation Johns Hopkins University had opened its doors in Baltimore, the first true university, in the European sense of graduate schools, in the country. Rabbi Szold offered to give a course in his home on Hebrew theology to Hopkins students, and soon the house was full of young Jewish men bent on heavy thinking. However Hopkins did not take women. A friend of Henrietta's, a young woman named M. Carey Thomas, who was refused permission to study at Hopkins, went to Cornell and then to the University of Zurich, where she won a doctorate summa cum laude.

But Henrietta could not go to Cornell or anywhere away from Baltimore, although she longed for a college education. She could not leave home—or would not. She felt she was needed there. By Adele, who was still an infant. By the household itself, although Sophie had the help of two servant girls, Maggie and Lizzie, who were capable, devoted and loving, who called the rabbi Papa, the rebbitzin Mama, and when either was away missed them as they would have missed their own parents. By the members of Oheb Shalom, which had grown to be the largest Jewish congregation in Baltimore.

All these duties Henrietta took with the utmost seriousness, but none was so important to her as her duty to her father. He had become a man of considerable reputation, not only in Baltimore. The fiery rebel of Vienna had all but disappeared, and Benjamin Szold was known as the mildest of men, humble, self-effacing, unfailingly generous. "Be like your father as to broadness of heart," his friend Rabbi Marcus Jastrow wrote to Henrietta when she was eighteen, "and like your mother as to coolness of reflection. . . ." Only in the pulpit did he speak in the old voice, making thunderous demands on his congregation, the Reform Jews, the Orthodox, the Gentiles. Henrietta remembered him before he grew bald and gray and was sorry for the others because they had no such memories. They knew only a part of Papa, but she knew the whole.

In time stolen from the congregation he was writing a new commentary on the Book of Job. His sermons were often in English now, which put fresh burdens on Henrietta, for she composed some of them herself. Everything he wrote, letters, sermons, manuscripts, had to be discussed with Henrietta, proofread by Henrietta, the news, the Jewish quarterlies and their debates talked over and analyzed with Henrietta. There had never been a time in her conscious life when her father was not the most important figure in it.

And there had never been a time when what she most wanted was to be like her mother. Now, when she might have been learning about love, sex, the mysteries of femaleness from other young people, she was still sequestered with Papa—not all the time, and never, never against her will, but there it was. An aspect of her character had never developed and was not developing now. Years later she was to wonder why she had never read Anatole France's sensual novel *Thaïs*. It would have taught her so much, she said. Nor did she read the poems of Swinburne or Dante Gabriel Rossetti or the novels of Flaubert. Or *Anna Karenina*.

Perhaps it was less a matter of what she read than of how she read it. Close at hand was the Song of Songs which is Solomon's, burning with lyrical sensuality, but it left no impression on her young mind. She would wonder later why she was never thrown into the company of newly married women exulting in their happiness; but she was often in the company of such women, if only when her sisters married. Her mind was simply somewhere else: in the study with Papa looking up references for the Book of Job.

By adolescence most girls have come to see that the first man they loved must be given up and another found to take his place. But Henrietta did not look for another; she was afraid of others, who were after all free to reject her. Papa's love was guaranteed. It was in no way seductive, nor was it ever intended to hold back or imprison a young life, but this was its effect so far as her sexual nature was concerned. The same touch, when applied to one instrument, summons a delicate, elusive tone but on another produces depths and resonances. Much depends on the instrument.

Her father could not possibly spare her, so Henrietta must remain at home. She was offered a teaching post at the Misses Adams's English and French School for Girls, run by three pale spinsters in black bombazine to the chin, with a rim of white ruching at the neck and richly beribboned black hats— gentlewomen ruined by the war. She was to teach French, German, algebra, for fifteen dollars a month.

Henrietta put up her hair, parted it in the middle, wore pince-nez and began to teach. Her style was like her father's; she started with the concrete— a flower, an insect, the rain—and went from there to the abstract. "It is the living, the organic, the concrete, that in which life throbs and pulsates like his own quickening blood, that attracts a child," she said, although she knew nothing about pedagogy beyond what instinct told her. She brought newspapers into the classroom. She was wary of textbooks. The students loved her.

But this teaching career, which she had more or less fallen into, was not what she was raised for. There was a little hinge-top desk in the upstairs sitting room, Henrietta's private domain, in which the pigeonholes and drawers were always scrupulously neat. Here she did some writing for the *Jewish Messenger*, a weekly paper published in New York. Using the name Shulamith, she reported on events in the Baltimore community; other women writers for the *Messenger* called themselves Stella or Ada, for women were not supposed to want fame or a byline. Naturally they did not want money, and she got none. These first compositions were stiff and short. They grew longer without acquiring any ease of tone, clearly the creations of a girl of eighteen repeating her parents' ideas.

One day the *Messenger* moved Shulamith from the back to an inner page under a boldface headline. She tried hard not to be proud of the promotion. Perhaps they had nothing better to put in that place; perhaps it would never happen again; in any case, it was only the *Messenger*, not *Blackwood's* or the *Nation*. But from then on her pieces appeared under the boldface headline, and in addition to reporting events in Baltimore she started to comment on Jewish life at large. Accents peculiarly her own began to be heard; anti-Semitic comments in a paper called the *Standard* elicited two blazing columns from Shulamith in which she called the reporter a Russian cur who might at any moment go mad and bite the editor.

Henrietta's epithet referred to the restrictive laws under which Jews lived in Russia, confined to certain areas, unable to own or farm land. In America, only the year before, there had been a shocking incident at a resort hotel in Saratoga whose manager, Henry Hilton, refused to admit a rich and important Jew. Now a number of other hotels did the same. American Jews like the Szolds, to whom anti-Semitism was a European malady, were totally unprepared for it. This too Shulamith wrote about, and anti-Semitism in Germany, and a scheme for settling Russian Jews in colonies and teaching them farming. Her style improved, the stiffness melted and the ideas were more often her own than her father's, although there was not yet anything strikingly original. But she was feeling her way and finding her voice as a Jewish essayist, a career that was close to the rabbi's heart.

2

In the spring of 1881 the Russian czar was murdered by revolutionaries. Under his successor the pogrom—the word is taken from the verb *pogromit*, to destroy— became an almost permanent feature of Russian life. In southern Russia, Jews were attacked by murderous, fanatical mobs, wave after wave of devastation exploding under the passive eye of czarist authority. The Russian rulers had always vacillated in their policy toward Jews. Now it became their declared intention to see that one third emigrated, one third converted, and the remaining third died. The Jews nailed up their houses with boards and waited for the fire storm to pass.

They had no weapons, no protectors, no way to defend themselves. Some set out for America. There were 5 million Jews in Russia and 200,000, mostly of central European origin, in the United States, which put no limit on immigration. This was the start of an unprecedented movement across a continent and then across an ocean to the Eastern seaboard, usually New York, sometimes Philadelphia or Boston, more rarely Baltimore. Whole villages and towns would be emptied in the two decades that followed.

In America the first arrivals were received with mingled pity and embarrassment, for they were poor and backward and often unattractive. A small number of American rabbis had already asked the government to stop further immigration.

That same year, in June, Henrietta and her father set off for Europe to visit relatives on both sides of the family, to see museums, monuments and the great centers of continental culture. During the two weeks' voyage she was thrown in with strangers day after day. For Henrietta this meant looking from a distance for the touchstones—name, accent, mannerism, whatever facial traits could be read as clues—that showed membership in what she called "the brotherhood" of Jews. It also meant being always on the alert for any hint of vulgarity on the part of fellow Jews, at which she would cringe inside and feel ashamed and hope no one saw; she was ashamed of being ashamed. And of course it meant letting people know as soon as possible who and what she was. On shipboard she made the acquaintance of a pleasant Gentile family with whom she took walks around the deck until the moment came to let them know. From that moment, they froze up. It was her introduction to the Old World.

The Szolds began their European tour in Germany with synagogues, opera houses and museums in Berlin, Hamburg and Dresden, then traveled down the River Elbe to what was then Upper Hungary, where Henrietta met first her mother's people, then her father's, crowds of them, including forty first cousins who called her *"Schwarzele,"* "the little dark one." The elders called her "the stout niece."

In Vienna one young cousin, an engineer, took her to the opera and paid court to her. He begged Henrietta to stay on for a year with his parents, even promised a trip to Italy in the winter. Another cousin would escort her home when the year was up. Perhaps she preferred to spend the year studying; they would find her a student's room. Letters flew back and forth to Baltimore, raising hopes on both sides of the ocean, including the half-expressed hope that if Henrietta stayed she might marry the engineer-cousin. Everyone wanted it, there was already a certain sympathy between the two, and Henrietta was sorely tempted, most of all by Italy.

Yes, she would stay after all, she said. There might never be such an opportunity again—didn't Papa agree? But Papa said, "The little ones will be homesick for you. Think it over. . . ." Henrietta packed her bags and left with him for Paris and London.

By mid-September she was home again, bringing with her a vague sense of unease. Something was not quite right with her life but she could not put her finger on it. She lacked activity, she longed for knowledge, she felt this longing as an "unhappy gift," although she had left the chance for both behind her in Vienna. She buried herself in busyness, teaching again at the Misses Adams's and at the weekly religious school of Oheb Shalom both Saturday and Sunday mornings. She tutored privately in Hebrew and German, attended public lecture courses at the Peabody Institute and Johns Hopkins and wrote pieces for the *Messenger* again, longer and more thoughtful than what she used to write. The unhappy longing was stuffed into the recesses of her mind. From time to time she took it out and looked at it, then pushed it away. By working hard enough she was almost able to forget it existed.

While Henrietta had been in Europe friends of Sophie's urged her to do something about the girl once she got back, to move her out into society more; she was well past twenty with no prospect of marriage. Had not Sophie noticed how prim and spinsterish she was becoming? And why, with all her accomplishments, did she still lack self-confidence? Apparently Sophie did and said nothing; perhaps she believed the situation would cure itself, eligible husbands being in good supply. The five Friedenwald boys, who lived nearby, had grown up alongside the five Szold girls; Harry, the eldest, used to trade stamps with Henrietta. He was a few years younger and looked up to her. The two sons of Rabbi Marcus Jastrow came from Philadelphia to visit for weeks at a time. Hopkins students, those who studied theology with Rabbi Szold as well as others who craved a little Jewish atmosphere and Hungarian food, were always welcome at the dinner table. Often they brought friends.

These young men discussed the most abstruse subjects with Henrietta, but with Rachel they sang under the grape arbor on summer evenings. Rachel played the guitar and had dark, liquid eyes and a somnolent quality; she took long naps in the afternoon. Henrietta did not nap or play the guitar, and she sang very badly; and with young men she held serious discussions that often became arguments. The sisters teased her about it. They teased her for many things: for being too serious, high-minded and self-sacrificing; for wearing white stockings with black shoes; for keeping her bureau drawers in geometric order; for belittling herself.

Henrietta's self-deprecation was not in evidence around the young men. Quite the contrary. They were college men, most of them postgraduates studying such specialized subjects as Assyriology. She felt they expected her to admire them and their views, to be silent and womanly, an odalisque like doe-eyed Rachel. Refusing to be anything of the sort, she flew to the opposite extreme.

When Harry Friedenwald went to Berlin to study ophthalmology, his mother wrote to remind him that Henrietta was several years older than he was and stubborn and moody besides. "Remember how angry she made you at times? I admit she is as good as you say, and that it is a great pity that she cannot get as good a husband as she deserves. Through her singular disposition she repels everyone who approaches her, and she has done this since she was young, and now we see the consequences. . . . *Please put this in your notebook for future reference.*" With her sisters, or with a few close friends Henrietta could let her hair down, but with young men she was stubborn, argumentative and, in one woman's opinion, repellant.

It almost seemed that she feared admiration. Compliments made her uneasy; sometimes they caused her actual pain. It was as if anyone's telling her she was talented or clever brought home to her the vast difference between their opinion and the ignominious truth. The most ordinary social encounter could become an ordeal followed by hours of painful raking through the ashes. Had she said the right thing? Had they thought well of her? What did they really mean by this or that remark? Why did I not say, why did I not do . . . ? Then back to the beginning. It was a circle of self-doubt that gripped her from time to time, most of all among people older, better educated and more worldly than she was. That she might be judged—laid bare, measured, dissected, with all her defenses ripped away—was one of her enduring fears.

3

In Baltimore the Russians were appearing in force. They emerged from the bowels of ships to sit on wooden benches in long wooden sheds at Locust Point Harbor, the women with shawls on their heads and shawls clutched around their upper bodies, the older men often long-haired, with tremendous beards that had never been cut. In winter men, women and children were sewn into their underwear.

The leaders of Baltimore's settled Jewish community, all German or German-speaking, came down to the docks to welcome the newcomers, and those who owned factories offered them work. But the welcome was highly tentative for the most part, and the work was at sweatshop wages. The German Jews of Baltimore had pulled themselves up in the world and were beginning to enjoy the fruit of their labors. It was an era of luxurious living and eating as well as the start of the American love affair with modern plumbing, and there were resort hotels with more and better facilities for washing and toileting than an entire townlet within the Russian Pale of Settlement, the area permitted to Jews. The German Jews were no less greedy than their Gentile neighbors for luxury; indeed it was their dearest wish to be indistinguishable from Gentiles. In Germany they had been Germans who happened to be Jews, now they were Americans who happened to be Jews. The new immigrants were simply Jews. No one in Russia mistook them for Gentiles, and the czar was spitting them out because Russia could not digest them.

To the delicate nostrils of the Germans it was apparent that the Russian Jews smelled. Among their possessions—for some no more than a single clumsy bundle containing featherbed and Sabbath candlesticks—there were sure to be bedbugs and lice. New York, Boston and Philadelphia provided sanitary facilities, showers, a semblance of comfort for the newcomers even in the early years of immigration, but Baltimore did nothing. And even if they had been showered and fumigated, how could one be sure? Superstition and ignorance were written on every face, and their ingrained habits were known to be filthy.

To acknowledge kinship with these Russians was an embarrassment, for they were everything the German Jews had buried in their distant past. Even their language was perceived as inferior, an ancient form of German mixed with Hebrew; this so-called Yiddish was hardly a proper language at all, more a jargon, a hodgepodge, almost a parody of the pure and elegant German spoken by the Jews of Baltimore.

But they were an embarrassment that had to be faced. Like them or not the Germans knew their duty. The Hebrew Benevolent Society gave a little money; the Ladies' Sewing Society contributed groceries and furniture. A number of community leaders established "Russian colonies," places where the newcomers were supposed to practice farming and self-sufficiency. There was one nearby in Pisgah, Maryland, another in Virginia. Attempts at farming by Russians were made in many parts of America with the aid of Jewish philanthropy, their chief virtue being that they pulled the immigrants away from the main centers of population and out of sight.

Rabbi Szold went down to the docks with the other leaders of the Baltimore

Jewish community, but unlike them he brought the immigrants home with him. He had always been a generous man; he had been hungry, homeless and lonely in his youth and preserved a quick sympathy for the underdog. The house on Lombard Street became an informal employment agency, the rabbi's study a social service center. Not until 1903, when the immigrants themselves formed a protective society (later a branch of HIAS, the Hebrew Immigrant Aid Society, founded in New York), would there be community-wide social services for the Russian Jews of Baltimore.

Soon the rabbi discovered the newcomers were not so ignorant. Many knew several European languages; all had a deep respect for learning; they had read Hebrew from childhood and the riches of the Old Testament were at their fingertips. He breathed it in like perfume. It was what he had missed for more than twenty years among the merchants of Oheb Shalom.

Henrietta fell into the habit of going with her father to the docks. She was a little shy of the immigrants and for a time confined herself to giving concrete help, running from Jewish shop to Jewish shop, from tailor to clothing factory, searching for jobs. Many were straggling back, bewildered, from the failed colonies; they knew nothing about farming and everyone had cheated them. The Baltimore Jews began to see that the immigrants were not only unattractive and embarrassing but an actual source of danger, for they could not be bundled off and kept out of sight, and those who were put to work in factories infected their fellows with socialism. Russia was a hotbed of dangerous ideas, the Jews, as a disaffected class, particularly prone to it, and now it was seeping into America.

But Henrietta was barely aware of their politics, a subject that had no interest for her then or in later life. Sitting in her father's study in a chair a little behind his, apart from the visitors because she was still shy in their presence, she watched and listened. She saw one young man in the group, fervent, eloquent, pale as death and spitting into his handkerchief. An old man with horn-rimmed spectacles resting first on his forehead and then on the very tip of his nose slipped down in his chair whenever the talk grew hot, until it seemed he might sink out of sight. They were discussing literature, modern Hebrew literature written in Russia, their arms flailing the air, their upper bodies moving backward and forward, the same motion made in the Orthodox house of prayer.

The rabbi broke in with a question, and a storm of argument rose up. Henrietta had never seen anything quite like it—bodies stiffened, eyes flashed, one man rose to his feet and orated, both arms in constant, eloquent motion. Two others leaped up to confront him; he fell back and sank into his chair, hands jammed in pockets, shoulders tense with suppressed anger. And it was poetry they were discussing, not politics.

So much passion had never before been set loose in the study of Rabbi

Szold. Henrietta saw everything the Germans saw: a people who were flagrantly Jewish, volatile, expressive, skeptical, noisy, addicted to argument for the sake of argument. No goal was ever so precious to them as the pleasure of arguing about how to reach it. The German Jews were self-contained and businesslike and addicted to order. They had the souls of bookkeepers, but these Russians had the souls of Jews.

She found them magnetic. Their wholeness, their unselfconsciousness, their passion and noise and volatility were what she wanted, what she felt to be most lacking in herself. For days on end she talked about nothing else but Russians. Her sisters teased her about it; she was being high-minded again, burying herself in the problems of others. Once she cried out, "We are in need, not they!" She sounded both angry and on the edge of tears.

On many nights the talk in the study was about Palestine and Zionism. Ten years earlier Rabbi Szold had written an article rejecting Zionism as outmoded and irrelevant; America was the Zion of the modern Jew, he said then. But that was before the pogroms. The rabbi was not rejecting now, but listening with the same close attention as his daughter. Some of what they heard was not new to them, but much was, for all they had learned about modern Zionism until now had come from newspapers and magazines.

There had always been a traditional Jewish belief in the redemption of the Holy Land, a yearning both vague and powerful and wholly unconnected with political reality. Scattered voices in the mid-nineteenth century, inspired by the rise of national movements, the romantic belief that each people had its own soul and destiny and language, spoke for a revival of Jewish nationalism. But it was not until the pogroms of the 1880s, when the great mass of Russian Jews were shaken out of the hope that the czars would come to accept them, that modern Zionism took shape. A pamphlet called *Auto-Emancipation,* written by Leo Pinsker, flew through the townlets of the Pale; the Jews must free themselves, he said, for no one would grant them their freedom as a gift.

Little societies sprang up in the townlets, Lovers of Zion, Returners to Zion. Coins were collected at their meetings; they would buy up land in Palestine from the Turks. Young people would settle on this land and farm; a few hundred were there already, known by the name of Bilu, an acronym for the Hebrew phrase, "O house of Jacob, come ye and let us go." To the Russians the Biluim were heroic figures living free and courageous lives in a landscape only dimly imagined but framed by olive trees and grapevines; they had already built a dozen agricultural settlements and attracted the philanthropy of Baron Edmond de Rothschild in Paris. One day a young Russian named Eliezer Ben Yehuda set off for Jerusalem to spend his life writing a modern Hebrew dictionary; he vowed that his infant son would never hear any other language.

This was what the Russians talked about in the rabbi's study for hours at a time: Zionism, Palestine, the Hebrew and Yiddish literature written in Russia and crystallizing the impulses toward modernity that stirred in a populace afraid for its life, clinging to the past, clutching for an unknowable future.

Zionism was dismissed by Orthodox Jews and Reform Jews alike, for different reasons. Henrietta knew all those reasons, but she did not rake them up and offer them to the Russians to be demolished. She felt that her father was ripe for conversion, that he was a Zionist unaware, but she herself never needed converting. All she had needed was to hear Zionism defined and declared by those who carried it in their hearts. "Zionism converted me to itself," she said.

Not because of the handful of farming communities in Turkish Palestine. There were millions of Jews in Russia, of whom only a few thousand might ever reach Palestine. But Judaism was a way of life, a code of law, a language and a literature—so her father had always taught her. With Palestine as their heartland the Jews of the dispersion would be armored against the monstrous anti-Semitism of Russia, the social anti-Semitism of Germany and the rational, sectarian embrace of democratic America, which threatened them with assimilation and extinction. They would have instead a spiritual home, a place where the Law could take root in holy soil. Once rooted there, it would grow and change and reshape itself to fit contemporary life, and the scattered Jewries of the world would become one people.

That autumn a handful of the young Russians formed a literary society, the Hebrew Literary Society of Baltimore. They appeared one night at the house on Lombard Street to invite the rabbi to give a talk before their society. He was delighted; he agreed to talk about poetry. Then the committee turned to Miss Szold and invited her to speak as well.

Oh no, she said, she didn't care to. The rabbi looked at her with a familiar look and asked why not.

She felt he knew quite well. The women's clubs to which she belonged asked her from time to time to prepare a paper and read it to the members; Henrietta suffered agonies in the process of writing these papers and often told her family she would have to go back on her word, it was too hard, it was beyond her meager abilities, she felt sick, physically sick with fear. Her father was the one who always persuaded her, luring her gently toward success. Now she was asked to speak before an audience of strangers, and worse than that, men.

What she would far rather do, she said aloud, was help them develop a night school, a place where adults could learn English after work. They would learn more than English; they would learn how to become Americans—they would vote.

The committee members smiled at one another, and someone took out the constitution of their society and showed her that a night school was written into it; it was one of their purposes.

That evening a bargain was struck. Miss Szold, a professional teacher, agreed to help and advise and guide them with their school and to represent them before the Jewish community; the members of the society would do everything else.

Her first step was to canvass the city for a small sum to pay the rent on the first schoolroom. It was a difficult and unpleasant task. According to the Germans there was no need for schools; "they themselves had acquired the good things of this life without night schools." The only argument that seemed to move them was her pointing out the faint but distinct odor of anti-Semitism rising over the American landscape. Help the Russians, she said, for you may soon be in the same fix yourselves.

Someone donated a gold watch and chain that was raffled off for $100, and with this Henrietta secured two rooms on the second floor rear of a store in a poor district inhabited by Czechs and Bohemians. It was a miserable place, with a long unlit hallway—they would have to grope their way at night—and a crooked, winding staircase leading to a large, utterly bare room. The committee came with buckets and mops; they scrubbed, painted, hammered, found kerosene lamps, chairs, slates and chalk and a few books, and in the fall of 1889 announced the opening of the Russian Night School. It was apparently the first such school in the nation.

Thirty men and women showed up on the first night, on the second so many that another class was started on the spot, one for those who could read a little English, the other for those who knew only the alphabet. Henrietta found two volunteer teachers, young ladies, who sometimes came and sometimes did not, which made her furious. Like Sophie she had a temper, fierce and sudden but cleansing. From then on teachers were paid fifteen dollars a month. The students also paid if they could, thirty-five cents a month. One hundred fifty adults were taught the first semester.

Henrietta acted as a kind of supervisor-principal, as well as part-time teacher, using methods that evolved from her work at the Misses Adams's. In the advanced class there was a single text, a history of the United States. The first lesson consisted of reading a brief paragraph, every word of which was explained by pantomime, analogy, quick sketches on the blackboard, the great goal being to use English and only English. Once the meaning of the passage was clear all its content was discussed, the geography, the economy, the historical figures, whatever incidental allusions could be brought in. Questions were asked, questions were encouraged and forced. Then lessons in grammar, spelling and writing made use of the same material. A single history book became a universal text.

Next spring the literary society gave a musical entertainment that raised enough to rent an entire building. Now they would have a library and a reading room, seven classes in English, also bookkeeping, arithmetic, Hebrew and dressmaking.

"I eat, drink and sleep Russians," Henrietta told Rachel. She was haunted by them—by the old men in her schoolroom who bent their work-hardened fingers around a pen, by the younger men she met at the office of the Baron de Hirsch Fund, the philanthropy of an immensely rich European Jew who sent money for food. Ninety souls jammed themselves into the little office one day, hungry and anxious about their hungry children. Some had come by foot from distant cities in search of work. There was no work. "It seems to me that I do not nowadays get rid of the heartache caused by these poor unfortunates."

It was her policy to refrain from influencing the young people of the literary society; at meetings of the board she spoke as little as possible. "This is their school, and they must run it." They were tremendously proud. Poor as they were and dependent on the charity of the community, the Russians often hesitated to take a donation for fear it might in some way oblige them to the donor. "My night school is not ready to beg at any rate. My Russians are glad to work for it and pull it through."

A student at the night school remembered Miss Szold in later years as an earnest young woman of almost painful intensity. For there was a quality of exaltation in the way she gave herself to the Russians—"my Russians." Riding on the horse-drawn tram late at night from Lombard Street to the Czech quarter, tired and cold and hungry because there were several days each week when she rose at 5:30 A.M. and worked straight through till nearly midnight without supper, she felt keyed up, almost transfigured. She rarely spoke about the Russian Night School afterwards. People who knew her in her fifties and sixties found she did not like to discuss it, as if the memories were too sacred to share.

She was in her late twenties now. Her mother's friends, who still considered Henrietta something of an oddity, praised her for her devotion to the Russians, for her considerable fame as a writer and for the distinguished circles she moved in as a member of several women's clubs. Privately they preferred their own daughters, who attended to the only important business of a Jewish girl, which was husband getting, and after that, babies. Henrietta did nothing along that line and her manner and appearance showed no improvement. She was growing stouter and plainer and always wore her pince-nez. She looked exactly like a schoolteacher, even to the mannerisms, the extended forefinger that admonished, the five fingers held up so that several points in an argument could be counted off. She was still proud of her slender ankles, her hair was brushed one hundred strokes each day when she rose long before the others to exercise and bathe and dress, and her clothing was meticulously kept. But she was plain. So were Sadie and Bertha, but Sadie cut her hair in bangs and Bertha laughed a lot, and somehow they transcended their plainness.

At a dinner party in honor of Rabbi Szold's sixtieth birthday Sophie served goose, turkey, duck, tongue, beef, chicken, fish, salad, cake and fruit. She weighed two hundred pounds but was as active and competent as ever. The guests were entertained afterwards by the daughters, who dramatized a part of *The Old Curiosity Shop*, with Henrietta as Mrs. Jarley, the stout, comfortable owner of a caravan of waxworks. She wore a large bonnet trembling with bows and took nips from a bottle concealed in her skirt pocket. The guests roared with laughter; Dr. Aaron Friedenwald actually wept. Henrietta would be thirty that year. If you were thirty and unmarried you were an old maid.

4

Henrietta was a woman who defined herself through work, who worked too hard and thrived on it, leaving no empty places in which she might be forced to look inward and take stock of herself. But when she was thirty-three her work and therefore her life came to a halt and she found herself compelled to stand face to face with the self she had become.

She did not like what she saw. The feeling she had had when she was twenty-one and newly returned from Europe—that something important was wrong—came back more insistently than before. Now everything was wrong. Her teaching career seemed unsuitable, even distasteful. She had taken it up by accident; she had no training for it; she was an amateur and a humbug. Without a college degree it would never lead to anything but frustration and penury. As for her writing, she had always done it more to please her father than herself, although not even Henrietta could continue to deny her fitness for it. By 1902 the *London Jewish Chronicle* was to call her the leading Jewish essayist in America. Nevertheless it was not congenial to her; writers must look within themselves and this was precisely what she most wanted to avoid.

Although she never stopped writing, she closed it off as a full-time profession. And month by month the feeling grew that her days were empty and all her labors a series of mechanical routines through which she hurtled without any sense of where she was going or why.

The time had come to take her life in hand, to make herself into someone she liked better. Yet such a conscious taking charge of herself and her destiny seemed beyond her. She had rarely done it before, had almost always fallen into things, backed into them, letting fate or others push her—not because her parents insisted on pushing their children. In this Henrietta was quite different from her sisters, none of whom had the same degree of passivity. In fact her sister Sadie, although physically frail, was a model of the self-realizing, self-directed young woman.

Sadie, the third of the sisters, was determined to go to college. Henrietta and Rachel never went because there was no money. Henrietta earned money; Rachel stayed home and helped her mother. But Sadie had applied to Bryn Mawr in 1888 and been accepted, having graduated from high school a year late because of repeated bouts of illness that were thought to be rheumatic fever.

Unfortunately a minor financial crisis intervened; the Szolds found they had less money than they had counted on, and Sadie never got to Bryn Mawr. Instead she spent a year teaching at the Misses Adams's and saving her salary. By the time Bertha was ready for college the Szolds were over the hump, and Bertha went at the usual age. But Sadie was twenty-three when she finally entered the Harvard Annex in Cambridge. Her hands were painfully arthritic, she had to come home for months at a time because her whole body was affected by the illness, but Sadie knew what she wanted and meant to have it.

Henrietta believed she wanted it too. The longing for a college education never left her, and even in old age she remained sensitive to the difference between herself and the college educated. Yet she could have done what Sadie did. She could have gone to college even in the 1890s—overage, like Sadie, in an era when it was not at all uncommon for a woman to enter college at whatever age she had the chance.

But no one forced her to go. Therefore Sadie went and Henrietta stayed home. For a time she satisfied her longing for education the same way other Southern women of good birth often did. She joined the Botany Club and the Women's Literary Club, both serious affairs whose purpose was not sociability but higher education. The members had served their time in church and temperance and missionary societies and learned thereby that women, when gathered together, can bring about important changes. Until then what they had done was for others, for Southern women realized only slowly that they might do something for themselves; Northern women had been joining clubs for a decade or more. Often the word "club" was not used—clubs were for men, they might be laughed at if they presumed to have clubs—so they called themselves circles or societies. Even then people laughed. It was a fad; it would pass; Southern women would return to their proper role as the passive and ornamental objects of Southern chivalry.

But it was not a fad. The movement spread almost telepathically. Some circles devoted themselves to the study of history or ancient civilizations or current events; others began with specific goals, building a public library, planting trees, improving garbage collection; in Rome, Georgia, a women's club built a hospital. Soon there would be federations of women's clubs. By the end of the century they were pounding on the doors of state legislatures and demanding the vote. Henrietta learned from them what the women's club movement did for women, what it gave them not only in self-improvement but in power. She would make use of it herself one day. But for the moment it was only another road leading nowhere.

The same was true of the Russian Night School, which she loved and had every reason to be proud of. During 1893 and 1894, the average attendance was more than 230, with a total of 900 actually enrolled; many were non-Jewish immigrants, and some were not immigrants at all, but third- or fourth-generation Americans. But even though she had once thought of them as her Russians, her school, in the end it was theirs alone; she believed she had no right to be proud of it. In fact she was unable to find a single accomplishment in her past that was cause for pride. She called herself "a very ordinary person, schoolgirlish in my views, worse than that in my expression of them, and extremely uninteresting and stupid . . . talking ambitious nonsense."

In 1893, the year of Henrietta's stocktaking, Sadie was home from Cambridge on Christmas vacation, confined to bed, where she read, sketched with her one good hand and wrote letters to her fiancé while shoring up strength to return to school. Bertha flung herself into all the small frivolities of college life at Bryn Mawr and got engaged to a Baltimore boy. Adele could hardly wait her turn, for there was a rebellious streak in her that longed to get away from home. And Rachel had already left. She had married Joseph Jastrow, the younger son of Rabbi Jastrow. For this marriage and everything it meant Henrietta had been totally unprepared.

She wept when she heard of it; she wept when they went off on their honeymoon; tears blotted a postcard she wrote a few days later to Rachel in which she described her own feelings of homesickness and a permanent lump in her throat. Of all the sisters Rachel was until then the closest to Henrietta.

Bertha and Adele seemed so much younger; Sadie, who was clever and intellectual, was somehow hard to get on with. She tended to push Henrietta away; there was always an unspoken, unacknowledged competition between the two. But Rachel was not intellectual, she lacked complexity, she was all warmhearted love and approval and sisterly teasing. With such a friend at her side Henrietta's abstract nature had a window on reality.

Now Rachel was gone, not only from the family but from Baltimore, for Joe was a professor of psychology in Madison, Wisconsin. The others would surely go in turn. Of the five sisters, four reached outside the family for adulthood and separateness while for one and only one the house on Lombard Street had become a magic circle she dared not venture beyond.

Even there, at the heart of the family where her father stood, was a sudden, baneful change. The congregation Oheb Shalom, which Rabbi Szold had led since 1859, voted to replace him. Overnight he became an old man and a dispensable one.

In the years since the war the shopkeepers, garment makers and petty businessmen of Oheb Shalom had been transformed into department store owners, clothing manufacturers and bankers. With prosperity came the need for a new synagogue in a new and fashionable uptown location; a new synagogue required a new rabbi, one at home in English rather than German, someone less traditional than Szold, less insistent on kashruth and Sabbath observance, and in appearance modern, smart, American. So the congregation had outgrown the rabbi, and he was to be retired and pensioned off. The decision left Henrietta heartsick. "I feel choked every time I look at his haggard face," she told Bertha. Moreover, when her father lost his post she lost her place of honor as his secretary-translator, his researcher and partner.

The family had scarcely accepted the fact of Rabbi Szold's retirement when Sadie's rheumatic fever became so severe that she was never out of bed. In March of 1893 she developed pneumonia; in April a trained nurse was sent for. On the sixteenth of April she died.

The Szolds received streams of visitors with a stoic calm, reserving their grief for moments when they could be alone. Henrietta remembered her sister's extraordinary courage during the last weeks, propped up in bed, working out geometry problems for the girls at the Misses Adams's although her body was racked. For years Henrietta had swallowed her grievances against Sadie out of a superstitious fear that something might happen to this sister; at other times her temper exploded and the anger flew out. Now she consoled herself with the thought that she had suppressed the worst.

Then one by one the family struggled back to normalcy. Rachel and Bertha left. The rabbi was invited by the Jewish Publication Society to help revise the Leeser Bible. Adele complained that all her friends had moved uptown and theirs was the last family stuck in the old neighborhood. A fresh blow fell—Henrietta herself was threatened with change. That spring the Jewish Publication Society invited her to serve as executive secretary to their publication committee in Philadelphia. She would be in effect editor and translator as well as secretary. It was a tempting offer, the salary modest, but they promised to increase it, the work in every way suitable.

She turned to her parents, hoping her father would refuse. "If Papa had only known how very little persuasion it needed for me to yield, he would have insisted upon my staying home." But for once her father failed her, and there was no insistence—she was thirty-three, there were servants, Adele, both parents in good health, the work was scholarly work and precisely what he always wanted for her. She had run out of excuses and was unable simply to throw up her hands and say, I will not do it because I do not want to. What else was there? Perhaps some inner voice murmured that after all it was time to leave home and test herself against the world.

In the course of the summer Henrietta resigned from the finishing school, the Russian Night School, the religious classes at Oheb Shalom, dismissed her private pupils and accepted the post. She was nervous to the point of numbness, so nervous it was an ordeal even to talk to people. Having burned her bridges, she looked at the wreckage without pleasure, and in her future the only crumb of comfort she could see was the possibility that the publication committee might be persuaded after a time to let her do the work from Baltimore.

In Paris, a Viennese journalist named Theodor Herzl wrestled with a similar feeling of aspirations unfulfilled, of life gone flat and savorless. He had been born in Budapest in 1860, the year Henrietta was born in Baltimore, but there were few other resemblances. Herzl's people were rich, worldly, totally assimilated Jews. He fixed early in life on a literary career, earned a degree in law, then became a successful writer of featherweight comedies, acquiring in his late twenties a rich and pretty wife. By the time he was thirty-three Herzl had learned that the marriage was a misery, his popularity as a dramatist evanescent, even the long-sought post as Paris correspondent for an important Viennese newspaper finally unrewarding. At the same time he became aware of a particularly virulent strain of anti-Semitism in France; it was to lead a year later to the Dreyfus affair. Herzl was familiar with anti-Semitism in Vienna and Budapest, but it seemed to be chiefly social, and like most men of his upbringing he believed that when the Jews of central Europe were finally assimilated, anti-Semitism would disappear. Russia, of course, darkest feudal Russia, was another story, but Herzl had no experience of Russia. Now a fantastic plan invaded his dreams—dramatic, for he was a dramatist, splendid, for he had a craving for splendor. He would go to Rome and ask the Pope for help against anti-Semitism. In return Herzl would "initiate a great mass movement for the free and honorable conversion of all Jews to Christianity." The mass conversions were to take place in a series of magnificent pageants in the greatest cathedrals of Europe's greatest cities, and Herzl himself, along with the leaders of his movement, would remain unconverted, the last Jews on earth.

But the editors of *Die Neue Freie Presse* were unable to take the plan seriously, and Herzl was persuaded to forget mass conversion. The direction of his life had been irrevocably deflected all the same. Everything he had accomplished became so many false starts, and his future, its shape still dim and unimagined, consisted of a splendid and dramatic fantasy in which Herzl led the Jews of the world—somewhere. Away from anti-Semitism and Europe, with the help, not of the Pope, perhaps, but of rulers and millionaires, through the force of his will, the power of his dreams to transform reality, they would go—somewhere.

Early that autumn Henrietta and her father received a visit from members of the Hebrew Literary Society of Baltimore, the same group that had started the night school. Now they were forming a local Zionist organization, which was to Henrietta an act of great daring. Would Rabbi Szold and his daughter join? They were to be the spearhead; if they joined, others in the community might follow. With her father and Harry Friedenwald she agreed to become a member of the Zionist Association of Baltimore, one of the earliest Zionist organizations in America.

Then she left for Philadelphia. She would live with the Jastrows, Rachel's in-laws. The two families had been visiting back and forth for years; Alice and Annie Jastrow were her girlhood friends, the Rabbi her friend and admirer. From this setting, familiarly Jewish and rabbinical, Henrietta would go forth each day by streetcar to grapple with independent life.

5

Rabbi and Mrs. Marcus Jastrow had five children, two studious sons and three pretty but empty-headed daughters whose chief concern was the high cost of dressmaking. Individually Miss Szold liked them all; together they were hard to live with, torn by half-expressed tensions she sensed but could not define. And she herself was in the worst of states, imprisoned within the numbing nervousness of her last months at home, dazed, unsociable, feeling faintly betrayed, as if her family had sent her into exile.

Philadelphia seemed changed since her last visit; it was a big city now, full of tall buildings where electricity was replacing the gentler gaslight. And at the offices of the Jewish Publication Society she found the room set aside for her utterly bare and bleak, its sole feature an empty fireplace on whose mantel a clutter of pamphlets lay like dead leaves. No books, no pictures, curtains or rugs. It looked like a cell.

Three whole days went by without a single letter from the family. "Going away from home is not pure delight," she reminded them. "I may as well confess that my courage has already oozed away." How was she to work in this blank room without a Bible or a Webster's, without her father's library and without her father?

At the end of the first week she fled home to Baltimore. When the weekend came to an end she went grudgingly back to Philadelphia. The second weekend was the same, the eager rush home, the slow return to work; the third time she forced herself to stay on and decorate the office, painting bookshelves in imitation of oak, putting up curtains, borrowing brass andirons and laying logs of wood across them. But it was already clear that Henrietta's going away from home bore no resemblance to her sisters'. She was away and she was not away, the time at home was real and the time in Philadelphia an interval to be endured. She made little effort to form a circle of her own, either at work or among friends of the Jastrows; she put down no roots, for she was already rooted in Baltimore. In January she wrote: "It somehow or other seemed harder for me to go away today than ever before. I am afraid of myself. I do not think I have the courage to undertake this for another year. . . . I wanted to say once more before I go to bed tonight, that I have the best mother and father that ever God gave to anybody, and that I love them more than I can tell."

Her work for the Publication Society was detailed, exacting, poorly paid, and became in time a form of genteel literary slavery. She had been hired to prepare manuscripts for the press, see them through publication, compose advertising circulars, keep the work of the society before the public in newspapers and, when she was not acting as public relations expert, editor and corresponding secretary, do such translations as the society thought fit to direct—all without typewriter or secretary, so that each letter had to be composed, then written out by hand. The salary was eighty-three dollars a month.

They had chosen her because she was a hard-working woman of exceptional scholarly training and a docile woman who would take direction, working herself to the bone while accepting a modest salary without complaint. Their choice was astute. She did all that was expected of her and much more, for the work grew with the years, and it became apparent that no matter how much the JPS exploited Miss Szold, she would stifle her complaints and agree to be exploited. Work was her drug, her remedy for homesickness and isolation and all other dissatisfactions with herself and her life.

She had been working by mail with the men of the publication committee since the JPS was first founded in 1888, a nonprofit educational venture whose purpose was to bring Jewish literature before the public. Since Jewish literature in English was in short supply they published mostly translations from Yiddish, Hebrew, German and French, for which volunteer translators like Henrietta and Rabbi Szold were enlisted. She had also worked as a volunteer editor; now she was the paid secretary of her former colleagues, one of the few among them with an avid, far-reaching interest in literature as well as a certain healthy soundness of editorial judgment.

Her immediate superior was Judge Mayer Sulzberger, president of the Court of Common Pleas in Pennsylvania and the first Jewish judge to win national recognition, a man of uncommonly forceful character, with a biting wit and the sublime assurance that he was always right. Miss Szold was afraid of him. She was awed by all the members of the publication committee, important men, men of affairs whom she respected but could not admire. As for the JPS itself, she found it tepid, bloodless and academic: "I had the feeling that it did not use its possibilities because it was afraid of life." The books she longed to see them publish seemed to perish or slip out of their hands to other firms. They lacked fire, they lacked what the Russians so abundantly had.

That autumn she moved from the Jastrows' home to another, closer to work, a well-run household free of the chaotic personality conflicts that marred the family life of Rachel's in-laws; here there was a lively young child and such an air of calm and thoughtful comfort that she thought her homesickness might begin to recede. It did nothing of the sort; it only grew worse with time. But in the spring of 1895, almost two years after Miss Szold first left home, the rabbi was suddenly taken ill and she rushed back to Baltimore for a long visit that proved to be a return for good.

She did go back to Philadelphia for a time, but the diagnosis had been a serious one, her father in great pain as well as danger, and the pall of homesickness that had clouded life before was darkened by fear and guilt. "It is too dreadful to realize! How can we bear it! Our dear noble father! If I could only bear this suffering for him! And to think that I have lost two precious years away from him! And that all my life I did nothing to give him real pleasure . . ."

The rabbi was apathetic, sleepless, unwilling to eat, and Henrietta resolved to watch his every movement, to meet each crisis while giving to the Publication Society the same limitless devotion she had given it before. Adele, her most persistent critic, was away at college in Wisconsin and wrote: "Henrietta, did you make absolutely *all* the indices and tables of Graetz's *History of the Jews?* You are a chump for doing so without extra pay. Do stop killing yourself, *in Gottes Name.* . . ." The five-volume history she had been editing for several years was brought out volume by volume beginning in 1891, and when the project was complete in 1898 it included an index 491 pages long, entirely Henrietta's work.

That year the family moved from the house on Lombard Street to an airy old place on Callow Avenue, and the work of the Jewish Publication Society went with them. Henrietta's first and last attempt to live on her own had come to a painless end; she would never again be separated from either of her parents except by death. "Now that I realize how dependent I am upon my intercourse with my parents," she wrote to a friend, "I marvel at my having been able to stay in Philadelphia nearly two years." Close to the surface of her letters during that period, close but never quite breaking through, is an awareness of how strange that was: to be thirty-five and unable to leave home for more than a few weeks at a time.

But from the work itself, from its diversity and responsibility, she had learned and would continue to learn. "She was all there was of the Society exclusive of its canvassers and directors," a Zionist colleague wrote years later. "She gathered all the work in her lap—whatever there was of the making of books, the editing or translating of its manuscripts, the proofreading of the galleys and the pages, the compiling of indexes and appendices . . . the motherly care of rejected and accepted manuscripts." Her care of manuscripts was more than motherly—that is, tenderly supportive—for when harsh judgments had to be made she made them, even fought for them. She spoke of hypocrisy, charlatanism, crookedness. It was a different matter entirely from teaching young girls of good family at a finishing school. She was matching wits with writers, sharp, often egocentric men, and learning an intricate trade. The revisions the JPS expected of her became at times extensive rewritings, and she was as much editor as secretary, as much translator as editor; when she left the post in 1916 Miss Szold would have translated a dozen books.

Yet the sense of crisis she had felt two years earlier, the awareness that life had reached a crossroad, that a new path and a new purpose must be chosen because the old ones were barren—this crisis had never been met. The work of the JPS challenged her mind without touching her heart. It was indeed something, it was far more than the schoolroom of a secular school, but it was not nearly enough. The specters that had gone into hiding would rise to challenge and torment her again.

6

In Vienna, Theodor Herzl's vision of himself as the savior of the Jews began to take solid shape. His book, *Der Judenstaat (The Jewish State: An Attempt at a Modern Solution of the Jewish Question)* was printed and ready for distribution. Herzl's diary for February 14, 1896, notes: "My five hundred copies came this evening. When I had the bundle carted into my room, I was terribly shaken. This package of pamphlets constitutes the decision in tangible form." In it Herzl proposed the establishment of a Jewish state—perhaps in Argentina, which he had been told was one of the most fertile countries in the world, perhaps in Palestine—to be governed by constitutional monarchy and based on political guarantees.

It was not enough to buy up bits of land in a nation ruled by others, he believed; the right of the Jews to settle on that land must be formally recognized. He made no mention of Hebrew; English or German would be the language of the new nation. Jewish tradition, Jewish religion and ethics, the Arab question, were all unknown to him, as unknown as the fact that a Jewish home in Palestine had been the dream of thousands of eastern Europeans since 1882, when Leo Pinsker's *Auto-Emancipation*, that bible of the young Zionists at the Russian Night School, was first published. Nor was he familiar with the ancient religious theme of the return to the promised land, a theme that Christians as well as Jews had resurrected in recent times, Napoleon, George Eliot and the convert Disraeli among them.

A month before publication of *Der Judenstaat*, Henrietta Szold had composed an essay that embodied her own views on Zionism. Herzl dreamed of himself as a prophetic leader, the king of the Jews; Miss Szold, a maiden lady of no particular importance, was merely composing a speech because the Baltimore chapter of the Council of Jewish Women invited her to make one. Her title was "A Century of Jewish Thought," and it was to be her first public advocacy of Zionism.

As a public speaker Miss Szold left much to be desired. Her delivery was dry and overrational; she never appealed to the emotions and would have felt that any such appeal was unnecessary, perhaps vulgar. Instead she spoke at great and erudite length about the revival of the Hebrew language and the work of Ben Yehuda, and the knitting together of diverse Jewries all over the world. "As there is but one God, so there is but one Judaism, and that Judaism has but one language—the Hebrew."

The Council of Jewish Women may have enjoyed the speech. Since they were well-educated feminists, the appearance of so impressively learned a woman must have been welcome to them. No one else was impressed. There was in fact great opposition to the speech in Baltimore as well as uncertainty about what it meant, for Zionism remained a mysterious and unsavory affair.

And reaction to Herzl's pamphlet was at first curiously hostile, not among Gentiles—antisemites frequently welcomed it—but among Jews. The German-Jewish press attacked him as a fraud. Orthodox Jewry was repelled by the idea of human interference in the return of the Jews to Zion, which could only take place when God willed it. In New York, a resolution by a group of Reform rabbis condemned any "formation of a Jewish state in Palestine in such a manner as may be construed as casting a doubt upon the citizenship, patriotism and loyalty of Jews in whatever country they reside."

But central Europe was crammed with young Zionist students who had left Russia because higher education, like the trades, the professions and the cities, was essentially closed to them, and flocked to the universities of Germany, Austria and Switzerland. There they starved on pittances earned by tutoring and plotted the redemption of their people. After the first wave of skepticism subsided they were amazed that a Viennese man of letters, a *Dr.* Herzl, was espousing their own, their secret cause. And in eastern Europe the Jews of Russia, Galicia and Romania heard the news as proof that the Messiah had arrived.

In the spring of 1896, Herzl started on the first of a series of pilgrimages that took him to the anterooms and palaces of the great. It was his unique contribution to Zionist theory that the Jewish nation must be housed on land secured to them by political guarantees. He had surrendered the idea of Argentina and was preparing to wrest those guarantees from rulers with influence over Turkish Palestine, where Jews had been settling since 1880 in amorphous and scattered little colonies and where they had lived since time immemorial in the holy cities. How was this to be accomplished? To Herzl it seemed simple: the sultan of Turkey needed money; there were immensely rich Jews, like Baron Rothschild, already willing to help the impoverished and persecuted Jews of

Russia. If the great powers—he turned first to Germany, later to England—would put pressure on Turkey and act as guarantors in the transaction, the millionaires would solve the sultan's financial problems in return for opening Palestine to legal Jewish settlement.

Herzl visited the German Kaiser, the Grand Duke of Baden and the court of the Turkish sultan, who refused to see him personally while suggesting to an emissary that the ideas were interesting, even sympathetic, and he might want to hear more. Returning to Europe, Herzl met Baron Edmond de Rothschild, who had been supporting the Biluim in their farming settlements in Palestine. The visit proved an utter failure, the Baron convinced that Herzl was a megalomaniac, Herzl equally convinced that Rothschild was narrow-minded, cowardly, without vision. A Russian Zionist named Menachem Ussishkin paid a call on Herzl and decided, "He does not know the first thing about Jews." Ussishkin took this to be a peculiar advantage, however, for Herzl thought he had only to deal with sultans and philanthropists; dealing with the fragmented and furiously contentious Zionists of eastern Europe, Ussishkin felt, would be a far more disagreeable task. And in England, Herzl met a young journalist, Jacob de Haas, whom he appointed as his London secretary.

Early in March of 1897, Herzl was in Vienna forming plans for a congress of Zionists from all European countries. Offices were rented and Zionist leaders instructed to stir the masses into action; de Haas was to contact the Jewish communities of America. Word of the plan had appeared in a July 1896 issue of the *Nation*, and opposition among American Jewry exploded from pulpit and press.

Throughout eastern Europe, young men like Chaim Weizmann, a Russian studying at the University of Berlin, raced from townlet to townlet within the Pale explaining what a "congress" was. Each of the Zionist circles scraped money together so that a delegate might make the journey to Basel, Switzerland, in August 1897. Herzl, meanwhile, had come to the full realization of what Ussishkin knew about Zionist bickering; he was heartsick over the carping, the vanity, the vehement personal quarrels. Yet he insisted on ruling like an absolute monarch and as a result managed to alienate almost all the leaders of real stature. On the eve of the Basel congress, Herzl saw himself as commanding "an army of schnorrers. I am at the head of boys, beggars and schmucks."

Delegates began arriving from Europe, Palestine and North Africa, most of them traveling third class, sitting up all night and eating the food they had brought from home. This was Herzl's first encounter with the Russians whom Henrietta Szold found so magnetic, and he saw in them the same authenticity and wholeness:

They possess an inner integrity that most European Jews have lost. They feel like national Jews but without narrow and intolerant conceit. They are not tormented by the need to assimilate. Their nature is simple and unbroken . . . they are upright and genuine, and yet they are ghetto Jews, the only ghetto Jews of our time. By looking at them we understood what gave our forefathers the strength to endure the most difficult times.

Almost all were desperately poor, and Herzl had written on the cards of admission, "Black formal attire and white necktie must be worn at the festive opening session." This was not entirely due to his craving for theatrics, for he believed the congress would succeed only if the delegates saw themselves and conducted themselves like men engaged in a high endeavor. Two hundred Zionists from sixteen countries descended on the rental shops of Basel to procure evening dress, which most wore for the first time in their lives.

The Basel congress was a personal triumph for Herzl, who had overseen all the arrangements down to the most minute detail. Twenty-six major European newspapers sent correspondents. Spectators overflowed the balcony and had to be accommodated below, behind the delegates. Herzl himself was received with cheers, weeping, hand kissing, repeated roars of sustained applause that made it impossible for him to speak, and a great wave of *"Yechi Hamelech!"* —"Long live the king!"

There were solid accomplishments as well. A world-wide Zionist organization was founded, to be headquartered in Vienna and run by an Actions Comité under Herzl's command; a Jewish National Fund to buy land in Palestine was discussed and later established; a Hebrew University in Jerusalem was discussed for the first time, and the Basel Program, the basis of political Zionism that was Herzl's unique creation, was here enunciated: "The aim of Zionism is to create for the Jewish people a homestead in Palestine secured by public law."

While most American Jews were horrified by the news of Herzl's congress, American Zionists found it exhilarating. There were already Zionist societies, chiefly in New York among the penniless immigrants, and Zionist discussion groups met in every city with a large Jewish population. But squabbles between Orthodoxy and Reform left most of them powerless, and the only group that sent a delegate to the congress was the Baltimore association. According to Zionist legend, when that lone delegate arrived in Basel someone asked, Why only one—are there no Zionists in America? Oh yes, came the reply, there are two, a rabbi and a madwoman: Stephen Wise and Henrietta Szold.

But in the wake of the congress, Zionist societies sprang to life all over America. Within a year a Federation of American Zionists united them, affiliating with the world organization. Richard Gottheil, a young Columbia University professor of Semitics, was elected president and would attend the second congress. When the second annual conference of the Federation of American Zionists met in Baltimore, Henrietta Szold became a member of its executive committee.

The other leaders of the federation were, like her, American-born and of central European origin, rabbis, scholars, professionals, many in their twenties. American Zionism looked impressive on paper, some 100 societies with a membership of 5,000 in New York alone, but it had no single leader of real prestige. It was still a dangerous movement, faintly crackpot, certainly déclassé. Even among American Jews of east European background Zionists were only a small minority. The children of the Russians were losing their Jewishness as fast as they could throw it away, scrambling after money honestly or dishonestly; they had fallen in love with America and would pay any price to be a part of it. Miss Szold had seen the seeds of change ten years earlier at the Russian Night School when she watched boys of fourteen mocking the old people who struggled with English. Their attitudes were epidemic now, and she faced it clear-eyed. She never sentimentalized her fellow Jews, not even the Russians.

Among her sisters, the parents' values had filtered down in varying strength. Rachel made only a half-hearted attempt at Sabbath observance in Wisconsin because Joe was indifferent to it. Adele was worse than indifferent. After a year of college she wanted to strike out on her own; she tried private teaching in Baltimore while raising mushrooms commercially, but the combination was unsuccessful. Baltimore was "stuffy" anyhow, so she left for New York to become an emancipated woman. There she found a job on the editorial staff of the *Jewish Encyclopedia*, for which Henrietta wrote scholarly articles from time to time; it was a haphazard affair intended to incorporate the biographies of Jewish prizefighters with those of big businessmen, the latter because they would surely contribute to production costs.

Interesting people worked off and on for the *Encyclopedia*, among them a "little Russian Jew" named Thomas Seltzer, who was very little indeed, not quite five feet tall, slight, frail, addicted to tea and cigarettes. Seltzer knew half a dozen languages and became a founder and editor of the *Masses* while living hand to mouth among avant-garde writers and artists in Greenwich Village. When Maxim Gorky came to New York a few years later, after the failure of the 1905 revolution in Russia, he named Seltzer as his official translator. It was just such an atmosphere Adele had hoped to find in the world beyond Baltimore: tea and revolution and heady talk and people who neither knew nor cared that she was a rabbi's daughter.

One day a man appeared at the offices of the *Encyclopedia* trailing clouds of that same rabbinical past. He was a young Talmudic scholar named Louis

Ginzberg, newly arrived in the States that year. Ginzberg began to work for the *Encyclopedia*, where everyone, even Rabbi Jastrow, who was one of the editors, recognized the presence of a brilliant mind. Adele was not impressed by Ginzberg, however. She thought he was too much impressed by himself.

Now there was only Bertha at home with Henrietta and the parents. Bertha had graduated from Bryn Mawr and was teaching school, for her fiancé had died quite suddenly. She was not "advanced," nor was she intellectual like Sadie and Henrietta; she was lively, intelligent and giggled a lot, but underneath was a solid Jewish matron, the competent mother of a large family, the preserver of established Jewish values, biding her time until a husband appeared.

A suitable candidate was a young lawyer named Louis Levin, who was also the editor of a weekly Baltimore paper, the *Jewish Comment*, a job that had first been offered to Henrietta. Miss Szold had declined because of the pressures of her work for the JPS, but she had promised to work closely with Levin and did so. Her suggestions show sound experience in every aspect of journalism: the physical make-up of the paper, the unreliability of printers, the best ways to beat out a rival when going after an important story. "Keep up your courage," she told Levin. "We are going to get out many a paper to blush for before a satisfactory issue comes along."

The sweatshop of the JPS had sharpened her wits and broadened her world, for everything she passed on to Levin had been gained there; but with her superiors Miss Szold was as muted as before. She had requested and been granted a raise and now earned $100 a month, less than she asked for and much less than she was worth. Far more than money, she had a poignant need for appreciation. How long and how unhappily she had longed for it was clear when the Publication Society celebrated its tenth anniversary. There was a banquet in Philadelphia preceded by a meeting. She wrote home about these events in the first daze of excitement, saying she had been praised, applauded; it was almost more than she could believe, for she "had not received a sign these eight years that my work was satisfactory, not acceptable merely because no better could be got . . . . " Judge Sulzberger's address "was masterly even before he said anything about me. I do not think I can make you appreciate what my feelings were when he began to eulogize me. First, I felt as though I might be dead . . . then the lump in my throat convinced me that I was alive. . . . I am not sure that I can repeat what he said. . . . I was so happy that I was positively miserable."

Her gratitude was put to a severe test when the JPS undertook to put together the *American Jewish Yearbook*, a massive reference work that soon became Henrietta's nightmare. She shared the labors of the first volume with Cyrus Adler, who had studied Assyriology at Hopkins, but all succeeding yearbooks were hers alone, and she was still without a secretary, working twelve, even fifteen hours a day for days at a time when the yearbook frenzy was at its height; there were years without a vacation.

In January 1901, Bertha and Louis Levin were married quietly at the Szolds' home; the rabbi's health was such that only the simplest ceremony and the minimum of guests could be thought of. By now he was in a wheelchair when he was not in bed, a demanding invalid who refused all food yet seemed to waste away for want of it before the eyes of the wife, daughter and trained nurse who cared for him.

"The chief thing," Henrietta wrote to Bertha, "is that Papa is very weak . . . and we are absolutely powerless. Dr. Gilpin says that we are killing Papa by giving in to him. I wonder how much holding out against Papa's will he would do if he were nursing him." She was more than a dutiful daughter caring for an aged parent. She breathed with him, suffering each pain in her own body. She was unable to put any distance between herself and her father, so that all her senses were keyed to an almost supernatural sensitivity and quivered at the slightest change.

Spring, summer, winter went by, and in the house on Callow Avenue life was measured by the spoonful, every drop swallowed a triumph, every drop rejected another defeat. But one summer morning Henrietta was wakened from an exhausted sleep by her mother and told that her father was dead. Her first thought was that she had failed him; she had gone to bed each night for eight years now reminding herself that her father might need her, prepared for the summons to his bedside, assured that he would die in her arms. He had died and she had slept. It was all failure and guilt.

For weeks she seemed to do nothing but sit at her desk before photographs of her father: in Breslau with university friends, as a young man looking stern and purposeful in rabbinical robes under a great black hat like half an inverted bowl, then older and older, the beard and mustache growing white. She raced from one picture to the next scrutinizing his features. They were only paper.

She was unable to remember his face, and this frightened her. Could she truly say she had loved him if she could not remember his face? All she could bring back was the pain, the noisy breathing, the hand that pushed away the spoon she held to his lips. It was a terrible thing not to remember your father's face. It was a denial of him; it meant that all those years were a mockery and an illusion.

If she loved him she would remember him. She went back to the pictures, scattering them in her anxiety to find one that would bring the *living* face before her eyes, feeling a tightness in her chest as if she had been running. Her eyes burned, she had a feeling of physical exhaustion, a lightness. The pictures were unreal and she hated them for that, but how could she hate them, how dare she, when they were all she had now?

It occurred to her, not for the first time since her father's death, that there was something unwholesome about her thoughts and feelings. She wondered what it was like when people lost their minds.

Even her mother, in the midst of her own grief, was troubled by Henrietta. While it was natural for her to mourn for her father, the extent of mourning, the compulsive preoccupation with what she had done wrong and how she had failed him, did not seem natural. When Bertha and Louis Levin had their first child, they named him Benjamin after the rabbi. For Mrs. Szold the new life brought a renewal of hope and faith, but for Henrietta nothing changed. A door had closed, and the room where she was left was a void.

Sophie Szold was always spoken of as the most practical of women, skeptical and level-headed, with none of her husband's rash generosity, and Henrietta came to think of her as someone bogged down in details, limited, even narrow. But what she did now was splendidly generous. She was entitled to the position of chief mourner, not only the widow of the deceased but a woman past sixty, who would have been within her rights if she had insisted her daughter put grief aside to get on with living, the proper work of the young, and leave the mourning to her.

Instead she reminded Henrietta that she was the legal heir of her father's manuscripts and the only one who could read the rabbi's arthritic handwriting. Perhaps she ought to put his papers in order now, even prepare them for publication.

Henrietta seemed to revive a bit. Yes, her father was gone, but she could hold on to him for years by working on the papers. He was a great man; the world of Jewish scholarship deserved to know his unpublished works.

But then she saw it was impossible. She did not know enough, she told her mother; she had no training in Talmudics.

She could get it, Sophie pointed out. She could write to Dr. Solomon Schechter in New York and ask if there were some way she might study at the new seminary, the Jewish Theological Seminary that would open for the first time in the fall, not to be a rabbi, simply to train herself for work on the manuscripts.

At first it seemed an outrageous idea, for there were no women at rabbinical seminaries. Yet Solomon Schechter was no ordinary rabbi; he had known her father, and he knew and liked Henrietta. Nor was his seminary an ordinary one.

It was the creation of a group of Reform Jews of German background, rich, powerful and addicted to philanthropy, the millionaires Jacob Schiff, Felix

Warburg and Solomon Guggenheim among them. Their purpose was to rescue the Jews of New York's East Side from crime and despair. For the hundreds of thousands of Russian immigrants jammed into tenement dwellings and coal cellars had suffered an almost total breakdown of social structure in the transition from feudalism to the machine age. Many gave up religion overnight because Orthodoxy hardly seemed to make sense in the New World; it was too difficult, too demanding. Reform Judaism was meaningless to them. Yet in Russia their social and communal organization had always been along religious lines. Unless the East Side could provide capable leaders the slums would remain an embarrassment as well as a heartache to the decent, prosperous German Jews of America.

Between Orthodoxy and Reform was a smaller, distinctive branch of Judaism that came to be called Conservative; it was to this branch that Rabbi Szold belonged before it had a name. Here the Reform philanthropists saw their solution. The Jewish Theological Seminary would train American-born rabbis in Conservative Judaism, and these rabbis, young, modern, conversant with Orthodoxy yet free of its narrowest limitations, would become the educators, organizers and leaders of the East Side Jews.

As head of the seminary the inevitable choice was a professor of rabbinics at Cambridge in England, a man named Solomon Schechter. Born in Romania, the son of a *shochet*, or ritual slaughterer, Schechter was eccentric, hot-tempered, charming and brilliant; the wife of one Cambridge scholar called him "that wild man of stupendous genius." Miss Szold, when she met him for the first time at the Sulzbergers' home in Philadelphia, called him "a lamb." Many of the leaders of the seminary were men she had known through the Publication Society—Cyrus Adler was president of the board, Sulzberger one of its members.

On second thought, therefore, her mother's suggestion appeared somewhat less than outrageous. Then the rebbitzin added that she, Sophie, would leave Baltimore after more than forty years and set up housekeeping in New York to make a home for Henrietta there.

It was a beautiful offer: to leave Bertha, the new grandchild and her intimate friends so that her daughter might come to terms with grief. For days Henrietta thought about it. Gradually her father's image seemed to return to her, "and then I realized the whole extent of my loss, and realizing it I was assured of my sanity." She told her mother she was ready to try.

The plan was put before Dr. Schechter, who was entirely sympathetic. It was true that women never studied at rabbinical seminaries; even the secretarial staff of Schechter's seminary was male. But Miss Szold was forty-two and her scholarly reputation as well as her character above reproach. He told her he would not object provided the entire board of the seminary were in agreement.

Early in 1903, Miss Szold got word that she would be admitted that fall

as a special student. She left immediately for New York to search for an apartment near the seminary, which was on West 123rd Street, close to Morningside
Park, Riverside Drive and the tree-lined campus of Columbia University. It
was during this exploratory trip that she went to a reception and was introduced
to Louis Ginzberg, the brilliant young man who wrote articles for the *Jewish
Encyclopedia;* Schechter had chosen him as the central figure of his new faculty.
She saw him again the following day and when they met held out her hand
to him, a curious gesture for a woman who was rarely impulsive. For some
reason the memory of it embarrassed her for weeks.

That summer Mrs. Szold and Henrietta moved to New York, where Adele
joined them. Mrs. Szold was to find her place among the wives of the seminary
faculty; Adele would work for the *Encyclopedia;* Henrietta was to have her
chance at higher education while continuing with the Jewish Publication Society.

She did not know that her father's papers would remain untouched; she
could not guess that she would fall in love for the first time and at the age
of forty-three with a blue-eyed professor of Talmud named Louis Ginzberg,
thirteen years younger and destined to become one of the most eminent Jewish
scholars of his generation.

II

NEW YORK:
IN THE SEMINARY CIRCLE

7

When the Jewish Theological Seminary opened its doors in the autumn of 1902, Solomon Schechter and Louis Ginzberg were most of the faculty. They went abroad the next summer and came back with two European scholars, Alexander Marx and Israel Friedlaender, both slightly younger than Ginzberg, who was generally expected to be the star of the show. After Schechter, that is; that imperious man, sonorous, belligerent, with the soulful eyes of a Hasidic sage and a wife who reverently brushed the bread crumbs from his beard, was the world's most illustrious Jewish scholar. It was a measure of his breadth of spirit that he had chosen as the main pillar of his faculty a man decades younger whose reputation was certain to rival his own one day, and had treated him from the first as an equal.

Although Louis Ginzberg was already a leading authority on rabbinic literature, in Schechter's estimation, he had written little besides his doctoral thesis. The Jewish Publication Society had agreed in 1901 to publish a Ginzberg volume on the legends of the Jews, but they had not yet seen a page of it. In 1902, with his lifework all before him, Louis Ginzberg never for a moment doubted its value; according to his son Eli, "He had already decided to become the greatest Jewish scholar living."

Before the seminary could judge the writer, they saw the teacher. It is the essence of Conservative Judaism, the movement embodied in the new seminary, that "there is no other Jewish religion but that taught by the Torah and confirmed by history and tradition." These were Dr. Schechter's words on opening day; Torah, the Bible of Moses, was the rock to which the accretions of history and tradition were added century by century. Which ought to be kept and which brushed away as unsuited to altered times and places were questions for the eye of faith informed by the scholarly mind, and to answer them required a process of constant sifting and examination, using the most rigorous techniques of the modern historian, linguist and anthropologist. Conser-

vative Judaism, then, gave first place to the scholar-scientist. Louis Ginzberg
was such a man. Some scholars and scientists are failures in the classroom,
but he was not.

From the start Ginzberg proved to be an exceptional teacher, radiant
with intellectual authority and a certain subtle, disturbing emanation that sig-
naled to his students the presence of someone with the power to change their
lives. One seminary graduate recalled the day of his first encounter with Ginzberg, when he presented himself to be examined for admission, eighteen years
old and serenely self-assured. He sensed a sarcastic note in the professor's manner:
"I left the room woefully deflated and strangely enough loving the man who
had put me to the blush. In the Students' Hall of the old Seminary building
where my friends and I reviewed our experience, I discovered that they too
had been smitten at first sight. We could not quite explain to ourselves how
it had happened. . . . And yet our pulses were in a great flutter." It seemed
to them the man was a giant.

Physically he was small, with well-formed features, abundant dark hair
worn short and a Vandyke beard, his eyes behind the pince-nez an extraordinary
blue. The students had noted his quizzical sarcasm; it was the air of one who
stands apart, who observes from beneath a lifted eyebrow, who knows the secrets
of the universe or at any rate those worth knowing, all others being by definition
trivial. Everything in his personal history had contributed to make of Louis
Ginzberg "the acme of the intellectual snob," as his son most affectionately
described him; "there were only three or four people he considered his intellectual equals."

He was born in 1873 in Kovno, Lithuania, a province of the Russian
Empire and the preeminent European center of traditional Judaism, populous,
poor, entirely cut off from the modern world, where Torah was the living
reality and Gentile history only a distant rumor, impermanent as mist. The
Ginzbergs were a family of scholars, influential for generations in the throbbing
intellectual and religious life of Lithuanian Jewry, men of substance as well as
learning, including on Louis's mother's side the Gaon (sage) of Vilna, the
most splendid name in Lithuanian Jewish scholarship. Founders and heads of
yeshivas, religious officials, saintly laymen were among their ancestors, and any
important personage in Lithuanian Jewry unconnected with the Ginzbergs by
blood or marriage was an intimate friend. Louis's mother, Zippe Jaffe Ginzberg,
was a learned woman. His father, Reb Isaac Elias Ginzberg, was a distinguished
scholar and an ordained rabbi, but, in the biblical tradition, his religion was
not his livelihood; one earned a living in whatever manner came to hand, for
the living was a necessity but otherwise of no importance. Although Reb Isaac
supported his large family by traveling as a commission merchant in textiles,

he was never identified as Reb Isaac the textile merchant; he was Reb Isaac the pious, the learned. Their sixth child, Louis, was the son Reb Isaac wanted and prayed for and deserved: a *matmid*, a perpetual student, brought up to emulate the Gaon, who was also blue-eyed. To the family he was a second Gaon, and to the father he was someone to be approached with respect: "My father was a great admirer of mine," Louis Ginzberg wrote, "not in that usual foolish way of parents but in that of a 'connoisseur,' so that he never allowed me to perform the smallest service for him because it is against the [law] to be served upon by a great scholar. . . ."

Ten rabbis attended Louis's bar mitzvah. At sixteen he was a learned innocent, spiritually experienced, deeply versed in rabbinic literature and Talmudic dialectic, his memory a library in itself, his mind at once profoundly rich and dangerously narrow. For he spoke no modern language besides Yiddish; he knew nothing whatever about the world. He was underweight, his health already eroded by study, his lungs fragile. A specialist was consulted; a year of "building up" on good Cognac and oranges followed. Then Reb Isaac prescribed a Western, secular education in any European capital with a Jewish population sufficiently large and Orthodox so that he could pursue his Talmudic studies.

Accordingly Louis was sent to Frankfurt, where in two years he completed most of the eight-year gymnasium course for university admission, including Latin, Greek and German. Then he entered the University of Berlin, concentrating on physics and mathematics, continuing Jewish studies on his own since the Orthodox rabbinical seminary failed to impress him.

But in Berlin, Ginzberg apparently entered into student life with more vigor than Reb Isaac foresaw. His German was now perfectly fluent and he had learned beer drinking as well, enjoying himself enough so that colleagues at the seminary would later refer to the "lewd life" he had led during his student days. The words can be taken to mean almost anything, for the seminary circle was composed of strict observers for whom indiscriminate theater going and drinking parties and a few fast friends were the outermost limits of dissipation. But it was not the life of a future Gaon.

After two years in Berlin, Ginzberg transferred to Strasbourg in order to study under Theodor Noeldeke, the greatest Orientalist of his day. For his doctoral dissertation he settled on the legends of the Jews as found in the writings of the Church Fathers, a project Eli Ginzberg later described as "the ambitious start of a search through the whole of the patristic literature for biblical legends. . . . The collateral descendant of the Gaon of Vilna had truly escaped from the confines of rabbinic literature. He was treading on ground that few if any Orthodox Jews had ever before explored. But he did so with a discipline and self-control that would have been worthy of the Gaon."

This was the young professor who came to America in 1899 equipped with a variety of traits associated with the addiction to study: poor health, lifelong insomnia, a photographic memory and the habit of omnivorous reading. He consumed the entire *New York Times* each day and retained much of what he read, whether related to the stock exchange or baseball. He had another trait less usual among scholars, and this was what the young students at the seminary reacted to when they felt their pulses flutter after their first meeting with him: he was charming because he intended to charm.

When Miss Szold first met him in New York in 1903, she was in the midst of a difficult transition, not only severing herself forever from the scenes and people that tied her to her father, but faced with a new setting altogether intimidating. At the turn of the century the five boroughs had been incorporated into Greater New York, and overnight the city became one of the biggest in the world. Bigness was a virtue. Progress was the preeminent virtue. Apartment houses sprang up everywhere, the most luxurious lit entirely by electricity. There were electric buses in Manhattan and thousands of electric signs. Horse-drawn traffic competed with automobiles in which drivers and passengers were muffled up against the weather. Bicyclists abounded. Horses drew trolley cars and fire engines, and most streets were cobblestoned, but the city was shooting outward because people wanted to live away from its heart and travel in to work. The great need was for cheap, rapid public transportation. They had entered the twentieth century, and everyone dreamed of shining bridges flung across bodies of water.

It was not gentle, *gemütlich* Baltimore, not even Philadelphia. In order to be near the seminary the Szolds would have to live in an apartment house. The flat Henrietta eventually chose was on the third floor of a small building with a brownstone front, the entry way decorated with the heads of Greek gods in bas-relief. It was diagonally across the street from the seminary, at West 123rd and Broadway; to the left was Riverside Drive, an impressive boulevard dotted with classical monuments to which Grant's Tomb had recently been added at vast expense. Bicyclists raced up the drive with the wind at their backs and the Hudson River below. It was always windy there, always splendidly remote from the city, a place for solitary walkers with lofty thoughts or lovers in search of privacy.

The Szolds moved into the new apartment in the summer, bringing whatever there was room for: the old Victorian pieces from the formal parlor, the Morris chair the rabbi used to use and Henrietta's hinge-top desk, which was placed under her father's portrait, with a picture of Herzl on the opposite wall. They would live a simpler, less encumbered life now; homes had generally begun to unclutter themselves, and housekeeping was not so elaborate, nor were women's clothes. Trim, tailored suits and shirtwaists were something of a uniform.

The high neckline and swelling bosom were unflattering to Miss Szold, who was short and weighed too much. But fashion was not a preoccupation among the women of the seminary circle. The professors' wives were serious-minded, cultivated, German-speaking. The entire tone of the seminary was Germanic. At services in the new synagogue frock coats and striped trousers were worn by the young professors, and they were frequently honored by the presence of board members Schiff, Sulzberger and others, clothed in the impenetrable dignity of their millions.

By the end of her first month at the seminary Miss Szold found to her amazement that everything seemed easier than she expected, perhaps because all she heard so far were introductory lectures. But there was one challenge she refused to accept. She did not enter Ginzberg's class on Talmud and during the first term went only once a week to his class on Aramaic grammar. She was afraid of him.

It had already occurred to her that she might be falling in love. She had had proposals before—proposals of convenience, she later decided—but she had never before been in love, nor had she ever had reason to believe herself loved. What she felt now was something like the early symptoms of a childhood disease, measles or chicken pox, descending on a middle-aged body that responded with the cry, "Now? Why now?"

Some weeks after the opening of school Rabbi Marcus Jastrow died. Ginzberg was asked to compose a eulogy, which he did in German, for his English was still uncertain. One day he stopped Miss Szold in the seminary hall and asked if she would translate it. She refused, although she felt it was ungracious to refuse, and when he pressed her she gave way. She did the translation and returned it to him as casually as possible in the hallway. For several months they had no other personal contact.

In the spring she had an earache that kept her home from synagogue one Saturday. Professors Marx and Friedlaender called at the apartment in the afternoon to see how she was and to learn if the informal lessons in English she had been giving them would take place as usual that evening. Ginzberg happened to be with them. She told Marx and Friedlaender to come back for dinner and their lesson, and it seemed impossible not to include Ginzberg in the invitation, although it was painful to do so. He came with them every week after that, and another barrier was breached. They saw each other regularly now; he was one of several visitors whom Mrs. Szold, Adele and Anna, their servant, recognized at sight.

During the summer of 1904—Ginzberg in Europe visiting his family, Miss Szold in New York slaving over the 460 biographies in the *American Jewish Yearbook*—Theodor Herzl died at the age of forty-four. He had been aware for some years that his leadership of the Zionist movement was not unquestioned. Although he was deeply and widely mourned, the young east Europeans had found Herzl's style too elegant and worldly, his pursuit of great men, princes and rulers who were to "give" Palestine to the Jews, the pursuit of a mirage. The movement was split into the left wingers, the Orthodox and the so-called Democratic Fraction, young academicians such as Chaim Weizmann who were centrists with a leftist leaning, all challenging the established powers. With Herzl's death a great weariness descended. "We had reached, it seemed to me, a dead point in the movement," Weizmann felt. "My struggles were destroying me; an interval was needed before the possibilities of fruitful work could be restored." He left the continent for England, where he could pursue the scientific career he had been neglecting. The University of Manchester offered him a research post, and he settled there with his wife.

The summer ended, the seminary opened and once again Miss Szold did not enroll in Ginzberg's Talmud class. He had stopped by at her house one day months earlier and been drawn into a discussion of higher education for women; Dr. Ginzberg believed that the home, the children's school and the exercise of loving kindness were the proper and only spheres for Jewish women, and Miss Szold took what he said that day to mean that women should not study Talmud—certainly they should not study Talmud in the company of men.

The Talmud is a compilation of Jewish civil and canonical law encrusted with detailed examinations into every likely and unlikely variant of human behavior. In the passages on *Kiddushin*, the sanctification of marriage, Talmudic analysis is trained on sex and the relations between the sexes. Aspects of genital penetration, frequency of intercourse according to the husband's profession or business, acceptable and unacceptable positions during coitus, all are considered in minute detail, in an atmosphere utterly devoid of squeamishness, by learned men anxious that no conceivable possibility should remain unexplored. Is a woman not a virgin when she has been accidentally deflowered by a stick? Has she committed adultery if she has been impregnated while bathing in a public place where the sperm of a male bather unknown to her has entered her body? These exotic situations and many more are considered in *Kiddushin*. What results is a dazzling analysis of human sexuality by those who sought to interpret the Almighty's intentions in the era preceding the sixth century A.D. If Dr. Ginzberg preferred to lecture on *Kiddushin* without a woman in his class, Miss Szold felt she could understand his reservations.

One day it happened that Friedlaender, Ginzberg and Miss Szold walked home together from a luncheon at the Schechters'. It was early October, the air radiantly bright and still warm. Friedlaender asked Miss Szold if she were going to a formal dinner being given for a visiting scholar. Oh no, she said; although she was a student and entitled to go, she had decided that as the only woman, she would not attend official seminary dinners. Friedlaender said he couldn't see why she should discriminate against herself. Dr. Ginzberg broke in with, "Ridiculous!" By which he meant, it seemed to Miss Szold, that he recognized her womanhood. She could not look at him for a while. She felt flushed, excited.

Some minutes later Ginzberg remarked that he had expected to see her in his Talmud class that morning. When she reminded him of what he had said that day at her house about women, higher education and Talmud and asked if this was not sufficient reason for her to avoid the class, he made no reply. But the following morning she had a note from him. Her hands shook when she opened it. He had just finished going through his projected lectures on *Kiddushin*, and he wrote, "I am quite satisfied that there is nothing in it which should prevent you from being present. . . ." He hoped she would be present; he wished he had more "disciples" like her.

She saved the letter, the first piece of paper with his handwriting on it that was hers to keep, and went to the class.

That first day he called her aside to ask if she would make note of his errors in English, and this too she did, coming up to him at the end of each class with the day's mistakes, each time remaining just long enough to explain the errors and her corrections.

She no longer feared falling in love; it had happened. Her fear was that she might expose herself, that someone, anyone, might discover the shameful secret, that Ginzberg might discover it. Her movements and her speech became even more guarded than usual; when others discussed Dr. Ginzberg, usually with admiration, she said nothing or was deprecating. She dissembled so well that for a time some of the professors believed she actually disliked Dr. Ginzberg.

But during class she watched and listened and devoured his presence with the undiluted attention of a young girl and with the same bodily responses, the visceral quickening that came long before the intellectual awareness that he was entering the room, that his eyes were fixed on her, that he was speaking directly to her. When she heard his voice, her heart banged.

To listen to Ginzberg was to be reminded of her father, her first love, now displaced. Worse than displaced; she could see there was no comparison between the two. The good and noble rabbi was not a scholar in the sense that Ginzberg was. Already the manuscripts she had brought seemed less precious, and in any case she had no hope of learning enough to edit them. She was learning something more complex and disturbing than rabbinics.

In January she heard indirectly that the troublesome *Kiddushin* passages were approaching and that he intended to make certain omissions for the sake of her feelings, so she sent him a note. "I want . . . to assure you that if you exercise your right to exclude me from the class when my presence is trying, I shall take it as an indication that ordinarily I am persona grata. . . ." There was no response, she remained in class, and Professor Ginzberg approached *Kiddushin*, that year at least, from a lofty distance.

In February he brought her a lecture of his written in German and inadequately translated by someone else; would she translate it for him? She translated and edited it, added suggestions about the best method of delivery and went to hear it at the synagogue. A little later he asked her to proofread one of his scholarly articles, and soon they fell into an arrangement whereby whatever articles or speeches he had in hand would be brought to her for translating, proofreading and similar editorial chores. She did as much for several other seminary professors, but what she did for Louis Ginzberg was an offering laid on the altar of the beloved. It took precedence over all her other work, her own occasional articles for Jewish journals, her JPS chores, her lessons at the seminary. She went without sleep to finish whatever Ginzberg asked of her and was happy only when she looked at him, heard his voice or worked at her desk with his handwritten papers at her fingertips.

That spring they began walking alone together after synagogue, west to Riverside Drive, then north or south along the railed walks high above the river, stopping from time to time to sit on the wooden benches. All week long she lived with the vision of that Sabbath walk before her, with last week's Sabbath walk burning in her mind. She had begun to spin out the hours she spent working over his papers; part of the time she was not working at all, just sitting, touching the handwriting, dreaming almost mindlessly. Nobody knew, not Adele, not their mother. Adele had never liked Professor Ginzberg, and she was full of her own concerns, her Greenwich Village friends and Thomas Seltzer, whom she called Toby.

Mrs. Szold liked Ginzberg immensely. He seemed to like her, and this reminded Henrietta of the way her own father used to say he loved Sophie's mother before he loved Sophie. But it never occurred to her to confide in her mother. Their relations were close without intimacy; and she was also a bit afraid of what Sophie would say about the difference in their ages, the difference between a plodding, methodical spinster and a brilliant scholar with all his life before him. So she said nothing to her mother, who was busy going back and forth to Baltimore. A second grandchild was born that summer. Rachel and Bertha were far away, and outside of mother and sisters there was no one Miss Szold could have confided in.

Her age began to weigh on her. She saw herself as middle-aged and aging and ineffectual. She was barely five feet tall and weighed about 150 pounds. She was fastidiously groomed, her eyes behind the pince-nez were said to be lovely (by her loving sisters), but she had never been pretty or lithe or vivacious even as a girl. Falling in love led her to despair of her appearance but not to change it. Her clothes were as prim as before, for it went without saying that a man like Ginzberg was above taking notice of clothes. Her hair was still in the knot at the back of her head, her sallow skin untouched by the film of powder worn by even the most respectable women. Fashion, frivolity, color were as foreign to her as flirting.

Young women passed her on the street with their rich hair piled up beneath flowery hats, their faces glowing and smooth. It was the era of the Gibson Girl, maidenly but athletic, corseted but supple. She saw those cheeks and waistlines with anguish; she was jealous even of Adele, who was young, mischievous, provocative, and bantered with Ginzberg from time to time, even expressed shocking opinions as if to tease him. Miss Szold was forty-four, a lovesick heart inside a middle-aged body.

Summer approached and Ginzberg announced he was leaving for Amsterdam to visit his parents; he would write to Miss Szold and Miss Adele if they would allow it. It seemed to Henrietta it was Adele he wanted to write to, and after he left she wept all night long, then the night after that, until Adele found her and the truth about her shameful love crept out.

Then the waiting began. She waited for a letter and no letter came, none for herself or Adele. She was working on the *Yearbook*, pacing back and forth in the living room on a hot July day, with her desk piled high with *Yearbook* papers full of numbers and dates and under them papers with his handwriting on them. She could not face the *Yearbook*, which was dead, while the papers he had written on were alive and electric.

The night before she had happened to read a love poem about a lonely, faded, rejected woman, "Thinking of this one thing alone—the love that never came to her." A sentimental and third-rate piece of doggerel, it gave her no peace. Only not now, she prayed. Only let him come back from Europe this one time with a free heart. After that she would force herself to grow accustomed to losing him. "Upon the mossed rock by the spring/ She sits, forgetful of her pail,/ Lost in remote remembering/ Of that which may no more avail. . . ." The name of the poem was "The Solitary."

She turned her back on the desk and the *Yearbook* and did something curious. She composed a letter as if in reply to a letter from Ginzberg:

I have been sitting with your precious letter in my hand all day long. . . . Perhaps before I reach the point of returning the treasure of love your letter gives me, my unreserve will have forfeited it. . . . In these hard months of my solitary struggle, I must have betrayed myself to your clear vision over and over again by my very efforts to exercise self-control. You must have divined it, that I was tranquil only when I was near you, only when you permitted me to do something for you . . . that at all other times I was restless, disturbed, unable to do the tasks I set myself, and which never before had found me distracted. Why then should I refrain from telling you in explicit words that my whole happiness lies with you—that you are the first to give my soul its woman's heritage, a soul that up to the time it was awakened by you—Oh! so many happy months ago—had known only filial passion. . . . You guess all the rest, all I have suffered to pretend indifference to you, all I would suffer to win you and hold you forever. . . .

Yet there remains a good deal to be said; and it is hard, bitter to say it, but it is better I send it across the waste of waters. . . . Somebody has sinned, or I should not have been exposed to the temptation of loving you—loving?— of adoring you—and you would have been spared the disharmony of being loved by me. Either I sinned against myself, or others sinned against me. But whoever sinned, one sin is not expiated by another. And I should be committing a grave sin against you, your young manhood, your high scholarship and ideals and gifts and prospects, were I to hang myself as a millstone about your neck. When you went away I wept and wept and prayed that this one time yet you might come back to me heart-free, so that I might have a space to grow accustomed to the idea that you would belong to some other woman. And then I grew bolder—I prayed for what has happened—I prayed that you would learn to love me. Happened, do I say? How we delight in deceiving ourselves! It has happened only because you guessed at the tumult in my soul and because you are chivalrous. For how can one like you spontaneously love one like me?

But whatever wild idea came into my disordered head and heart, I never lost sight of this one—that in the end I should have to practice renunciation. . . . I dare exercise no claim upon you. You belong to a happy, sprightly young creature, one that has not known the heat and burden of life, who will not so much give you intellectual sympathy . . . as she will give you warmth and color to glorify your life. With me you would walk in the gray shadow of sorrow.

Only one thing I ask of you, my dear friend. Do not think it easy for me to give you up. If you would see what I see before me now, my own future dark as night, cold as death. . . . I can never go back to the ignorance of my passionless days. You have made me to eat of the fruit of the tree of knowledge, and my eyes have been opened—only to behold my own misery, only to pity my past self which was so stupid, to pity my future self which is doomed to unhappiness. . . . I give you back then what you offer me, I shall bear my lot bravely. You will see how I shall control myself though my heart break. . . .

She folded the letter and stored it away along with the poem that inspired it.

Why had she written such a letter? To rehearse the painful need to reject Louis Ginzberg's proposal? But there was no proposal and no reason in the world to imagine he thought of making one. They were on terms of friendly formality; they were "Miss Szold" and "Professor Ginzberg" in all their conversations. There was nothing approaching intimacy between them, not even the staid Victorian intimacy Miss Szold might consider as leading toward a staid Victorian proposal. The letter was an exercise in fantasy. A dream.

It is the nature of dreams that they say what our waking selves cannot. "Someone has sinned, or I should not have been exposed to the temptation of loving you. . . . Either I sinned against myself, or others sinned against me." What sins could she have been thinking about in that blameless life, and who could have sinned against her? One thing is clear: whoever exposed her to the temptation of loving Ginzberg was the same person who kept her from loving others when she was young. Who kept her soul from its woman's heritage, confined her to passionless days, averted her sight from the tree of knowledge.

Her father had wanted an apprentice and heir, someone who would live the life that was denied to him. He shaped his daughter's character to fit his needs. His love had been everything to her; now for the first time she began to suspect it was not only the love of a wise and noble parent but also of a human man with selfish goals. He had not loved her for herself alone, as everyone wants and deserves to be loved, but as an extension of himself. Moreover, in shaping her a certain way, he had cut off the other ways—the woman's heritage. That it was one of the commonest parental sins was small comfort to the sinned-against.

Once she put these thoughts on paper she shoved them back into the realm of dreams, where they bided their time.

Later that month Louis Ginzberg did indeed write, not to Adele but to "my dear Miss Szold." It was a travel letter, rather stately in tone: "The weather and the sea were splendid all the time of my voyage. . . . The grandeur and monotony of the sea has always a melancholy-producing effect on me, and it is very good for me to be in the gay city of Paris again. . . ." She answered it instantly. A month or so later there was another, sending his mother's regards; his father had said that if it were not against Talmudic law he would have liked to send his regards as well.

A third letter was written in September as he returned from Europe. Responding to Miss Szold's remarks about the characters in a play she had read, Ginzberg wrote: "From the moment she declared her love to Gilbert she became unfit for real work, her socialism and all her other 'isms' only her playthings while poor Gilbert was going on planning, scheming and thinking. In other words I believe that a woman can't master more than one strong feeling at once, when in love nothing but the object of her love exists for her, while the man is strong enough to love a woman and have other passions at the same time."

8

Harry Friedenwald, who grew up near the Szolds in the German quarter of Baltimore, was a physician now, charming, kind-hearted, well-connected, active in Jewish affairs and a long-time Zionist. In 1904 the Federation of American Zionists elected him president, somewhat unwisely, for he still lived in Baltimore and its headquarters were in New York. Moreover he lacked aggressiveness, a quality the American organization sorely needed at that point.

But the FAZ was in no position to choose. The great majority of its members were eastern Europeans and greenhorns who needed a prestigious figure at their head. Prestige was a monopoly of the Germans, few of whom had any use for Zionism. Friedenwald, like Miss Szold, was one of the few.

The real work of the Zionist organization, the everyday business of bringing in members and raising money and keeping track of everything, was carried on by volunteers and a few salaried workers, all Russians, the same passionate, mystical people Miss Szold had fallen in love with in Baltimore. But passion will not keep an office in order. Not only were the financial affairs of the FAZ chaotic, but the Russians considered this fact unremarkable. Loyalty counted, not neatness.

In the summer of 1905, Friedenwald was on his way to Basel for the seventh Zionist congress. He stopped off in New York to confer with the executive committee of the FAZ and visited the Szolds his first evening in town. No one was home but Henrietta, and the two of them talked Zionism till one in the morning. The next day they went to an executive committee meeting in a little room on the upper floor of a building on East Broadway. Street sounds floated through the wide-open windows. Miss Szold in her light summer dress and the men in their shirtsleeves grew sweat-beaded and steamy. Everybody talked. Between the heat and the talk, which seemed to hammer relentlessly at the most trivial points, she had to fight to stay awake. When the meeting was over they all went to a cafe and drank vile celery tonic till midnight.

That was the leadership of the FAZ eight years after the first Zionist congress: a dozen or so sweaty conspirators in a two-room office. Small and ineffectual as they were, the FAZ was not the whole of American Zionism. There was always an ebb and flow of groups breaking off and forming rival organizations. Mizrachi, the Orthodox party, was born in 1903; Poale Zion, the labor wing, in 1905. All were members of the international movement, but the FAZ was the acknowledged official body in America.

The summer ended, and Louis Ginzberg returned from Amsterdam. Miss Szold found him waiting for her at the apartment with gifts, some Dutch china and an inkwell. When Saturday brought her to the synagogue she purposely moved out of his path through the foyer after services, but he found her, and soon they were walking home together as before. He had not fallen in love abroad; he had returned in spirit as well as in fact. She told herself she would be leaving New York in two years' time to go back to Baltimore forever. She was no danger to him. She had already given him up. Secure in this knowledge she offered to write out her notes on a new series of lectures he was giving that term; he agreed, and they spent a good deal of time together going over the lectures, which she transformed into a handwritten volume of more than 400 pages.

In October a wave of Russian pogroms drew the German and Russian Jews of New York together. They were pogroms of a new type, larger in scale and more devastating, which had first erupted a year and a half earlier in the Russian town of Kishinev, where forty-five Jews were massacred and every attempt at self-defense aborted by police. Anger and pity united workers and capitalists, the greenhorns of the East Side and the Yahudim of "uptown." One hundred thousand strong, they marched as in a funeral procession up Broadway and Fifth Avenue, with Dr. Judah Magnes at their head.

Magnes, who was twenty-eight years old, had recently been called to the pulpit of a Brooklyn congregation. Miss Szold had met him a year earlier when he appeared at her door on a Saturday afternoon, "a young man looking full of youth. He said, 'My name is Magnes, and I have been thinking we ought to know each other, so I came.'" Handsome, sunny, enthusiastic, he was a

Reform rabbi who nevertheless called himself a Zionist. One year later he was to become associate minister of Temple Emanu-El, the richest and most influential Jewish congregation in America, fiercely anti-Zionist. Nevertheless Magnes agreed to act as honorary secretary of the FAZ. So there were contradictory aspects to his beliefs and an unmistakably quixotic streak in his character, and altogether he seemed to be everything Miss Szold was not: young and daring and impulsive, unsullied by study and the hesitations of the intellect. The parade up Broadway was the greatest Jewish demonstration New York had ever seen.

The winter that followed was hard on Miss Szold. Her decision to leave New York evaporated and with it her peace of mind. She spent sleepless nights praying for strength. Sometimes the apartment seemed to imprison her; during a long day of rain and icy sleet, when walking was impossible, she wanted to run outdoors. She waited till evening, then flung on hat and coat and ran to Morningside Park, where she raced across the paths with the wind slapping her cheeks. Then back upstairs to the quiet apartment, walking, not running. Sedate, contained; that was the most important thing, to keep it contained. No one must know.

One day an old friend from Baltimore appeared at the door. His name was Benjamin Hartogensis; he had worked with Miss Szold at the Russian Night School and married one of the teachers. His wife had died five years earlier, leaving a little daughter. It occurred to Miss Szold that he needed a mother for the child, but she had promised to go walking down Riverside Drive with Ginzberg. She saw no reason to wait about for a proposal and after a brief visit left Hartogensis with her mother, put on her coat and hat, tied a veil over the hat and went to meet her beloved.

It was a cold day; even before they reached Riverside Drive they were moving briskly to keep warm. The moment they turned onto the drive the full force of an icy wind flew up at them. Ginzberg had brought parts of a new lecture, and he read it aloud as they walked. They seemed to be somewhere on top of the world and utterly alone, for the narrow parkway along the drive was deserted and his words fought the winds. When he finished he gave her the lecture to translate and edit; she tucked it into her purse, and within minutes the wind grew fiercer, ripping her veil partway from her hat so that the ends flapped about. She tried to pin it back, but the wind snatched it away. Sit down, Ginzberg told her, pointing to a bench. She sat; he bent forward and tied the veil while she stopped breathing and her heart banged against her chest. They walked on for a bit, but the river below was gray as steel and the skies were gray and every step was a battle, so they turned and went home with the wind at their backs. As soon as she was alone in her room Miss

Szold took off the veil with the greatest care so as to preserve the knot intact. She put it in the same drawer as the notes and letters he wrote her. From time to time she took the veil out and touched it.

Winter became spring and nothing changed. All her promises to stop loving him came to nothing; she learned nothing at the seminary, did nothing whatever with her father's papers. There was even the ugly suspicion that it made no difference, for the splendid heritage the rabbi had left her shriveled in the presence of Schechter, Ginzberg and the other professors, and for this she was ashamed. Overcome by guilt and overwork she had a crisis of nerves. She fled to Baltimore and Bertha, and when she came back she gave up the seminary courses.

But the walks on Riverside continued. Often they sat silently for hours at a time watching the river, the tugboats and barges, the rocky reaches of the Palisades on the other side. One summer evening they went together to a downtown synagogue and came back on the elevated train; it was hot, Miss Szold wore a short-sleeved dress, the train moved and jiggled and she was lightly thrown against him so that his bare hand brushed her bare arm. He snatched the hand away so quickly it seemed he could not bear to touch her.

In the fall Adele married Toby Seltzer and went to live with him in his tiny Greenwich Village flat; they had no money for a honeymoon. Seltzer's literary income was so fitful that Adele took on two jobs, one in the mornings as social secretary to Mrs. Jacob Schiff, who lived in staggering splendor on Fifth Avenue, and one in the afternoons as secretary for a child study association. Henrietta had discouraged the marriage, not because of Seltzer's poverty but because of his temperament, which seemed likely to clash with Adele's. He was very Russian: disorganized, dilatory, a great talker and theorist.

Now there were just a widow and a spinster in the flat, with a spinster for a servant. All that winter Miss Szold worked with Ginzberg on his *Geonica* and on the translation of what was to become *The Legends of the Jews*, of which the projected one volume promised to the JPS in 1901 had already extended itself to two, then three. In 1909, Louis Ginzberg was to publish four major works: the two volumes of *Geonica*, examining contributions to Jewish life of the spiritual leaders of Babylonian Jewry in the seventh, eighth and ninth centuries; *Yerushalmi Fragments from the Genizah*, an exploration into the Palestinian Talmud, and volume one of *The Legends of the Jews*. The latter became in time a vast and intricate construction of seven volumes, a work of historical and literary scholarship that can be read with pleasure by the lay person, while to the specialist it remains one of the basic research tools of Jewish learning, for scope, profusion and originality comparable to Sir James Frazer's *The Golden Bough*. A Jewish scholar once remarked that *The*

Legends of the Jews alone "would have required from almost any other scholar, no matter how brilliant and how tenacious his memory, two lifetimes."

Miss Szold had persuaded herself by then that Ginzberg would never marry, for he told her repeatedly how happy he was in his bachelorhood, how little he understood women. These were unusual sentiments on the part of the observant son of a devout family, for Orthodox Jews disapprove of celibacy. Virtue lies in early marriage and many children. But he transcended the rules that bound others, as he himself pointed out to her from time to time; his arrogance was never concealed from her, and she found it charming, like whatever else was his.

If he did not mean to marry, she need not give him up. At all costs she must continue to hide her love for him, but she could go on as she was, his literary servant and walking companion. They fell into the habit of spending every Tuesday together between his afternoon lecture and dinnertime. It was more than enough for her. It was an abundant feast.

One day in March, Ginzberg told her his father was ill; he would leave for Amsterdam that spring and spend five months with his parents. For a moment she was unable to say anything at all; the thought of so many months without him chilled and frightened her. Then she blurted out, "Do you mean you are leaving in less than five weeks?" A few days later he came to take her for a walk and asked why she seemed so unhappy, and she told him about a series of vexations with the Publication Society, then added, "There is something else I dare not tell you." But he did not ask, and she could not offer more.

He was to sail on a Saturday, the Sabbath. The day before, he came to say goodby to the Szolds, but Sophie was out. The living room was filled with the clatter of the typewriter—Miss Szold had a part-time typist now—so they went into the dining room and sat at the round table. He would have to walk several miles to the docks tomorrow, and she asked if she might go with him. He seemed pleased by that. Would she wear the new hat she had ordered, the one with the roses? Yes, she told him. Avoiding his eyes when she said it. No matter what he asked of her the answer could only be yes.

Then, in an almost offhand way, he told her his father hoped to see him marry. In that moment she noticed something strange; she had no physical reaction to his statement, no trembling. He would come back engaged, to please his father, and she would be saddened by it, but no more. . . . Then he pushed back the chair and went out to the hallway to get his coat, saying goodby to Anna and telling her to take good care of Miss Henrietta.

The next day they walked to the docks. Dr. Marx joined them, and later so did several others, including Adele and Toby. Miss Szold, who had taken with such calm the news that her beloved was supposed to find a bride for his father's sake, was no longer calm; she felt herself gripped by a hysteria she had to fight to suppress. Once Adele whispered under her breath, "Get hold of yourself!"

The little group of friends had lunch together, Miss Szold sitting beside Ginzberg, but she was unable to eat. By the time she saw him boarding the ship her face was streaming tears. He was gone, and his father wanted him to marry.

In Amsterdam, Ginzberg learned that his father had cancer of the throat. "There is absolutely nothing we can do but wait patiently," he wrote to Miss Szold. His father suffered, and the sight of his suffering was terrifying to the son; he gave up his usual careful diet in order that his parents might not notice there was anything wrong with him, and the pain of watching his father in pain was compounded by acute physical discomfort.

Their correspondence continued, accounts of Reb Isaac's condition mingled with gossip from the Jewish press and news of the progress of the manuscript of the *Legends*. All this flying back and forth of letters, some of them very long letters, did not go unnoticed in the Amsterdam household. The parents asked questions about the American woman who sent her regards to Reb Isaac's wife, and Ginzberg explained that she was an editor, thirteen years older than he, that they worked together, that while she was also a friend the letters were mostly about his manuscripts. To his parents such a relationship was beyond understanding. In their world men and women did not work together and were never friends. Once Miss Szold sent her regards to Reb Isaac by way of a legal evasion that permitted a woman to address a man unrelated to her, and Reb Isaac expressed his admiration for the learning of this American woman; his own good wishes were sent by way of the same legal evasion.

But no matter how learned she was they saw her as a threat. Although both parents longed to see their son marry, his bachelorhood being a source of continued sorrow to them, they never had in mind a wife past forty-five, too old to bear children. "That the apple of their eye should be running around with this older bluestocking," as Ginzberg's son later expressed it, "was part of an uncouth and dangerous American environment." Whether they ever said as much to Louis, it was in the air, it was surely in their eyes and voices, and Louis must have seen and heard and breathed the knowledge of it.

Therefore he must have known as early as 1907 that some people believed he was interested in marrying Miss Szold. These people were mistaken, which was another matter; if anyone, even his unworldly parents, suspected him of courting her and let him know they suspected, the possibility that she had the same suspicion must have occurred to him.

In early June his letters stopped for a while. Miss Szold, alone in New York—every one else had fled to Europe or the Catskills while she remained chained to the *Yearbook*—grew bitter and pessimistic. Surely he was sick from having given up his diet. But Ginzberg's three-week silence was caused by a sudden and unlooked-for blow. It was his mother who was ill, only briefly, as it happened. "The physician feared the worst. Her precarious state affected the health of my father considerably, and you can imagine what I suffered. . . ." As for Reb Isaac, "we hope very little but fear much." The Zionist congress was to be held at The Hague, but there was no chance of his going, and in any case "Zionism is dead here! Holland Jewry produces now only Kosher *Käse* and *Yomtov Chokolade,*" kosher cheese and holiday chocolate. Although Ginzberg had declared himself a Zionist before he ever came to America, he had nothing to do with Zionist politics abroad or at home. His Zionism was deeply felt, but he left the fighting to others. He had no appetite for controversy, except in scholarly matters; Ginzberg was a man who preferred to be comfortable.

Finally a letter from Amsterdam announced the death of Reb Isaac. "Father lived the life of a saint and died the death of a martyr. His suffering was such that death came to him as a deliverance from evil. And have I any right to think of what I have lost?" A week later, after the formal period of mourning when writing was not permitted, he expressed the first bitter sorrow darkened by guilt, to Miss Szold an echo of her own loss and her own imagined guilt:

> I cannot yet realize the fact that my father is dead. I still suffer with him as I did for the last three months. I read that people who have parts of their limbs amputated still feel pain in the part amputated. . . . I do not mourn but suffer indescribably. . . . I was yesterday to see a nerve specialist as I did not like the state of my mind. He made a very grave face and ordered me to leave Amsterdam at once. . . . If you want to confer a favor on me —and I know you do—please write to me so often your time will allow it. . . .

Yet he understood at what cost to herself she would read his letters and answer them—"Now I am asking myself is it right for me to cause you such pain and open old wounds. But what can I do?"

A few days later: "I cannot help thinking that my presence partly increased the mental suffering of my father . . . how many a time did he suppress a sigh that this his son did not become a Gaon . . . but a scholar!" That summer Reb Isaac had realized even more clearly that his son was not truly *frumm*, pious to the letter. Quite by accident he had set out for a walk on the Sabbath with money in his pockets, his father, again by accident, discovering it. "I doubt whether my presence was beneficial to him. I cannot say more."

Another doctor advised travel, so he went to Berlin and stopped on the way to visit his maternal grandmother:

> Of course it was not an easy thing for me to answer her questions relating to my father without betraying any emotion as I had decided to keep his death a secret from her. The strain on my nerves is so enormous that I fear I may break down every moment but it seems that I am physically stronger than my physician ever thought. The sleepless nights with the suffering of my father all the time before me are becoming unbearable! A specialist for nervous diseases whom I have consulted advised me to go to a sanatorium for some time, but imagine what will become of my poor mother!

He had booked a return trip to America for late September and was on his way to Amsterdam now, having drugged himself during the German trip with work and company; "it is only the sense of duty that keeps me up and I hope that I'll come out victorious from this struggle."

That it was a struggle had by now become apparent even to Miss Szold, for whom Ginzberg was godlike. She too had struggled when her father died, seeing in the manner of his death—herself asleep, although for years she had gone to bed each night expecting to be awakened, to be at his side when the moment came—a metaphor for all her shortcomings. She was selfish, impatient, imperfect; her inadequate love or overweening self had caused or intensified the sufferings that ended in death; she had never given him a single reason to be proud of her.

But however sympathetic Miss Szold was with Ginzberg's struggles, they were not the same as her own. The ties between father and son are different from those between father and daughter.

Louis Ginzberg's feelings about Reb Isaac were mixed and unusually intense. The death set up "fantastic reverberations," according to Eli Ginzberg. The looming figure of Reb Isaac in life had dammed up Louis Ginzberg's creativity so that the great works that churned within him had waited, not merely to ripen, but to meet the light of day after, and only after, Reb Isaac's eye could no longer inspect them. At any rate this is what Louis Ginzberg himself believed and later told his son: had Reb Isaac lived, "I could not have published my life's work, because it wouldn't have met my father's standards." He was free now to work and publish, but the freedom was poisoned by the suspicion that he was implicated in the death because he profited from it. Who he was, what his life was for, what would become of him now that he was free, guilty and free, tormented him unbearably. He felt himself in danger of coming apart.

He turned to Miss Szold as his safety valve. The accounts from Amsterdam continued full of "frightful nights with physical and mental agony," and she took upon herself the task of reassuring him that his presence had not been a cause of suffering to his father, that his father understood and accepted the differences between them. "I am convinced as though I had heard the words from his mouth, that your presence was a solace to him." For a time she tried to see herself as an equal capable of comforting an equal, but the illusion was impossible to sustain. To stand beside him even for a moment was to feel the need to abase herself again. Agonies of self-effacement suffuse her letters during this time. Her ego had always been fragile, but this was something apart, something connected with the nature of love itself, the dwindling of the ego before the onslaught of love, the pouring of all the supply of self-love into the worship of the beloved, who becomes more and more precious, more and more sublime: "I know I cannot measure the depth or express the force of your emotions. . . . What I mean is, if I cannot follow you to the highest heights and the deepest depths, I know at least that there are heights and depths, and when their times come and go—in short I can be sympathetic, I can feel with you. . . ." Another time:

> When I wrote to you yesterday, I felt that for once—a sad once—we stood upon the same level, eye to eye. . . . Today, after a little while, I have to admit to myself that even now you stand above me. Our fortunes may be the same objectively, my loss as great as yours, even our capacities for sorrowing equal, but in one respect you must outrank me. The well-springs of your consolation flow deeper, fuller, more spontaneously. . . . We all, it is true, are subject to the same fortunes and fate; the elect alone emerge from them equipped for ampler life.

From time to time more mundane subjects lightened the correspondence. The state of American Jewry was frequently discussed, an old topic between Miss Szold and Ginzberg, in which he was always the prophet of doom and despair, poking among the ruins with elegant contempt for America in general and the Jews of America in particular. More recently Miss Szold had begun to share his despair. "Do you remember the Galician canvasser who offered his services to me for the Directory? Some time ago he presented himself to bid me goodby. After four years of struggle with American conditions in the effort to live as a Jew, he is returning home. He could not make up his mind to bring his children to this country."

Even the seminary seemed an uncertain venture now, for the East Side Jews refused to accept seminary graduates as their rabbis; not all the power of Schiff could force them to it. So the generosity of the seminary's backers began to waver, and Miss Szold had to report that Schiff himself had spoken of Dr. Schechter's "conversion" to Zionism since his removal to the United States. In the years directly ahead, Solomon Schechter would have to beg for the coals that heated the seminary buildings.

As the date of Ginzberg's return approached, he assured Miss Szold that he had regained his serenity, although at the expense of great physical suffering. But his return this time would be different from those of other years, for their letters had been different; he had reached out the groping hand of a man about to fall, and she had met him with a firm clasp, but all on paper. To sustain this relationship in person would be another matter, and she could not look forward to it tranquilly. "There are only three more weeks of letter-writing from me to you," she wrote, "and after that it will lie with you whether we shall walk and talk on Riverside."

Travelers were returning to the seminary every day from Europe and the Catskills; Dr. Magnes came back from his first trip to Palestine glowing with hope. He stopped by to see Miss Szold and told her his secretary belonged to a women's study group, a circle of fifteen that called itself the Hadassah Study Circle and met at weekly intervals to discuss the works of Herzl and the pre-Herzlian Zionists. It occurred to him that she should join it; they were all young women who would be rather shy in the presence of a distinguished older person like Miss Szold, however, and she might prefer to become an honorary member.

She said no, she would be a working member like any other and was happy to join, although privately she knew that study groups had come and gone, several even using the name Hadassah, after Queen Esther. But she believed in study; she believed in women's clubs and the power of women to educate themselves. Perhaps they could take up conversational Hebrew.

From the moment of Dr. Ginzberg's return in the autumn of 1907, it was clear that he intended a change in the nature of their relations. They began to see each other more and more frequently until it became a daily routine. At first their old habit of spending part of Tuesday together extended itself until it encompassed the afternoon and evening; he would come for lunch, they would work together on the *Legends* until it was time for his afternoon lecture, he would return at five so they could walk along Riverside, he would stay on for supper. By December he was coming several times a week, giving Miss Szold dictation in German, English or Hebrew, standing beside her desk, looking over what she had written, once putting his hand on hers to keep her from writing again while he thought about it. Minutes went by and his hand was on hers.

They joked together; they had a kind of shorthand in which familiar subjects and familiar attitudes were referred to, such as his cool dislike of the rich men who backed the seminary. Often he was the only one who did the joking, for he dearly loved an audience, and he told Talmudic anecdotes with a little chuckle she adored. There were times when she felt no one in the world had as much as she did: the hours of his company, the glances, the precious aloneness when he was entirely hers. Now and then she would be called to the phone when he was there, and when she passed the hall where his hat and coat were hung, she stopped to run her hand over his hat because she could not caress his hair.

After synagogue services each Saturday he would catch her eye, and they would leave together and talk together, sometimes joined for a few moments by others, whom Ginzberg always shook off. It seemed more and more frequent that he looked at her in a particular way; it was a look of intimacy, a look that presupposed a peculiar understanding. He had brought her from Europe, not a conventional gift, but a prayer book of his mother's that he had found among his father's possessions, and this too seemed to Henrietta a token of the peculiar and special understanding between them—unspoken. For all the hours they spent together and the thousands of words that passed between them now, much remained unspoken. Not one word was ever said about their feelings for each other.

Everyone saw that they were constantly together. No one, not even her mother, spoke to her about it. Mrs. Szold rejoiced that her daughter's happiness was secured at last—she even said a special prayer of thanks for it in synagogue— but since Henrietta said nothing, she would not intrude. Dr. Marx saw it another way; he believed that Ginzberg was pursuing Miss Szold but that Miss Szold for some reason drew back. Others simply counted the weeks and months of their togetherness and waited, assuming a marriage would be announced in good time. What Miss Szold did was write poems and prayers in Hebrew on tiny slips of paper in her minute handwriting, carrying them with her wherever she went. The moment she thought about him she would take one out and study it and learn it by heart. At home, on the elevated, walking down Broadway, anywhere, when she found him gliding into her mind she defended herself with her bits of paper. She was still fighting against it, still believed she had renounced him.

But by midwinter she was overtaken unawares and in spite of all her precautions by the certainty that he loved her. It came from nowhere yet it was irresistible; he loved her and needed her. He might or might not marry her, but if the idea of marriage came to him, she prayed, let it be soon enough so that she could bear a child.

She was forty-seven years old. Childbearing at forty-seven is not unknown, although it is uncommon, but Miss Szold never debated the possibility. In fact she prayed that when she became pregnant she might bear twins, a boy and a girl, so that he would not be deprived of the whole range of the parental experience. There were no twins in her family or in his. He had never proclaimed his love, he had never proposed, but Miss Szold, encased in a dream, left it all in his hands and waited passively.

That spring Ginzberg began the introduction to his Genizah studies, and when it spun itself out to nearly twenty pages he seemed to realize what a burden he was placing on her with the translation that kept her up late at night or pulled her out of bed early each morning, so that days had to be taken from the work she was paid to do. He suggested she find another translator. She told him that would make her unhappy. It seemed to her a dangerously forthright statement.

How much did Louis Ginzberg know or sense at this time? According to his son, "I would guess that my old man finally woke up in the spring of 1908 and realized he was on the kind of ice he never figured on. . . . He had lost his balance in the summer of 1907, since then he had given signals that could be misinterpreted. . . ." At last he understood how his behavior looked to others. And if Miss Szold had been a different person, capable of pursuing him, a word would have been enough. She had only to declare that he had created between them an intimacy others took for courtship and that she expected the rest to follow. He had not regained his balance yet; because he had no other source of succor or support, he might well have gripped the outstretched hand and with it Miss Szold. He was hers for the asking.

But she never asked. She fully believed he loved her. To her it was a miracle that prevented her from sleeping, and when she finally fell asleep woke her with a little shock of joy that preceded the memory of just what it was she had to rejoice in. The proof of it was everywhere: he saw her every day; he visited nobody else, not even the Marxes. With a look, a word, she might have had him. Instead she sat beside him on the wooden bench overlooking the river and breathed in the aroma of his Dutch cigar. And waited.

In June he had to leave for Amsterdam. On the next to last day they walked together to the post office and stood on the steps saying their farewells. Her lips were trembling. She went home and wept all night, full of love and longing and completely unaware that she had lost him. He telephoned next morning, saying he wanted only a word with her before he left and she cried out, "God bless you!" feeling certain now that they belonged to each other.

She wrote as soon as he was gone to say the heavens had poured rain for four unbroken days. "The purpose of all the water . . . must have been to bemoan your going away. . . ." Then the letter becomes an exercise in girlish high spirits, a tone as strange to Miss Szold as waltzing:

> And as for me, I sorely miss Gal and Gak, and Shat and Shash, and Hag (with a dot) and Hat (without), not to mention Albargeloni and Aaron of Lunel, and Isaac, he of the Or Zarua, and Rabbi Jehudai (with or without, as you like). . . . My butter does not even come from Gischala and I have received no news from the scholars of Kairwan. And Riverside is wet, but not with the waters of the Hudson alone. . . . I ought to thank you for all the pleasant hours you made for me this summer—I ought to, but I won't.

She watched the progress of his ship with the help of the newspapers and an atlas, but when a month had gone by without a word from him all her happiness drained away; "there has not yet been a letter or anything from you. So I have neither time, nor brain, nor heart for writing."

At last there was a brief letter from the ship, then a longer one from Copenhagen, where Ginzberg attended a conference before going on to Berlin and Amsterdam, and then a gift for her, a book on Jewish literature. She kissed the inscription, and after a silence of two and a half weeks started writing again.

9

Ginzberg's sparse correspondence revealed nothing of a dramatic turn of events in his personal life that began when he left Denmark for Berlin in the summer of 1908.

In the spring of that year, having come to realize the potential dangers of his friendship for Miss Szold, he had resolved to go to Europe and come back engaged, appeasing his father's ghost and escaping a childless, loveless marriage. This at least is Eli Ginzberg's conjecture, and the events that followed with such amazing rapidity bear it out. He said nothing to Miss Szold about his resolve, neither that he was going to find a bride nor that he would no longer allow himself to take up so much of her time. He had always been a man who shrank from painful confrontation, a human and understandable weakness for which Miss Szold was to suffer grievously. He told her nothing, hinted nothing and saw her every single day until the moment he left for Denmark.

From there he went to Berlin, where he stayed with Isadore Wechsler, an old friend of Frankfurt days. Ginzberg often stayed with the Wechslers, but his visits were usually in midsummer when the city was deserted. Now it was late August, and a friend of Mrs. Wechsler's, a pretty young woman named Adele Katzenstein, was in town. She was twenty-two years old and precisely what the Amsterdam family had in mind; perhaps they had even urged the Wechslers to bring the two together. Ginzberg and the Wechslers went to the synagogue. Mrs. Wechsler, sitting up in the women's gallery beside Adele, pointed out to her the American professor below. Downstairs with the men, Wechsler pointed to the gallery; Ginzberg looked up and saw his salvation from the dilemma of Miss Szold.

That afternoon Adele Katzenstein came for a visit to the Wechslers' home. When she came again on Sunday the Wechslers suggested she go out to buy a delicatessen meal and bring it back, and Ginzberg was told to go with her. That night he said he would write to her; the next day he left for Amsterdam.

Two weeks later he proposed by mail and was accepted by mail. Eventually he returned to Berlin and paid a long visit to her family. "One reason that I was able to make such a quick decision was that Adele was very fond of children," he told his daughter-in-law years later. "She acted very motherly with the two children of the Wechslers. . . . However it's difficult to tell why a man at a certain age makes a certain decision. It very likely was gland trouble."

Perhaps it was too quick a decision to allow him to fall in love, but there was every reason to believe love would follow. Adele Katzenstein was remarkably pretty, and more than that, she was a woman determined to enjoy life. Her education had been modest, her interests never intellectual. She was lively, she promoted liveliness in those around her; she had a light heart and a quick tongue as well as quick wits and spoke her mind, often bluntly. She had wanted to become a nurse, and when her father refused she presented herself at his office and proceeded to work there. She was a person who knew what she wanted. Her decision, after all, had been as quick as Ginzberg's.

Adele Katzenstein saw the letters of Miss Szold when they were forwarded to her home in Berlin during the family visit; noticing the delicate handwriting on the envelopes, she handed them to Ginzberg saying, "I'm not so sure I ought to give you these letters. . . ." He explained, as he had explained to his parents, that Miss Szold was a friend, a very good friend; her mother too was his friend. Perhaps Adele would like to write to his friend Miss Szold. Adele pointed out that for her to write to this unknown woman would not be proper. Privately, she wondered about the friendship. She herself did not believe in platonic friendship, not even with older women of a scholarly temperament.

When Ginzberg left for New York it was understood that he would return the following summer for the wedding and bring Adele home with him.

Miss Szold, who had spent the last two weeks before his return in a state of radiant expectation, became depressed when there were no more letters. A note from Rabbi Magnes announced his own marriage. He was as boyishly happy as only he could be. His bride was beautiful, rich, well-connected, and Miss Szold, who should have rejoiced at the good fortune of someone she liked as well as Magnes, broke down and wept instead. Happiness was made for everyone, it seemed, except herself.

She did not go with the Marxes to meet Ginzberg's ship but stayed at home and worked with her typist. They were at her desk in the living room at twelve-thirty when the bell rang and Ginzberg came in. The moment she saw him she knew he must have come straight from the ship. They exchanged a few words; then he asked if they could go to another room because he had something to tell her. She followed him to the other room on a surge of hope. What else could have been so urgent that he had run from the ship with the words in his mouth, except that he loved her? Only, before she reached the room she felt a sudden, chilling cold, an apprehension. She went in and closed the door behind her.

He was standing with his back to her, leaning against a bureau. He said that she would be surprised to hear that he was engaged.

She was still cold and very calm. He described the meeting with Adele in the Berlin synagogue as her mind raced back over the letters and she realized the day they met was the day he had sent the book on Jewish literature, the book whose inscription she had kissed. He described the girl's family and the girl herself: beautiful eyes and mouth, a sound German education, very domestic.

She told him she hoped he would be very, very happy. Still cold and calm. She asked to see the girl's picture, and he showed it to her. With a sudden, spirited gesture he added that the person he talked most about to his fiancée was herself, herself and her mother.

He knew nothing. She could see that for herself. He did not know how she felt or what he was doing to her. She felt sick, dead inside, but he was quite animated now. He was asking her to write to his fiancée, and she agreed to do so.

Somehow they were in the hallway. He said that he would come back and take her for a walk that afternoon. She told him she would not be free until six; she had a speech to make before the Council of Jewish Women, and they could take their walk after that.

He opened the front door, calling out to Anna that he would be there as usual on Tuesday. Then, without warning, he said to Miss Szold, You *are* happy about this, aren't you?

Yes, she breathed. Then he was gone.

It was very strange, the way she sat down at the hinge-top desk and wrote in German to Miss Katzenstein, as strange as the nerveless way she had endured the interview. For a moment she wondered if there were something seriously wrong with a woman who could hear such news and take it as she had, without screaming, without fury.

Then she wrote:

Dear Fraülein Katzenstein,

Dr. Ginzberg was just here and shared with me the joyful secret that he has indeed found the woman who will bring light and beauty to his life . . . you are the last person I need to tell what a fortunate woman you are to have won the love of such an extraordinary man. I have been in almost daily contact with him for five years and I know every fiber of his being for true and upright. A gift of God indeed is his clear, penetrating and richly stocked mind. For you, life at his side will be a sacred and beautiful feast. And when you come to follow him to America in a short time then you must promise to become my friend even as your fiancé has been up to now. Bear with the strange language if I have expressed myself clumsily; it comes from the heart.

That afternoon she made the speech before the Council and rushed home to be there at six, and when Ginzberg failed to arrive she telephoned his home and learned he was not back yet. Her teeth had been chattering ever since she finished the speech; she sank into a chair feeling cold and feverish. Ginzberg telephoned to say he could not come. But she wanted to show him the letter, she said; he told her he was sure it was all right, but she insisted, and they agreed to go for a walk the next day.

Then she went to bed, where she was sick all through the night, and Anna nursed her, not knowing what was wrong.

She met Dr. Schechter the next day at the seminary, and he remarked that she did not look well. She told him she had not slept; she realized that the seminary knew everything, that they were talking about it and pitying her, that the daughter of Rabbi Szold was on everyone's tongue, an object of sympathy. Amused, even mocking sympathy.

Ginzberg came that afternoon to take her for their walk; she showed him the letter, but he barely glanced at it. He gave her his European gift, a handsome belt buckle in art nouveau style, and when she started to refuse it he looked as if he were about to become angry so she accepted. They set out on their walk, but when they had gone a little way she felt so weak she said they had better go back. What was wrong, he asked—so innocently that she decided on the spot that he had never loved her, he had known nothing, suspected nothing, he still suspected nothing. They could continue to be friends.

They came home from the walk, and he stayed for supper. On Tuesday he came for lunch and rang her later at five when his lecture was over so they could take a walk. But she began to suspect it was wrong to continue this pretense of friendship as before. He belonged to someone else, and she was not his friend; she was a woman who loved him to distraction.

She packed his letters away, along with the veil he had knotted and his gifts. She went to Baltimore, where her mother was staying with Bertha, afraid of pouring herself out to her mother; she still feared that Sophie, with whom she had never once discussed her feelings for Ginzberg, would tell her she was a fool for believing such a man could ever have loved her.

She said nothing in Baltimore, but when they were home again in New York—Ginzberg coming and going for working sessions on the introduction, for walks, for dinners—she forced herself to confess. Half expecting a look of derision on her mother's face, she saw instead that Sophie was at once angry and moved. Yes, she knew about the engagement; it had come as a shock to her, a very great shock. Before that she had been certain Henrietta and Professor Ginzberg would be married. He was a traitor, she said. He had acted shamelessly.

Oh no, her daughter retorted. He knew nothing. He was innocent all along; he was an honorable man. Say nothing against him.

But inside her head she debated and debated, endless, circular arguments in which she told herself that he was innocent, his every daily action proved it, and a voice would break in to say he was guilty, Mama had seen that he had acted as if he loved her. But no, Mama was partial to her; he was after all innocent. He had never loved her. How could such a man love someone like her?

On November 17, she decided to exorcise her anguish by writing an account of her love story and its ending: "Today it is four weeks since my only real happiness was killed. . . . Today for the first time I have been calm. . . . Today the thought comes to my mind that if I put all my memories down . . . so as to have them before me as an object, so to say, outside of myself . . . perhaps it will help me."

When Bertha's husband, Louis Levin, came from Baltimore, she told him everything, and he comforted her for a time, advising her to break off entirely with Ginzberg. Bertha heard the story from Louis and wrote an exquisitely loving letter. But the reassurances of those who were close to her were never really reassuring for long; she needed more. She made an appointment with Dr. and Mrs. Marx and with the greatest difficulty told them everything. She had not been a fool, they said. There was every outward appearance of a courtship; they could not explain what ultimately happened because Ginzberg never explained it to them.

The record of the love story she was writing continued all this time, an outward expression of the inner repetitions, for she was always retracing not only the present question and answer but the tormenting past, digging for clues, burrowing farther and farther back in time. What was the meaning of those intimate looks of his during the year that followed his father's death? Why had he spent every single day with her, eaten day after day at her home, accepted the total immersion of her desires in himself and his work? Granting that he was innocent, unsuspecting all along, with no thought of love on her part or his, how had he justified to himself the taking up of all her time, all her energies? It wasn't as if she were an idle woman with hours to occupy. What did he think he was doing? What did he imagine were her motives?

And again, granting that he was innocent to begin with, since his return she had made it clear beyond any doubt that she suffered horribly. Why did he never ask the reason? If he was innocent and she used to be the friend to whom his own sufferings were unburdened, why did he not ask her the cause of her present anguish?

It was a plan, she decided. He wished to present himself as innocent; therefore he acted as if he saw and knew nothing. He was a deceitful schemer; he was a coward. She poured herself out to the Marxes again. She bared herself to Dr. Schechter. She gave way to self-pity that verged on self-hatred: "I realize more and more the mediocrity of my character. My virtues are too small, my faults are too small, for full, deep-breathed living. The self-discipline that enabled me to control myself when the blow first fell counts against me."

But by February all control, all discipline were so far demolished that she wrote a note to Ginzberg himself asking him to call on her, for she intended to hear an explanation from his own lips.

During all the happy months when she believed herself loved, she had sealed up her joy, not only from Ginzberg, but from her mother and sisters as well as the world. With the rejection, her defenses shattered and the flood waters poured out, bringing with them all the bitterness and disappointments of the past that had been dammed up for years, all previous losses, all old jealousies and self-doubts, the repressions of the good sister who swallowed down her envy, the good daughter who was her mother's camel. Everything came out, so fast, so intense and hot an outpouring that it swept her with it like a bystander caught in a flood of someone else's emotions.

This was surely not herself, this distraught female who ran from friend to friend, thrusting on them her innermost hurts and demanding explanations. This could not happen to her, this public nakedness, this baring of powerful feelings so utterly at odds with her outward appearance. She was not who she thought she was. She was a woman she did not recognize and could not control, a woman who summoned Louis Ginzberg to give an accounting.

When he came they talked for two and a half hours. She told him everything: which of his actions led her to believe he loved her, what Dr. Marx,
her mother and the others thought. "Don't you know that you absorbed me
and my time completely?" she asked.

"I know it now, and for that I must apologize." He assured her he had
never felt anything but friendship for her, that he still cherished that friendship,
that he never for a moment suspected she had misinterpreted his behavior. . . .

And what was she to do now, she asked him.

"You will get over this," he said. It seemed to her he wanted to add,
"and hurry up about it." They could go on being friends if she found it comfortable; she was the only one to be considered, since she was the only sufferer.

As soon as he had gone she went through the interview again in her
mind. And again. She repeated the conversation to everyone in their circle
who would listen, Mrs. Schechter, Dr. and Mrs. Marx, Mrs. Friedlaender, her
sisters, her mother. The seminary people were consoling, perhaps too consoling;
it seemed to her that those who had never criticized him before had only
criticism now, as if they said it just to assure her she was well rid of him.
Even the criticism failed to comfort her, for she believed she would rather
hold on to her ideal of him than see him cut down, unworthy of her love.
And from time to time she stood back and wondered what she was doing.
"Other women have suffered as I am suffering," she wrote in her journal,
"and so far as I know they have not suffered so obviously—the world has not
known so much about it, and they have not obtruded their suffering upon
the cause of it as I have. Why?"

There was a letter from Ginzberg asking Miss Szold's permission to acknowledge, in the preface of the Genizah book, her "kind assistance without which
this book would never have been published in English." It was a work of 600
pages with which she had been helping him for five years and whose 200-
page introduction she translated the past summer; was she or was she not to
be publicly acknowledged in it? She decided to refuse, not wanting her name
coupled with his, aware that she would be "cutting my nose to spite my face
because I lose recognition for really good work. But that seems to be part of
my tragic life."

But soon the first volume of the *Legends* would appear. "Should I take
my name from that too? There it appears on the title page as the translator.
But the title page is not yet printed and I can still remove it. . . ." She wrote
to her mother in Baltimore asking her to consult with Bertha and Louis Levin.
Sophie was staying with them during the birth of their fourth child, and Miss
Szold's letters to Baltimore played an anguished counterpoint to that happy

event. She went to synagogue in February, and as soon as Ginzberg came in her head began to throb. The Song of Songs was the text that day, sensual, tender, perfumed with youth, and the words sent a sort of panic through her body, the fear that she might scream out in public. During Purim she went again, and again she nearly broke down.

Louis Levin advised her to put her name on both books "as a matter of truth and history," but Miss Szold's final decision was to omit it from the Genizah studies while allowing it to appear on the first volume of the *Legends*.

That spring, at a meeting of the JPS, she asked Judge Sulzberger for a six-month leave; it was granted most generously, for she was to have a leave with pay, and with her mother she began to plan a European tour that would start in England and bring them eventually to Austria and Hungary for reunions with both sides of the family. If the money held out they might even go on to Palestine.

She had also asked Sulzberger for permission to do no more work on Ginzberg's books after July 1. This proved a more difficult request, not because the Publication Society resisted, but because Miss Szold herself was of two minds. Ginzberg wrote to her that he was leaving for Europe in May, that if she could not complete the proofs before then they must wait until his return in October; in effect, she must work on them when she came back from the vacation that was supposed to cure her of Ginzberg. A little later he offered to read the corrected proofs abroad and suggested that perhaps Miss Szold ought to hire another translator if the present arrangement was inconvenient. She could not bring herself to do this, so the proofs were to go to Miss Szold in Europe for correction, and she was to send them on to Ginzberg. In the midst of the cure, she would continue to reinfect herself.

Her last sight of him was on the street one sunny day where she was walking with her brother-in-law Louis Levin and his little daughter. Ginzberg came toward them, but when he caught sight of her he turned on his heel and crossed the street. Then he sailed for Europe.

She heard he had been married in London. She was still tormenting herself and every one of her friends with the unending repetition of what had been done to her, and thought of herself as dried, wasted, full of "the quiet of a churchyard"; but the assurances of some of the seminary wives that Ginzberg was arrogant and self-centered began to make inroads. Miss Szold knew it all along—she used to find it charming—but seeing that others perceived the same faults and were not charmed had a certain effect. Little by little she learned to think of him as a flawed and mortal being, although he was still the one desirable man in the world. During the years in New York, Miss Szold had had three proposals of marriage, all from respectable and somewhat colorless widowers; the third proposal took place just before Ginzberg sailed. There was no need for her to think twice before refusing. She was not really free to marry, she felt. She was like an *agunah*, a deserted wife, whom the Talmud says may not marry. She could never belong to another man.

Some weeks before Miss Szold and her mother were to leave for Europe, she received a gift of $500 from the Publication Society with their "earnest hope that you will have a pleasant and restful vacation," by which they surely meant an end to the public breast beating and self-pity, a return to the sealed, decorous, chilly Miss Szold of before. She put this $500 aside to take them to Palestine.

No one encouraged her in the decision; indeed the family apparently feared her Zionism would never survive a visit to Palestine. Moreover there was a good deal of disagreement about the route; everyone who had been there insisted Marseilles was the only port for the Holy Land, but Miss Szold, who would be in Hungary seeing relatives, was determined to travel from there to Constantinople by rail, then across the Mediterranean to Alexandria, then to Beirut, then by train to Damascus, then south again to the Sea of Tiberias, from whence the tour of the Holy Land would begin.

It was an eccentric approach. She wondered later how she ever hit on it. By taking this long and redundant journey, she would visit a number of Middle Eastern cities before the Holy Land, so that she would approach Palestine with a mind already "Orientalized," whereas the trip from Marseilles to Alexandria to Jaffa would have plunged her almost directly into Eastern realities. She made another alteration to the usual tour of Palestine, one that took wisdom and stubborn courage. It was her intention to see not only the holy cities but the agricultural settlements, the "new" Palestine of the Zionists. Everyone pointed out that her desire was prompted solely by ignorance, that a woman of forty-nine and her mother of seventy—weighing 160 and 200 pounds respectively—could not possibly get about from settlement to settlement on roads that were little more than rutted trails, in a country where the automobile was unknown. She thought vaguely of going on horseback.

Palestine, an outpost of the Turkish Empire, was populated by some 600,000 Arabs, Christians and Jews, the latter numbering 80,000. Many were pious Europeans who had come to pray and study and die on holy soil, others were descendants of Mediterranean Jews who had lived there for centuries. Only a handful were Zionists who had come to build a homeland. Almost every American who visited Palestine agreed it was holy and picturesque and unspeakably poor, a wretched and disgraceful place. When Jacob Schiff returned to New York after a recent trip, he said he would rather give half a million to get all the Jews out of Palestine than one cent to add a single Jew to its present population.

10

The Atlantic crossing was so restful that for a time Miss Szold believed her mother had been right in urging the European trip as a cure. But when they reached Edinburgh and began their tour of that bewitching city, she was overcome by a sense that she had no one to share it with. "I still feel bottled and corked, I cannot speak out to any one as I did to him—nor could he to any one as to me, that I will believe to my dying day." Her mother, who trudged bravely along beside her, making friends with everyone, shoving her nose into everyone's business, was no comfort; except in Palestine the travel diary barely mentions her mother.

They went from Edinburgh to York, where they admired the cathedral and found the synagogue little better than a stable. "Why have we no such treasures?" she wondered. After London and Cambridge they were invited for several days to the country home of a large family of English Zionists, the Bentwiches, the parents of young Mrs. Friedlaender and of Norman Bentwich, a writer whose *Philo* Miss Szold was editing. The Bentwiches had been to the Ginzberg wedding in London, and after dinner one evening they told Miss Szold all about it, assuring her the bride was:

> a florid beauty, attractive to some men, patently able to look out for No. 1
> . . . she had been engaged before, and when he asked to be presented she
> asked, before consenting to meet him, whether his intentions were serious.
> It is all as I suspected—she "roped" him in! . . . Dr. Friedlaender said very
> emphatically that a man of his age had not the right to engage himself as
> he did. Was it to escape me?

They returned to London, where it rained all day, and the proofs of the *Legends* came. "No, I cannot finish his book when I get back, I cannot stand the sight of his handwriting." They visited museums and saw a vaudeville show, and her mind ticked off each day according to what had happened a year ago: "A year today since 'they' robbed me of him, and I was so happy in my unconsciousness of what was happening and in his letters to me."

They went to France, dragging the *Legends* proofs with them. By September 6, Miss Szold had finished them. "Now only the page proof of a half chapter and I have done with him forever." They went to Munich, then to Vienna and her mother's relatives, then to Hungary, to the towns of Pressburg and Cziffer, where her father's people lived, then back to Vienna. There she heard of a meeting of leading Zionists and attended it; not one of the sixty men present asked her a single question about conditions in America. Several offered to escort her back to the home of the cousins she was staying with, but she had the distinct feeling it would be a chore to them. Even her presence at the meeting had probably been a chore. For the first time it occurred to Miss Szold that she had come to Europe without proper letters of introduction to Zionist circles. "Why didn't my learned Jewish friends look out for me?" she wondered.

There were more relatives to be seen in Budapest. Then they set out in mid-October for Constantinople on a train that became more Oriental by the hour, increasingly crowded, noisy and disorganized as they approached the meeting place of East and West. Two days' journey brought them to a city unlike any they had ever seen, and their first reaction was nausea. "I was sickened and heavy-hearted—the rain, the dogs . . . the overloaded donkeys and horses, the still more overloaded men, the filthy streets, the dirty hovels." Crowds of beggars greeted them at the entrance of their hotel; the room and beds were unsanitary. Sophie, who was prepared for everything, had brought insect powder.

In Constantinople, quite by accident, they saw three familiar faces. Professor Richard Gottheil, the Orientalist from Columbia University and former president of the FAZ, was touring the Middle East with his wife and his wife's sister, Eva Leon. They were headed for Beirut and Palestine, and the two families arranged to meet later.

After the Gottheils left, the Szolds visited the Jewish sections of the city, inspecting schools and synagogues. In the neighborhood of the Ashkenazic Jews they stumbled across a red-light district. The sight of the painted women and their customers was like the city itself, vile and pitiful yet somehow riveting, and Miss Szold wrote in her diary after a description of the brothel, "God forgive me, I thought only of him!"

At the end of the month they set out for Beirut on a mail steamer. A newspaper from home caught up with them, and in it she saw that the seminary had opened and Dr. Ginzberg was "at home with his bride." She passed a sleepless night; "neither change of time nor place makes a difference to my feelings about the wrong done me and about my sorrow for him and for myself, that I must go through life without his companionship." The journey across the Aegean and the Mediterranean took them to Smyrna, to Piraeus and Athens, to Alexandria, to Port Said, with excursions ashore, all of them heady assaults on the mind and the senses, but Ginzberg was with her throughout. She dreamed of him night after night, argued with him, forbade him to see her now that he was married, scorned the false air of innocence that was his only answer to her arguments.

Heading north for Beirut, the ship dropped anchor by moonlight off Jaffa, in northern Palestine; some passengers were rowed ashore by clamorous Arab boatmen. When they awoke next morning they were still at anchor, still opposite Jaffa, "our first sight of the shores of the Holy Land. . . . There can be no doubt that the thrill this morning was different from the others." Throughout the day they sailed north along the Palestinian coast on smooth seas beneath a cloudless sky, following Miss Szold's plan that they must enter the Holy Land from the northernmost point in order to visit the colonies before the cities; they must see Zionism and the new Palestine before their hearts were shriveled by the old. That was not entirely possible—the town of Tiberias was to be their headquarters for the northern colonies—but Jerusalem came afterward, Jerusalem was to be left for the end. They would go to Beirut and Damascus and enter from there.

At three in the morning, with white moonlight pouring down on the sleeping city, the two women left Damascus for the train to Tiberias and the Holy Land. Past a string of camels, their Bedouin drivers riding on donkeys, past Arab towns with the look of fortresses, past black Bedouin tents, black mountains covered with black sheep, great stretches of black basalt and lava, all of it wild and harsh and superb. The soil, when one had a chance to examine it, appeared to be rich. There were terraced fields near the riverbank and evidence of the most loving cultivation, Miss Szold learned that the Arabs plowed between the stones and their yield of grain was extraordinary. "We saw them fanning the grain as it was fanned in Bible times—'the chaff which the wind driveth away'—we saw the maidens (alas! they were tattooed on their chins! I hope Rebecca was not!) go to the wells and carry jars of water home."

The Arabs used the wooden plow, unchanged by 3,000 years. But in certain soils—she learned this later—deep upturning was harmful and the superficial scratching of the wooden plowshare with its small iron attachment exactly right. Some Jewish farmers were willing to copy the Arab method where it suited the terrain. Miss Szold believed such examples of mutual helpfulness were certain to multiply, to lead to better understanding and tolerance. But more than anything else the quality of the soil reassured her. The soil was fertile. She smelled it. She crumbled it in her hands. She turned to her mother, that earthy and practical countrywoman, and saw in her mother's face the assurance that the land itself was capable of fulfilling the biblical promise. Until now Sophie was barely mentioned in the travel diary, as if her opinions about landscapes, paintings, architecture, were of no interest to her daughter. In Palestine she became a valued companion.

The sight of Tiberias, their first extended stop in the Holy Land, was sobering. They saw a network of filthy streets whose houses seemed like blind and devastated faces. A large Jewish population lived there in indescribable poverty, entirely dependent on Halukah, the communal charity of European Jews. The synagogue was a horror, "the gabardined, side-locked Jew strolls through the narrow streets or crouches in his subterranean room with his equally gabardined and side-locked sons. . . ." The women found it literally sickening, and the sticklike legs of the children were to haunt them for months.

Still, Tiberias was not the Palestine of the Zionists—that lay ahead. Tiberias was Palestine in its timeless aspect, the place where devout Jews came to study or die. Almost all the 80,000 Jews of Palestine were town dwellers in Jerusalem, Hebron, Safed, Jaffa, Haifa and Tiberias. Half of them lived on Halukah.

The Zionists despised the Halukah system because it pauperized, leaving those who received it drained of volition and pervading the country with a sense of the long wait before death. Moreover, the Zionists looked on those who lived on Halukah as an insult; their passivity seemed to taint all Jews. The new Palestine was to be built by the young and active, those who were prepared to work hard and take risks, and in this new Palestine there would be no place for Halukah. No one would hand out charity; no one would want or receive it.

Miss Szold had intended to begin her tour of the colonies from Tiberias, riding on horseback through the settlements of the Galilee while Sophie remained in the town. But by now it was clear that she could not do it. The hotel was almost as squalid as Tiberias, and her mother could not endure to be left in such a place. Before she could think of an alternative, a man of striking appearance—a handsome, middle-aged Russian, mournful and bearded—arrived at the hotel to hand her a letter. His name was Jehoshua Hankin, he had been connected for twenty-seven years with colonization in Palestine, and two years earlier had guided Chaim Weizmann on a first tour of the Holy Land. When she described the trip she wanted to make he suggested she do it in a horse-drawn cart, the kind farmers used; both women could ride in it. Hankin laid out the route, hired the wagon and secured as their guide a laborer from the colony of Mizpeh.

As for the letter, it was from Israel Shochat, another laborer. Miss Szold had met his wife, Manya, in New York a few years earlier and found her extraordinary, "a warm, palpitating and yet Tolstoian personality." She was a leader and visionary formed by Russia and the secret revolutionary movements. As a girl of twenty Manya Shochat had killed a czarist spy, dismembered the corpse and shipped its portions to Siberia. She was in Europe now, the letter said, but her husband would meet the Szolds in the course of their Galilee tour and come part of the way with them.

They left Tiberias for the colonies of the Galilee on the first of November.

From then on the tone of Miss Szold's diary changes, the entries coming in brief phrases joined by dashes, with nothing ever fully explored, as if the writer were afraid to examine even in private the impressions that flew at her hour by hour. Even Ginzberg disappears for the time being, and all the entries of the next two weeks take on an elliptical quality. She had plunged into Zionism, real Zionism, the world of the Biluim. She was to inspect it with a critical and fearful eye, wary of disappointment.

The earliest settlers of this new Palestine were the pioneers who came in the 1880s. In Zionist history theirs was called the first aliyah, or wave of immigration, and their agricultural settlements on land purchased from Arabs were what the young people of the Russian Night School described to Miss Szold and her father. These Biluim, some of whom were Orthodox believers, others student radicals, came to a country they knew only from legend. The news that drifted back to Russia pictured them riding horseback in the robes of desert Arabs or sitting down to tables glowing with olives and figs and grapes they had grown themselves, marvelous stories to the dwellers in the Russian townlets where Jews had always been landless shopkeepers and peddlers.

These stories were true only for the rarest individual. The whole reality of the Biluim was harsh and tragic. They knew nothing about agriculture, possessing no implements or animals or money to buy them; they had no choice but to work the soil with their bare hands. To keep from starving they became day laborers at the Mikveh Israel Agricultural School. Many returned to Russia or fled to America; many died of exhaustion in a climate they found unendurable. Those who stayed lived in tents or caves or hovels. Snakes glided past them; scorpions bit them. Great rains spilled down on them. Families were wiped out by malaria. Whole communities perished leaving only a few headstones in an abandoned cemetery.

But by the end of the century these brave and stubborn souls had created twenty-one agricultural colonies with some 4,500 inhabitants—Petach Tikvah, Zikhron Yaacov, Hadera, Rishon l'Zion among them. The settlements had been saved from collapse by the generosity of Baron Edmond de Rothschild, who bought up the land on which the Biluim remained as farmer colonists. During the 1880s, Rothschild spent about $5 million on the colonies.

In some the chief industry was wine making, in others the cultivation of the silkworm, and during the early years of the new century citrus fruits were grown. The stony soil the Biluim had worked with their hands was blooming and productive now, and the colonists were said to live in comfort, even in ease. Unfortunately the settlements remained isolated from each other, physically detached and scattered as if they had been tossed at random into Turkish Palestine. A new wave of immigration began in 1904 and 1905, and in 1908 the Zionist organization established a Palestine office in Jaffa under Arthur Ruppin so that the buying of land by the Jewish National Fund—land that was to belong forever to the Jewish people, land that could never again be bought or sold by any individual—might proceed in more systematic fashion.

This was the Palestine Miss Szold and her mother set out to see in the horse-drawn cart, the Palestine of modern farming where Jews lived self-respecting lives on Jewish land. They traveled through hilly country; wild oleander bloomed by the roadsides, and there were traces of ancient terracing although the land had not been tilled for centuries. The road itself was miserable, deeply rutted and in places knee deep in mud. They headed first for the settlements of Kinneret and Yemma, only a short distance from the southern shores of Lake Tiberias. Well-tilled fields of cotton and fruit trees came into view. Men were at work in the fields, and there were donkeys and geese. This was Kinneret, where they stopped only long enough to eat a meal, then went on to Yemma.

"Colony fairly presentable," Miss Szold noted in her diary, "and yet not attractive. . . . Fields and cattle look fine." There was fresh spring water and a simple supper, and after that they retired to the administration building, where they slept on cots. Although she said nothing about the sanitary arrangements, they had been a source of amazement to Ruppin when he toured the colonies a year or so earlier. He had visited Kinneret, wondered at the lack of toilets, been further dismayed that the colonists themselves seemed indifferent to the problem and "When I asked the . . . manager of the Kinneret farm for the lavatory there, he gestured munificently, as much as to say, 'The whole world is at your disposal!'"

The next morning they were joined by Israel Schochat, a slender young man with a heavy mustache. He planned to take them westward to Mesha, then to Sejera, where he lived. The road grew worse, Miss Szold and her mother clinging to each other to keep from being thrown from the cart, but the earth looked fertile, light-colored and crumbly. Sejera proved to be one short street with tiny houses set close together on each side and garden plots in front, the whole surrounded on all sides by deep-furrowed Jewish fields.

There at the foot of Mount Tabor wheat and barley were grown, poultry and cattle raised, the farm itself having been established in 1898 as a sort of training ground for modern agricultural methods. Shochat explained all this with pride. Experts were hired, he said, special attention being given to the hitherto neglected subject of manure and other fertilizers, and Arabs from nearby villages were called in to teach the Jewish laborers. For the last four years workmen at Sejera had gone off to colonize other settlements. They were much sought after.

The women stayed overnight at Sejera, rising early next morning to leave for Haifa with Shochat. At that hour workmen were setting off for their fields, and Miss Szold watched them in the chill of the first white light, young men in the smocks of Russian peasants or battered, European-style suits, with great broad-brimmed hats on their heads; many were barefoot. Suddenly she realized that five of the workmen were women, girls really, barefoot like the men, marching off to the fields with hoes slung over their shoulders, to work all day in drenching rain or harsh sun and come back at night to a supper of bread and cheese and sweetened tea. They asked no quarter.

The Szolds set off on the westward journey toward the Mediterranean coast and the town of Haifa. There in a little German hotel Miss Szold sat down to write a long letter home, her first in over a week, describing the railway journey, the trip to Tiberias, Hankin and the Galilee tour:

> Here my letter ought to begin. I ought to tell you what impression the land made upon me, what impression the colonists. I cannot yet. . . . One thing more. Do not infer from my silence that I am disappointed in anything Palestinian. My impressions are not yet in order, that is all, and I am tired after my day's trip. . . .

But disillusion followed her from Haifa to the little colony of Athlit, where ten people had lived for the past two years in a single row of two-roomed cottages whose front doors faced a range of stables. Disillusion lurked in Zikhron Yaacov, which was ugly and planless, where everything seemed sad and neglected and some unhappy instinct had produced the look of a Russian village, squat and narrow and turned in on itself. The hired overseers of the Rothschild colonies, she learned, were dishonest and took no real interest in the settlements; the man who managed Zikhron lived in Haifa. It was common gossip that the overseers seduced the young schoolteachers and married them off later on, when they were tired of them.

Miss Szold had noticed many Arabs living in the villages. They were workmen, she was told; Jewish workmen were too expensive. So the Jews of the Rothschild colonies, who were pensioners of the baron, living on his bounty, paid Arabs to do their work and complained about the baron's administration. It was not what she had expected, not what she had read about in Baltimore or New York, not what Zionism was supposed to mean.

Next morning they set out to visit two daughter colonies of Zikhron, and now Shochat talked about himself. He had been a university student of agronomy at Halle, but after six months had run away to Palestine without a cent. His father implored him to return to Russia. Shochat refused. He lived as a common day laborer and would never go back.

For the first time Miss Szold began to sense what had drawn the extraordinary Manya to this man, who was in no outward way extraordinary. He told her about a union of workers at Sejera who were pooling the money they earned by their hourly labor. With it they would set up a fund to provide shelter, clothes and food for new chalutzim, pioneers, for a period of two years. The newcomers were to go wherever needed, do whatever service, like soldiers. Above all they were to work on the Jewish settlements the way the Arabs did, for the purpose of the scheme was to replace Arab workers with Jews. Shochat was also active in Hashomer, the organization of Jewish watchmen who guarded the colonies; Manya had been one of its founders. Until now Arabs had been the watchmen, but the Arabs must be replaced.

This was the voice of the second aliyah, the wave of immigration beginning in 1904 and 1905; they believed that the exploitation of Arab labor must cease, that the Jews could not build a homeland on the cheap labor of others. The land must be worked by Jews themselves, for only by doing the hardest and most menial tasks could they redeem the soil and make it their own. What was most striking about the men and women of the second aliyah was their youth, their socialist fervor, their need to see everything as black or white. They were people who could not compromise.

It did not occur to these young idealists that if hard and menial labor constituted a just claim to the land, the Arabs already had such a claim. Nor were the probable results of their high-minded doctrine apparent to them. They knew the Arabs must lose their jobs when Jews did all the work on Jewish land, but they saw this as only a temporary setback—in the end the Arabs would profit from the economic improvements that followed, from the increase in trade, the higher standard of living. What they were unable to foresee was that these measures would ultimately serve the ties that grow from working together. If Jews had labored side by side with Arabs, or even if Jews had continued employing Arabs, they would have had a common meeting ground in daily life. As it was, the two peoples grew increasingly estranged. Neither learned the language of the other. And the move toward Jewish labor on Jewish land would also serve to confirm Arab suspicions that the coming of the Zionists meant the displacement of Arab peasants and workers.

There were other forces at work. A year earlier the Young Turks party had staged a revolution in Turkey and deposed the sultan. The Ottoman Empire was henceforth to be ruled constitutionally; elections were held, newspapers founded. In this heady atmosphere a long-suppressed Arab nationalism finally found its voice and in Palestine took the form of a struggle against the Zionists, the new Jews.

But Shochat said nothing about the Arabs, and Miss Szold apparently did not ask. To her he personified the mystical young Russian populists who were establishing their first foothold in Palestine. Like the young women at Sejera, like David Ben-Gurion—who had left his home in Russia three years earlier at twenty, arrived in Jaffa with his worldly possessions on his shoulder and walked on to Petach Tikvah to work on the land—they were common laborers competing with the Arabs for wages. The first kibbutz—or agricultural collective, where all property and work were shared and no individual owned anything, not even his clothing—was born at Degania a year after Miss Szold's visit, but the kibbutz movement was already in the air at Sejera, at Kinneret, where little bands of laborers tried to live together on a temporary basis, pooling tools and earnings.

Miss Szold had seen a glimpse of the future, but the present continued gritty and abrasive. She disliked the desolate air of the Rothschild colonies, and the colonists somehow irritated her. They lived a singularly unattractive life without harmony or passion or the love of work. They were not particularly attractive themselves. They were lazy. They complained too much. What the baron failed to do for them usually remained undone. Where was the fire of Zionism, the high sense of national purpose, the collectivity? The cadences of the Bible filled her mind, her feet were on biblical land, but the Jews she saw were simply Russians transplanted, unkempt, without grace or manners or toilets.

At the end of two weeks they had visited fourteen colonies, some superficially, others at close hand during an overnight stay and all in the company of Shochat or someone like him. According to Miss Szold's plan they were now properly fortified for Jerusalem, a city of 70,000, where more than half were Jews.

They approached it by train, a noisy, rattling, sooty train with no water supply. Climbing upward through the bare and mournful Judean hills, they passed little Arab settlements. The land was terraced; infinite labor had gone into the tending of Arab farms that clung to the steep, arid hillsides. The two women hung by the windows straining for their first sight of the city. "Up, up and again up," until they reached Jerusalem the golden, the citadel of the heart that every Jew everywhere in the world remembers each year at Yom Kippur and at the Passover, with the vow, Next year in Jerusalem.

It was noon when they arrived. Dr. Gottheil was waiting for them at the station on a donkey. After a meal at the hotel he took them out to the Mount of Olives for a view of the Old City: the silver dome of El Aksa, the golden dome of the Mosque of Omar rising above the rock where Abraham was said to have offered his son as a sacrifice, the massive, crusader-built walls. It was ethereally beautiful at a distance, but when they traveled back to the crenelated walls and looked through, first the Jaffa Gate, then the Damascus, they saw narrow alleys crowded with beggars. Then they went inside, pulling their skirts around them.

They plunged into a thick, slowly moving stream of camels, donkeys, goats, mixed with humanity in all its shapes and colors. Stacks of firewood rode past on the backs of donkeys. Trays of sweetmeats, bloody raw carcasses on the way to butcher stalls, tea sellers, fruit sellers, hawkers of water snaked through the crowd. These water sellers carried their wares on their backs in nightmare form, poured into bladders of goatskin that were nothing more than the outer hide of the goat with its limbs and head lopped off.

Jerusalem's water was collected during the rainy season in dirty cisterns, then peddled through the streets in the goatskin bladders. These cisterns were twenty to thirty feet square and so constructed that the water from the streets and buildings flowed into them unscreened and unfiltered. December was cold and rainy. Water mingled with the dung of camels and donkeys and goats. The air was putrid.

The women trudged on. They entered the marketplace and saw piles of rotting garbage and flies on the fruit, meat and sweets for sale at open stalls and on the faces of children. Flies were a fact of life, like the dung and the unspeakable water; not even the mothers troubled to wave the flies from the faces of infants they carried in their arms.

There were scores of maimed and blinded beggars, many young, most of them patient, all with an air of Oriental resignation to fate almost maddening to the American women, for trachoma, the chief source of blindness, was caused by an organism that flourished only under crowded conditions where hygiene was unknown. It was not sophisticated medicine these blinded beggars had needed, but simple medication and cleanliness.

Yet the city was seductive, at once lurid and gripping, and nothing so fascinated Miss Szold as the variety of its inhabitants. In the midst of the jostling, yelling mob she saw priests and monks of a dozen different Christian sects marching in stately procession, some of them black. She saw Arab women completely veiled, shawled and cocooned, followed by servants. There were Kurdish Jews, Bokharan Jews, small-boned black Falashas and Yemenites, sturdy, tubercular, rachitic, dressed in rags. These Yemenite Jews, each with several wives and a great box of books, arrived by the hundreds to do the hardest work of the colonies and the cities.

A few days later the Szolds made a tour of Jerusalem's several Jewish hospitals, beginning with Shaare Zedek, "a thoroughly modern institution with scientific appliances," but modern was a comparative term, for there were no microscopes, no x-ray apparatus, no laboratories and no maternity ward; there were none anywhere in the city. That evening a nurse from Shaare Zedek called on Miss Szold at her hotel to tell her that doctors who insisted on cleanliness were simply turned away.

Life in Jerusalem was hard. "There is so much strife, so much misery, so much to make the heart ache," Miss Szold wrote, "and Mrs. Gottheil and Miss Leon are very tender-hearted. Every minute they wish for the end of their stay."

When, at the end of ten days, the Szolds were ready to leave, Henrietta may have been glad of it herself. They went to Jaffa on November 22, passing through a green and bountiful countryside, but Jaffa was another miserable place, the streets unpaved and filled with heaps of rubbish, an unpleasant smell hanging over the town. It was in Jaffa that Arthur Ruppin had contracted typhoid a year earlier. He was taken to a hospital kept open a few months each year by Rothschild money; when the money ran out, the hospital shut down. It was open when Ruppin took sick. He was put in a room without a door, water, utensils or linen. Cats wandered in and out all through the night, waking him with their noises, staring at him with phosphorescent eyes from the top of his coverlet. When he needed a bath the water was carried up in tins from an outdoor well.

In Jaffa an incident occurred that Miss Szold was to remember with precision for the rest of her life. She had gone with Sophie to the Girls' School. On their way they passed a group of children playing in the sand, children who seemed to have a sort of dark wreath about their eyes. When they came closer they saw these were wreaths of flies. Flies on children's faces, especially at the eyes, where the exudation of the early stages of trachoma attracted them, were no novelty to the Szolds, but this time they seemed so thick that Sophie was struck by it.

Inside the school they saw that none of the children had trachoma. "How is it that all these children are perfectly healthy," Mrs. Szold asked the principal, "while outside there are children in such awful condition?"

He said a physician visited them once a week at the school and a nurse came daily, "and we take care of the eyes." When they went outside afterward Mrs. Szold told her daughter, "That is what your group ought to do," meaning the little Hadassah group Dr. Magnes had persuaded her to join, the fifteen or so young women who studied Herzl and Pinsker and Ahad Ha-Am, the fathers of Zionism. "You should do practical work in Palestine."

From Jaffa they traveled to Port Said, to Cairo, to Alexandria. On November 28, aboard the steamer *Hapsburg* bound for Venice, Miss Szold finally wrote to her sisters. Twenty-five days had passed since her last letter home. She had seen the pyramids, she told them, and the Sphinx by moonlight, and a splendid museum, and all the "truly beautiful evidences of ancient Egyptian life. . . ."

> All this we saw, and I was apathetic. Palestine has used me up. . . . Even now I hardly know how to tackle the great subject. It is not that I am afraid of putting down my true impressions nakedly. . . . I am really afraid of fixing my impressions, of giving them a definite form . . . and I am not ready to do that.

She had spent twenty-five days getting ready for this letter, most of that time, according to the diary, sleeping badly, often in poor temper, because she had been measuring what she saw against an inner vision that was nowhere confirmed. Yet she knew her sisters were waiting, skeptical of Palestine but vaguely hopeful, for Henrietta's sake. They knew and she knew that if she had any future at all it must include Zionism. Without it she was only a maiden lady who did literary housekeeping for a small, pedantic, penurious publisher.

So the letter moved ahead with determined step: she had emerged, she told them, the same Zionist she went in.

> There may be two opinions as to the value of Jewish colonization in Palestine for the regeneration of the Jewish race, but I fail to see how there can be more than one concerning the fertility of the land. Where there is a handful of earth an olive tree can be planted and under Jewish cultivation gives a return of fruit in seven years, though the Arab had to wait twenty before he learnt a thing or two from the Jew. The casual observer will see only stony ground. . . .
>
> It is true, Palestinian farming in the first place is far from easy. The neglect of 2,000 years must be made good, the mismanagement of the present government must be counteracted, the lack of water must (and can) be remedied. But once the thing will be set agoing the land will blossom like a rose.
>
> So far as the products of agriculture are concerned the colonists have done well. The fields and orange groves look well kept and well-worked. But the administration! That is a long chapter. . . . There is so much to say of the heartless, planless way in which things have been done, the homes built, the streets not arranged, the sanitation disregarded. . . . The country is strewn as thickly with failed experiments as the Mount of Olives with graves. . . .

As for the cities, which were all most travelers saw, they were dens of filth and poverty. "If it were not for the presence of new men . . . the men that live the law of beautiful skies and wide prospects . . . Palestine would not be possible." These new men, the socialists of the second aliyah, became in time the nucleus of Labor Zionism and the shapers of the state of Israel.

She had not reached her conclusions lightly or easily. Twenty-five days of disillusion weighed down the start of the letter, but once she began she seemed to gather momentum. The letters she wrote afterward to her friends sounded almost buoyant. The Zionism of the Gottheils might not last out their trip, but hers would last because she had determined it must: "The result is that I am still a Zionist, that I think Zionism is a more difficult aim to realize than ever I did before, and, finally, that I am more than ever convinced that if not Zionism, then nothing—then extinction for the Jew."

11

Miss Szold and her mother returned to New York in late January 1910. Two weeks later their seminary friends gave them a dinner party at the Hotel Premier in honor of Sophie's seventieth birthday the past December. Dr. Schechter's son Frank remembered her on that occasion as a woman of "genial urbanity, a noble serenity, and repose." There were toasts and sonnets, a birthday cake with seventy candles, and a speech by Miss Szold in praise of the new Palestine.

The evening was intended as a loving tribute to both women, but the seminary people may also have been trying to atone for the fact that the Ginzbergs, triumphant bridegroom and beautiful bride, were at home and apparently happy, whether or not they deserved to be. And the bride herself was after all a charming, spirited young person, not easy for even the staunchest of Miss Szold's friends to dislike.

The new Mrs. Ginzberg, now twenty-three, had come to a strange country where she did not speak the language; she was alone, her sole ally and supporter a husband fourteen years older, a professional scholar whose work she could not understand and whom she had married after the briefest acquaintance. She had seen the letters from Miss Szold that were forwarded to Berlin and elicited Dr. Ginzberg's explanation. She had received Miss Szold's first letter to herself and written in return, referring to her husband as *"Professorlein"* and *"Schatzelein,"* to the dismay of Miss Szold, who could not imagine using such pet names before a stranger.

Now Mrs. Ginzberg was troubled by the suspicion that more was afoot than her husband had revealed or even known. She saw it on every face, "here a word, there a word," everywhere the conviction that she was usurping another woman's place. With Miss Szold's return, it became clear that everyone would conspire to keep the two women apart. "It was goddam foolish of them to try to protect Miss Szold from me," she said many years later. She began losing weight; by the end of her first year in New York she had lost twenty pounds and was weeping a lot.

But when she was not weeping she was reveling in her position as the wife of a brilliant scholar whose first published works, the four books that appeared during the year of his marriage, seemed to have been called forth by the sunshine of her presence. The sight of this young bride and her unabashed high spirits and pleasure in the company of her husband were fresh wounds to Miss Szold. All the old wounds had started aching the moment she left Palestine. The dreams began again and with them the obsessive, circular thoughts, the greeting of each day with the recollection of what had happened a year ago, what she had been thinking, what he had been doing: "sporting with that woman in Berlin."

Miss Szold could avoid that woman on social occasions and with the help of friends who juggled invitations, and she could avoid Dr. Ginzberg on the street because he was prepared to go to fantastic lengths to avoid her. But at synagogue there was no protection; at synagogue she saw them entering arm in arm, leaving arm in arm, smiling into each other's eyes. Again she was gripped by the need to pour herself out to old friends and to her diary:

> I cry out against fate! I feel so deep a capacity in me for happiness and making happy, and I must seal myself up. The books and the wise people tell you to help others and you will help yourself. Am I not putting most of my time into other people's work? Does it make me forget myself or even him?

She was still the secretary and slave of the Jewish Publication Society and therefore the secretary and slave of the prolific Ginzberg, whose works had become the society's most glittering product. At a meeting of the publication committee a letter of Ginzberg's was read; his material for the *Legends* on Moses was so abundant that he asked for a fifth volume, which meant more work for her: "One sentence of the letter made me boil—the old arrogance is in it—indeed the whole letter is himself." And as the secretary, she was required to answer the letter. The society agreed to the fifth volume. It seemed to her Ginzberg had his way in everything.

His manuscript had pursued her on the continent; now his letters pursued her at home. There were four in one week, all in connection with the editorial work, and she broke her glasses over one of them. When he sent her an introduction in German written out on a scrap of paper, she hurled it back at him with the demand that he let her have it in English. "I hardly know myself when I do these things to him—I who used to spare him every vestige of drudgery.

Is it malice on my part? Or is it truly a measure of self-protection. . . ." As for Mrs. Ginzberg, "I cannot face her, as though I and not she had done the wrong, and her wrongdoing is as great as his—almost as great."

There was a lump in her throat all the time. She was "full of ugly envy," aware that she looked at every woman she met only to measure the extent of her own misery against the other's good fortune. Young women she saw as radiant with the joys of newly declared love or reveling in the presence of an infant; older women seemed always to be flanked by accomplished husbands, loyal children and adorable grandchildren. Her speaking triumphs—she had begun making speeches about Palestine to small groups, women's groups, the YWHA, the Council of Jewish Women, temple sisterhoods, the little Hadassah Study Circle—brought her no satisfaction. She envied her sister Adele her ailing husband, envied her sister Rachel the illness that brought forth so much tenderness from Joe, envied Bertha her children, "and I hate myself and my life." She was fifty years old; she had done nothing and she was nothing.

Along with her work for the JPS she had taken up all her old self-imposed chores, the translations and editorial work for seminary professors done as a matter of course. And within weeks of her return, Miss Szold accepted a position as secretary for the Jewish Agricultural Experiment Station. This was a project near the colony of Athlit founded by a young agronomist named Aaron Aaronsohn. A group of rich, non-Zionist American Jews were ready to back him financially; there were hopes of scientific exchanges with the U.S. Department of Agriculture, and someone was needed to coordinate matters at the American end. When Miss Szold took it on, the Agricultural Experiment Station became her first official connection with a piece of constructive work in Palestine.

But nothing could distract her for long from Ginzberg. Dr. Schechter was to spend a year abroad, some member of the faculty must take his place during that year, and the obvious choice was Ginzberg. Dr. Schechter told her one day that he was troubled about it. There was no reason to be troubled on her account, she told him; he had no choice but to leave the senior professor in charge.

Presently Mrs. Schechter made an appointment with Miss Szold to take a walk and talk about Ginzberg. It became apparent now that there had been a certain long-standing strain between Ginzberg and Schechter, to which the jilting and subsequent misery of Miss Szold added fuel. Mrs. Schechter was not willing to state the source of this strain; she said something about Ginzberg's life during his *Jewish Encyclopedia* days having been "irreligious." He was not pleasant to people. He took no interest in communal affairs. . . . Miss Szold said nothing, but she thought to herself that he could so easily win his way. She knew his winning ways. . . .

To appoint him as substitute now, Mrs. Schechter went on, would encourage him to lay claim to the presidency after Dr. Schechter's death. And Dr. Schechter did not trust him.

Miss Szold took up Dr. Ginzberg's defense. Not to appoint him would be destructive of morale. She knew he would acquit himself brilliantly. She had "confidence in his ultimate honesty, in spite of his action towards me."

Mrs. Schechter replied that everyone knew what he had done to Miss Szold. Could Dr. Schechter disregard public opinion?

If his behavior was reprehensible, Miss Szold retorted, he must be dismissed. If it was not—and she held it was not—he must get what was his due.

Then she went home and seethed. "It was cruel that I should have been drawn into this—I love him too much and hate him too much not to be over-fair with him."

At the wedding of pretty, refined Molly Jacobsen to a man Miss Szold called "a coarse little herring," Mrs. Ginzberg's eyes met her own from a distance. Miss Szold shivered. She was told later that Mrs. Ginzberg had nearly fainted. When a tea was planned for faculty ladies Mrs. Ginzberg called on Mrs. Marx to ask pointedly who else was invited. Mrs. Schechter reported it later to Miss Szold and asked whether Miss Szold did not pity her. "And then the pent-up storm of the day burst out. Pity her? No! . . . Why did she marry with such unseemly haste? Why? And why? No, I pity only myself, my blighted existence. . . ." And when she learned Mrs. Ginzberg had nearly fainted at the wedding she could only think it was because of the sight of her own haggard and tormented face. Impossible to pity her. "In me everything is dying, dying," she wrote in her diary, "and in him and in her life is welling up in joy and happiness, and they actually draw the elements of youth from my dreary—" She put her pen down, unable to go on.

One day Miss Szold took a long walk with a friend, Alice Seligsberg, whom she had met just before the storm of Ginzberg's rejection broke upon her head. Miss Seligsberg was an unmarried woman in her late thirties, gentle, pretty, delicately refined, with a hunger for the spiritual. Born into a liberal, cosmopolitan Jewish family and raised as a member of the Ethical Culture movement, she had wandered to the brink of Catholicism, then retreated into a vaguely Anglican stance. Pictures of the Holy Family attracted and frightened her. It was Miss Szold's hope that Miss Seligsberg could be reclaimed for Judaism.

Miss Seligsberg looked up to her as a wiser, stronger figure, and Miss Szold was drawn to Alice because she was spontaneous and all of a piece: "You are so earnest and single-minded, so stimulating to me, so whole a personality, that I recognize unity in all you do and say. . . ." She was sorely alone now, desperate for someone to love and trust. Rachel and Bertha were far away, and Adele had her own demanding life. Miss Szold loved her family with all her heart, but she needed someone's full and unwavering attention, someone who would serve as a sort of mediator with the world of things and ordinary people. Now Alice began to fill the place Rachel had occupied when they were girls. She was the confidante who would never judge, whose sociable, impulsive, enthusiastic temper acted as a balance to Miss Szold's arid intellectualism.

In the course of their walk Miss Szold told her friend her eyes had been troubling her for some weeks. She felt generally unwell, but that could be ignored; her eyes were a more serious matter.

Miss Seligsberg begged her to see a doctor, but she did nothing about it, not even when she had to put her work aside a few days later because her eyes were so painful. At a meeting of the FAZ leaders someone told her she ought to become secretary; the present secretary was considered dangerously inept and a fool. "Out of the question!" she cried. She knew better than to take on such a burden at any time, and now she was hardly able to attend to the work she was paid for.

Sometimes, working on the preface to Ginzberg's *Yerushalmi Fragments*, a phrase would come back to her that she had used in her letters to him, and "for an instant I fear that my sanity will give way. And then I remember his superior air, his placid tranquillity, or the assumption of it, in our interview in February, our last interview . . . and I fear that some day I may do him physical violence. . . ."

An elaborate dinner was planned for Dr. Schechter for late May, in honor of his forthcoming trip to Europe. Miss Szold was one of the planners, her task being to arrange the seating of 131 guests. The dinner was to take place on a Sunday; the night before, she realized she had placed herself at a table alongside the one at which she had seated the Ginzbergs. Instantly she shifted her own place. But on Sunday morning another rearrangement became necessary, and in carrying it out she once again placed herself next to them: "So close that I could feel his breathing—and she might have heard my habitual sighs that I cannot control any more." Once their eyes met; after that Mrs. Ginzberg took care not to turn toward Miss Szold again.

In the crowded, overheated hotel dining room Miss Szold watched without watching. Yes, Mrs. Ginzberg had beautiful eyes but not a beautiful mouth, and "her whole face is meaningless. She had on her wedding dress, her hair was overdressed, she has no style and no manner. . . . Him I could see in the mirror opposite. . . . His chief expression was haughty disdain and jealousy of Dr. Schechter."

A day or so later she watched the Ginzbergs through her window, seeing

them walk down the seminary steps with someone else. Mrs. Ginzberg hopped
along, one minute putting her arm through her husband's, then withdrawing
it, then patting his shoulder, patting his back, and going through the whole
series again. "And she chucked him under the chin! And then she folded her
hands up against her back, and again she snatched them out and took off his
hat. . . . That seemed too much for him and he drew back . . . that is the
sort of woman he prefers to me. It excited me beyond words, and the storm
that gathered force within me all day broke loose at the Marxes that evening
and I denounced her."

Mrs. Marx—one can only admire the inexhaustible patience of that young
woman—defended Adele Ginzberg, explained that she was young, innocent,
playful. Mrs. Marx also said that once when Miss Szold was visiting them
the servant had answered the front door and found Mrs. Ginzberg, who was
ushered into the dining room. When Mrs. Marx went to her later she was in
tears.

But what did *she* have to weep about? Miss Szold, at home at her desk,
faced the manuscript sent by Dr. Ginzberg in his own handwriting, on paper
she had given him for that purpose, wrapped in an envelope addressed to
Mr. and Mrs. Professor Ginzberg in Berlin. The notes, which were incorrectly
numbered, were written part of the way through in childishly perfect handwriting
she identified instantly as that of Mrs. Ginzberg. And the whole was sent,
not by mail and with a note or letter of explanation, but by a messenger, by
way of his translator. The man was almost a stranger to Miss Szold, but she
broke down in front of him, weeping uncontrollably. Take it all back, she
said. Tell him the notes must be numbered correctly. .

The translator told her she ought to be able to correct the manuscript
of Dr. Ginzberg with the same devotion she put into all the other work of
the Publication Society. "Let him try to go through life for two years with a
lump in his throat, with a burning coal on his left side, with eyes that threaten
at any moment to run over with tears," she told her diary.

She seemed to make no effort to control herself even before strangers, as
if she had become so accustomed to giving way that now she welcomed the
slightest opportunity to do so. If people found it frightening, let them. She
hurt inside; why should they not know and feel the extent of her hurt? There
was something almost larger than life about the earnest schoolteacher transformed into an avenging angel while Mrs. Ginzberg wept alone in the Marx's
dining room. Something powerful, abandoned. Everybody knew. The story had
spread far beyond the seminary. The Jewish circles of Columbia knew. The
JPS knew and pitied her. Impossible not to pity her. But was there not perhaps
a certain amazement—who would have thought she had it in her?—and with
this amazement, perhaps the faintest tinge of admiration?

It was clear to Miss Szold that something must be done about her work on the *Legends*. Adele's handwriting had defiled it for her. "If I put myself into his book that is now hers, I shall be driven to suicide. That is the horror of the last two days. I feel the idea of suicide becoming more and more familiar to me. . . ."

There was another outburst a few days later, again in the presence of a stranger, a Mr. Breuer, who brought more manuscript and a letter from Ginzberg saying that because he was to sail in a few days' time he was unable to make further corrections but would make them in galley proof. So Ginzberg refused to take his work along with him but was willing to put it on her. She broke out in a rage that terrified her and Breuer:

> Oh, he *is* utterly selfish. . . . I contrasted my life of never-ending toil, which he had not scrupled to increase during five whole years, with his and her life of ease . . . and I raged so that my poor mother wanted to carry the manuscript to him and tell him what she thought of him. . . . Oh how he has murdered my soul. . . . And in my pain and anguish I cried out to my mother that I must give up the position with the Publication Society because I cannot, cannot bear the handling of his book. . . .

One day in early June a committee from the FAZ came to ask if she would serve as secretary, and to her own amazement Miss Szold told them she would. Dr. Friedlaender came over a few days later to say it would be "the salvation of organized Zionism in this country."

At last the Ginzbergs left for Europe. Miss Szold slept that night, hours of refreshing sleep for the first time in many weeks. She could breathe freely now. She could walk out the front door of the black-and-white entry downstairs without the fear that she might meet him and be cut by him. She woke next morning with a new resolution: she would ask for permission to employ someone at her own expense to see volumes three and five of the *Legends* through the press.

That night she had a dream. She dreamed that a particular book was lost, that she went into the study of the house in Baltimore and her father was there, and she asked him where the book was. With his characteristic precision he told her just where it was. She went to the shelf and found it.

She awoke early next morning. It was four-thirty. She felt as vigorous as she used to feel before October 1908. She sat down and wrote a letter to Judge Sulzberger asking to be relieved of the responsibility for the two volumes of the *Legends* and to employ someone else for that purpose at her own expense, for "being a human woman as well as a proofreader, I may not be in a condition to do my literary duty to the author properly."

Then she mailed it, prepared to offer her resignation and look for other work if he did not agree. As for the money, "I shall spend that money with the same spirit as I would pay for a hospital operation on some diseased organ of mine."

She did not refer again to the dream, for Miss Szold was not a connoisseur of dreams, but its spirit suggests she had begun to look for a way out. What was lost—her self-respect, perhaps—would be found. She did not know where to look for it yet, but with the help of what was best and wisest within her, she would learn.

At last Sulzberger and the JPS agreed to her request for a translator. Dr. Israel Davidson, a professor at the seminary, was suggested, and he called on Miss Szold, but the visit was unlucky. An outburst of self-pity and indignation overcame her, and Davidson refused to take the job, perhaps fearing that part of her resentment would rub off on him.

A Mr. David Blondheim consented to do the *Legends*. Within days, he wrote that he had trouble with his eyes and could not do the work after all. It had become an incubus, but she resolved to give up her position rather than handle it herself. At the same time she resolved never to do any extra editorial work. She had "cheapened myself all my life . . . until they only look upon me as a proofreader," and she was never thanked. They all took it as a matter of course.

From then on she would try to do something of her own. She thought about a travel book describing the trip through the Middle East; she considered a book that would be a Jewish portrait gallery. She was anxious to begin, anxious to prove to herself either her own utter incompetence to be anything but a proofreader the rest of her life or else that she had the ability to do something with a tiny creative spark in it.

She looked about her now and saw for the first time that there were other women who suffered as she did. Before she had seen only the happiness of others; now, in her own circle, in the newspaper, in fiction, she saw that women's lives could be destroyed by love. She copied out one novel, lent to her by Rachel, for pages, word by word, into her diary. Why had she never read such books when she was young, she wondered. How had she gone through life altogether unaware of sex and marriage and what they meant to women? . . . Others knew, but she knew nothing. Something that awakened spontaneously in them slept inside her until Ginzberg woke it up. Why? What had gone wrong with her early life?

Summer approached, and it was going to be a very hot summer. She had a new responsibility to the FAZ, and in spite of her resolve not to do menial tasks for others she agreed to index the first ten volumes of the publications of the American Jewish Historical Society, some 600 hours of work, according to her estimate. This time the *Yearbook* was overwhelming, 180 pages longer than it should have been, and there was no chance of even a week's vacation.

An old phrase floated to the surface again—"I hate myself and the life I have made for myself"—but she had not remade it. Her "own work," the work she said she yearned to do, was still undone, and she had not really determined what it was. Worst of all, she thought she saw some sort of pattern behind this mismanagement of her life, some grain in her character that doomed her forever. Their servant, Anna, threatened to leave. Miss Szold watched her mother's reactions and found in them a certain "hard tactlessness and childish insistence on minor points. . . . She has, in spite of her fifty years' housekeeping experience, no executive ability—I am exactly like her, I too am wearing myself out in detail work, in which I excel as she does. So it is fate with me! And I am meant to suffer until the end."

That scorching summer she began going down to the offices of the FAZ on East Broadway, consisting of two bedrooms and a hall in an old-fashioned house into which the Jewish National Fund, the Yiddish newspaper *Dos Yiddishe Folk* and the FAZ were all crammed together. Miss Szold inspected the bedrooms and the hall, a dark, nasty room, and decided she would establish herself there. No one was to interfere with her hall; no one was to take her crayons or use her light. They had the bedrooms, she had the hall and it must be hers absolutely.

Then, for the next seven months, she went to the house on East Broadway every day between four and five in the afternoon when her JPS work was done, remaining until three in the morning. She found membership receipts accumulated during all the years of the Federation's life, a safe deposit box full of bits of paper containing the records of Jewish National Fund contributions, and Colonial Bank shares, all stuffed together without order or chronology. Miss Szold set about putting them in order.

She loved order and had a weakness for filing cabinets; she had freely chosen to do this work against all common sense, and in the heat of a New York summer. A voice inside her must have told her she was punishing herself, for she sent a letter to a friend remarking lightly, jokingly, that she was working on the Historical Society Index and contemplating suicide. To Dr. Schechter, some months later: "I cannot flatter myself that I am doing Zionist work; cleaning up other people's Augean stables is too far removed from Jewish ideal hopes. . . . I am not living—I have committed suicide. . . ."

In the early months of 1911 it became apparent to members of the seminary circle that Adele Ginzberg was pregnant. During this same period Miss Szold's health gave way entirely. The eyes that had troubled her so sorely the year before were only part of it; there was pain extending from her head to her foot on one side of the body. Repeated examination by eye doctors revealed nothing about the eyes, but for the bodily pain surgery was recommended. Sometime in April, Miss Szold entered Baltimore's Hospital for the Women of Maryland, where she underwent surgery and remained for two weeks. During the same month Mrs. Ginzberg gave birth to her son Eli. Possibly Miss Szold's operation was a hysterectomy; perhaps whatever was wrong with her was brought on by overwork following heartbreak. The light talk of suicide, the vision of herself as a shoveler of dung, a prisoner of her own deformed and blasted character, may well have left her helpless before the final blow, Mrs. Ginzberg's confinement.

In any case the pain remained after surgery, and the doctors insisted on complete rest for months. The pain meant nothing, they assured her. But her eyes were no better; if her sight failed her utterly she would have to start anew in some other field. Meanwhile, she could read no more than half an hour a day.

At Mount Desert, Maine, where Bertha had taken a place for the summer, Miss Szold sat on the porch while Mama read to her. They went through Jakob Burkhardt's *Civilization of the Renaissance in Italy* followed by Renaissance literature, punctuated by the comings and goings of the children and Rachel and Bertha. It was a pleasantly noisy household which she found somewhat dismaying, for she was used to a much more formal life. People ate when they liked and wore what they liked while she and Mama sat upright on their chairs and considered Venetian sculpture. But the children made up for everything; she loved them all, especially Benjamin, the eldest, a bright, studious boy who was never without an armload of books, English and Hebrew. Mama and Rachel said he was just what Henrietta used to be, so serious. When he was very little he had burst into tears one day because someone told him Hebrew was not an American language.

She thought how sensitive he was, how keenly appreciative of what was beautiful and good. Sometimes her eyes filled with tears when she watched him. "I hope life and the world will deal gently with him. . . ."

That autumn she returned to New York after six months of convalescence.

III

NEW YORK:
A SECOND LIFE

12

For the past three years Miss Szold had been making a public display of herself. She had been wallowing in her emotions, ugly emotions, the chief of them naked jealousy. Also her sharp regret for the youth she had thrown away. Also anger and petty vengefulness, for her behavior to Ginzberg and his bride was spiteful, and she knew it and would not change.

She taught herself bit by bit to see him as a mortal man and in the process came to see that her father was also a mortal man. Much of the rage against Ginzberg echoed her resentment of a father who had brought her up to asexual duty for his own sake, depriving her of her rightful heritage while her mother stood by. Her mother, who did not know or did not care, had allowed her to bear the burdens while Rachel and Sadie and the others were initiated into a richer, fuller life. Nowhere in her diary does she blame her parents, but the questions she repeatedly asks herself imply only one possible answer: that she was lured into an emotionless half life because of the needs of Mama and Papa, the projection of their own desired images onto her.

This anguished process, this explosion of resentment that she did not and could not suppress, lasted so long because there was so much to accomplish, so many losses other than Ginzberg that the loss of Ginzberg reawakened. But when it was over she had won something far more precious than freedom from Louis Ginzberg. At long last, she had left home.

What Philadelphia could not do for her, rejection did. She would live from now on as an adult rather than a dependent child. Her father was no longer a living presence temporarily and unjustly snatched away by death, he was truly dead, and she could go on without him because his ideas were part of her, woven forever into her mind and spirit. She was free, as she had never been before, to act on them.

Age had freed her as well. She had surely passed through menopause whether or not surgical menopause put its dramatic seal on the change. There was less to repress now, less to fear, not because her sexuality ceased to exist, but because it was not longer such a momentous issue.

The diary, the letters and the veil were packed and hidden away in a trunk with other souvenirs of her love. One wonders why she kept them. Perhaps it was because she kept everything, perhaps because she wanted to remember those three years of abandon as well as the years of her disembodied romance. The dimensions of that public display were so awesome she may have felt unable to part with them entirely.

For the faculty wives, motherhood permanently altered the status of Adele Ginzberg; she was no longer an interloper but one of their own. Three years later she gave birth to a second child, a daughter. Although Ginzberg had chosen his wife too quickly for comfort, the choice proved a brilliant one, for the girl from Berlin had remarkable talents for mothering and wifehood. The marriage was long, happy and seldom dull.

Louis Ginzberg was not chosen to replace Schechter during the year abroad, nor did he become president of the seminary after Schechter died. This might have been 'due to bad feeling over his rejection of Miss Szold, but more likely it was not. He did become one of the preeminent Talmudic scholars of his day and the seminary's most beloved teacher. According to Louis Finkelstein, chancellor of the seminary in the 1940s: "To his students he was a father, suffering a father's aches, as well as partaking of a father's joys . . . a saint as well as a scholar. . . . Huddled in his tallit, reciting the ancient prayers, appealing for divine help on behalf of Israel and the world . . . Professor Ginzberg was transfigured."

Miss Szold went back to the flat across the street from the seminary, to the old life and the old activities. There were no more public displays, no private preoccupation with the Ginzberg family. The past was past, out of sight and out of mind and, like her childhood, irrevocably a part of her. Outwardly she was much the same woman who came to New York almost ten years earlier, with the same diffident bearing of a Victorian lady. Her hair, a little grayer now, was still brushed a hundred strokes a day, parted in the middle and fixed in the back in a chignon; her dresses were as plain as ever and topped by a broad white collar as meticulous as a nun's wimple. But beneath this demure exterior her backbone was stiffer than before. She was less patient, less inclined to let others run over her, less willing to suppress feelings of anger or annoyance.

Meetings of the FAZ executive committee rarely began on time. Sometimes they were forty-five minutes late, sometimes three hours, and Miss Szold wrote several acidulous letters to the committee on the subject. She herself was always several minutes early, which the others took as a reproach. Her very person was something of a reproach to them, for she sat with her eyes closed, either to rest them, although the eye trouble had receded, or to shut out the endless, pointless wrangling. Whatever the reason, she must have looked disapproving. In her presence they had to swallow down some of the juicier epithets that sprang to their lips when carried away by argument, as they so frequently were. They were almost all Russians and almost all quite young, for their organization was exactly the kind that attracts the young: a lost cause. Most American Jews were new immigrants consumed with learning the language, getting jobs, joining unions and becoming American, concerns more immediate than Zionism.

Miss Szold closed her eyes and saved her energies for something else.

When Emma Gottheil had attended the second Zionist congress with her husband in 1899, she had been urged by Herzl to organize American women for Zionism. During the intervening years, little Zionist groups, like the Hadassah Miss Szold had joined, sprang up in several parts of New York, often calling themselves "Daughters of Zion," to which the name of a Jewish heroine would be added: Deborah, Rebecca, Rachel or Hadassah. Emma Gottheil belonged to a Daughters of Zion on the East Side; Miss Szold's group was centered uptown in Harlem. All were essentially study circles, an outgrowth of the leisure of middle-class women as well as their desire to learn and share their learning. They studied Herzl and other Zionist writers; occasionally they made a stab at conversational Hebrew, and most were very young, like the men. But by the fall of 1911 the Harlem group had suffered the usual fate of women's Zionist circles: it had dwindled, it was all but dead. Miss Szold made no effort to revive it. She had something far more extensive in mind. She wanted a nation-wide organization that would continue with Zionist education but whose goal would no longer be study alone. It must do something practical, along the lines of Jane Addams's social work in Chicago, perhaps, or in the area of public health.

The men of the FAZ were also interested in a nation-wide organization of American Zionist women. They wanted a women's auxiliary that would be molded and directed by the men, with the goals of increasing membership and raising money. Social work of the sort Miss Szold had in mind was in their opinion philanthropy, which they equated with charity, a bourgeois catering to the helpless, a form of self-indulgence that was outmoded, even dangerous. It reminded them of Halukah. They despised Halukah.

But for the time being the interests of the FAZ and Miss Szold were one. A member of the executive committee of the FAZ, a young lawyer named Bernard Rosenblatt, was given the assignment of meeting with some of the leading Zionist women and helping them organize. Accordingly Rosenblatt and Miss Szold called together a group with the former members of her Hadassah circle as a nucleus. There were three meetings during the early months of 1912, at which Rosenblatt guided the women through the drafting of a constitution. Actually two constitutions were worked up, one for the national organization, one for its first chapter, which was to be called Daughters of Zion, Hadassah Chapter.

Provided with a constitution, their next need was a membership, and a letter was circulated inviting attendance at a public meeting to be held February 24, 1912, in the vestry rooms of New York's Temple Emanu-El. Seven women, Miss Szold, Mrs. Schechter and Mrs. Gottheil among them, signed the letter, which read:

> The undersigned, in consultation with other women Zionists in New York City, have reached the conclusion that the time is ripe for a large organization of women Zionists, and they desire to invite you to attend a meeting for the purpose of discussing the feasibility of forming an organization which shall have for its purpose the promotion of Jewish institutions and enterprises in Palestine, and the fostering of Jewish ideals.

Thirty-eight potential members came to the public meeting, at which a women's Zionist organization was established. A few days later officers and a board of directors were elected, and Miss Szold chosen as chairman. The old Hadassah circle then graciously handed over their entire treasury of $19.16.

Sophia Ruskay, a member of the first board of directors, remembered how she had been "pulled in." Two of her friends were vaguely interested in Zionism, and "Miss Szold was eager for acolytes, people who would listen to her dream." The three women lived in Far Rockaway; they gathered together a group of six or seven and invited Miss Szold to meet with them. "Week after week she schlepped herself down on the train. She electrified everybody— yet it wasn't the way she spoke, it was the humanity and the knowledge. We were ignoramuses in our early twenties, Miss Szold was a scholar, an important person who moved in important circles. Nothing was ever said about women's rights but we had the feeling she was living women's rights."

From then on, board meetings and general meetings proceeded at a rapid clip; minutes record a constant preoccupation with the exact nature of the "institutions and enterprises" that were to be promoted in Palestine. A day nursery was talked about; so was the possibility of providing work for young women in lace making or the pearl industry, but they always returned to the subject of public health. Letters of inquiry to doctors and institutions in Palestine brought conflicting advice. No one in Palestine thought much of Miss Szold's particular favorite, a system of district visiting nurses. Lillian Wald had pioneered in New York in this field, which required trained nurses capable of working semi-independently and visiting the people of their neighborhood house by house to search out health problems. To Miss Szold it was the ideal beginning for country-wide public health work, no matter what the physicians of Palestine wrote. Perhaps it might lead to a school for nurses.

There are a few grandiose phrases in the early minutes, an occasional statement of policy almost breathtaking in its largeness of vision, but by and large Hadassah's first year was spent in ladylike discussion over tea and cakes. The women met afternoons at one another's homes, and it was the duty of the hostess to send written invitations to all her friends asking them to come to a talk on Palestine "illustrated by stereopticon views." Every session started on the scheduled minute; all business was conducted with precision and formality. The meetings were everything the meetings of the FAZ executive committee were not.

The star of these early meetings was the stereopticon machine, projecting homemade slides of miserable quality on an improvised screen until a few pitiful houses or the sand dunes of Tel Aviv appeared, wavering and flickering. Yet the women had gone to a good deal of trouble and expense to buy the machine, and if the pictures showed nothing beautiful or inspiring, they were satisfying proof that all the talk was somehow real, rooted in an actual piece of earth, however distant and desolate.

With the help of Dr. Friedlaender a motto was chosen, "The healing of the daughter of my people," a shortened version of a moving passage in Jeremiah: "Behold the voice of the cry of my people from a land that is very far off. . . . Is there no balm in Gilead? Is there no physician there? Why then is not the healing of the daughter of my people accomplished?" For their seal they took the star of David against a blue background, encircled by branches of myrtle, in Hebrew *hadas* or *hadassah.*

The membership of Daughters of Zion, Hadassah Chapter, now stood at 122. Their aim was still practical work in Palestine, preferably public health, but they refused to start anything they could not pay for in the immediate future. Until they had a membership of 300 they felt they must bide their time.

In December 1912 the pace suddenly changed; events accelerated and pushed Miss Szold before them. One day she picked up a Jewish newspaper and read that Mr. Nathan Straus and wife, having recently returned from the Holy Land, planned to go there again in January. Straus, then in his mid-sixties, belonged to a family of department store owners and merchants who were also public servants. Public health was one of his lifelong interests; he had served as president of the New York Board of Health and on his recent trip had set up a soup kitchen and embryo health center in Jerusalem.

He was an impetuous and strong-willed man, a true original. In the course of a long life, Nathan Straus gave two-thirds of his fortune to Palestine, mostly for Jewish causes and occasionally for the specific needs of Arabs at a time when no other Jewish philanthropist knew or cared that there were Arabs in the Holy Land.

Miss Szold got in touch with him, which resulted in Straus's offer to pay the traveling expenses and four months' salary of a trained nurse chosen by Hadassah; Hadassah had only to pay her salary for the rest of a two-year period. There was one other stipulation: the nurse must be prepared to leave with the Strauses for Palestine on January 18.

An emergency meeting of the board was called for January 1, at which Miss Szold gave an account of her meeting with Straus and added that Hadassah would need the sum of $2,400 over the course of two years to pay the salary and expenses of the first nurse. According to the minutes, "It became evident that in order to meet such an obligation, Hadassah would have to appeal for donations on a large scale." The sum seemed frightening. If the venture failed the women would become the laughingstock of the FAZ, who made no secret of their disapproval of Hadassah's aims and independence. Nevertheless Miss Szold and Mrs. Gottheil swept all before them, the offer was accepted and it remained only to find a nurse who could leave the country in eighteen days. A committee to pass on applicants was formed and advertisements placed in two Jewish newspapers.

A Mount Sinai nurse named Rose Kaplan was engaged. But in the meanwhile Eva Leon, Emma Gottheil's sister and a Hadassah member with a maddening habit of acting on her own, had raised a sum of money among non-Zionists in Chicago for use in Palestine. Nathan Straus was eager not only to bring a second nurse with that money but to bring Miss Leon as well. A non-Zionist nurse was therefore hired, Rachel Landy of Cleveland. Eva Leon was already employing two midwives in Palestine with money she had raised through non-Zionist channels. There seemed to be no resisting Miss Leon.

The party for Palestine now consisted of Mr. and Mrs. Straus, Eva Leon and the two nurses. A settlement house would be rented for them in Jerusalem, where they were to become district visiting nurses, concentrating on the needs of women and children and supervising Miss Leon's midwives. But Hadassah's purpose was something larger, not so much the relief of the individual as the organizing of a thorough system of public health nursing throughout the towns and colonies of the Holy Land. It was a precarious venture, launched on less than three weeks' notice, frowned upon by the men who led American Zionism and backed by a women's club less than one year old, without funds or experience.

No sooner were the nurses off to Palestine than Miss Szold arranged visits to Baltimore, Cincinnati, Chicago, Boston and Philadelphia to organize chapters of the Daughters of Zion. The support of the nurses would depend on expanded membership, and they were still a single chapter rather than a national organization. Then she took to the road. We see her in Baltimore looking fit and fashionable in a new hat, in Cincinnati in July, where it was hotter than hell, or, as she put it, "the nether regions have no terrors for me any more." Three new chapters sprang up in her wake: Philadelphia, Baltimore, Boston.

"We need Zionism as much as those Jews do who need a physical home," she wrote to Alice Seligsberg. She was speaking not only for American Jewish women but for the two of them, Alice, who was gentle and spiritual and forever in search, and herself, an independent woman now, in need of a use for her independence.

As soon as they reached Jerusalem, Kaplan and Landy installed themselves in the Orthodox Mea Shearim section, in a little stone house with a lemon tree in the courtyard; the interior was fitted up for them as a gift from Mrs. Straus. The nurses were shown through the Straus Health Bureau, one of whose physicians, Dr. Wilhelm Brünn, was to supervise their work; they were put in touch with a number of health and medical centers in the city, the Pasteur Institute, recently begun by German physicians, an eye clinic under Dr. Albert Ticho, an antitrachoma project run by Dr. Arieh Feigenbaum. Then they hung a sign outside their house announcing in Hebrew and English: AMERICAN DAUGHTERS OF ZION NURSES SETTLEMENT HADASSAH.

The Strauses and Miss Leon returned to America. Dr. Brünn left for Tiberias, where there was a cholera epidemic. The two nurses felt lonely, rudderless, for the physicians of Palestine did not welcome them. Although visiting nurses were well accepted in America, they were unknown in the Middle East and Europe, where most of the Jewish doctors had been trained. A nurse was supposed to be a robot placed in a clinic or hospital, awaiting orders from her superiors. These women proposed to go about the city on their own, to penetrate the subterranean dwellings, to exhort, cajole, explore and gather statistics. It was a system perfectly suited to the public health needs of Jerusalem, which were vast and hidden and embedded in the ignorance of a superstitious population who shrank from doctors and hospitals. But because the concept was foreign to them, the physicians remained aloof. "Those two nurses were like lost souls, wandering through Jerusalem, not knowing what to do," Dr. Feigenbaum recalled. Rose Kaplan was a dark, stocky Russian, Ray Landy a tall blonde, so he called them Short and Tall, and he pitied them.

What they saw during their wanderings was a city where malaria, typhoid, cholera and typhus flourished along with trachoma. Quinine and bismuth were the cure-alls, often dispensed by physicians who practiced medicine on the street in front of the pharmacies. One doctor sat on his donkey throughout examinations; most cooperated as partners in trade with the pharmacists. Poor people went to pharmacists instead of doctors because they were cheaper; cheaper still was the folk medicine practiced by Jewish women at home. They relied on amulets, melon juice and dung.

Through courage and persistence the nurses eventually established working relations with a few of the doctors. They did maternity work, and trachoma prevention in the Jewish schools, but systematic district visiting nursing was put aside, either because there were more pressing needs or because of the physicians' hostility. About a year after the nurses arrived, a young woman named Helena Kagan came to Jerusalem directly after medical school in Switzerland; she was twenty-four years old and wanted to be among her own. Kagan got much the same reception as Landy and Kaplan. Nobody believed a woman could be a doctor, and she simply "hung around," waiting and hoping for work. Meanwhile she joined forces with the Hadassah nurses.

By 1914 it was evident to Hadassah's board that the work in Jerusalem needed stronger direction. They decided that a third, perhaps even a fourth, nurse would leave for Jerusalem, and Eva Leon, who planned to go there herself, would send back frequent and precise reports. Above all, no action was to be taken in Jerusalem without first checking with New York, even at the risk of delay, for the nurses' settlement in Palestine was an American undertaking. Miss Szold and the others felt strongly on this point. To Miss Szold, after all, the work in Palestine had been intended not only for the benefit of Palestine but equally for the benefit of American Jewish women. Without it they would be spiritual drifters—comfortable, charitable cultivated but soulless. Their ties to Palestine were their stake in the future of their people.

13

The third and fourth nurses never got to Palestine, nor did Miss Leon return to issue her precise reports, for in August 1914 the First World War severed Turkish Palestine from America and the rest of the world.

The effects in the Holy Land were immediate. No steamers came or left from Jaffa, prices rose instantaneously, there was a run on the banks. Hadassah's board voted to release Landy and Kaplan from their contracts, but both women replied that they would stay on.

In November 1914, Turkey entered the war, and Jerusalem became a military center for the Turks and their German allies. Citizens of the Allied nations—France, Russia, England—were expelled, sometimes brutally; those who had Ottoman citizenship were pulled into the army or forced into labor paving roads. Noncitizen doctors were deported or returned voluntarily to their homes to serve in their own armies; the few who remained were drafted by the Turks. All hospitals were shut down because the military requisitioned the buildings; drugs simply vanished. Cholera, typhus, malaria stalked the city, and everyone starved.

"Since the war began," Rachel Landy wrote to Hadassah in January 1915, "we are not having the usual good luck with our infants. Quite a number are dying after a few weeks. . . . Needless to say, it is all due to starvation." In February: "It is all I can do to treat the Sepharad Talmud Torah. The children seem to be getting smaller and thinner every day. They are developing idiotic expressions. . . ."

In the autumn of 1915, Hadassah ordered Landy home because her mother was sick and needed her. She sealed up the settlement house, leaving the trachoma work in Dr. Ticho's hands and the maternity work with Dr. Kagan and the three midwives. Dr. Kagan requested that Hadassah open a small clinic for women and children under her direction. They agreed to do so, provided the work was carried on in Hadassah's name.

Rose Kaplan had also returned to America to ask the board to sponsor her as a nurse in the refugee camps set up by the British in Alexandria for the thousands of Jews expelled from Palestine. But she had other business in New York of which they were only partly aware. During the months between her arrival, in January 1915, and November, when Hadassah sent her to Alexandria, Miss Kaplan underwent surgery for cancer, returning to the refugee camps with the knowledge that she had at most three or four years to live.

From Alexandria she reported regularly to Hadassah, describing her trachoma work and the equally important project of teaching hygiene to the children of the camp. A hot water supply was rigged up; everyone in the encampment had to bathe once a week: "We began with the school children yesterday, four hundred of them. I received a supply of soap . . . a huge flat tin pan, the kind Jerusalem people wash their clothes in, a bucket, and a dipper. . . ." The refugees lived in three apartment houses set apart for them, several families to a room, and throughout Miss Kaplan's accounts were cheerful; boxes of linen and baby clothing sewed by Hadassah were received with rejoicing; the

British commandant of the camp arranged for a sweet bun with raisins in it to be given to each school child daily, and the children were delighted with the feast. Each little conquest over privation was a triumph to her, and the tone of her letters, with their sturdy, wholesome concern for the daily lives of others, nowhere betrays the anxiety of a woman who harbored a fatal disease. Kaplan continued in the camps until August 1917, when she died of cancer.

Thus, in the opening years of the war, although the settlement house had been shut down, Hadassah's work was carried on among the women and children of the Alexandria refugee camp by Rose Kaplan and in Jerusalem by Dr. Kagan. Young, ardent, courageous, Helena Kagan saw the population of the city dwindle day by day. She moved among corpses that littered the streets. She bought a cow and kept it in her back yard in order to give a little milk to her child patients, and she contracted malaria, from which she suffered throughout the four years of the war. She sent meticulous accounts of her work to America and Hadassah, to which they replied, also meticulously. But as it happened, none of their replies reached Jerusalem, and in the dying city Kagan felt helpless and alone.

The year 1915 brought a revolutionary change to Miss Szold, one that left her feeling "as though I were reading in someone else's book of life, not my own."

First her mother became seriously ill. For fourteen or fifteen months Miss Szold fulfilled all her obligations to the JPS and Hadassah while caring for an obese and feeble woman of seventy-five. Then, toward the end of the year, help came from an unexpected quarter: a man named Julian Mack, a federal judge and the first American Jew to attain such a distinction. Generous, kind, plain-looking and unbuttoned, possibly the only Harvard-educated judge in the country willing to belch in public or to walk unselfconsciously down Fifth Avenue eating an apple, his background was German, his chief interest social reform.

Mack was a devoted admirer of Jane Addams, and Miss Szold was another of his enthusiasms. He now took it into his head that such a woman ought not to have to work for a living but should be free to devote herself to Zionist causes. Therefore he arranged an annuity for her. Julius Rosenwald, Mary Fels (whose husband made his fortune with Fels-Naphtha soap), Mack and others would contribute to it. Between the annuity and some savings and investments of her own Miss Szold should be able to live in comfort, nurse her mother and eventually return to Zionism. She was confused and bewildered by the offer. It was peculiar, she said; it had happened too suddenly. In the end she accepted.

Because of Sophie's illness, the two women left Morningside Heights and moved to a house on Pinehurst Avenue on the outskirts of the city. It was there that Mrs. Szold died in the summer of 1916, conscious to the last. A month later a family friend wrote to Miss Szold offering to recite the kaddish, the traditional prayer for a dead parent given by the eldest male child in synagogue throughout the year of mourning. When there is no male child, a stranger may recite the prayer. But Miss Szold, who was touched and grateful, nevertheless insisted the duty must be hers: "When my father died, my mother would not permit others to take her daughters' place in saying the Kaddish, and so I am sure I am acting in her spirit when I am moved to decline. . . . But beautiful your offer remains. . . . I know full well that it is much more in consonance with generally accepted Jewish tradition than is my or my family's conception. You understand me, don't you?"

She was alone now in an empty house. For the first time in her life, at the age of fifty-five, the dailiness of existence had to be met undiluted, for there was no one to consult or defer to in the small matters in which larger affairs are always embedded. There was no more slavery for the JPS, from which she had resigned six months ago. She was free to devote herself to Zionism, to the building of what she called "a sanctuary for the Jew . . . a center from which Jewish culture and inspiration will flow," words that expressed her father's vision.

The methods she had used so far were those of her orderly, practical mother. But Zionist affairs had grown considerably since 1913 when the two nurses left for Jerusalem. They had grown because of the war, and the small-scale undertakings of Hadassah grew with them until, a year or so after her mother's death, Miss Szold was to find herself heading a project of staggering proportions.

World Jewry was particularly threatened by the war, compelled in eastern Europe to bear arms for nations that had persecuted them and endangered on the eastern front by the clash of German and Russian armies in the areas of Poland most densely populated by Jews. The Yishuv, the Jews of Palestine, either starved or spun out a makeshift existence in refugee camps. At the same time, all the mechanisms through which Jews helped Jews—victims of hunger or persecution in eastern Europe, Halukah paupers in Palestine—were disrupted. The Zionist movement itself had come to a halt, headquarters remaining for a time in Berlin, with members of the executive committee scattered throughout Europe.

It was apparent that whatever relief measures were to aid the Jews of eastern Europe or preserve the Yishuv in Palestine must come from America. More than 130 Jewish agencies—eventually under the umbrella of the

American Jewish Joint Distribution Committee, created for that purpose—rose to the needs of European Jews. But Palestine remained the specific charge of the FAZ, a weak, impoverished organization without influence in high places or among the masses. In the entire country, with a Jewish population of 3 million, dues-paying members of the FAZ numbered 12,000.

Those meager resources were tried within weeks of the outbreak of war. Arthur Ruppin, chief Zionist official in the Holy Land, sent the Americans an urgent call for a relief fund of $50,000. The FAZ responded by holding an emergency meeting of American Zionists at the Hotel Marseilles in New York, on August 30, 1914. Among those invited was Louis Brandeis, a crusading attorney of national reputation, a Jew who had never played any part in Jewish affairs. The FAZ hoped for nothing more than the use of an illustrious name.

Brandeis was then fifty-eight, tall, loose-limbed, rumpled, with a halo of white hair and a noble face, aquiline and aristocratic. Born and raised in Kentucky, his parents were German-speaking immigrants from Bohemia, prosperous intellectuals who neither denied their Jewishness nor proclaimed it.

At nineteen Brandeis had entered Harvard Law School, where he was accepted into the loftiest circles. Soon after graduation he established a law practice in Boston and became "in practically all respects . . . a Brahmin," according to one biographer. By the end of the century he was a successful lawyer, increasingly identified with the Progressive movement and reform, an enemy of large corporations, of giant monopolies and the brutalizing power of big business, a protagonist of citizen action and the individual entrepreneur. Also the supporter and friend of Woodrow Wilson. For the latter reason, and because he had joined the FAZ in 1912 at the urging of Jacob de Haas but without taking an active role in it, Brandeis was invited to the meeting at the Hotel Marseilles.

There he was offered the leadership of the committee that would face the emergency in Palestine. He accepted. It was expected that he would remain a figurehead. Instead, to the consternation of Zionist leaders, it became apparent that Louis Brandeis intended to take charge of the American Zionist movement.

The Boston Brahmin had been transformed into a public Jew, and not merely a Jew but the chief of those East Side Russians who subscribed to the dangerous delusion called Zionism. The reasons behind the transformation remain mysterious, as all true conversions ultimately are, hidden within the mazes of an unusually complex character. Nevertheless the Zionists now had a leader of such uncommon authority and attainments that the movement must inevitably alter its shape and direction in his hands, a man whose name guaranteed perfect respectability, the assurance that Zionism was compatible with Americanism, and direct access to the sources of national power.

The committee formed at the Hotel Marseilles with Brandeis at its head was called the Provisional Executive Committee for General Zionist Affairs, referred to as the PC, and its members included old faithfuls like Friedenwald, Magnes and Miss Szold. But the presence of Brandeis attracted new men, men of stature, not only rabbis and professional scholars, but lawyers and businessmen with an aura of money and good connections. Julian Mack, a lovable and generous figure, became Brandeis's right hand. Felix Frankfurter, a member of the faculty at Harvard Law and a brilliant young man with little Jewish identification, entered the movement at the request of Brandeis. Rabbi Stephen Wise, a long-time Zionist who had left the American organization some years earlier, came back now because of his respect for Brandeis. He was tall, jut-jawed, vital, with a voice of muted thunder and the strength of an ox, according to a female admirer. A fearless, sometimes reckless fighter for many good causes, such as labor reform and birth control, he was a formidable orator and to the end of his long life a formidable womanizer. Jacob de Haas, who had been Herzl's English secretary, now became Brandeis's secretary for Zionist affairs. Essentially a propagandist, de Haas was unswervingly loyal to the movement and to Brandeis, who forgave him much.

This was the nucleus of the Brandeis group, chiefly men of German background and American education, successful men, progressives and social reformers. Their vision of Zionism was shaped by Louis Brandeis and was therefore a very American vision, organized and businesslike and reformist. Because Brandeis was the enemy of big business, he saw Palestine as another America that was better for being smaller. It would serve as a laboratory for new forms of social institutions as well as a place of refuge for the oppressed Jews of Europe. American Jews would naturally remain in America, investing their money in the upbuilding of small-scale business enterprises in Palestine. "The highest Jewish ideals are essentially American," Brandeis wrote.

In the years that followed it would become apparent that Brandeis and his inner circle saw Zionism in an entirely different light from the rank and file of the FAZ. To the latter, Palestine was no laboratory but an ancient dream. It was not essentially American or essentially Russian, German or English; it was essentially Jewish.

What was equally important, they were to find Brandeis himself an enigma. Still a Boston Brahmin, righteous and puritanical, he knew nothing about Judaism or Jewishness, and his character was almost diametrically opposed to that of the Russian Jews, although he was nevertheless attracted to them, not, perhaps, as individuals, but in the abstract. Among the Russians everyone, no matter how accomplished, had a weakness, whether for women or herring or noodle pudding or schnapps; some even told lies. The weakness was what made them human. Brandeis never spoke to a man he had once caught in a lie. He believed in the perfectability of the human race, not its weaknesses.

No matter. For the time being Louis Brandeis breathed life powerfully into the movement. The emergency fund initiated at the Hotel Marseilles would far surpass Arthur Ruppin's original request; a new era in American Zionism had begun, and the days when its leaders met over celery tonic in a Grand Street cafe were clearly past.

Miss Szold's associates now were men whose opinions she heard with deep respect. We may assume she no longer closed her eyes during meetings of the PC. To Louis Brandeis she was not a worthy and tiresome old maid but an admirable woman, a born leader as well as a fellow puritan; and her Hadassah, which she had created, in which she believed and which had doubled in membership during 1914 alone, was not a group of bourgeois women indulging in "diaper Zionism," a favorite accusation of the FAZ, but an important arm of the movement.

And it was to Miss Szold that Brandeis turned in 1916 when the European Zionists sent the PC a cry for medical help in the Holy Land. The country had been stripped bare of doctors, drugs, food, linen, clothing. Cholera and typhus and typhoid were epidemic.

What could Miss Szold and her Hadassah do? She told him a corps of ten doctors and two nurses should be sent with a supply of drugs; it would cost $25,000, which Hadassah would provide.

Hadassah now numbered somewhat less than 2,000, with chapters in twenty-seven cities, and their receipts for the past year were close to $3,000. At their third annual convention in July 1916 the assembled delegates heard the news that an American Zionist Medical Unit (AZMU) was to be outfitted and maintained by Hadassah for one year in Palestine. Understandably stunned, they accepted the task all the same.

By fall the cost of the venture had risen to $30,000. Miss Szold suggested saving on carfare; if every Hadassah member saved fifteen dollars by walking instead of taking streetcars they could raise even $30,000. By June 1917 the original estimate had quadrupled.

Costs were not the only problem. From the start the idea of a relief ship to Turkish Palestine raised diplomatic hackles. In August 1916, when the French, having blockaded the coast of Palestine, refused to consider a landing by a medical ship for fear the drugs would be used by combatants, it was suggested that the doctors and nurses travel instead by way of central Europe, Constantinople and the Anatolian Railway. Three months later Jacob de Haas was told by a representative in the Holy Land that the Turkish pasha was against it because the mission was entirely unnecessary; health conditions

1. Rabbi Benjamin Szold and his wife, Sophie

2. Henrietta Szold at sixteen

3. Rabbi Szold's study in the house on Lombard Street

4. The Szold daughters in 1888: from the left, Henrietta,
Bertha, Rachel, Adele, and Sadie

5. Louis Ginzberg and his fiancee, Adele Katzenstein (Berlin, 1908)

6. Miss Szold, Dr. Rubinow, and the nurses of the American Zionist
Medical Unit (AZMU), 1918

7. Hadassah institutes a milk supply for the babies of Jerusalem.

9. Miss Szold on shipboard

10. Dressed (atypically) in work garb
in the fields of Palestine

11. Dr. E. M. Bluestone

12. Theodor Herzl, the founder of political Zionism (1903)

13. Chaim Weizmann and Albert Einstein (1921)

14. Sir Herbert Samuel, first British High Commissioner under the Mandate

15. Louis D. Brandeis in 1914

did not warrant any such emergency measure, in his opinion.

Miss Szold heard otherwise. A letter from Helena Kagan was sent to her by the American ambassador in Constantinople: "The mortality rate now is nearly four times as great as it was before the war." Typhus was endemic; even the less contagious diseases had become fatal because of starvation. The ambassador himself had lent Dr. Kagan and Dr. Ticho $500 to carry on. The American dollar, he said, was worth only thirty-five cents, their funds were exhausted, but the two doctors were throwing themselves "body and soul" into the work.

Miss Szold concluded that the relief ship must and would sail. She made a series of fund-raising tours to Eastern cities, and Hadassah raised money by selling nasturtium seeds at five cents a package. They did not neglect more substantial sources of money. Negotiations were begun by Eva Leon with the "Joint," as the Joint Distribution Committee, the non-Zionist umbrella organization for American Jewish relief, was called; she believed they might be induced to make a large gift.

Once America entered the war, all hope of Turkish permission ended and the expedition simply waited on events. Letters that came to Miss Szold now gave a heart-wrenching picture of life in Jerusalem: bread that used to cost one franc selling for eleven, meat and eggs tripled in price, the roads lined with starving men and women begging for a mouthful. Helena Kagan wrote that she was being harassed by police, as were all suspected Zionists. Her letters had to be smuggled out. She begged for help, for money. She had started a little nursing class in Hadassah's name and continued the polyclinic, although she was sorely troubled by the fact that she was acting independently now, without their orders or approval. Not until 1918 did any of Hadassah's letters reach her.

It was against this background—Miss Szold on fund-raising tours that took her as far afield as Texas or at her desk reading smuggled letters describing the misery of the Yishuv—that certain events took place threatening not only her leadership of the relief mission but her leadership of Hadassah, even her place in Zionism.

She had been born in a home in which Germany, its language and culture, were deeply revered; as a young woman she had been stirred to the depths of her being by the rape of Russian Jewry. Both attitudes were jolted by the European war. From the start American sympathy lay with the Allies, England, France, Russia, and against Germany. However most American Jews, Miss Szold among them, were repelled by an alliance that included Russian murderers. The only Yiddish newspaper to support the Allies lost so much circulation that it went out of business.

But the second stage of the war was marked by German submarine attacks on neutral shipping, and American Jews turned increasingly toward the Allies. Miss Szold no longer admired Germany. She still hated the war but on religious and philosophical grounds, as a pacifist. In this she was one of a small but vocal group of dissidents like Jane Addams and Lillian Wald, who clung to the belief that international problems are never solved on battlefields.

In February 1917 the U.S. broke off diplomatic relations with Germany and in April entered the war. During the weeks between, emergency peace organizations sprang into action: petitions against the war flooded Congress, thousands of telegrams reminded President Wilson that he had been elected to keep the country out of war. Perhaps the most active organization fighting for a quick peace was the People's Council of America for Peace and Democracy. Scott Nearing and Morris Hillquit, both well-known radicals, were members of its executive committee, and Miss Szold joined in January or February, as did a number of her friends, fellow members of Hadassah, including Alice Seligsberg and Jessie Sampter, a poetic semi-invalid.

Their attitudes were exceptional by then. American Jews had always been sensitive to accusations of conflicting loyalties; they were equally sensitive to suggestions that because some were socialists, the entire community was socialist, radical and now pacifist. They hastened to declare their support of the Allies and the war. That summer Brandeis made the following statement at a meeting of the PC: "I cannot help feeling that the pacifistic attitude of some Jews is a danger to all Jews. . . . There are therefore these two things before us: being good belligerent Americans, and active disciplined Zionists."

Yet there was the problem of Miss Szold, who openly allied herself with the People's Council and who wrote to Dr. Gottheil: "I am afraid you will have to bracket me with Dr. Magnes and Miss Wald. I am anti-war, and anti-this-war, and anti-all wars. . . . I believe 'Thou shalt not kill' is a law in force." What was to be done about Miss Szold and her friends?

For a time, nothing. The women struggled privately with their consciences until they came face to face with a clear-cut conflict of interests: in September 1917 it was proposed that the Medical Unit attach itself to British expeditionary forces in Palestine. It was a way of moving past diplomatic hurdles that might be otherwise impassable and therefore a way of getting relief to the Yishuv— perhaps the only way.

Their first thought was that they must resign from Hadassah. Their second, Sampter's and Seligsberg's at any rate, was that they must not resign. Let the others force them out. They seesawed back and forth and left Miss Szold confused. "You may be right," she wrote to Miss Sampter, "that I am muddle-headed and not honest with myself, and seeking to maintain my own personal position, and am too impressed with my own importance. . . . I don't know whether you actually said all those things. . . . Perhaps it was my conscience speaking." But she did not want to resign; she wanted to stay and protest.

A long letter from Jacob de Haas explained to Miss Szold that there were a number of delicate diplomatic negotiations to be considered. If Britain won the war, he wrote, the Ottoman Empire would be dismembered and divided among the conquerors. Perhaps the Jews would come in for a share of the postwar world, as the Czechs, Poles and other nationalities hoped to do. De Haas mentioned Chaim Weizmann, now president of the English Zionist Federation, and the Pope, and the provisional government of Russia; and he hinted at transactions so tenuous and vital that the governments of the great powers did not feel it desirable to make public disclosures of them.

If all these negotiations were to reach fruition, he continued, it must be demonstrated "in each of these countries that the Zionist idea is the wish of the majority of the Jews." In America, therefore, it was incumbent on each and every Zionist to show solidarity, to uphold his government and its policies, to avoid rocking the boat.

On September 23, Miss Szold and Jessie Sampter met with a formidable group of PC leaders: Rabbi Wise, Harry Friedenwald and Judge Mack among them, headed by Louis Brandeis, who was now Justice Brandeis. The year before he had been elevated to the Supreme Court, resigning his position as chairman of the PC, which Julian Mack took up; but he remained the de facto leader of American Zionism, and the tone of the meeting was set by his presence.

Miss Szold began with a statement signed by herself and five Hadassah colleagues: they were pacifists, she said, but they were also patriots. "The methods we have espoused are legal and constitutional, and cannot justly be interpreted as obstructionist. . . ." However it had recently come to their attention that their views diverged sharply from the official Zionist position. Was it indeed their first political duty to urge active military participation of Zionists in the present war? And in working for the Medical Unit, must they agree to see it attached to British military forces?

Discussion followed, somewhat mealy-mouthed in tenor, in that everyone who spoke declared pacifists ought to resign from the movement while insisting they would not be ordered to resign. Brandeis spoke at length: "I think myself that Miss Szold and the ladies with her have taken a position which is very harmful to the Zionist cause. . . . What we have here is the question presented during our Civil War, and the people who claimed to have a conscience and to be acting upon their conscience, are doing exactly what they did during the Civil War, and came very near breaking Mr. Lincoln's, not only his heart, and his health, but would, if they had had their way, have broken up the country into two countries. . . ." He did not care what any individual did or said, provided they were not in the Zionist organization. "What Miss Szold or Miss Sampter or any other person thinks on this subject is a matter of which we have no concern. . . . We may regret it, but that is the end of it; but I do think it becomes our business when they join an organization which is hostile to the Government or Administration." The People's Council was not hostile to the Government. Miss Szold knew it but did not contest the description.

Eventually a resolution was adopted declaring that for Zionists to join the Peace and Democracy movement was detrimental to the Cause, although no one was to be read out of the organization, and Brandeis finished by saying, "When a person who is as conspicuous as Miss Szold . . . takes a position and is known, then the injury that is done is obvious."

The meeting was at an end. Miss Szold asked for a copy of the minutes, Rabbi Wise informed her it was not their practice to issue copies of minutes, although a summary would be available, and then Miss Szold and Miss Sampter went home.

She thought it over for two agonizing weeks, discussing and arguing with Jessie, asking for another meeting of the same PC committee. She was no rebel. She was a great admirer of Louis Brandeis; authority in general impressed her, especially the authority of men, especially men with degrees and achievements, and the achievements of Brandeis were robed in all the potent mystery of the highest court. At the same time much of what Jessie Sampter said to her over the telephone, or what Miss Szold thought she said, was equally true. She sought to maintain her own personal position within the movement, a position that was now her profession, her family and her life. If she severed herself from the movement Hadassah might well survive and the Medical Unit would surely set out for Palestine under someone else's direction, but for Miss Szold the chance to make her life matter would be lost and at fifty-seven she would never have another.

Yet the convictions that prompted her to join the People's Council remained unshaken. She wrote to them on October 13: "To my great regret I must ask you to remove my name from your membership list. My request is prompted by reasons extraneous to the purpose of your organization, which continues to have my endorsement." Six months later Jessie wrote to her, "While I know my position is inevitable, I am not happier for having relinquished my pacifism." Miss Szold replied, "You have described my state of mind. . . . I am so glad the [military] uniforms have high collars. I cannot bear to look at the strong young necks . . . of the marines. I see them mangled and gory."

She had been reading some of the scathing antiwar novels edited by Toby Seltzer, who had joined the publishing firm of Boni & Liveright. Whatever Toby edited, Adele urged her sister to read. Some of the new books left her "writhing with the pain of the wounded soldier."

But it was done, behind her, and in time it came to seem the only possible course of action. It was also to be a recurrent theme in Miss Szold's long life: guided by her conscience to take a stand at odds with that of the Zionist establishment, sometimes she kept her own counsel because the establishment, who were wise and powerful men after all, might really know better than her conscience; at other times she fought staunchly for her position but was beaten down, and in the aftermath wondered if she had been right to go along with the others, or should have resigned, or fought harder, letting the chips fall where they might. The over-all result was a good deal of swallowed-down bitterness, whether directed against herself or others.

14

A new act in the Zionist drama was about to begin. It was called the Balfour Declaration. The curtains parted, and the leading actor appeared on stage, not Arthur James Balfour, who hovered in the wings with Herbert Asquith, David Lloyd George and other members of the British power structure, but a Russian Jew. A most extraordinary Russian Jew. Indeed, the world has rarely seen his like.

The same Chaim Weizmann who used to frequent the cafés of central Europe with his impoverished fellow exiles was now Dr. Weizmann, a chemistry professor at the University of Manchester, bearded, mustached, broad-nosed, already bald in his early forties. A British contemporary saw in him the following qualities:

> An almost feminine charm combined with a feline deadliness of attack; enthusiasm and prophetic vision. . . . Ruthless and tolerating no rival, yet emotional; contemptuous but (I have ultimately found) a fair dealer. He was a brilliant talker with an unrivalled gift for lucid exposition. . . . As a speaker almost frighteningly convincing, even in English . . . in Hebrew, and even more in Russian, overwhelming; with all that dynamic persuasiveness which Slavs usually devote to love and Jews to business, nourished, trained, and concentrated upon the accomplishment of Zion.

When he came to Manchester in 1904 after Herzl's death, Weizmann found a city full of Jews but almost devoid of Zionists. British Jewry as a whole was anti-Zionist, especially those with money. Soon after the outbreak of war he met the editor of the Manchester *Guardian*, C. P. Scott, a Bible-reading man who had once hoped to become a minister and was drawn to the passionate religion of Zionism. Through Scott, Weizmann learned that if the Jews of Britain were anti-Zionist, a number of the more powerful Gentiles were not.

Scott decided to introduce Weizmann to Lloyd George, then Chancellor of the Exchequer, a Welshman of lower middle-class origin, champion of the underdog and firm believer in the biblical prophesies, including the return of the Jews to the promised land. At Lloyd George's suggestion Weizmann went next to Arthur Balfour, then First Lord of the Admiralty. Although Balfour was thought by his friends to be unable to take anything seriously—he had the upper-class British manner to an exaggerated degree, cool, negligent and cynical—he was immensely taken with Weizmann. "It is a great cause you are working for. You must come again and again."

Thus far Weizmann had been spinning a web of connections. His dazzling personal charm, his identification with an emotionally appealing cause, carried him from the office of one important political figure to another but without concrete result. Perhaps it was too soon for results, which must wait on the winning of the war. Still there was one particular stumbling block he seemed unable to get around or climb over: the powerful British Jews who were prepared to go to any lengths to defeat Zionism.

In early 1916, Weizmann gave up political activity for the time being and under pressure of war devoted himself full time to science. Some years earlier he had experimented with techniques for synthesizing rubber and by a fermentation process like that used to make whiskey had created an artificial acetone, a by-product for which there was then no earthly use. Now, however, he was summoned to the offices of the British Admiralty, where the head of the powder department explained that there was a serious shortage of acetone, vital in the manufacture of the explosive cordite. Thirty thousand tons were needed immediately. Weizmann, who had never made more than a few hundred cubic centimeters, "was given carte blanche . . . and I took upon myself a task which was to tax all my energies for the next two years, and which was to have consequences which I did not then foresee." A pilot plant was started in London, so Weizmann left Manchester and moved there. First in a gin factory, then in distilleries all over England, acetone was eventually synthesized by the tens of thousands of tons.

At this point the British government was divided in its attitude on Zionism and the leaders of British Jewry united in ferocious opposition. The most telling arguments in its favor were not, of course, found in the Old Testament; Lloyd George would never have exerted himself for the Zionist cause without first making sure the policy did not conflict with British interests. In the postwar world a Jewish Palestine under imperial protection would constitute a barrier separating the Suez Canal from the Black Sea and any hostility that might come from that direction: "England would have an effective barrier and we would have a country," as Weizmann put it.

The next scene opened abruptly. Asquith's cabinet fell in 1916, Lloyd George became Prime Minister and Balfour Foreign Secretary. Weizmann's friends were in power now, still pro-Zionist and more than ever pro-Weizmann, for he had made an impressive contribution to the war effort. Early the following year he was invited to the first of a series of conferences on Zionism, while in the Sinai Desert a British expeditionary force assembled the greatest collection of camels ever seen in one place and prepared to invade Palestine.

Month by month the conferences proceeded. Although the important statesmen were whole-heartedly pro-Zionist, the Jewish leaders continued to natter and nudge, and the French hovered hungrily in the background, for they had their own designs on the postwar Middle East. An ugly, public power struggle developed within Anglo-Jewry.

By summer the first drafts of a declaration of British support for a Jewish homeland in Palestine were submitted to the war cabinet. The leaders of Anglo-Jewry accelerated their bitter rear-guard action, and the great danger now was not the loss of the declaration so much as its being watered down to placate those leaders. In fact Weizmann thought the first drafts were appallingly cautious, mollifying and weak. All fronts now mounted a do-or-die effort. The Zionist leader Nahum Sokolow was sent to Paris and Rome to elicit sympathy from the French, Italians and the Vatican (the delicate negotiations hinted at by de Haas to Miss Szold), and Weizmann turned to America for support. For months he had been urging Brandeis to get from President Wilson a statement of sympathy with the concept of a Jewish homeland under British protection. Balfour himself had gone to the United States, met Brandeis and discussed with him British-French rivalries and the possibility of an *American* protectorate, which Balfour favored. Brandeis retorted that the Wilson administration had no interest in the Mideast, would never agree to such a role, and that American Zionists were all in favor of British protection.

Pressure for the American statement increased. If the United States approved of British dominion in Palestine, it could be used as a lever against the French. In May, Brandeis finally secured from President Wilson, in confidence, his personal approval of the British position, although couched in guarded language. When the French agreed, Brandeis said, American sympathy could be made public. Weizmann was sorely disappointed. The Americans, and Brandeis in particular, seemed to be delivering too little too late.

In mid-October a cable announced President Wilson's public support of the British declaration. "This was one of the most important individual factors in breaking the deadlock created by the British Jewish anti-Zionists," Weizmann wrote, "and in deciding the British Government to issue its declaration."

The result was a brief letter addressed to Lord Walter Rothschild, as symbolic head of England's Jewish community, made public on November 8, 1917. It read:

> Dear Lord Rothschild:
>
> I have much pleasure in conveying to you, on behalf of His Majesty's Government, the following declaration of sympathy with Jewish Zionist aspirations, which has been submitted to, and approved by, the cabinet.
>
> His Majesty's government views with favour the establishment in Palestine of a national home for the Jewish people, and will use their best endeavours to facilitate the achievement of this object, it being clearly understood that nothing shall be done which may prejudice the civil and religious rights of existing non-Jewish communities in Palestine, or the rights and political status enjoyed by Jews in any other country.

The Balfour Declaration was at once magnificent and nebulous. It avoided any mention of the borders of this national home, its full extent being nowhere described, the very words "national home" rather than nation or state giving rise to endless debate. Nor was there any hint of how the "sympathy" of the British government was to be embodied in international law or of which country was to serve as Palestine's protector. But for the first time in modern history a major power officially recognized that the Jews were a people with aspirations fixed on one earthly place, the Holy Land.

Quantities of ink have been spilled in succeeding years in an attempt to decide what political motivations, imperial or strategic, lay behind the Balfour Declaration. Balfour himself was not eager to see Britain in Palestine; he held out until the last for an American protectorate. Other motivations certainly played their part, but it seems inescapable that one strong theme uniting the Zionism of Balfour, Lloyd George, Sir Mark Sykes and the others responsible was a deep-seated humanism of religious origin. They had done what was noble and generous. In time the stresses of a more pragmatic age corroded the impulse behind the Balfour Declaration, but it was no less noble because of its consequences, no less generous because it also served British aims in the Near East as they were seen at the time.

The Jewish masses throughout the world felt an upsurge of hope as great as Herzl and his first Zionist congress inspired. In America, Zionism became not only respectable but popular. In 1918, 210,000 members paid dues to the FAZ.

One month after the release of the Balfour Declaration, British forces under General Edmund Allenby captured Jerusalem.

15

Allenby's entrance into Jerusalem revealed a people on intimate terms with death. Twenty thousand of the city's inhabitants had already perished. The streets swarmed with beggars, the prisons stank, the sight of the prisoners froze the soul. Dazed and homeless children roamed the streets and slept where they fell.

British Tommies were stationed before all Jewish and Christian holy places, and British Indians at the Moslem sites. Thus began the rule of the Occupied Enemy Territory Administration (OETA), a branch of the British military, for much of Palestine was still held by the Turks, and in Jerusalem the British were merely the temporary governors of a conquered city whose sufferings they would try to alleviate while carrying on a war. The healing of a population of more than 50,000 without medicine, civilian doctors or even thermometers still depended on the relief ship.

Three weeks after the capture of the city Miss Szold read a telegram from the U.S. chargé d'affaires in Cairo, received at the New York offices of the Joint: "Military authorities will allow entry into Jerusalem American Medical Unit when transport facilities permit. They believe this will be possible within two or three months." It had been a year and a half since the women of Hadassah first agreed to outfit and send a medical rescue ship to the Holy Land.

But so far there was no ship. Week after week was consumed by a series of paper battles for diplomatic or military clearances.

Hadassah had charge of the Unit, Miss Szold had charge of Hadassah and in the first months of 1918 her office became purchasing headquarters for supplies for the Unit. Even as Miss Szold in her methodical fashion set about buying up medicines and medical equipment, cables from Weizmann, acting on the advice of British authorities in Palestine, informed her that what was really needed was equipment for a 100-bed hospital. Other cables followed

requesting machinery Miss Szold had never dreamed of procuring: oxygen-mak-
ing devices, disinfectors, pumps, even ambulances and trucks.

What had begun as an emergency mission, quick and versatile and light
on its feet, was becoming something far more intricate and many-faceted. The
AZMU now required a budget for its first year of $450,000. Although Brandeis
favored the Unit to such an extent that he gave Hadassah most of the American
Zionist funds from that and the years immediately following, it was not enough.
More came in the form of a gift of $100,000 from the non-Zionist Joint followed
by another $100,000. Great quantities of clothing and shoes and a special sum
of money were given by Nathan Straus for the particular use of Moslems in
the Holy Land. Hadassah women donated clothing, linens and baby layettes
they had made themselves. Eventually the massive store of supplies, weighing
400 tons, included equipment for a small hospital, hundreds of cases of drugs,
medicines and bandages, six automobiles, several dental outfits, an immense
supply of food and over 100 large cases of clothing.

By mid-April, Miss Szold's somewhat leisurely proceedings came to a sudden
halt. The time had come to hire doctors and nurses, and in this aspect of the
Unit's preparation she was to have the help, like it or not, of Jacob de Haas.

Legal contracts were drawn up and typed, specifying that the employee
agreed "to minister to the needs of the people of Palestine (Jews, Arabs and
Christians equally) for the term of one year's actual service." A typical physician's
salary was $3,500 a year. Then hectic interviewing began. Those nurses who
were hired were given a list of required and suggested items to take with them
and $125 to cover their cost. Among the suggested items were a rubber bath
tub, air cushion, knife, fork, spoon, paper cups and napkins, a drinking cup, a
bed frame, a smaller frame to be worn over the head and mosquito netting
to cover the frames.

By the end of May, twenty doctors and twenty nurses organized into
eight departments—obstetrics-gynecology, eye-ear-nose-throat, pathology and
pediatrics among them, as well as several sanitarians—were ready to sail. But
there were further diplomatic delays, and some of the nurses spent their waiting
time taking refresher courses or meeting with Miss Szold for talks about Palestine.

Many of them were women of a new breed: "advanced" young women.
Some had cut off their long hair; most wore makeup. The war was pulling
women out of their homes into factories, shops or other work places vacated
by men and in the process changing the way they thought and felt about
themselves. Miss Szold, an overworked, graying woman sitting at a modest
desk in a modest office of the FAZ, spoke to these women across a gulf much
greater than the thirty years' difference in their ages. The advice she gave
them was not only sound but wise; she told them, for example, to live with

the people and learn from them. But there was much she did not tell them because it never entered her head.

An air of romance hovered about the nurses. They were leaving their homes in wartime for a country they had never seen, a fabulous country where anything might happen, in the company of equally adventurous young men. Their uniforms were gray crepe, with white collars and cuffs, a red star of David on the sleeve and large panama hats with gray veils. They expected to look lovely in those gray-veiled hats. Since it had never occurred to Miss Szold that many of them were going off in search of romance, she never warned them against being exploited by their doctor superiors. Neither did it occur to her that the doctors would be leaving not only wives and children but the restraints of a familiar society where everyone knew them for the freedom of an exotic setting, perfumed with intrigue and keyed up in the wake of a terrible war.

Some doctors were going because they were failures in America, a country where it was in any case hard for Jews to get good posts. Others were trying to escape from something, perhaps an unpleasant domestic life. Still others went out of a sense of Zionist duty and at considerable sacrifice. The physicians of the Unit were a mixed bag.

Among the nurses even those blithe spirits who went in search of personal freedom were at the same time dedicated and professionally serious. This was all Miss Szold saw, for she had not yet become aware of the new woman. Most of her friends were unmarried and high-minded and middle-aged like herself. Alice Seligsberg had just endured the same sort of disembodied love affair Miss Szold had with Ginzberg, one that came to the same sad end. They commiserated with each other. Sometimes they laughed together. Alice's friendship was a steady rock, and Miss Szold wrote to her once: "No, life has not been mean to me, since you are my friend." But Alice knew nothing about the new woman either.

One day in June the personnel of the AZMU, with Alice Seligsberg representing Hadassah, met together in utter secrecy and rode in covered trucks to New York Harbor, where they boarded a troopship. There were no flowers, no music or bon voyage parties, no farewells. They were without a medical director, for Dr. I. Seth Hirsch had withdrawn at the last minute under pressure from his family. Only two well-wishers came to the dock: Jacob de Haas and Hirsch, who thrust his face against the palings of the fence and wistfully watched them off. With eleven other troopships they slipped quietly out of New York in a military convoy; their own vessel held a cargo of 3,000 American men and women, mostly troops, with a sprinkling of Red Cross people and some volunteers for the Jewish Legion, which was fighting with the British in Palestine.

The medical supplies of the Unit went separately on another ship.

In the calm that followed Miss Szold sat in her neglected apartment, where all her possessions were filmed by a thick layer of dust, and wrote to Alice. The Unit troubles had left an indelible mark on her soul, she said. The spring had gone out of her step; even her mind felt dimmed by the last four months of crisis and disappointment and fresh crisis. Much of her suffering stemmed from Jacob de Haas, whose assistance must have been maddening and whose selection of personnel one of the Unit leaders later called "irresponsible." The rest was due to the sudden defection of the medical director.

Miss Szold turned to Dr. I. M. Rubinow, knowing only that he was a physician and statistician, suggesting he head the Unit. When Rubinow told her he was no Zionist, she assured him it did not matter. He accepted, tentatively, despite his family's reluctance.

Between the time the Unit left and the time Miss Szold herself arrived in the Holy Land in the spring of 1920 on a rescue mission of her own, a number of changes took place in American Zionism. Some were of interest chiefly to Americans, to Miss Szold and Hadassah and the FAZ. Others, especially the persistent struggle between Louis Brandeis and Chaim Weizmann, affected the role the Americans were to play in world Zionism.

In the summer of 1918 the Federation of American Zionists, a collection of clubs throughout the country, became a single organization, the Zionist Organization of America (ZOA), divided according to regions. The need for this united front was seen by Brandeis as early as 1915, when he realized the hodgepodge of clubs and circles was inefficient administratively as well as politically. In their relations with the international organization, a single spokesman for a single group promised the authority the FAZ had always lacked.

Miss Szold claimed to be entirely in favor of the plan; indeed it was she who designed the regional divisions. Certainly it was more efficient and progressive, and although many of the original clubs within the FAZ balked at losing their authority, Hadassah was assured that they might continue as before. Their board was to remain intact, acting as an advisory body to the administration of the ZOA, but the actual work of Hadassah's Palestine Bureau was transferred to the ZOA's executive department.

As for Miss Szold, she became head of the Department of Education of the ZOA. She found herself in charge of an amorphous undertaking including youth clubs, publications, leaders' training and adult education. Much of it she enjoyed, especially the contact with young people. On the other hand, Brandeis was away in Washington and the day-to-day affairs of the ZOA were in the hands of men who did not believe in Zionist education. Neither did they believe in Henrietta Szold.

Jacob de Haas was one of these men, Louis Lipsky another. Lipsky was a Zionist writer and teacher in his early forties, tall, thin, unsmiling, with ears set almost at right angles to his face. He was a fervent lover of Yiddish who spoke it atrociously. Zionism was his life—not the American Zionism of Brandeis, but the Zionism of Weizmann and the eastern Europeans.

Lipsky was never comfortable with Gentiles or with women, and Miss Szold bored him. As for Zionist education, in light of the Balfour Declaration he could see no point to it—all the Jews of the world would pour into the Holy Land during the next few years while Miss Szold continued to turn out pamphlets for schoolchildren. When a young man named Alexander Dushkin came to work for her, Lipsky and de Haas took him aside and told him to forget about Miss Szold and her nonsense. If he wanted to do important Zionist work he ought to make out "a complete and very detailed inventory of all the educational needs for units of one hundred thousand" immigrants to Palestine.

Dushkin did not agree that all of world Jewry would or should pour into Palestine, nor did he agree with their estimation of Miss Szold. "They respected her, but they knew she was a woman. They used to argue her down. She used to be very bitter about them . . . very openly. She had a bitter streak in her. But at the same time there was something so beautiful about her. . . ." What was beautiful was the way she felt about Jewish education. Dushkin was field secretary for the ZOA's education department; he toured New England, the South and parts of the Middle West organizing youth groups and Zionist study circles. In the eyes of Miss Szold, "I was a missionary setting out to preach Zionism as basic Judaism, and everything I was to do had in it the quality of holiness." Her exaltation embraced and inspired him, confirming his sense of vocation. If such a woman saw it as a sacred task, clearly he had chosen well.

Another young man who came to the education department and Miss Szold was Emanuel Neumann; he too would make his career in Jewish teaching. Dushkin and Neumann occasionally visited Miss Szold in her apartment. She seemed to expand in their presence; sometimes her mood was so easy and relaxed that she would do her imitations of people being called up to the Torah or the style in which various dignitaries took snuff. The young men laughed till their sides hurt. They adored her.

Many of the idealistic college students attracted to Zionism by Brandeis and Frankfurter adored her, although few were on such an intimate footing as Dushkin and Neumann. A young man named Max Cohen came to her directly out of college and was put in charge of Young Judea, the organization for high school students. "I arranged a citywide basketball tournament," he recalled.

> The games were played in high school gymnasiums. Each school had its own basketball which we were able to use, but a second ball was needed before the game so each team had a chance to warm up. I decided to purchase the ball first and answer questions later. Miss Szold now had the bill for an $8.00 ball. . . . A directive had been issued to keep to the budget, and there was no margin for sports. I was in trouble. I went to my desk and pulled out a photograph. Then I went into her office.
>
> The secretary for Zionist Education let me have it—"If Zionists would discover that the money donated for a Jewish state is being used for balls . . ." Instead of answering I put the photograph on her desk, a picture of a winning team in their basketball suits, a white shirt with a Mogen David on it, and blue trunks with white stripes. She warmed up to that picture, her anger disappeared. "How many teams like that do you have?" she asked. I said, "Forty. And they all paid for their uniforms out of their own pockets." She just looked at the picture; she never gave it back. She put her okay on the bill. "One more question, Mr. Cohen—can you get a good enough ball for eight dollars?" I said, "Remember, this is Zionist money." She was flexible.

Max Cohen was young and full of Zionist enthusiasm. To him Miss Szold was a heroic yet fragile figure in need of protection, a warm-hearted, motherly, even a loving woman. If de Haas and Lipsky saw her as futile and boring, if she was embittered by their opinion and let the bitterness show, he knew nothing about it.

Yet she was disappointed with the reorganization, the change from FAZ to ZOA, almost from the start. Nothing seemed to be working out as she expected. The individuality of Hadassah was supposed to be preserved, their board to act in an advisory capacity. Nobody asked the board for advice, however, and no one paid attention to the advice they offered. Apparently Louis Lipsky hoped the Hadassah chapters would melt into oblivion or limp along as sewing circles.

But to Miss Szold it was clear that the women were not satisfied with sewing alone. They wanted to do "distinguished work," Zionist work. She spoke of their hearts' hunger for well-organized projects serving the Medical Unit or its nursing school under the leadership of their own elected board.

There was one consolation. The Hadassah circles seemed to be ignoring the ZOA, ignoring the snubs to their board, existing in fact although they had disappeared on paper. They met, they held discussions, followed the work of their pride and joy, the Medical Unit, and carried out projects the board was literally forced to invent. And they did this without their newsletter, which had been sacrificed to centralization.

Throughout the war an air of general distrust had permeated relations between the Brandeis men and the Europeans. With the Balfour Declaration, the Americans recognized Weizmann as de facto leader of the European movement, and by war's end both sides realized the need for some sort of coordination.

Yet the more they knew of each other the less likely it became. Before Louis Brandeis was able to travel to England he sent Rabbi Stephen Wise. Wise wrote back: "The Zionist movement in Europe admits that there is a Zionist movement in America, because occasionally, much too occasionally, remittances come to hand, but if those remittances for any reason should cease . . . we should speedily be cut off from London or France. Our friends there do not know us, do not believe in us, and do not believe in the reality of our Zionism."

In 1919, Brandeis made his first and last trip to Palestine and on the way back met Weizmann and his associates in London. Now the full extent of the differences between Zionism in Europe and in America was laid bare. Brandeis wanted to see Palestine built up with care and thought, not in one great rush, but slowly. First of all the country must be cleansed of malaria. Sanitation first, colonization later. Instead of pioneer farmers, the early settlers should be small-scale capitalists. He disliked the idea of a powerful international organization headquartered in London, with its Palestinian arm, the Zionist Commission, seated in Jerusalem. Everything he had seen of Zionist finances in Palestine and London confirmed his suspicion that they were wasteful, disorganized and irresponsible.

The Weizmann party found the Zionism of Brandeis as foreign and indigestible as they found the Boston Brahmin himself. They wanted Palestine settled immediately and by millions of Jews, preferably pioneers, chalutzim. The more Jews there were, the sooner the rest of the world would grant them a state. It would take more than one generation, of course. Weizmann himself was in no hurry for statehood. Others were. They would get rid of malaria, but immigration came first. As for small-scale capitalism, the Almighty had not promised the Holy Land to capitalists but to all Jews. Besides, they were socialists.

The American Zionist Medical Unit, according to the Russians, concerned itself chiefly with women and infants and people who lived in the towns. But the homeland was to be built by young and vigorous pioneers. The Unit must be controlled by the Zionist Commission, and its primary task must be the health of the chalutzim. Moreover the 400 American medical people who came with the Unit persisted in speaking and writing English. Hebrew was to be the language of the homeland. Let the Americans send money and keep their English-speaking medical people at home.

As for the accusation that Zionist finances were chaotic, the Russians scarcely blinked. They had not built a movement on bookkeeping. They were not businessmen but prophetic leaders.

The differences between Weizmann and Brandeis were, of course, far more intricate than those summarized here, but in the end they seem to have been fundamental differences of temperament. Even at those times when their philosophies were parallel the estrangement never healed. Neither was capable of compromise. They were strong-willed men, each certain of his own rightness, his own capacity for one-man rule. The progress of the Jewish homeland would have been smoother if Russians and Americans had worked hand in hand from the start, but revolutions are not mounted by compromise. The birth of the Jewish homeland was a revolution.

Little of this dissension reached the Zionist masses in America. The women of Hadassah knew only that their rescue ship had arrived and was at work in the cities and towns of Palestine, in Tel Aviv, Safed, Haifa and Jaffa, where refugees poured in from the internment camps of Egypt. Camels, donkeys, goats and people, "filthy dirty, covered with flies, flies in their eyes, nostrils, ears and mouths," choked the little outpatient department in Jaffa. A young boy with one eye gone still wore an amulet against the evil eye wrapped in his hair; a young woman with a skin infection applied manure to it for protection against evil spirits. Somehow everything worked; supplies that did not exist were improvised, and the nurses who had never been out of New York found themselves at home among a people with whom they had no language in common.

In Jerusalem the Unit took over the fifty-year-old Rothschild Hospital and established its headquarters at the Hôtel de France nearby. A school for nurses was officially opened; actually Dr. Kagan had started it some months before the Unit came. In mid-September 1918, British forces finally freed the country of Turkish occupation, and Palestinian physicans began to trickle back from their military service abroad.

Many joined the Unit. Yet they were resentful of foreigners in their midst, with the rules of medical practice being made by those foreigners. The Jews of the Yishuv seemed antagonistic to the Unit; having suffered bitterly during the war, they resented those who had not suffered. The Americans brought luxuries that had never been seen in Palestine—ice-making machines, an x-ray laboratory, ambulances—as well as the subtle condescension of the well-fed for the hungry they had come to feed. The nurses had record players and records, and in their free time they danced American dances with the young doctors; no one had told them how their high spirits would be perceived by a population that lacked beds and clothing. And the language problem became a concrete symbol for those elusive feelings. English, the language of the so-helpful visitors, was also the language of the new imperial rulers.

But by early 1919 the Unit was firmly established under its new director, Dr. Rubinow. Dr. Harry Friedenwald arrived when Rubinow did and wrote to Miss Szold that all the rumors they had been hearing at home were true. There was no esprit de corps among the Unit physicians; a great deal of money had been unwisely spent; the nurses were not models of morality. "On the other hand a *great* deal of good is being done."

From Rubinow himself she had less encouraging news: dissension among the physicians, attacks on the Unit by the Zionist Commission, scurrilous articles in the newspapers, anti-Americanism on all fronts. Yet he too was awed by what the Unit was accomplishing. He only prayed he could stay to see it through; several of his letters had the tone of a man driven to the breaking point and crying for release.

By the winter of 1919 relations between the AZMU and the Zionist Commission were dangerously eroded. The Unit had become a symbol of the antagonism between the Russian Zionism of the Weizmann party and the American Zionism of the Brandeis men. An open rupture threatened the integrity of the movement itself. Once again Louis Brandeis turned to Miss Szold. He asked her to go to Jerusalem for a two years' stay. She was to restore inner and outer harmony with the Zionist Commission and establish some sort of esprit de corps among the doctors. Above all she was to make clear to the Commission that the Unit must retain its integrity as an American organization; it could not be centralized. Its money came from America, and the Americans had no intention of giving it over into Russian hands.

Miss Szold's reaction was equal parts of elation and fear. The Jewish homeland as a political entity, recognized by the League of Nations, was only now coming into being. She would be present at its creation, then. She would be in Palestine within months of the first British civilian government.

And more. This was the first substantial sign that Zionist leaders took her seriously. Over the years she had been conscious of slights that seemed to have no basis. She had never once been sent as a delegate to a Zionist congress, although she had served the cause from its earliest days. She had not even been sent in the autumn of 1909, when she was already in Europe. Nor had she been nominated to the Zionist Commission when Weizmann requested the names of leading American Zionists to go to Palestine. Brandeis had approached Rabbi Wise, who could not go; he had turned to Judge Mack and been refused again. Finally Brandeis cabled Weizmann: "International situation definitely renders American membership in Commission impossible."

He had never asked Miss Szold. "We need not fool ourselves," she wrote to Alice at the time, "the Commission will not consider seating a woman." And it rankled. Brandeis and Mack were men she deeply admired; they admired her, certainly they thought well of her Hadassah. But they could not take her seriously enough to challenge the Commission on her behalf.

They took her seriously now. Yet the seriousness of the whole adventure, her doubts that she could live up to it, almost spoiled the pleasure. She was too old for such a trip and the responsibilities that went with it; her Hebrew was inadequate, her gifts as a diplomat inadequate. What was more important, she had fundamental doubts about the validity of the mission on which Brandeis was sending her. She was not sure she agreed with him, not certain the Unit ought to remain an American project.

But at the farewell party given her by the ZOA on the night before her departure, one of her young employees remembered Miss Szold as radiant. "She kissed me," he said. "She was so excited she threw her arms around me and kissed me." For several hours he was aware of that side of his face as being different from the other because of Miss Szold's kiss.

Then she set out at the age of fifty-nine for the great adventure of her life, having first packed all her personal belongings, including her father's papers and the letters of Louis Ginzberg, which she sent to Bertha in Baltimore. Leaving the Zionists of America, she headed for the Yishuv and Palestine.

IV

JERUSALEM:
AT THE HÔTEL DE FRANCE

16

The Italian steamer S.S. *Giuseppe Verdi* left New Jersey in late February 1920, bound for Naples. The sailing had been postponed several days because of storms, and when at last it took off a great wave of cheering broke out among the passengers. Most were Italians, middle-class families who had prospered in America, as well as working people who had not. There were many whose return had been delayed by the war, others who, it was said, were escaping Prohibition, but from steerage to first class the excitement of an Atlantic crossing was intensified by the knowledge that they were going home. So was Miss Szold.

She shared her first-class cabin with a young woman named Julia Aronson, a dietitian who would join the Medical Unit. On the first days out the weather was so fierce that Miss Aronson lay supine and moaning in the cabin. "A wild night followed by a wild day, though sunny and magnificent," according to Miss Szold's diary. "The foam and spray dashed mountain high, were superb, and the air soft, enveloping. . . . At lunch the dishes danced around in their pens, and in the kitchen there was crash after crash of breaking crockery. Marconi wireless reports pogroms in Russia." The dining room was almost empty, but Miss Szold survived the wildest weather. One of the few who managed to struggle to her table was a dapper young Italian whom she tempted into a "Jewish conversation." In his opinion Jews were the worst anti-Semites.

As the weather improved some of the other passengers struggled out of their cabins, "happy families, somewhat vulgar and superficial," a count and countess beginning to thaw a little, a buxom, good-humored, petted wife wearing diamonds bigger than peas on bust, fingers and ears. Miss Szold observed them from behind the pince-nez, her first glance always intended to discover if they were Jewish. The diamonds irritated her—"It is curious how those who indulge in them seem to lose all sense of humor on the subject"—and she saw in the smug, prosperous company unhappy reminders of the comfortable, comfort-ridden Baltimore Jews she had grown up with.

The rest of the time she sat on deck, reading, studying, writing, arranging notes. Sometimes she took walks. Whatever she did was done energetically, as if she had keyed herself up for the Holy Land. She did not move like a woman of nearly sixty, and her face seemed less lined now. She looked almost young.

On March 8, the *Verdi* reached Naples. Miss Szold had left New York without her permit to enter Palestine, hoping to find it waiting at the British consulate in Naples; it was not there and they had no news of it. She settled into the Hotel Royal. Julia Aronson and another American woman who had crossed with them and was headed for Palestine already had their permits. They went on a few days later to Brindisi, leaving Miss Szold to follow when she could. So soon after the war Mediterranean sailings were too infrequent for them to miss one.

Weeks went by with no word about the visa. Miss Szold felt cut off from Palestine and America alike, at times almost paralyzed by the fear that something had happened to her family and they had no way of letting her know. The other tourists in her hotel and those she met on expeditions seemed to be ignoring her, even snubbing her. None of them was Jewish. She felt alien, solitary, painfully homesick. She wept easily.

At the end of March she left Naples for Florence to spend Passover near Rabbi Samuel Hirsch Margulies, a veteran Zionist whom she had visited with Sophie in 1909. And it was in Florence that the outside world caught up with her in the form of ugly news from Palestine. It was in all the newspapers; it was all anyone could talk about at the Margulies home.

In 1920, Passover and Easter coincided with the Moslem festival of Nebi Musa. Jerusalem was swollen with Jewish soldiers on Passover leave. There was a tautness in the atmosphere. Overnight, placards appeared as if from nowhere: "The Government is with us, Allenby is with us, kill the Jews: there is no punishment for killing Jews."

In the narrow passageways of the Old City the Arab mayor harangued Moslem agitators with a patriotic speech. The crowds took fire; a riot exploded. Jewish policemen were absent, assigned to other towns out of respect for the Moslem festival, and Arab policemen were slow to turn their arms against fellow Arabs. Before the riots could be stemmed by British troops, six Jews were dead, almost 200 wounded.

Miss Szold talked this news over at the Margulies' one night with a visiting Englishman, a former cabinet minister, a Zionist and a Jew named Herbert Samuel. He had been sent by Lloyd George to Jerusalem and was now on his way to San Remo, Italy. It was said that Samuel would be the first civil administrator of the Holy Land. He was dark, handsome, heavily mustached and in bearing the ultimate British gentleman, well-tailored, emotionless and exquisitely patient. He told Miss Szold his experiences in Palestine gave him an optimistic view of the future, "but he admitted that the Arab situation was serious and was held by the British to be serious."

A few days later Samuel left Florence for the San Remo conference that would decide the fate of the Middle East. The Balfour Declaration had not yet been formally adopted by the League of Nations, nor had the Mandate for Palestine been awarded to the British. Until these hurdles were past, the future of the homeland remained uncertain. It had been uncertain since the end of the war, partly because England and France haggled over it, mostly because the Middle East was not the most pressing of their concerns.

Miss Szold remained in Florence and waited for her visa. She studied Hebrew six hours a day. She revisited churches and museums she had seen with Sophie. Faint echoes of world happenings reached her from time to time: at San Remo the Balfour Declaration had been incorporated into the peace treaty with Turkey, and the Mandate over Palestine was awarded to England. Then one day she was summoned to the American consulate to receive a cable; Judge Mack and Rabbi Wise had been pulling strings in a frantic attempt to release her from captivity, and the cable told her to proceed to Cairo, where the visa would be waiting. She packed and returned to Naples, boarded the S.S. *Umbria* and sailed for Alexandria.

Among her fellow passengers was Dr. Montague David Eder, an Anglo-Jewish psychoanalyst and member of the Zionist Commission, a kind and tactful man. The chief of the Commission, Menachem Ussishkin, was neither; he was a Russian, the terror of Rubinow and the Medical Unit. Dr. Eder told Miss Szold he held the British military chiefly responsible for the Easter riots. He also told her the results of the military courts-martial that followed the riots: long prison terms for twenty-one members of a Jewish self-defense force hastily thrown together by a man named Vladimir Jabotinsky, who had fought with the British during the war; the Arab mayor of Jerusalem sacked; stiff sentences imposed on two Arab leaders, Haj Amin el Husseini and Aref el Aref, who had managed to escape the country. Most Moslem rioters got light sentences or were let off.

They reached Alexandria on April 30. In Cairo, Miss Szold found her permit at last. Three days later, on a train packed with British soldiers, she and Dr. Eder traveled to Kantara. From Kantara another train brought them through the desert toward the Holy Land. She slept a little that night in her upper berth, and in the morning the desert they passed through was Palestine.

Blue thistles, red poppies, golden sand dunes and the gleam of blue sea beyond. Once, when the train stopped, Dr. Eder jumped off and gathered her a bouquet.

In the broiling hot sun they came to a stop at Ludd. Miss Szold climbed off, stepped over a mountain of boxes and trunks, moved past a mob of howling Arabs and saw that except for the presence of a pack of insolent-looking British soldiers, nothing was changed. There was the same white sun, the dust, the camels, with their gentle eyes and brilliant trappings, leaving a trail of dung, the same crowds in their layers of rags with flies at their mouths and eyes and nostrils. Everywhere dust, chaos, stench and that lurid excitement. You could not be indifferent to it. In no respect was it ordinary or forgettable.

She felt a sudden, overpowering wave of homesickness, of wondering what she was doing there, what in the world she hoped to accomplish among the welter of foreigners. Tired, dirty, thirsty, she realized the adventure had been doomed from the start, plagued by mishaps and misunderstandings. Then she saw three familiar faces: Alice Seligsberg, Nellie Straus, another friend from Hadassah, and Dr. Rubinow. Instantly she felt soothed. Face to face with people who represented home, pushing her way through the crowd toward the beacon of Alice's gentle smile, everything became right and normal.

They surrounded her with a storm of questions while they moved past bodies toward a battered and tremulous automobile. All the questions were about the delay in Italy, but Miss Szold was not interested in Italy; she wanted only to put Italy behind her forever. As they climbed into the automobile she stared into their faces. Alice looked worn, as well she might, for her letters had not been happy; she found the doctors so discouraging she spent most of her time working with war orphans. And Rubinow? Dark, choleric, temperamental, a man of deep feeling, his letters from Jerusalem had revealed to her that the strains of running the Medical Unit were taking a heavy toll. Rubinow had come to Palestine without the slightest suspicion that he would be fighting anything except disease. Certainly he had not foreseen the bull-necked Ussishkin.

As the four climbed into the automobile—there were perhaps two or three ancient civilian automobiles in the land, only one road suitable for motor traffic and that road always in disrepair—the three women talked and smiled into one another's eyes with lively affection and gazed through the windows at the hills, with their stony gray outcroppings that looked like grazing sheep, dotted by clumps of brilliant wildflowers, a landscape hauntingly beautiful even to those who saw it every day. Alice and Rubinow refused to say anything about the Unit's affairs, and that seemed ominous. Still more ominous were the looks they exchanged when she asked specific questions about one or another member of the Unit. Rubinow was strangely morose; they talked mainly about the riots, the British court of inquiry that was examining its causes, the stirring of world opinion over the merciless sentence of Jabotinsky: fifteen years at hard labor. But now they were in sight of the Judean hills. They were climbing up a winding road under the piercingly beautiful domed skies of Jerusalem, walled, gated and pinnacled with legend. Although she would make many visits to America, this was to be Miss Szold's home for the rest of her life.

In 1920 the Yishuv, the Jewish community of Palestine, numbered about 64,000, some 10 percent of the population. They included Sephardim, of Mediterranean or Middle Eastern ancestry, who had lived in Palestine for generations, and Ashkenazim, Jews of central or eastern European background, the great majority sent by eastern European communities to study, to contemplate or simply to exist in the Holy Land on Halukah. These Halukah Jews were fiercely Orthodox and resentful of the young Zionists who first appeared in the 1880s. When new waves of immigration started just after the turn of the century they aroused far stronger resentment.

The Balfour Declaration, the Russian Revolution, which released an outburst of peasant anarchism and pogroms, and the general unrest and displacement of populations following the war had all combined to loose a stream of eastern European migration into Palestine. It was this stream the Zionists had been dreaming of ever since Herzl's first congress in 1897, but they had dreamed more effectively than they had planned.

The Jews were coming to Palestine from only one part of the world, eastern Europe, and they were coming at the rate of about 1,000 a month, a third of whom soon left. The Zionist organization was on the one hand ferociously eager to increase the numbers of immigrants and on the other almost totally unprepared for their arrival. A young lawyer who was sent to Palestine in 1919 reported to Justice Brandeis: "They come in boat loads—and there is a panic every time a boat comes in. Nobody knows about it until it arrives."

In 1920 the situation was the same. The underlying cause was a philosophical and temperamental conviction on the part of east European Jewry that passion conquered all. Zionist passion would pack the Holy Land with Jews so that ultimately the world powers would recognize that a Jewish homeland must give way to a Jewish state. Planning, bookkeeping, details and preparation were the antithesis of Zionist passion. They were suspect; perhaps they were American. Certainly they did not express the true Zionist spirit, described by Felix Warburg in 1932 when he said: "I am certain that if the [Jewish] Agency had money for one new colony the movement would decide to create two and trust to the future to complete them." This was the policy of the World

Zionist Organization: through bold leaps of the imagination to create a need and trust to the future and the heart of the Jewish masses to fill that need.

So the Jews of eastern Europe arrived in the Holy Land in numbers at once too large and too small, and the young chalutz, a type of being not totally unknown in Palestine before but certainly unknown in such numbers, was the single most striking element in postwar Palestine. Why did they come to the Holy Land at all, these chalutzim? Why were they leaving Russia, now that the revolution and the pogroms had passed, for a country so primitive that there was no water supply except from wells and cisterns, no drainage system other than cesspits forever overflowing; no roads, no factories, no universities; where more than half the population suffered from trachoma and loathsome skin diseases and malaria was endemic? Why did they not follow their relatives and neighbors to America? Between 1881 and 1925, when the United States put an end to open immigration, more than 2.5 million Jews left eastern Europe for the United States. It was the land not only of religious liberty and economic opportunity but of free education for all, the place where one's children could grow and expand, become teachers, lawyers, doctors; it was the land of possibility.

Those who went to America generally went as families, and their aspirations centered on the future of the family. But those who went to Palestine in the years just before and after the war had other goals; they were for the most part unmarried young men and women, the prewar arrivals often in their teens. Their intentions had nothing to do with family, schooling, opportunity. What they wanted was to found the absolutely perfect society.

They were the products of several different but closely intertwined cultural influences, all of them ultimately romantic: nineteenth-century nationalism, according to which every people had its national soul, its language, its "myth"; the German youth movement that spread like a mystical fire across the continent, antirational, Dionysian; the literary influences of Tolstoi and Dostoievsky, glorifying hard work, the simple life, the soil; and socialism in its various forms. There were of course specifically Jewish elements: Jewish tenacity and single-mindedness and the awareness that there was no nation on earth of which they could truly be a part. If they were to express the national soul it could only be in Palestine, a land formally, if ambiguously, promised them by the British in 1917 and by the Almighty before that. But in the deepest sense these young people were largely indistinguishable from thousands of young non-Jewish Russians of idealistic bent who wore the peasant blouse and believed that wisdom came from simple men of the soil, like Tolstoi's Platon. They carried Russia, its forests and streams as well as the introverted but deeply loved *shtetl* world, with them into the Holy Land, and in a sense they never ceased being Russians—fiercely argumentative, dream-haunted, righteous, rather humorless and puritanical Russians—who spoke Hebrew, another of their passions, although they rarely spoke it well.

Manual labor, salvation through work, was an article of faith basic to the chalutz life:

> We must raise a generation of men who have no interests and no habits.
> . . . Bars of iron, elastic but of iron. Metal that can be forged to whatever
> is needed for the national machine. A wheel? I am the wheel. If a nail, a
> screw or a flying wheel are needed—take me! . . . I am the pure idea of
> service, prepared for everything. . . . I know only one rule—to build.

So Joseph Trumpeldor, an officer in the Russian army who came to Palestine in 1912 and died in an Arab attack on Tel Hai in 1920, is supposed to have defined the chalutz.

The young immigrants came either from lower-middle-class families in Russia or Poland, where they would normally have gone into the trade or business of their fathers, or from middle-class professional families. Thus the escape to Palestine was also an escape from parents, home, education: the expectations of others. A young chalutza, Zipporah Bentov, told about the feelings of her father when at the age of seventeen she ran away from home and fled to Palestine, where she was assigned the task of breaking stones for the roads. He wrote: "Please, if this is work which must be done, if you feel it to be of such importance, let me send you a goy from our brickyard here, a first-class day laborer, to work in your place. And please, we beg of you, come home to us and continue your studies." Not only did the young chalutzim look for salvation in hard work, they yearned for the pain of the hard work, craved the blisters and the fevers, for there was an element of masochism in the chalutz character. Sometimes they even craved death; next to disease—malaria, typhoid, typhus, pneumonia—suicide was one of the most conspicuous causes of death in some of the early settlements.

Almost all came from observant Jewish homes. The earlier arrivals, those who emigrated before the war, usually kept a respect and affection for the forms of Judaism although not observant themselves. But most of the postwar immigrants were atheists. They discarded all forms of the parental religion along with all bourgeois values: the pleasures of dress, of good food, of cleanliness, of manners. This stern philosophy was nowhere so apparent as among the dwellers on the kibbutzim, a form of agricultural commune invented by the prewar pioneers, where all property was held in common and every member was a working member; the kibbutz was not only a way of farming but a total way of living. Kibbutz dwellers took pride in wearing grossly ill-fitted clothing from the common stock. They took a fierce and utterly sincere pride in the absence of all pretense, comfort, tradition. "In the early days kibbutz funerals were marked by the strangest behavior. . . . People simply came to the burial ground, the body would be lowered into the grave and the grave would be covered, all in absolute silence. Then the mourners simply walked away," one kibbutznik recalled.

If they had a religion it was socialism. To speak lightly of the class war and Marx to a group of chalutzim was like mocking the Bible before an audience of English workingmen. Socialism was both a unifying and a divisive force, for there were a number of different socialist parties, shifting, exploding apart, forming shaky alliances that fragmented again. The would-be chalutz belonged to a Zionist club of one party's persuasion in his home townlet of Minsk, Pinsk, Mohilev, Plonsk or Bobruisk; under his party's sponsorship he sailed to Palestine and joined an agricultural settlement, sent his children to school there, read the newspaper of his party and voted accordingly. Thus from Europe to Palestine, from youth to adulthood to the grave, he was to be encapsulated within the party, bound by ties that went all the way back to the *shtetl*. It was a closed world, difficult for outsiders to penetrate.

The pioneers of the early 1920s built roads with hand tools while living six to eight to a tent where they frequently slept on the ground; they founded the kibbutzim; they drained the malarial swamps that were to become the glowing farmlands of the north. Young people of fanatic dedication who were determined to create the perfect society along socialist or communist principles, to suffer, to work, to share everything—not only possessions but thoughts, dreams, the love affairs for which they had scarcely the strength or the time— they were a strange new breed of worker and a totally new kind of Jew. And if the European Zionist leaders seemed to treat them like pawns it was largely through ignorance and mismanagement, for they did not know how to build a homeland out of the leavings of the Turkish Empire. They had no models. Nothing like it had ever been done before.

The British rulers of Palestine, accustomed to governing "native" peoples in Egypt or India, hardly knew what to make of these young Zionists. Until the spring of 1920 the British rulers were OETA, the military occupation force, a mixed lot blown to the Holy Land by the winds of war and including among their officers a cashier from a bank in Rangoon, two assistants from Thomas Cook, a picture dealer, a clown and a Glasgow distiller. With a few striking exceptions, OETA was pro-Arab, antisemitic and anti-Zionist.

In the spring and summer of 1920 the military gave way to a civilian government responsible to the Colonial Office in London. Unfortunately the change was not total. Many of the old faces put on new hats and remained. It was one thing to replace a few high officials, another to alter the public tone of a governing class. Some of those who could not agree with the Balfour Declaration resigned; others who should have resigned did not. A sizable military force remained until the mid-twenties, a hotbed of anti-Jewish feeling. Many clerks and other low-ranking employees stayed on, sometimes exerting an uncanny influence on daily affairs, as did the wives of British officials, who were often less enlightened than their husbands. There were also a few fervent Hebrophiles, men of singular and lifelong dedication to the Zionist cause, as well as a greater number who were just as fervently in love with Arab culture, yearning to be primitive sons of the desert. Others were simply civil servants, good, bad, mediocre.

In the end perhaps none of this counted—the social antisemitism, the indifference to Zionist aspirations on the part of some administrators, their wives, clerks and the military—because it had become apparent to those in power in Britain less than two years after the Balfour Declaration that oil was what would matter in the postwar world. The friendship of Arabs would matter. The Balfour Declaration had been made in the midst of a war when America, where it was supposed that Jews were in positions of influence, had to be reckoned with; America was withdrawing now into isolation. Nor did Zionist influence in Russia signify any longer. It was oil, only oil.

The men who composed the Balfour Declaration were brought up on the Bible. They had leaped at the chance to right a historic wrong while at the same time serving the wartime interests of the Empire. Overnight, their impulse toward the generous and noble gesture seemed to have receded into the shadowy past, into the God-fearing nineteenth-century world of before-the-war. The Balfour Declaration was still there, of course; it was His Majesty's policy; the honor of Britain was irrevocably intertwined with it, but it had never been entirely clear what those so carefully chosen words meant. To Britons on the decision-making level who had the duty of preserving the interests of the Empire, only time would tell what the Balfour Declaration meant.

The framers of the declaration were of course aware of the Arab presence in Palestine. Unfortunately they tended to think of the Arabs as natives in picturesque costume rather than a people capable of national aspiration. To the Zionists they were fellow Semites, backward cousins who would benefit tremendously once modern agriculture and manufacture were set in motion. How could they fail to approve of a situation that would better their lot or fail to welcome those who made it possible? That the same spirit of national self-consciousness that moved the Zionist Jews should one day kindle the Arabs had not yet occurred to anyone.

Indeed many of the chalutzim, with their Tolstoian outlook, admired the Arab peasant as a man of the soil. Young Jewish men in the 1920s often copied the small mustache, the *kefiya* and robes of the Arabs; Herbert Samuel's son Edwin was married soon after his arrival in Palestine and at the wedding reception wore Bedouin robes and headdress, the gifts of a sheikh. Everyone knew there was nationalism in Syria, in Mesopotamia, but in Palestine they believed there were only Bedouins and peasants.

Nationalism was there, however, although barely visible. Totally repressed under the Ottoman Empire, when all political dissent was forbidden, Arab nationalism had made its first undeniable appearance in 1909 with the revolution of the Young Turks. It was further fanned by the Allies during the war in the hope of securing Arab military aid against the Turks. By the war's end the Arabs of Palestine began to suspect there was an Arab nation and an Arab language crisscrossing several borders and they were part of it.

When the first Zionist Commission arrived in April 1918 on the heels of the Balfour Declaration, it put the fear of God into Arab and British alike. Truculent and overbearing, its members were not the instruments of British presence in Palestine so much as a shadow government preparing for a huge Jewish immigration. The Arabs were already alarmed by the new Zionists. The communal life of their agricultural settlements, the mingling of the sexes, the socialism, the atheism—all were terrifying signals of change to a deeply traditional people. Now the Zionist Commission made it apparent that these thousands of chalutzim were the forerunners of an army of millions.

To one educated Arab the realization that the Jews meant the Arabs of Palestine "to become a minority in an alien national state set up in their own country, aroused in them not only the deepest fears of the survival instinct, but the burning hatred which comes of an outraged sense of justice. . . ." It was argued that:

> The Arabs had all the Arab world and the Jews wanted only Palestine, a small corner of that world. Was it too much to ask for? Could not the Palestine Arabs find a home in Syria or Iraq? To understand how the Palestinian Arabs felt about this argument, it is only necessary to imagine how the people of Devon or Cornwall would greet a suggestion that they should surrender their part of England to the Jews and find a new home in Scotland.

The writer, a Christian Lebanese educated at British universities, was Edward Atiyah, a man of large views and considerable sophistication, politically not far from the Fabian socialists.

If Atiyah found the Zionist vision absolutely opaque, what could it be to the representative Arab of Palestine, a semiliterate tiller of someone else's land? The Zionists had stated their case in appealing and moderate terms to the Gentile leaders of England and profusely to the Jews of America; the Jews of eastern Europe had required no explanations, but they had debated interminably and exquisitely about every political shading of Zionism. To the Arabs alone the case for Zionism was never explained.

With the 1920 riots, the Jews of the Yishuv as well as the British were shocked into sudden awareness of the danger of a major conflict between Arab and Jew. But they did not yet diagnose the malady of the Arab as nationalism. They spoke instead of British weakness, British pro-Arabism, foreign interference, and comforted themselves with the knowledge that their intentions were honorable, as indeed they were. Jewish doctors had already benefited Arabs as well as Jews. The American Zionist Medical Unit had helped stem epidemics that threatened both populations, and its hospitals and dispensaries were open to both on an equal basis, one of the contractual conditions under which the staff of the AZMU had been hired in America.

Miss Szold was unusually perceptive about the Arab question when she pointed out that people do not always want to have good done to them by others.

The automobile that took the Americans "up, up and again up" arrived at last in the northwestern section of the city, not far from the offices of the Medical Unit and the Zionist Commission. It stopped before an Arab house set in a garden, with two steep staircases inside and high-ceilinged squarish rooms and a few large pieces of furniture brought from Europe. This was the home of Helena Kagan and her mother. Dr. Kagan was away in Europe for several months of rest and study. Her mother welcomed Miss Szold to the two rooms she was to occupy, where everything had been prepared for her, even mosquito netting over the windows and a little maid with a room of her own.

Tea bubbled in a samovar, and around the samovar gathered several friends, among them Alex Dushkin, the young American interested in Jewish education, and Colonel Norman Bentwich, the British Zionist and writer Miss Szold had met ten years earlier in England. There were homemade cakes, fruits, flowers, marmalade, biscuits and little gifts. More friends came and more the next day, Americans as well as the Palestinians she had met on her first visit. It appeared that she was to have an "establishment," not hide herself away in a simple room with some family, as she had wanted to do. The reason for the establishment was that she was expected to assume a position of importance. It was hoped that she would entertain not only well-connected British women but Arab women. She would give teas. In Palestine, where Englishmen, Moslems and Jews of Russian extraction eyed one another with uneasy suspicion, tea was one thing all had in common; the English drank theirs with lemon or cream, the Russians with sugar, the Arabs with mint. Miss Szold, as it happened, never drank tea at all. She disliked it.

17

Miss Szold rose early next morning to carry out the fastidious rituals that went back to her girlhood and Lombard Street: calisthenics, hairbrushing, then bathing and dressing and setting herself so precisely in order that close to two hours were used in the process. Only when the lace pin had been fastened at the exact center of her white, lace-trimmed collar a certain way and no other was she ready to greet the world.

She had come to a land where most aspects of life, such as work habits, sanitary arrangements and finance, were pervaded by a sort of Oriental languor, an acceptance of things as they were. Her many-layered underclothing, her dainty handkerchiefs, hats, collars, cuffs, purses and gloves were as foreign here as her financial arrangements. For decades she had been both frugal and obsessively meticulous. Tiny notebooks in which expenses were recorded in her minute and elegant hand—five cents for carfare, pennies for a newspaper, fifteen cents to take her nephew and nieces to the zoo, three cents for peanuts for the zoo animals—some of the notebooks thirty years old, had been stored with the letters that lay in the attic of Bertha's house in Baltimore. Her personal expenses were always kept rigorously separate from public expenses, those that could be rightfully covered out of Zionist funds. When she traveled on Zionist business, for example, she sometimes gave way to a craving for thick, sweet cream. Zionist money paid for her fares and her meals, but to Miss Szold it was inconceivable that an indulgence in cream could be charged to a Zionist expense account. She kept a separate list of such luxuries in order to pay for them out of her private funds.

Combed and dressed, she was ready to meet Rubinow and examine the Unit's finances. But first a formal call must be paid to Menachem Ussishkin, chairman of the Zionist Commission. Rubinow called for her, escorted her there and left her, for he had no desire to see Ussishkin unless expressly summoned. What Miss Szold found was a man as Russian as the steppes, with a powerful head, totally bald, mounted on a powerful neck, vast energy, vast obstinacy and a demeanor almost menacing in its autocratic power. Weizmann spoke of Ussishkin as a "steam tractor trying to weave fancy lace," and Rubinow was not the only one who found him forbidding, vain, petty and contentious. Yet Ussishkin was possessed of a logical mind, unshakable honesty and considerable executive ability, and he expressed as did no one else the hopes and instincts of the Jewish masses, who trusted him implicitly.

Miss Szold did not record her reactions to Menachem Ussishkin. The meeting was brief and formal and must have been infused by her awareness that while Americans were incomprehensible to him, their choice of a woman to represent them verged on the insulting.

Then she went across the street to the Hôtel de France, which served as headquarters for the Medical Unit. Its offices consisted of five interconnecting rooms of which the most elaborately furnished, the director's, held a desk and two chairs and a pot-bellied stove. In a carpentry shop under the hotel most of the office furniture and all the furnishings for their hospital were made out of the wooden packing cases in which supplies were received from America.

In the director's office the staff of the Medical Unit gathered to meet Miss Szold, doctors and clerks, the lowest as well as the highest, for she told Rubinow she wanted to see them all. Reuben Katznelson, Rubinow's young assistant, had looked forward with some apprehension to the meeting; it was his understanding that the American woman would take the director's place during the long leave Rubinow hoped for. Katznelson was a Russian, one of a large family of devout Zionists for whom "Zionism was the sickness in the family," and the idea of being directed by a woman was not congenial to his Russian temperament. Moreover, when the woman appeared she proved to be very small, hardly taller than a child, plainly dressed, not a commanding person at all and with manners that confounded him.

She insisted on being introduced to everybody and shaking every single hand, "from the *shomer*, the watchman, to the highest official, and she pressed the hand—that was something. For us it was exceptional, unknown. . . . Then, going to the *shomer* she said, 'Ah, where is the other man,' because there were two *shomrim*, and she had to meet both of them. In my view it was something not permitted."

It was out of order and it boded no good, this openness, politeness. Officials in Russia, as well as Arab officials both petty and grand, were never polite. They were fierce, impatient, contemptuous; they picked their noses, they smoked, they kept people waiting and dismissed them with a hand wave. The notion of a woman like Miss Szold that she was a public servant, that her purpose in life was to help as patiently as possible with whatever expert knowledge was at her command—this was "not permitted" to the east European. The patience was suspect, perhaps not even honest. It would surely be taken advantage of, Katznelson felt at the time.

Then the staff straggled out and left Miss Szold alone with Rubinow in a bare little room with a floor of large, uneven stones, surrounded by stone walls one meter thick. Outside it was spring, the sun was hot, birds sang all day long, but the winter's chill clung to the floor and walls and to Rubinow as well. Whatever he had to say to Miss Szold, she knew it would not warm her.

On the desk before her he placed the books that contained the financial mysteries of the Unit. There in figures was the story of the Unit's struggle for survival in the face of Brandeis-Weizmann warfare and continued shortages of money.

Zionist finances in London and Palestine had always been chaotic. For this reason the Americans had recently begun to send their money to London headquarters earmarked for the use of the Unit. It was then forwarded to Palestine intact, so that Rubinow could dispense it as he saw fit and according to American instruction. London took this as confirmation of what they had long suspected in the Americans: impudence, separatism, rebellion. Therefore they proposed to convene a Jahreskonferenz in London in the summer of 1920 at which the question of the Unit—whether it would become an instrument of the world organization and the health department of the Yishuv or a medical philanthropy administered entirely from New York—would be once and for all resolved.

But Rubinow was not happy with the Americans either. They promised more than they furnished; their collections lagged far behind. Prices were rising. When the money failed to arrive he was forced to borrow. Then, some months ago, the Zionist Commission had ordered the bank to cut off his credit. Brandeis sent a sum of money to bail him out, but prices went on rising. There were emergency expenses connected with the riot. Members of the Unit demanded salaries, clinics needed supplies, patients had to be fed. The only way out was to pay doctors, nurses and shopkeepers with chits to be redeemed when the money turned up. It was disgraceful and shabby.

He paused only long enough to gather breath, then plunged on again, his gestures rapid, fluid; intellectually Rubinow was a statistician, but emotionally he was a Slav with a Slav's dark mobile expressive face. He was talking about Ussishkin now. He believed he was under personal assault by Ussishkin, defamed in the press, on the very streets, because of Ussishkin's insistence that Hebrew and only Hebrew be used by the Unit. Every letter, every prescription, every report must be in Hebrew, yet Rubinow knew no Hebrew and had made that clear from the start. Most of his doctors knew no Hebrew; Dr. Eder, Ussishkin's colleague on the Commission, knew no Hebrew, but the use of the language had become the symbolic club with which Ussishkin flayed his enemy, America. And *"Rack Ivrit!"*—"Only Hebrew!"—was the battle cry.

Rubinow felt the Unit was living from hand to mouth, and so was he, emotionally speaking. For it had been reliably reported to him that Ussishkin "made the statement privately that he would make that man (meaning me) take orders from him or drive me out of the country." Rubinow would rather leave quietly and give up the cause that had become dear to him than precipitate a world war within Zionist ranks.

What Rubinow did not say, although Miss Szold learned it soon enough because it was common knowledge, was that his troubles were compounded by his having fallen in love painfully, unexpectedly, without his wishing it, the way such things sometimes happen to a man of forty-five. He was in love with his Russian secretary. She loved him in return; therefore she left her job. Everybody knew, and outside the Unit everybody accepted it, for Old Palestine was in no way discomfited by extramarital romance; Old Palestine was Oriental. But Rubinow did not belong to Palestine. He was a Westerner with a powerful Western conscience. He found no consolation in the knowledge that any number of Unit physicians took up with a succession of women, usually nurses because they were handy. He was torn between the possibility of a new life with his beloved and his family, the wife and three adolescent children who waited in America.

Later he took Miss Szold on a tour of the Rothschild Hospital, the heart of the AZMU, a beautiful building of rose granite lent them by the baron in Paris. She was impressed by the hospital. When the Unit first arrived in 1918 it had had ninety beds but no heat, electricity or running water. Now, staffed by the specialists of the Unit, the Rothschild Hospital treated men and women of all ages and hordes of children, Jewish and Arab. She visited the eye clinic, the surgery, the pediatric clinic. There was a pharmacy, an obstetrical clinic, a dental clinic and 120 beds. Much of this expansion was crowded into a series of humble little annexes, the whole crying out for a single, permanent, unifying building.

Next she interviewed each of the doctors of the Unit. And for the first time she learned what she had only suspected in America: "that the internal relations of the members of the Unit to one another and of nearly all of them to the Director are strained to the breaking point." In fact she learned they had been strained from the first coming of the Americans, almost a year before Rubinow had landed. Dr. Arieh Feigenbaum, who had been in Jerusalem when the first two Hadassah nurses arrived, told her the Unit had descended on the country like so many avenging angels, shoving men like him aside: "They disregarded everything that was done here by Jewish doctors before. Because they came from America and had money, the newcomers thought they had to teach us everything. . . . They treated us like nonentities. The Americans behaved as in an enemy-occupied country."

Feigenbaum's attitude was typical of most of the Unit physicians now; there were few Americans among them, for Palestinians and incoming Europeans had replaced most of those who had left from the States in 1918. Yet these same physicians complained about their salaries; they wanted, insisted on, raises. They said they must be paid on the American scale although everyone else in Palestine lived on next to nothing. Miss Szold, who had always thought doctors were noble beings, found it hard to comprehend their greed and rapacity combined with contempt for America because it was rich.

Within days of this series of interviews Rubinow resigned. His self-esteem had been injured because the press made it appear that Miss Szold had come to check up on him. Out of sympathy, the medical council of the Unit then resigned in its entirety. Within days the student nurses of the Hadassah School of Nursing went on strike, "seventeen walking out of the wards in one fell swoop."

Rubinow withdrew his resignation and announced he was leaving next month on vacation. He would go to America and on the way visit London and the Jahreskonferenz. "I am not going with the intention of returning," he told Miss Szold, "nor am I going with the intention of not returning." She knew his insistence on going home was based largely on the imperative need to learn if his marriage was still intact. Moreover, at the Jahreskonferenz he could fight for the Unit more effectively than anyone else, since he knew its needs better than anyone else. But the thought of his absence made her heart contract painfully. While he was gone there would be no one to take charge but herself.

She felt that she too was ready to flee back home. During the weeks and months in Italy, when she had waited for deliverance so she could reach Jerusalem and see firsthand the work of the Unit so painstakingly built with American dreams and American money, she had known there would be problems. What she had not known was how petty they would be, how infused with spitefulness and avarice. She could hardly sleep at night, for she began to suspect she had devoted twenty-two years of her life "to an ideal that had turned out to be a will o' the wisp. For what is a Zionist who no longer believes in the Jewish people? . . . A voice kept shouting inside of myself: These are not your people. You have no part and parcel in them."

A year went by before she could write any of this to anyone outside the family, and even from them she kept the full extent of her disillusion a secret.

The day came when the Unit salved its feelings sufficiently so that Miss Szold could walk across the street to the Zionist Commission. It was housed, like Unit headquarters, in a former Arab hotel, a bare and primitive stone building. Here she tackled Menachem Mendel Ussishkin, whom Jew and Arab alike referred to as Menachem Pasha. Even Sir Ronald Storrs, the civil governor of Jerusalem, stiffened before the onslaught of Ussishkin: "To us he might well have been Czar Menachem; and when he was announced for an interview I braced myself to take my punishment like a man."

Miss Szold was aware almost from the start that her nogotiations with Ussishkin made no progress, that he did not want to make progress, that he was in fact fencing with her. Apparently he wanted immediate control of the Unit, "complete surrender," as she put it. He must have been confident he would get it at the Jahreskonferenz.

Yet if he had taken a conciliatory attitude and shown himself open to compromise, Ussishkin would have found in Miss Szold a most willing listener. When she was first asked to go to Palestine, Brandeis had instructed her to safeguard the Unit's identity as an American organization. To this Miss Szold had replied that, on the contrary, she believed the Russians were right: the Unit must submit to central authority; it could not remain autonomous and American. Brandeis had retorted that of course he agreed. In time, he said, it would naturally be taken over by the Zionist Commission on behalf of the international organization. But only when the time was ripe.

Where Miss Szold and the Brandeis faction parted ways was on the matter of time. To the Americans, the time would be ripe in some distant, barely foreseeable future. To Miss Szold, the sooner the better. But now that she was in Jerusalem herself, she had to agree with the Americans. She was increasingly suspicious of what would become of the Unit if Ussishkin and the Russians took it over at that point.

Much later she would come to feel that she had succumbed to the Brandeis leaders against her better judgment. Now, however, she stood up to Ussishkin and his demand for total surrender, telling herself there were times when it was best not to cling to principles. It was best to protect the Unit for the time being.

Certainly the Unit cried out for protection. A bulletin of the labor party, Hapoel Hatzair, informed its members that

> The Zionist Organization must fight against this [American] usurpation by all means. It has to organize the medical relief in the country at once. . . . And if we shall be obliged to be satisfied with less automobiles and less other luster, we shall do it; we shall not be dependent on people who mock at us by the rich contribution they give us. "The AZMU does not exist for us any more, we have nothing to do with it," this ought to be the answer of the Palestinian public.

Two distinct processes were going on side by side, then. The Americans were reaching out toward the Yishuv, eager to help, to be part of the great adventure, and they brought their help in the form of American efficiency and money. The Yishuv recoiled because it was painfully eager to stand on its own feet, which blinded it to the need of the Americans: the need to be needed. Nobody thought of pooling the needs of America and the needs of the Yishuv.

Since Miss Szold first came to take over Alice Seligsberg's position as Hadassah representative with the Unit, Alice had been waiting for an American social worker who would carry on her work with Jewish orphans. Now the social worker had arrived, and Alice sailed for New York. Miss Szold wrote to her sisters a few weeks later, "I miss her terribly." She missed them all, the sisters, Bertha's children, the infant boy her sister Rachel had adopted. She was hungry for all the intimate details. "I feel very far away from you all and I can't deny that I am distinctly homesick."

The woman who came to take Seligsberg's place was in her own way quite remarkable. Her name was Sophia Berger. She was thirty-eight years old, and an English friend remembered her as "the ugliest woman I ever clapped eyes on; she grew uglier with time." She was thrifty; she saved string; she was sociable and gossipy, "a mine of information, much of it incorrect," another friend recalled, and she had a certain bossiness. She decided to take charge of Miss Szold. Dr. Kagan had returned from Europe, and Miss Berger offered to find "an establishment" in which she and Miss Szold could live together. She would manage all domestic details while Miss Szold managed the Unit.

Now the heat of spring gave way to the brazen heat of summer. Indoors the rough stone buildings were deliciously cool; outside the sun clamped down without mercy and flies settled in black crusts on the garbage heaps. Old men sprawled in the sun by the Western Wall, dazed and motionless, babies lay torpid in their mothers' arms, and from the Arab cafes gramophones shrilled monotonous Oriental chants, hypnotic, piercing. In New York the Hadassah circles dispersed for the summer, to take up their business again in the fall. Miss Szold had been hearing heartening news from Hadassah's board. Their little newspaper was struggling back to life, an impoverished undertaking sent only to officers to be read aloud at chapter meetings. Although she despaired of Hadassah's ever regaining their original life as a separate organization within the ZOA, the newsletter was a sign of tenacity. Louis Lipsky hoped they would melt away, yet it seemed the women had wills of their own. The Medical Unit and the nursing school were what held them together, along with Miss Szold, their president and founder, who was also their representative in the Holy Land, their link with those two precious creations.

They had no way of knowing that in Jerusalem Miss Szold's life was a daily battle, not with the heat, the filth, the discomfort, but with her own belief in her own dream.

18

On June 30, 1920, a new era in the history of Jewish Palestine began with the arrival of the first British High Commissioner, Sir Herbert Samuel, knighted for the occasion. To the Yishuv the awareness that a Zionist and a Jew embodied all the powers of the British Empire was inexpressibly moving. Ronald Storrs was sent to meet Sir Herbert's ship: "As I stepped ashore with the man chosen to execute so tremendous a decision, and presented to him the assembled leaders of a people almost faint with happiness and moving as if in the glory and freshness of a dream come true, I was acutely conscious that I was walking in something stranger than history—the past summoned back and made to live again."

They drove toward Ludd, the man beside the driver heavily armed, and Storrs concealing a loaded and cocked Browning pistol in his left hand, for the countryside was placarded with notices declaring that Sir Herbert would not live four days after his arrival. The news of the appointment had been a severe blow to the Arabs. For a man of Jewish blood to be placed at the head of government seemed an outrage, an insult even worse than the Zionist Commission. Allenby had warned the Foreign Secretary that the appointment of a Jew would be tantamount, in Arab eyes, to handing the country over to a permanent Zionist administration; raids on Jewish villages, outrages, murder would inevitably follow.

Yet here was Sir Herbert, with his perfect Edwardian posture, sitting with Storrs as the automobile climbed to Jerusalem. To the accompaniment of a seventeen-gun salute fired from a knoll where the Hebrew University was one day to rise, Sir Herbert stepped out of his car before Government House. The outgoing chief administrator, General Sir Louis Bols, handed him a slip of paper on which he had written, "Received, one Palestine in good order." Samuel glanced at it unsmiling and added, "E. and O.E.," meaning "Errors and Omissions Excepted."

Palestine, having been conquered from the Turks, was to be governed by Great Britain under a League of Nations mandate; each year the British would send the League voluminous accounts of their trusteeship. Nevertheless they would administer Palestine in much the same way they ran a colony like Egypt. They provided services—police, hospitals, schools, sewers, a water supply—levied taxes to pay for them and encouraged autonomy among the native population in certain aspects of life, especially religious institutions.

The sewers and the water supply provided by the British were admirable, but their hospitals were inadequate and the schooling they offered the Arabs a bare minimum even in that undereducated part of the world. The schooling they offered the Jews was simply refused; the Jews preferred to furnish their own school system, paid for out of international Zionist collections and administered by the Zionist Commission, accepting from the British the minute sums that would have been spent on Jewish students. With regard to health care, again the Jews preferred to ignore what the British offered and provide their own: the AZMU, which the Zionist Commission was so greedy to take over.

In most of its relations with the Yishuv the British government dealt through the Zionist Commission, which was elected by the world organization to serve as the government within a government as well as the link between the British and world Zionism. The British never expected the Zionist Commission to behave in so lordly and independent a manner as it did, and one official believed Sir Herbert had been chosen as the first High Commissioner in order "to pare the nails of the Zionist Commission," to steal its thunder. They themselves could not control the Commission, especially the Russian bear Ussishkin. They could surely control Sir Herbert.

In any event Sir Herbert was sent to run a penny-pinching colonial regime, neglectful but on the whole well intentioned, a regime whose greatest problem would be its "native" population, two peoples with conflicting desires, both of whom he must serve according to the will of the Colonial Office and that murky document, the Balfour Declaration. The chief bone of contention in this and all succeeding regimes would be the number of Jews allowed to enter and settle in the country.

In the weeks that followed, both British and Arabs began to modify their opinions of Sir Herbert. The Arabs were impressed with his physical courage; in the face of their threats he appeared everywhere in public, a tall, upright figure in close-fitted white suit and cork helmet, always with the same patient courtesy for plain people as well as dignitaries, Arabs as well as Jews. He was very British, very fair-minded, determined to do justice to both sides. Moreover he worked hard, which impressed the British. But Miss Szold was not especially impressed. She did not share in the mystical glow of hope that followed Samuel's arrival, not so much because she found him wanting in any important respect, but because he represented imperial England and military conquest. She was at heart a pacifist, and the knowledge that the Holy Land had been won for the Jews on the battlefield and was being held for them by force of arms stuck in her throat.

Sir Herbert's first acts were well received. He established Hebrew as an official language and reached a generous agreement with the Zionist Commission on immigration: for all practical purposes unlimited. He pardoned those who took part in the Easter riots, Jabotinsky as well as the two Arab leaders who had escaped the country. Aref el Aref became a British civil servant, working in Palestine for a quarter of a century with diligence and distinction. Haj Amin el Husseini was appointed the following April to the lifetime position of Mufti of Jerusalem, spiritual head of all Moslems. Regarding the Arabs, Samuel followed the well-worn British ploy of choosing the class bullies to be his monitors in the hope of coopting them for the administration. With Aref he was successful, but the choice of Haj Amin proved disastrous.

That summer Miss Szold and Sophia Berger set up housekeeping together in a little rented house in a mixed European and Arab section on the outskirts of the city, overlooking the Mount of Olives. They had a large garden with olive trees, plums, figs, oranges, vines as well as flowers and an area that was completely wild, full of tall grasses. Miss Szold walked among them with the copy of Gray's *Botany* she had brought from Baltimore, bending the grasses back to search out the tiniest wildflowers. The house itself was quite primitive, their only heating system a smelly kerosene stove, and she wondered how they would get through the winter. In the searing heat of the Palestinian summer, it was shadowy and delightfully cool.

Because Sophia loved company, picnics, expeditions and unexpected treats, Miss Szold was drawn into a life of pleasant sociability. Norman Bentwich and his two sisters, Alex Dushkin, the American poet Jessie Sampter and Nellie Straus Mochenson and her husband formed the nucleus of their group. On Saturday mornings they met for Sabbath prayers in Miss Sampter's rooms on the Street of the Prophets; on Saturday afternoons friends came to Miss Szold's and Miss Berger's for tea. During the warm months Sophia served it in the garden, dragging out chairs and rugs and a low Oriental table that was a gift from Alex Dushkin. There they would sit for hours watching the skies change color and marveling at the sunset, a little island of English speakers in a sea of Hebrew.

The house and the friends made a difference in Miss Szold's feelings. Until then she had suffered not only from disillusion and homesickness but from having no one to share her homesickness with, no community of fellow Americans. On the Fourth of July she had wandered through Dr. Kagan's garden humming all the patriotic songs she could think of, having first made sure there was no one within earshot, because her singing was always off key. Now, thanks to Sophia, she had an American circle. In Jerusalem, people said, If you want to get to Miss Szold, you must see Sophia Berger. Sometimes it was Alex Dushkin or Julia Aronson one had to see, but mostly it was Sophia. For Miss Szold still hung back from people. She had the same tendency to withdraw to a distance and from that distance cling to one or two close friends.

They acted as her mediators, her bridge to the rest of the world. Those she chose were either the very young, like Alex and Julia, with whom she felt entirely at ease because they would not judge, would not criticize, would sit at her feet like students, or those somewhat closer to her own age who took her as she was, people with a certain healthy ordinariness.

She wanted to be admired, yet she was afraid of it. People who adored and sentimentalized her might lose their illusions, might come to see her flaws and inadequacies and hold her to account, as if she had deceived them. With Sophia, Miss Szold felt, "She does not admire me, but she does love me." Best of all, Sophia tied her to real life, the life of ordinary people and sociability and picnics.

Helena Kagan was entirely different. Meeting her for the first time, after she returned from Europe, Miss Szold found a tall, thin, intense young woman, not at all like the doctor's gentle mother, who had cooked for her, gossiped with her, spoiled and petted her. Alice Seligsberg was very fond of Dr. Kagan, and Kagan was very fond of Seligsberg. But Kagan and Miss Szold did not get on.

They had much in common, much in the past to compare and mull over as well as shared hopes for the future: Hadassah's pasteurized milk station, the first in the country, was to join forces with Dr. Kagan's little hospital for infant diseases, forming the nucleus from which public health work in Palestine eventually grew. It was one of Miss Szold's cherished dreams for the Yishuv, as it was Dr. Kagan's. All the same they did not get on.

Helena Kagan came to see Miss Szold as impressive: "awe-inspiring and very single-minded . . . I told her she was hard sometimes, yet she was so modest. She was extraordinary. She wasn't a usual person. She wasn't easy."

To Miss Szold, whose education never went beyond high school, who was struggling at the time to learn the fundamentals of public health and medical administration from a pile of pamphlets, this young woman, with her expert knowledge and her history of defiant courage during the war, must have seemed awesome herself. Miss Szold's reaction was defensive; she became stiff and hard and unapproachable, and Dr. Kagan felt a sense of loss.

Rubinow had left, having neither resigned nor promised to return. Miss Szold moved into his office and set about learning the business of the Unit; she plunged into filing cabinets, studied correspondence, receipts and accounts. For the next two months she was to work at it seventeen hours a day, six days a week, while half of Jewish Palestine streamed into the little room demanding work or medical services.

The Unit was the largest single employer of labor in the Holy Land. Beyond the Unit the only work to be had was on road-building gangs. Miss

Szold learned about the living conditions of these gangs from such letters as the following, addressed to Rubinow several months before her arrival by a physician in the little settlement of Rosh Pinah: "More than one hundred young men are lying, literally like dogs on the hard floor . . . how awful is the scene which presents itself to the eyes of the observer! cases, boxes, packages, sacks, scattered leaves, mud, water, food-supplies, sick persons all mixed up. A bad smell meets me on entering the room. From every corner sighs are heard, and there is no ear to hear them. . . ."

Now the road builders and swamp drainers sent delegates to Miss Szold, demanding that the Unit furnish them with clinics or field hospitals. The Unit had no money. She explained at length that they had no money, to which the chalutzim, whose unions and newspapers denounced the Unit for being rich and American, made no reply but simply repeated their requests.

In fact the Unit had not been entirely ignoring the chalutzim, as it was accused of doing. From their first arrival, sanitary inspection teams had gone out to serve the old Rothschild colonies, and the Unit furnished drugs, equipment and personnel to the workers' sick fund, the Kupat Holim. But there was no denying the basic truth of what the Europeans claimed: the AZMU did not put the chalutzim first.

Two things became clear to Miss Szold as she sat in the director's office: something would have to be done about the pioneers in the Galilee, and for the Unit to do everything that needed doing would cost roughly a million dollars. They had half that amount, at least on paper, but actual receipts were long overdue. The only organization that sent their pledged payments on time was the non-Zionist Joint.

That autumn she set out on a series of tours to immigrant reception centers at the ports and the tent camps of the road builders and swamp drainers, fifty-two in all, some of them served by field hospitals run by Kupat Holim with the Unit's equipment. It was the same territory she had traversed with her mother in 1909, a barren wasteland shimmering with swamps, crisscrossed by primitive paths fit only for camels or mules. On those paths the ancient Unit car broke down repeatedly. All around, the earth was harsh and dry. There was a sense of bareness, brilliant and iridescent. Olive and fig trees, blooming purple thistle and teazle were dusted with chalk.

One day that fall a young chalutz named Arieh Lifschutz was working on the *kvish* (road) between Afuleh and Nazareth with two companions, all in their teens and newly arrived from eastern Europe. They lived in a tent camp nearby, sleeping six or eight to a tent, "without beds, without food, with nothing. . . . It was terrible to live like that." They had no shoes. Sacks that had contained sugar were folded four layers thick and bound about their feet, and with their chisels and hammers the chalutzim broke up the rocks that would form the roadbed while standing on stone rubble in cloth-bound feet.

To this forsaken spot came two visitors, a man and a woman. The man was a Russian Jew named Pinchas Rutenberg, thickset, powerful, dressed all in black, with a granitic head and a voice that seemed to issue from between clenched jaws. He was an engineer who took a particular interest in the pioneers, and chatted now with the three young men in an easy, friendly manner. He promised them shoes.

The woman was Miss Szold, dressed in heavy sweaters, breeches and thick woolen stockings under boots, the first and apparently the last time in her life she appeared in such a costume. She picked her way across the stony rubble with brisk movements, quick little steps so vigorous one might have taken her for a woman of forty. She questioned the men about their health needs, food and living conditions with a concern Lifshutz always remembered as motherly, and she was the first person in Palestine to ask them such questions. Some time later Rutenberg fulfilled his promise by buying a huge supply of used shoes from the Egyptian army and distributing them among the *kvish* builders. Miss Szold got them a hospital barracks.

The chalutzim she met during her autumn forays before the coming of the rains were pouring into the port of Jaffa now at the rate of 300 weekly. Their kitchens were tents and their sewage flowed into the Sea of Galilee, from which they drew their drinking supply. When physicians of the Unit tried to inoculate them against typhoid they fought inoculation. They wanted to be strong, like the Arabs. Nobody inoculated Arabs. For the same reason they tried to ignore malaria. Everyone succumbed to it within a week of their arrival, and they lay on the ground in the tents, gnawed by fever or torn from sleep by terrifying nightmares and delirium. Some made their way to the towns, to hospitals or clinics of the Unit where there was no room for them. With fevers of 103° they had to be turned away because there were no free beds.

When she returned from the Galilee, Miss Szold wrote to her sisters: "If we had all the money in the world, these first immigrants would be bound to serve as dung to this land. Our task must demand the sacrifice of young lives. It is *war* with nature. But it is hard—awfully hard." She began an educational campaign, her first battle in the war with nature, by dictating to one of the Unit's public health men a series of popular leaflets on the diseases of the country and their prevention. She organized the immigration work at the ports, medical, sanitary, prophylactic, including a delousing station, for many of the immigrants came from typhus-infected areas. "Isn't it absurd for me to be doing this sort of thing when I am approaching sixty?"

Much of Miss Szold's energy that summer went into dealing with students of the nursing school, a rebellious crew who embodied the earliest dreams of the Hadassah women. She wrote to the Hadassah chapters about them with great pride, describing the quarters of the pupil nurses as spartan yet cozy, speaking of the satisfaction it gave her to see a path of professional opportunity thrown open for young women in a country where women, especially in traditional families, had never had any occupation or training whatever. And this first class, its members from twenty to twenty-five years old, contained few with more than a grade-school education.

But Miss Szold's description of the nurses' training school in her Hadassah letters did not reveal all her feelings. She told her family, "the pupil nurses, who will graduate next year, hate Americans and Hadassah so much that not even the fine salaries will keep them." They did not want to work in the Hadassah clinics, where they were sorely needed; they wanted only to serve among chalutzim.

They had other ideas at odds with those of Miss Szold and the administration. They refused to take instruction in any language other than Hebrew, although most of their teachers, the Unit physicians, knew no Hebrew and there was not a single textbook in the language anywhere. They set up committees aimed at self-rule; they went on strikes, insisting on a voice in the running of the school, and in Miss Szold's authoritarian presence they smoldered. She came to believe it might be better to bend with the wind. Of the forty who entered the first class, only twenty-two survived the three-year course, and there were several suicide attempts, one successful. Miss Szold therefore practiced understanding and acceptance with the pupil nurses; she tried not to see what was too painful to see and encouraged them with treats, such as a moonlight picnic on Mount Scopus in early July, with their young men invited. Each of her attempts at improving relations was launched with the highest hopes, but the distance between her nunlike ideals of public service and their fiery need for freedom and modernity could not be reconciled.

It was no wonder Miss Szold found frequent relief that embattled summer in losing her temper. There would be a sudden banging of her fist on the desk top, followed by her voice "so loud you could hear it in Jaffa," then a stamping of the feet, her face flooded with color. Then a pause, as if to say now that's over and out of the way, now we can proceed. She was not proud of her temper. As a child in Baltimore she had looked with wonder at the Quaker women, with their composed and placid faces, and thought she might be like them when she was old. Throughout her life she had believed in self-mastery and self-control, and had succeeded all too well in developing those qualities. Now she was nearly sixty; but the temper remained. It grew worse with age.

The hours she kept were a source of amazement to members of the Unit. Indeed Miss Szold herself continued to amaze them. If Reuben Katznelson found her strange because she was democratically American, his wife found Miss Szold incomprehensible because she was herself: "Miss Szold had let it be known, jokingly, that Katznelson had one fault—'He loves his wife and the new baby, and goes home at one in the morning,' " while she stayed on in the office. It was a joke and it was not a joke; Mrs. Katznelson was aware of that. She felt Miss Szold was hard to know, even though they were to work closely together some years later; about the inner self, the woman behind the machine that worked so hard, "I think it was very, very covered, the inside. . . . Yet she was such a big person. I liked her and disliked her at the same time."

It is curious that many people took her for much younger than she was that first year in Palestine. One woman guessed thirty-eight. "I am not yet a nebbish," Miss Szold said when she heard it. She did not dress like a young woman, nor did she talk like one. Apparently it was the outpouring of energy, the sheer staying power that deceived them. There were other contradictions. Precise and exacting as she was, her speech meticulous and literary, her concerns impersonal, there was nevertheless an elusive quality of femininity in the whole. Certain gestures, a particular movement of the hand, could only be described as dainty. Some Europeans said of her, "She was 'coquette.' " A man who came to know her well in the late twenties said, "If it is possible to speak of the sex appeal of an elderly virgin, one could use this description for Miss Szold."

19

In London the 1920 Jahreskonferenz had dragged on for two months, an acrimonious affair from which Brandeis came away feeling that Americans and Europeans had no common meeting ground and no common language. But to both parties it was apparent that the Americans still held the purse strings.

The shattered Jewish communities of Russia had no money after the war; they were in need of extensive relief themselves, and there were no Zionists to speak of among continental Jewry. Even in America the great Jewish fortunes belonged to Reform Jews of German ancestry who considered Zionism about as sympathetic as syndicalistic anarchism. Chaim Weizmann hoped in the near future to effect an alliance with these Yahudim, a task that would challenge to the utmost even his splendid gifts of diplomacy. Meanwhile, because only the American Zionists had money, they were able to fend off European attempts to take over the Unit.

At the same time the dollar was shrinking. So was membership in the ZOA, 180,000 at the height of post-Balfour excitement in 1919, 25,000 now. There was a spirit of isolationism in America, a turning inward from which American Jews were not exempt. The Joint was interested in war-stricken communities in Europe, and they too were ready to leave Zion to the Zionists. The air was frosty with Retrenchment.

In Jerusalem Rubinow had returned, bringing his family with him. Miss Szold handed back the Unit whole and intact, perhaps even somewhat improved from the organizational standpoint. Then she moved out of the director's office. He wanted her to stay and share it with him, but she transferred her things to a little table in a room with the clerical staff and would not budge. Rubinow offered to find her a rug for the stone floor by the table, and this too Miss Szold refused, but the rug appeared one day and remained, for which she scolded him. Together they decided that she would stay on with the Unit for a while to ease his transition. Later she would take charge of the nurses' school.

One day quite by accident Rubinow learned that Miss Szold's sixtieth birthday would take place in December. He arranged for a surprise party and invited the doctors and nurses of the Unit to a dinner before it, with Sir Herbert and Lady Samuel the chief guests. Sir Herbert asked in a whisper, "Shall I wear my decorations?" Rubinow told him no; knowing the limitations of Miss Szold's wardrobe he realized that if the party were to be a surprise, she would not be equal to Sir Herbert's decorations.

After the dinner there was a reception for 150 guests at the Hôtel de France. There were gifts, a warm Persian rug among them, dancing and a tribute from the Unit employees that was especially touching to Miss Szold, since they knew quite well that "I haven't too much respect for some of them." She had been taken completely by surprise and felt almost stupefied. "Fortunately I didn't feel as though it was meant for me. I felt impersonal. But it *was* wonderful."

The day before, there had been a birthday picnic in the countryside near the Arab town of Ramallah, with Sophia, Alex, Julia and Miss Szold. They had passed a party of Arab stonecutters chipping away like the chalutzim, and one of them had called out to Dushkin, "Try your hand at some work and see whether you like it as much as being a gentleman." Miss Szold understood the gestures if not the words and took up the challenge before Dushkin could, sitting down beside the stones with chisel and hammer to "work" for five minutes. "You should have seen the amusement and loud laughter. Since then Arabs have ceased to be only figures in the landscape. I wish I knew Arabic."

Certainly she had not been lucky with Hebrew. What she had learned as a child in her father's study was the biblical language, read rather than spoken. Her acquaintance with the modern tongue began with her 1909 trip; ever since, she had struggled to conquer a language that rarely surrenders to the Westerner. She could read it; she could deliver a speech in it if the speech was prepared ahead of time; but to speak, to exchange not only ideas but feelings, was a slow and miserable business. If she ever left the country, she said ten years later, it would be because of the language.

There were other obstacles to confront, such as the weather, for which her wardrobe was entirely inadequate. The torrential rains of autumn melted the unpaved earth—and in the suburbs of Jerusalem there was a good deal of unpaved earth—to glutinous mud. No lightweight raincoat was sufficient for those rains; one had to be covered head to toe in cape, boots and hood made of the heaviest rubber obtainable. Miss Szold got a British policeman's rain gear eventually, a single enveloping garment from which only her face emerged.

In the Berger-Szold household, two spinsters of thrifty and methodical habits were waited on by little Rivkah Cohen. Rivkah attended night classes four times a week, and on those nights Sophia rushed home from work to prepare dinner. She did it with ease, even slapped up a meal for six people after office hours gaily and successfully. But now that Rubinow was back, Miss Szold felt constrained to share the cooking, to furnish dinner on alternate nights. And she had never cooked before. In the rough stone kitchen set up for an Arab servant, without icebox or oven, with neither electricity nor water supply, she studied the cookbook, wrote out a menu, reached for the dictionary, examined the larder, chose, debated, scratched out and started over again. She was too precise and detail ridden to be a cook. Besides, there was nothing to cook with. Palestine was full of fruit; oranges and tomatoes flourished. If nations could be built on oranges and tomatoes, the Jewish homeland would have sprung up overnight. But there was no milk, butter or eggs to speak of; the milk was bluish water, the eggshells half empty because the hens were undernourished. So was most of Palestine. Julia Aronson called it "a museum for undernourishment," where children with bloated bellies scrounged in garbage pails.

Miss Szold and Miss Berger, both observant Jews who kept a kosher kitchen, decided to become vegetarians in order to simplify *kashruth* and avoid buying another set of dishes. For even dishes were expensive and hard to get. The stores were empty, there seemed to be nothing in them but strings of beads.

Clothing, housewares, furniture, even shoelaces had to be bought abroad. To ask for books was lunacy.

Miss Szold read the books Adele sent from America. Toby Seltzer had his own publishing firm by then and since the summer of 1920 had been publishing the works of the English author D. H. Lawrence; they had never been printed in America before. In November of that year he brought out *Women in Love,* which no one in England would touch after the sensation created by Lawrence's *The Rainbow.* The new book was also sensational— people called it salacious—and when Miss Szold received her copy she wondered if she was going to feel about it as Adele did. "I'm pretty sure I'm not."

What Adele felt was that it was a tremendous work, that Lawrence was "overpoweringly beautiful and a gigantic intellect besides," and she was proud of her husband's connection with such a man. Otherwise her life was not happy. She resented having to work for Mrs. Schiff, who was much too rich and extravagant for Adele's socialist tastes. Often she resented being married; if she were twenty again, she told her sister, she would never marry but support herself and live with any man she loved. Even now she was sometimes tempted to escape from the box that marriage was: "But for the debts, I'd throw up everything. I shouldn't care. I'd go to a farm as a maid, anything, just not to have to be a flunkey any more."

Henrietta wrote soothing letters urging her sister to think positively, to be grateful for the intellectual affinity between herself and Thomas. Adele, in turn, wrote inspiriting letters to Henrietta. She thought of her as someone whom life had subtly cheated, who never got the praise and recognition she deserved, partly because she hid from them. She urged her sister to put herself forward, to move toward life and people. Henrietta recognized this as valid and hung back nevertheless. Now, after her successful leadership of the Unit during Rubinow's absence, Adele told Henrietta to mix more with the English ruling class. Henrietta mulled it over.

In January 1921, she received an invitation to a gala dinner at Government House. It stated that decorations would be worn, which she took to mean that women would come in décolleté. Therefore "my first reaction was that I wouldn't go—I'd decline." On second thought it seemed wiser to go. "As for décolleté—well, I was a Jewish Quaker. If they invited me, they'd have me as I am. . . . So I went in my demure . . . [light silk evening] gown, cut into v-shape so that no more skin showed than can be covered by the fourth part of an American lady's handkerchief."

She had asked her family for a warm sweater as her sixtieth birthday present, a big, thick, heavy sweater, the very best that could be got, the kind that would surely be found at Abercrombie & Fitch. She hesitated to ask for things, but there was no such sweater to be had in Palestine, probably not in Cairo or Alexandria either. The sweater arrived at last. "If I tell you that it comes up to the topnotch of my expectations because it looks like everyone else's, will you understand how satisfied I am? Or don't you remember that it has always been my desire—unfulfilled for the most part—to look exactly like other people?" But the sweater proved to be only near perfect; there was something wrong with the pocket. It was of course just what she had wanted; she appreciated the trouble they had taken; yet the pocket nagged at her. Perhaps it was her destiny never to reach that pinnacle where she could look and be exactly like other people.

A fancy dress ball was held by the Unit in the spring of 1921. Miss Szold could not bring herself to go in fancy dress, so she wore that same demure gown of thin, satiny silk and cotton. All the others were done up as Orientals. There were men in long dark Arab robes, with swords in richly chased silver scabbards swinging at their sides and short silver-handled daggers thrust into sashes. There were women in dresses of silvery stripes on a darker fabric, with great shawls almost as voluminous as the dresses enveloping head and shoulders, their faces completely covered by gauzy, patterned muslin; it was the costume of a Moslem lady. Miss Szold moved among these fantasy figures wondering what everything had cost. Several of the women had come in elaborately embroidered Bedouin gowns, clanking with silver coins and massive silver necklaces studded with amber or garnet. No wonder the doctors of the Unit grumbled about their salaries. They and their wives were wearing their salaries.

Adele continued to chip away at Henrietta's claim that she was a failure in Palestine on the personal side. "I feel pretty sure I understand exactly what led you to have that impression—you, a systematic person, a disciplinarian, a martinet even—they, loose and rebellious; you, a dry American, they, full-blooded Russians." Henrietta acknowledged both descriptions as painfully correct.

Dry she certainly was; American she certainly was. And the Russians? Graceless, self-indulgent, lazy, a people who were finished with idealism. They felt they had done their share, let the rest of the Jewish world support them now. Adele spoke up for the Russians; her sister's criticism, she said, sprang largely from her own fine and aristocratic nature. But Henrietta would have none of it: "I cannot, cannot accept them."

The young chalutzim were a different breed, and for them she felt a shy admiration mixed with curiosity. She visited the kibbutzim of the Galilee, the agricultural collectives where some of the chalutzim had settled down to farm. Life was almost as harsh there as in the *kvish* builders' camps; people ate in a wooden barracks at a bare wooden table. They gulped down their food with heavily sugared tea as if they grudged the time it took to eat. Something within her cried out against what she saw there. Admirable though they were, those men and women lacked the slightest particle of social courtesy. Because they were atheists they also lacked all the beautiful rituals associated in her mind with Judaism: they lit no candles on Friday night, said no prayers on Saturday morning, and married abruptly. She learned that their infants were being raised in collective nurseries. The purpose of this innovation was to free the mothers for work in the fields; a dozen or so infants could be cared for day and night by one or two women while the other women worked or slept. It seemed to her that social experiments rather than life were carried on in the kibbutzim. "At present, loads and loads of money are sunk in the experiments, and all my eyes have seen is a disorder that keeps one uncomfortable in mind and body."

But she was drawn to them. Perhaps it was the schoolteacher in her, perhaps a long-suppressed taste for adventure that made her fantasize a life for herself among the chalutzim. She thought of organizing a group whose living conditions she could supervise. She tried to picture herself out in the fields with the young people or in the kitchen cooking proper meals for them. "Or I ought to be in America collecting money for 'social' work in the camps— better tents, better food, recreation, well-equipped field hospitals, scoutmasters, games. . . ." In the end she shrugged it off. She was afraid of being laughed at.

By 1921 she had passed the earlier stage of defeat and disillusion and broken sleep, when her life in Zionism seemed the pursuit of a phantom, but was not yet sure what had replaced it. Not a day went by, she told her sisters, when she did not long for her father's calm wisdom. He seemed to her a modern of moderns while she was a Victorian flung into a disordered world, uncertain about everything except that she did not fit. She put her hopes in the perplexing chalutzim and in the land itself, the rich but long-neglected, long-abused soil of Palestine.

On a long trip with Sophia, Julia and Alex in April of that year, she slept on the ground wrapped in a rug, with the cool breezes blowing over her nose and the sky quivering above. It was a botanist's paradise; everything was woolly or prickly or spiny or had sinuses. She had never slept on the ground in America and had probably never wanted to.

To a Baltimore friend she wrote that she was undergoing the biggest adventure of her life, "so big that in spite of my age and in spite of the burden I have been carrying, I feel young and strong. It is very very wonderful, this experience in these last days of my life."

In the spring of 1921, Winston Churchill, now Colonial Secretary, went to Cairo and with quick, decisive strokes intended to clear up the tangled postwar affairs of the Middle East, set up Emir Feisal as king of Iraq and

Feisal's brother Abdullah as king of a newly created country, Trans-Jordan, the part of Palestine that lay east of the river Jordan. The severance of this territory made little impression on the Yishuv at the time, for there were no more than two or three Jews living in it.

Then Churchill came to Jerusalem, where a Moslem-Christian delegation called on him claiming to represent the entire Arabic population of Palestine. They asked him to rescind the Balfour Declaration and put a stop to all Jewish immigration. This Churchill resoundingly refused to do. Moreover he assured them the present government would remain in power for several generations. To the Arab leaders it seemed that the British and the Zionists were united in a subtle plot to keep the Arabs of French-held Syria and British Palestine permanently enslaved.

Then Churchill left, and a period of brooding ensued. In the face of anti-Zionist propaganda, the Jews had begun to organize for self-defense. There was a certain amount of arms smuggling, which the British purposely overlooked. When spring brought Nebi Musa and memories of the previous year's tragic events, the Yishuv sucked in its breath and braced itself.

Nevertheless Miss Szold and Sophia joined the ceremonial procession of Moslems that marked the opening of that festival, pouring through the gates of the city, then up along the road to Gethsemane. They were the only women in the crowd and two of the few Jews. They saw British machine guns bristling on all the hills and the Unit's trucks prepared for any emergency, so they felt safe. Besides, Miss Szold was resolved to feel safe. If one showed no fear and went about one's ordinary business, people would not be tempted into violence.

At the head of the procession rode the newly appointed Mufti, Haj Amin el Husseini, his palms upturned in a dignified attitude of prayer. What Miss Szold found most striking about him was the way he seemed to float above the hysterical crowd, encased in a timeless serenity. He was a small, delicate man with an elfin expression, possessed of a natural dignity and the remarkable power of sitting as still as a statue for hours at a time. He never gestured, he never raised his voice, he made others seem vulgar by contrast.

The festival passed without incident. Passover and the Latin Easter, followed a few days later by the Greek Easter, also passed, and the Yishuv began to breathe again. On the first of May, the day of workers' parades throughout the Western world, Jewish workers paraded in Tel Aviv, among them the small but vigorous Communist group called Mifleget Poalim Sozialistit, and known as MOPS. They handed out leaflets in Arabic calling for the overthrow of the British imperialists.

But the great majority of the Zionist workers resented the Communists and ousted them from the parade, sometimes forcibly. The sight of Jewish belligerency inflamed the Arabs, as if the brooding resentment that lay beneath the surface of Nebi Musa and Easter suddenly took fire. A small riot broke out. A tide of armed Arabs swarmed toward Immigration House, where defenseless men, women and children waited to enter the country. Thirteen were hacked to death with primitive weapons.

Miss Szold had been vacationing in Rehovoth, one of the old Rothschild colonies, a serene, well-ordered place just outside Jaffa and not far from Tel Aviv. Early on May Day she left for Jaffa, riding with Sophia, the American Zionist Mary Fels and a young Palestinian. During lunch in Jaffa they heard shots, but the men at the table assured her it was nothing, a display of authority, they said. The explanation failed to satisfy her. She felt a sudden, indescribable tension.

When lunch was over they waited for the auto that was to take them to Jerusalem, but it never came. Miss Szold decided to go to the Unit's hospital in Jaffa, first walking, then running, realizing as she ran that there was a war on. At the hospital she saw the yard packed with dead bodies on stretchers. A long line of wounded and dead were being carried into the hospital; the little building itself held eighteen wounded. The operating room was jammed with wounded waiting to be bandaged. She learned from the nurses that the massacre at Immigration House had triggered a wave of murderous rioting in Jaffa.

She made her way to the office and telephoned Jerusalem for hospital supplies and nurses and doctors, then with Sophia took charge of the crowds of relatives who descended on the place to search among the wounded and dead for their people. Body after body was brought in, and she heard there were hundreds more in the school nearby, at the French hospital in the city, in private homes. The next morning she telephoned Jerusalem again, this time for bread and eggs; there was nothing in the city to eat, and the wounded had somehow to be fed. The shops were tightly shuttered, Jews and Arabs alike paralyzed by terror. Everybody was armed with sticks bristling with nails. Among the wounded she had seen bullet wounds, knife wounds, wounds from clubs and iron utensils. She moved through the morning like a sleepwalker.

At noon Rubinow arrived with supplies, then Sophia and Miss Szold rode back with him through Tel Aviv toward Jerusalem. On the road they saw crowds of Arabs armed with clubs. Miss Szold learned later that "there had been murdering done in the Jewish houses between Jaffa and Mikveh Israel. In one of them the poet Brenner with the whole family whom he was visiting was hacked down . . . closer to Jerusalem, we came across a group of Arabs dancing to their own music. They seemed to be jeering at us."

Inside Jerusalem shopkeepers put up their shutters, white with fear. She begged them to open their stores again; it seemed to her their very fear was a suggestion to the Arabs who stood about on the streets in groups. But panic was everywhere, and the panic terrified her far more than the bloody sights in the Jaffa clinic. Panic was the acknowledgment of fear, the recognition that one was in danger, and she could not bear it. Her character was such that she could only suppress and deny her own fears and wanted everyone else to do the same.

She stalked into the offices of the Zionist Commission. She would tell them to organize a band of young men and "let them keep up the courage of the Jews in different parts of the city." But none of the heads of department seemed to be in the office. She went up to a young man—she felt calmer now and somewhat more reasonable—and began to talk to him. "I used some strong language about the Jews being chicken-hearted. I got my lesson. He asked me—he was a stranger to me—'Madam, how many pogroms have you been through?' Of course I said, none. Answer: 'I have been through twelve.' Do you understand that I was silenced?"

All that week there was news of outbreaks in Jewish villages. Self-defense groups were organized in Jerusalem, and friends urged Miss Szold and Miss Berger to move into the Hôtel de France, at the heart of the city, but they refused. Arab children in her neighborhood threw stones at her when she went by until the sheikh who lived next door went to see their parents. On the second morning after the Jaffa outrage, an Arab neighbor had come to her window with a bouquet of roses and murmured sadly, "Jaffa, Jaffa!"

Two and a half weeks went by before Miss Szold could bring herself to write an account of her experiences to her family. "I feel utterly perplexed; I feel soiled," she said. It was as if she had been made aware of some secret shame, perhaps the knowledge, felt now for the first time by some Zionist leaders, that they had been lulling themselves all along with a fantasy of Semitic brotherhood. Her sense of guilt and humiliation lingered for weeks, and throughout that period all Jewish newspapers were censored by the British and immigration stopped.

One month after the riots Sir Herbert made a speech. There would be certain limitations on immigration from now on, he said; only people with independent means or with a sure prospect of employment could come in. Privately he told Miss Szold that unless he had spoken and acted as he did, there would have been a massacre of every Jew in the country. She took his speech as a policy of cowardice. "There isn't one of us who would not rather fall in a general massacre than be saved by such methods. Of course, I admit that Sir Herbert cannot say for me that I would prefer to be killed to being saved—by him. But he could have resigned!"

Like the Yishuv, she felt Sir Herbert had been influenced by anti-Zionists among his advisers and hypnotized by Arab violence, the violence of ignorant people incited by agitators who were the hirelings of the Arab landowning class. The limits set on immigration were precisely what these landowners were after, a whittling away at the Balfour Declaration, surely the first of many.

But Miss Szold was her father's daughter. For her the Jews were at fault as well as the rich Arabs and indecisive British. Her feelings of guilt and humiliation subsided in time, and she was left with the certainty that the Jews had failed to create economic opportunities for Jew and Arab alike. They must reinspect their national aspirations, she wrote, and remove from them every possible admixture of injustice. Then they must seek out the best and wisest of the Arab leaders "to cure what is diseased in us and in them." It was a point of view strongly rooted in prophetic Judaism but one that would not endear her to the Yishuv.

20

In April 1921, Chaim Weizmann, who had given up his scientific career to head the international Zionist organization, made his first visit to America. Among those who accompanied him was Albert Einstein, then in the first flower of international fame. They reached New York Harbor on a Saturday, remaining aboard ship until after sunset. In the course of the day the Jews of New York set out on pilgrimage to meet them, walking by the tens of thousands to the docks from Manhattan, the Bronx and every section of Brooklyn. Evening approached, the Sabbath ended and thousands more took off in wagons, trucks, carts and private cars flying the Zionist flag. Every car horn blared its greeting in a kind of joyful defiance; on that day New York was a Jewish city, intoxicated by the presence of the man who had won a homeland for the Jews.

Weizmann came to America in order to launch a Palestine Foundation Fund, the Keren Hayesod, which would raise $100 million for colonizing work in the Holy Land. Zionists and non-Zionists alike would be asked to contribute to it, some in outright donations, others as investors. The Brandeis people welcomed him most reluctantly. They saw Weizmann's presence in America as an insult, an attempt to go over the heads of American Zionist leaders in their own territory. The insult was all the more stinging because Weizmann was personally irresistible even to those who disagreed with him.

To Brandeis the Keren Hayesod was repugnant, financially irresponsible and morally debilitating. To pour money into the kibbutzim, as Weizmann proposed, would be to create a new form of Halukah. The Americanized leadership of the ZOA looked on the communal settlements as chancy experiments. They had done nothing so far but eat up money, and the conviction of the east Europeans that one day the kibbutzim would be self-sufficient seemed a socialist dream.

There were other sources of disagreement that boiled down to disputes over the uses of money and signified something far larger than money: the difference between the methodical American Zionism of Louis Brandeis and the organic Zionism of people born with it in their blood. The origins of east European Zionism were not rational any more than love is rational, or loyalty, or the bonds that tie a family together.

Since his return from the Jahreskonferenz in London, Brandeis had refused to attend Zionist meetings, although his followers implored him to speak, to fight, to explain his position. Profoundly certain that he was right, he saw no reason to fight for his beliefs, and the Europeans came and went while Brandeis refused to meet with them publicly or privately.

The staff workers and rank and file of the ZOA, Europeans all, began to wonder about him. They had not followed Brandeis because they were entirely captivated by his doctrine of small-scale capitalism or the separate destiny of American Zionism but because Brandeis, Mack and Frankfurter were eminent men, success stories in the New World that the recent immigrants hoped to emulate. Now there was a stirring and ferment in the wake of Weizmann's visit. The electrifying awareness that a Russian Jew arriving in America on official Jewish business had been received by President Harding and welcomed by important Americans, as a statesman is welcomed, forced them to look with fresh eyes at the differences between Weizmann and Brandeis. If the American Jew was a worldly success, so it seemed was the Russian. Moreover, Weizmann had given up science in order to devote his life to Zionism, but Brandeis refused to give up the Supreme Court bench, as he would have had to do if he were to take an active role in international Zionism; he preferred instead to work behind the scenes through Julian Mack and other lieutenants. Small wonder that Weizmann's eloquent presence suggested there might be something half baked about the Zionism of the American leaders.

As a result staff workers and rank and file came to the annual convention of the ZOA in Cleveland that June with a new assertiveness. At the opening of the convention wild applause greeted every speech in Yiddish, but those in English were received with chilling silence.

The women of Hadassah watched and waited. As political tacticians they were the merest innocents, hardly aware of Robert's Rules of Order, but they were tenacious innocents who felt a stirring and ferment of their own. Their organization had been merged with the ZOA in 1918 and nearly extinguished, but in the intervening years they had struggled back, and now Hadassah leaders hoped to see them move toward semiautonomy. Most of the Hadassah leadership were Brandeisists so loyal that Weizmann's arrival had triggered angry disputes about the propriety of sending him even a formal greeting.

In Jerusalem, Miss Szold followed the news of Weizmann's visit with avid attention. Torn between the two factions, each of which believed her loyalties belonged to it, she spent a small fortune on cables begging for more information, weighing the future of the Medical Unit—it would be safe only in businesslike American hands—against her heartfelt conviction that the Zionist movement must be one and indivisible, the Weizmann view. It was the Brandeis side she ultimately chose.

But the Weizmannites and their Keren Hayesod won overwhelmingly at the Cleveland convention, striking a body blow at Hadassah leaders, for the Weizmann faction would surely transfer control of their precious projects, the Unit and the nurses' school, to the Zionist Commission. And in those hands they would shrivel and die.

There was a more immediate result. No sooner was the convention over than Lipsky turned on Hadassah's board, accusing them of disloyalty. Their desks and files were removed from the office, which they were not allowed to use henceforth, and office supplies and stationery were refused them. Much of the ZOA supported Lipsky in this vendetta. They had watched the birth and growth of Hadassah with dismay, their success being the most dismaying spectacle of all. Moreover, the Lipskyites feared the lingering presence of the Brandeis party within the ZOA, and Hadassah's leaders were precisely that.

The trick would be getting rid of the leaders while holding on to Hadassah members at large, more than 10,000 of the ZOA's total 30,000. Lipsky therefore reached out to Miss Szold. He sent her a cable denouncing Hadassah's officers for their failure to support Keren Hayesod. The officers cabled her too, imploring her to come home and make peace, to protect Hadassah, placate Lipsky and assure the life of the Medical Unit. Brandeis cabled Miss Szold to stay put, and she did.

She would stay put the entire summer as well, even though the Unit physicians urged her to go to a meeting of the world organization at Carlsbad, Germany. They wanted her to fight for the Unit, but she could not bear the thought of losing and being publicly pitied: "I should be a dear little old lady, so devoted! so idealistic! come to plead for a cause to which she has devoted so many years. . . . Poor dear! it's a shame, they'd say, but . . . she must be swept aside. . . . Why should I go to Carlsbad and plead and arouse pity of myself and be a victim to adorn the triumphal chariots of the victors?"

In the course of that autumn the Lipsky men finally came to grips with the problem of Hadassah's leaders, whom they could not live with and could not live without. A compromise was arranged, uneasy, fragile but face-saving for the men and for the leaders of Hadassah a distinct triumph. They would remain with the ZOA. For this they extracted the following price: American support and American control of the medical work would continue; Hadassah was guaranteed their status as sole agency for Zionist work among American women, and for the first time would have direct representation at the World Zionist Congress. The innocents had taken their first important step toward political maturity. And at Carlsbad the world organization grudgingly agreed to continue the Unit's work for one more year. After that some bourgeois philanthropy had better take it over, they said, because that was what it was, a charity, the proper occupation of well-meaning middle-class American women with time on their hands.

Three years earlier the Nurses' Training School had been dedicated on Balfour Day, the second of November. Since then the women of Hadassah had followed every aspect of its development with the bemused pride of those who can scarcely believe what they have accomplished. Was there really a nursing school in the Holy Land, were the classes really held in Hebrew, and was it all their doing? It was real and they had done it, those women who went to evening meetings in one another's living rooms when the children were in bed, bringing their "little bits of things," the sewing, the reports, the stereopticon slides, everything the men despised. Now the first class of the nursing school was ready to graduate, and ceremonies would be held on November 2, 1921.

Invitations in Hebrew and English were sent out by messenger. Programs were prepared, designating the language of each address, whether in Hebrew— Miss Szold and Lady Samuel would speak in Hebrew—or English—Colonel George Heron, head of the British health department, would be one of the English speakers. But there were rumors of an impending Arab attack, and the Zionist Executive, the former Zionist Commission, asked Miss Szold to delay for a week. She did so. On Balfour Day a riot erupted in the Old City; five Jews were killed, twenty wounded. Governor Storrs and his police were ineffectual or too late or both. Two days later a massive funeral procession left the Rothschild Hospital, more than a thousand people marching in silence behind stretchers on which the bodies of the five were draped in blue-and-white prayer shawls. A month of mourning was declared.

It was Miss Szold's second exposure to violence and the second time her pacifist faith had been shaken. She spoke with admiration of the Jewish self-defense forces and their stockpiling of bombs: "A bomb is safer than constantly carrying firearms and knives concealed. Bombs are not carried around; they are kept at strategic points." It seemed clear that the Jews must rely on themselves, since the British did not protect them.

The graduation was now postponed for the entire month of mourning. A pall of depression hung over the city, and there seemed no point in fixing a date for the ceremonies; all the bloom had been rubbed off. At last December 7 was decided on. They would use the new nurses' home, profusely decorated with flowers. Miss Szold would preside. Lady Samuel would hand out diplomas.

The audience was a distinguished one composed largely of British officials and Zionist leadership, some of whom were supposed to sit on the platform with the speakers, the entire Palestine Zionist Executive among them. But as audience, nurses and speakers assembled, Miss Szold realized that no one had arrived from the Zionist Executive except Dr. Eder, who had been asked to speak toward the end of the ceremony. The seats put aside on the platform for Ussishkin and the others stood glaringly empty.

The solemn prayers, the speeches, the music, the parade of nurses unrolled in their predetermined order, and the seats on the platform remained empty. As the moment for Dr. Eder's address approached a note was handed to Miss Szold, written on the back of a card of admission. It was from a member of the audience, none other than that pioneer of modern Hebrew, Eliezer Ben Yehuda, who begged Miss Szold "not to profane the sanctity of the occasion by allowing Jews to speak in a language not Hebrew."

Then Dr. Eder stood up, and Ben Yehuda and his wife ostentatiously left the hall.

When the last speech was over and most of the audience gone, Miss Szold covered her face with her hands and wept. She forgave Ben Yehuda. He was an old man whose health had been broken by his fanatic dedication to the Hebrew language. But the Zionist Executive? They had known for an entire month that Eder would speak in English, yet they had waited until the day itself to administer this affront, this cruel public humiliation. She would not tell Hadassah; how could she possibly spoil their picture of the dream fulfilled? But she told her sisters at length and in scorching detail.

Even the nurses helped mar the triumph of their own graduation by complaining about the salaries of the jobs that had been found for them, which they wanted to equal those of American graduate nurses with ten or twelve years' experience. They had been overwhelmed with kindness and attention—a dinner party, a reception, individual gifts for each of them, telegrams of congratulation from Europe and America—yet "up to this moment not one—do you understand? *not one*—has come to me and said a single word of recognition of trouble taken, or of appreciation of the beauty of the celebration."

But it was done, accomplished; Hadassah and the Yishuv together had created twenty-two trained nurses. Several graduate courses were initiated almost immediately in midwifery, operating-theater nursing, public health. Hadassah women in America began collecting money for the translation and publication of the first Hebrew text on nursing. Equally important, the professional training of Jewish women had begun in the Holy Land.

A Jahreskonferenz was scheduled for Carlsbad in August 1922. Hadassah cabled Miss Szold asking her to go as one of the two delegates they were now entitled to. The conference was to take place under circumstances both auspicious and flawed: the Jewish homeland had just received the final, formal seal of approval of the League of Nations, yet the precise wording employed, the conditions that prompted that wording, left a bitter taste in the mouth.

Churchill's visit to Jerusalem the year before had culminated in a White Paper that reaffirmed the Balfour Declaration, stating that the Jews were in the Holy Land by right and not on sufferance. But the national home was said to be *in* Palestine, the implication being that it did not consist of the whole of Palestine but rather a section. Perhaps a very small section. Perhaps they might be expected to share sovereignty of the whole with the Arabs, or they might have to live forever under British rule.

Moreover, "immigration will not exceed the economic capacity of the country to absorb new arrivals." The emergency measures that followed the Jaffa riots were thus carved into law. Appended to the Mandate, the Churchill White Paper was then ratified by the League at the second San Remo conference, at which the British Mandate for Palestine was formally confirmed. This White Paper remained the basis of government in Palestine for the next eighteen years.

Weizmann and the Zionist Executive accepted it only with bitter reluctance and under the most intense pressure from the Colonial Office. Jews and Arabs alike found it unwelcome, the Jews because they had never anticipated a permanent limit on immigration, the Arabs because their hopes for an independent Arab state in Palestine were permanently crushed. And Miss Szold felt that the White Paper had interpreted the Balfour Declaration into nonexistence; she had just driven to Haifa, five and a half hours "through an empty, deserted country. What harm to the Arabs if the Jews develop it?"

She went to Carlsbad with mixed feelings, unsure of what she was to do there: Plead for more money when there was less and less? Plead for the medical work in particular, when education, colonization and immigration cried out for money? Louis Lipsky and several others from America would be at Carlsbad, and she expected them to upbraid her for her "defection" to the Mack-Brandeis group. "I am not alarmed at the encounter," she assured her sisters.

She found Carlsbad to be a small and elegant town where those who could afford it came to take the waters and enjoy the cafes, the promenades, the sedate entertainments and the exquisite countryside. There was silken grass, soft moss, tumbling streams and mountains shaded by dense forests—everything she had missed in Palestine. The delegates themselves were a source of fascination at this, her first international Zionist conference, presided over by a portrait of Theodor Herzl eight or nine feet high, brooding and visionary in his impeccable evening clothes.

In the years since the first congress called by Herzl, the Zionists had won their homeland. What they had not won was the support of world-wide Jewry; out of 12.5 million Jews, only 100,000 belonged to the Zionist organization. Lacking mass support, they lacked the support of the rich as well. Few men of great wealth contributed to Zionism, and so far Keren Hayesod had not drawn much from the non-Zionists. Already it seemed that Weizmann's plan to raise $100 million in five years was a fantasy. After two collection seasons only $2 million had been gathered in. The trend Miss Szold had seen in the summer of 1920—diminishing financial support of Palestine from America as well as from impoverished Europe—had not been reversed.

Now, in Carlsbad, her head was full of the misery of the Yishuv, where children plundered garbage pails and bubonic plague swept through Jaffa. Yet the congress was compelled to cut their medical budget by one quarter, leaving less than $250,000 for all the health needs of Jewish Palestine in the forthcoming year.

Hadassah begged her to return to America and run the organization. Their board was exhausted by continued struggles with Lipsky, which not only sapped their strength but damaged collections, for the ZOA still seemed determined to sabotage Hadassah. If all else failed the ZOA might even create a rival women's organization.

Yet Miss Szold was afraid to return. Throughout the spring Rubinow had talked about nothing but his desire to resign. Unless he meant to spend the rest of his life in Palestine, which he did not, it was time for him to make a place for himself in America. He had never trained anyone to succeed him. If he left there would be no one to lead the Unit but Miss Szold.

She thought over both possibilities, medical work in Jerusalem, peace making and fund raising in America, while she headed for Vienna to visit her maternal relatives, the Schaars. She had met them for the first time when she was twenty-one, traveling with Papa; she had visited them again in 1909 on her way to Palestine with Sophie. Would they find her changed? "I warn you there are pathetic little puckers all around my lips, and my hearing is impaired, and I think a lot of my comfort, and my hair is whiter than it was—but I don't *feel* older."

Between visits she ran from shop to shop, for Vienna was said to be full of "things," and she had not seen fashionable things for two and a half years, had not even seen shoelaces. She needed everything, and Vienna was known as a bargain-hunter's paradise. Miss Szold was not cut out for bargain hunting, however. She thought it was a contemptible activity. "I feel mean, mean," she wrote. "In Vienna I was a mighty shopper before the Lord—may the Lord forgive me."

Still undecided about whether to return to Palestine or go on to America, she was assaulted by cables from Rubinow saying he had no money to pay the doctors and nurses. He urged her to go to Paris and put the case of the Unit before Baron Edmond de Rothschild. Expecting nothing, she went to Paris.

There she walked down a narrow, crowded street lined with antique shops, clothing shops, hairdressers, until she came without warning to the gates of the baron's residence. Past the gates she found princely gardens. Within doors, surrounded by art treasures, was the seventy-seven-year-old baron himself, slender and deaf and exquisitely dressed, his heavy-lidded eyes and skeptical eyebrows suggesting an Edwardian roué.

Miss Szold was afraid of feeling like a supplicant, but his manners were so gracious, so flattering when the work of the Unit was discussed, that she began to relax and observe her surroundings. There were two paintings standing on easels in the salon, and she imagined the baron waving his hand toward one and saying, "There is a little thing of the school of Leonardo . . . take it," and the Unit's fortune would be made.

But the baron did not wave. Behind the courtly manner was a certain peremptoriness, an almost brutal consciousness of his vast powers, of which he may have been somewhat afraid. He launched into an attack on American Jewry in general and the Zionists in particular; they did not even support the little they started, he said. He told her to go to America and tell the rich Yahudim, the Guggenheims and Blumenthals and Warburgs, their duty. "My usual ability to see both sides made me a poor advocate," Miss Szold noted. Perhaps it was impertinent to ask any more of a man who had been working steadily and logically for Zionism for more than forty years.

She went back to her lodgings knowing she had failed as a *schnorrer*, a beggar. She had a miserable cold; she wrapped a wet cloth around her throat, read French novels, which she found "nasty," had a supper of roasted chestnuts and brioches in her room and washed her handkerchiefs. The cables from Rubinow continued, telling her to hurry back to Palestine since "he saw no reason why he should stay to suffer the pain and ignominy of deconstruction."

Hadassah collections were declining and London remittances uncertain, said his next cable; he could not carry responsibility alone much longer. Miss Szold abandoned the idea of America and returned to Jerusalem.

There she found the Unit essentially bankrupt. The process of dismantling had begun—the Tiberias hospital closed down, the Jaffa hospital reduced, a clinic in the Old City shut, all salaries cut by 5 to 10 percent, ninety-three employees discharged—and it was not nearly enough. She looked about her and saw that all of Palestine was suffering. If her doctors and nurses were unpaid, so were the schoolteachers; they had gone unpaid for five months, and their salaries were far smaller than the medical staff's. Settlers in the new colonies lived for months at a time on raw tomatoes. Important colonization work was interrupted. Hardly a day went by without one of the schoolchildren fainting from hunger.

But Miss Szold had not come to Palestine to run the entire enterprise; she had come to help with the medical work, the specific task of Hadassah in America. And in spite of the agreement reached by the ZOA and Hadassah in autumn 1921, Hadassah's collections were being hampered by the ZOA, Hadassah's very existence threatened by them.

She had read about a grand rally held in the spring at the Hotel Pennsylvania in New York, with Emma Gottheil presiding as chairman of a women's committee of Keren Hayesod. Jabotinsky and Manya Shochat were speakers. Mrs. Gottheil's sister Eva Leon delivered lectures at the slightest provocation about the beginnings of Hadassah, its two district nurses sent, she said, through her own efforts and those of her friends; an unspoken resentment of Hadassah's claims for priority in the medical work suffused all her recollections.

A new women's organization, to be controlled by Lipsky and Keren Hayesod, was in the air. Miss Szold smelled it and shivered. When a commission of inspection arrived from the Joint she felt "the harpies gather."

Now she sat down and wrote a long letter to Emma Gottheil, accusing her in four and a half pages of single-spaced typing of starting a rival organization to Hadassah. Hadassah was supposed to be the only women's Zionist group in America, yet Mrs. Gottheil's committee had taken measures to adopt a constitution and establish dues lower than Hadassah's.

Mrs. Gottheil's reply was ten pages long. She opened with the assurance that Miss Szold was after all in a very disturbed state of mind, a prey to many misapprehensions. She unfolded past history. Miss Szold and her supporters had run Hadassah and its medical projects like their own personal empire from the start, she said, refusing to acknowledge the contributions of others. What the long tirade amounted to was that Hadassah must melt into the American Zionist organization, raise money for Keren Hayesod like everyone else, and surrender their medical projects to the world movement. The Yishuv's new health department would take over the hospitals and clinics, for who knew better than this Jewish health department seated in Jerusalem what the health needs of Jewish Palestine were? Certainly not the officers of Hadassah who lived in New York.

Miss Szold read it and thought about it and did not reply, for there was just enough truth in Mrs. Gottheil's point of view to make her very uncomfortable. Suppose Hadassah submitted, collected funds for Keren Hayesod and gave up the medical work? Quite aside from the matter of the Unit's survival was the matter of Hadassah's survival, and Miss Szold's feelings about Hadassah were indeed proprietary. The organization was her child, the Unit their joint "pride and boast," as Mrs. Gottheil put it, but she was also extremely perceptive about the purpose of Hadassah.

American Jewry needed the Yishuv. The whole of American Jewry was not Miss Szold's immediate concern; the needs of American Jewish women were. She believed Hadassah suited those needs. They had never ceased to be an assemblage of study circles; Zionism was studied, Judaism, Jewish culture, history, current events, literature and Hebrew. For those women who were cut off from organized intellectual life this was important. Far more important was the work Hadassah did in America, the work of tying Jewish women together, uniting rich and poor, German and Russian, college-trained social worker and the peddler's wife. And it was their work for Jewish Palestine that made this possible. The work was real, organic, creative, uniquely theirs.

Here was the paradox, the contradiction that Emma Gottheil's letter put so sharply before her: the Yishuv must manage its own affairs according to Palestinian realities that no American mind could gauge from America. Yet American women would lose their Jewish identity unless they were bound to the Yishuv by more than fund raising, against the will of the Yishuv and perhaps to its detriment. For if the affairs of the Yishuv were to be run by well-meaning women in America, how would it ever grow up?

These were Miss Szold's ambiguities, but they were not Hadassah's. The leaders were absolutely clear in their intention to continue running the medical affairs of the Yishuv so long as they decently could. In time, her point of view and theirs would collide. She had created in Hadassah a daughter with a craving for independence, and her future relations with the daughter were to be troubled by this same paradox, the contradiction between Hadassah's needs and that of the Yishuv to work out its destiny alone.

In the meanwhile she tried to keep up the women's courage. Her letters to the Hadassah newspaper told them with great pride that of 1,000 Jewish babies born each year in Jerusalem, 500 were delivered at home by Hadassah-trained midwives; 350 were born in the obstetrics ward of the Hadassah hospital. Hundreds of mothers brought their babies to the two infant welfare stations, and scores of them bought milk from Tipat Halav, the pasteurized milk station. Those who could not come to the milk station in the Old City went to the hospital, where some of the same supply arrived each day by donkey in wooden boxes fitted with bottle trays, each bottle packed in ice and labeled for the baby for whom it was intended. Intertwined with the work in infant care was a voluntary organization, the Histadrut Nashim Ibriot, the Society of Jewish Women. Miss Szold had nudged and prodded it into existence in the spring of 1920. In the course of its existence the Nashim Ibriot had gathered statistics on 600 mothers; now she was able to tell Hadassah members that in a number of instances a baby born under the guidance of the society was a woman's first living baby after ten, sometimes twelve, miscarriages or stillbirths.

This was the news that made the rounds of the Hadassah circles in their monthly bulletin—news of an undertaking they had paid for and supervised, one that was changing the face of Jewish Palestine by scratching away in the most fundamental manner at the crust of Middle Eastern filth and ignorance.

Then Rubinow left. His leave-taking was a miserable affair, for some of the physicians with whom he had worked for three and a half years actually refused to say goodby. He was to build a distinguished career in American social services and become known as the father of the social security system, a prolific author and friend of Franklin Delano Roosevelt. But Miss Szold was alone now at the head of a dying enterprise, lacking even the money to bury it. The Joint offered to increase their support by one quarter if they could assume complete control of the Palestine work; she called it a "vile proposition" and refused.

During that miserable winter two people sustained her. One was Abraham Berkstein, a boy of thirteen whom Sophia took from the orphanage she supervised to live in their home. Sophia did all the work connected with the boy; Miss Szold had all the enjoyment. Her letters referred to him as a dear little chap, delightful in manner and keenly intelligent: "I love him. My one fear is that his mother will come from Poland and claim him. She writes heartrending letters to him in vivid Yiddish, which I must spell out to her boy, who sobs. . . . He hasn't seen his mother for seven years."

The other was her old friend Judah Magnes, who came with his family in time for Miss Szold's sixty-second birthday; Sophia, Dr. and Mrs. Magnes and Miss Szold celebrated with a ten-mile walk.

Magnes intended to settle in Palestine. He was forty-five and as boyish as ever, with the same sense of youthful mischief Miss Szold had always found so endearing. But he was a complex person; handsome, charming, impulsive, he had nevertheless a certain air of autocratic assurance. He was not what the Yishuv expected in a rabbi, nor had he come to be a rabbi. Indeed he was not sure why he had come. He had left the Reform rabbinate in America because he had been drawn toward Orthodoxy and Zionism; but as the head of an important Conservative synagogue he had still felt dissatisfied. An outspoken pacifist during the war, eventually he had made his position in New York untenable. Because he was financially independent he was free to follow his conscience, so he left the rabbinate and came to Palestine, bringing a gnawing discontent. "I seem to sow, sometimes to sow well, but seldom to reap. I at least have the excitement of the combat."

That was his great love, the combat, the rousing oratory in which he excelled, the unpopular cause. When the unpopular cause succeeded it lost its charm for him. In Palestine, Magnes was to find another cause, that of Arab-Jewish rapprochement, in which Miss Szold would join him. He fought for it with sincerity, persistence, a stunning lack of tact and absolute naïveté. Even the Arabs came to see him as an earnest naïf, too pure for political realities, and this too was what Miss Szold loved in him.

The Magneses settled into an Arab house a few minutes' walk across a field from the home of Miss Szold and Sophia, and there was an active coming and going between the two houses. Every morning Magnes presented himself at the office in the Hôtel de France to help Miss Szold with affairs of the Unit. He had a practical turn of mind and a command of figures and knew the Joint inside out. They sat in the cold room and counted and calculated and faced together the creditors who pounded on the door demanding payment for drugs, for groceries. "I know the agony of an honest bankrupt," Miss Szold wrote to her sisters. "I feel like a hunted animal!" She had called herself contemptible in Vienna when she searched for bargains; now she was forced to refuse honest men who demanded what was theirs by right.

One day a gift of $20,000 came from Nathan Straus. She was to spend the money as she saw fit, and of course she would spend it on the Unit. It looked as if the Joint would continue their support after all. Ussishkin decided to leave the Executive and was replaced by the British Colonel Frederick Kisch. So the fortunes of the Unit were, if not looking up, at least possible to contemplate.

But in April of 1923 Miss Szold got a cable with the news that her sister Rachel was seriously, perhaps mortally, ill. Leaving the Unit in the hands of Dr. Magnes, she sailed for home.

V

JERUSALEM:
MISS SZOLD CROSSES
THE STREET

21

Three years passed. During much of that time Miss Szold kept an apartment in the Hotel Alexandria, on West 103rd Street in Manhattan, from which she was ready at a moment's notice to run to Rachel in Wisconsin, to Bertha in Baltimore, even to Palestine; at Hadassah's insistence she had made three voyages there and back since her return to America in 1923. She was now sixty-six years old. She looked and felt her age, yet the extraordinary physical endurance, the ability to work day after day after day on six hours' sleep, remained. It never failed to amaze her. "I don't understand what keeps my machinery oiled," she told Bertha. "I ought to be dead according to all the rules of the game."

Her teeth troubled her; so did her temper. But at an age when people begin to look backward she looked across the seas with hungry eyes into the homes and hospitals and growing factories of Jewish Palestine. She wanted everything for them.

This aunt with a foot in two worlds was a perplexing figure to her nephews and nieces. Bertha's daughter Sara remembered her during those years as a brisk, energetic, quick-walking little woman who adored and frightened them. "I know she loved us very dearly. . . . When she came to our house she would get so emotional, there were times when she could hardly eat her supper." Jastrow Levin remembered his mother and his aunt at the piano playing duets; at intervals the two women would look at each other and giggle, then laugh, then drop their hands in their laps, helpless with laughter. Jastrow also remembered his aunt's telling him not to dirty the towels, not to scuff his shoes against the walls. She never played with him; as far back as the children could remember none of them had ever played with their Aunt Henrietta.

The family of Zip and Robert Szold, Henrietta's distant cousins, had much the same reaction. As Zip put it, "I wanted my children to know Henrietta. I'd bring them to her apartment for lunch one Sunday or another. How did they take it? They stood it. They found her forbidding—she tried not to be. She made a serious effort to talk to my children on their level; they recognized it as an effort."

The family was infinitely precious to her, and during the past three years they had made no secret of how sorely she was needed. There were times when she was torn between two death beds, Rachel apparently dying of a brain tumor while Bertha's husband, Louis, suffered a sudden onset of kidney disease from which it was certain he could not recover. Rachel's husband, Joe, implored Henrietta to come back to Wisconsin, where she had nursed Rachel for months, but she dared not desert the Levins, and she lived with the fear that whatever choice she made would be the wrong one.

Now Louis Levin was dead, leaving Bertha with little money and five children. As for Rachel, the doctors claimed she had recovered, but Henrietta refused to believe it. She didn't like the way her sister looked, listless and lifeless and too heavy. Something in that once-beautiful face told her Rachel would die within months.

But in December of 1925 Hadassah asked her to go back again to Palestine to initiate the new director of the Hadassah Medical Organization (HMO), as the Medical Unit was now called. Miss Szold had originally left it in the hands of Dr. Magnes; an American physician had succeeded him but quit before a year was up. A Palestinian had filled in for a time, but his health was poor. Now Hadassah's board believed they had found someone who would stay. From all accounts, especially Alice Seligsberg's, Dr. E. M. Bluestone was a paragon, thirty-four years old, a Hebrew speaker and the son of a fervent Zionist Miss Szold had known for years.

Summoned to her apartment for an interview on December 1, Bluestone expected to meet a kindly and academic spinster with a romantic past, for he was a Columbia graduate familiar with the Ginzberg story. No doubt she would be a good deal like her friend Miss Seligsberg. They might even reminisce about his father or mutual friends in the seminary circle.

But his first impression was disappointing. Miss Szold had a lapful of darning, and while they spoke she darned, glancing up at him at intervals stolen from her work, which was apparently more important than he was. There was a chill about the woman, he thought. She was like an old-fashioned radio that took forever to warm up. There were no gentle reminiscences, no gossip about old friends. Instead she conducted a running quiz, examining him in Hebrew, inquiring closely about his training, his beliefs, his hopes and his marriage. He felt secure about his Hebrew and equally secure on the subject of his wife, who was loyal, compliant and ready to follow him to the ends of the earth.

His views about modern medicine, preventive and sanitary work, public health and medical insurance were similar to Miss Szold's. Yet he was as uncomfortable at the end of the visit as he had been at the start. Why had she refused to give him her full attention? It was a trivial matter, the business of the darning, but Bluestone found himself returning to it again and again in later years. He also wondered again and again why so much was left out of that initial interview and of all the discussions between himself and Hadassah that preceded his going to Palestine.

They told him nothing about Rubinow's ordeal at the hands of the Zionist Executive, nothing about the Yishuv's profound antagonism for America and all its works. Nor was he told about the growing power of Labor Zionism.

Yet the Histadrut, the country-wide labor union founded in 1920, would become in time the most powerful nongovernmental force in Palestine, and even by the mid-twenties the scope and nature of its undertakings pervaded the life of the Yishuv. In order to provide work for the Jewish workingman, Histadrut went into business, into agriculture, building, fishing, retailing. It built cooperative stores for its members, also banks, a newspaper and medical clinics run by Kupat Holim, the workers' sick fund. Socially the workingmen were the aristocrats of the Yishuv, whether they labored on kibbutz or in Histadrut-owned factories. Politically their foremost articles of faith were rapid, large-scale immigration and a society based on social justice. For the middle class, as for bourgeois America, they had mostly contempt.

But Bluestone knew nothing about any of this. The women of Hadassah told him only that he would run an American hospital with American money for the benefit of the Jews of Palestine. He would be responsible directly to the 20,000 women of Hadassah, the board and Miss Szold. If they said nothing more, it was because they were afraid of losing him.

Bluestone was in many ways uniquely suited to the post. He had worked for five years as assistant director of Mount Sinai Hospital in New York, having turned his back on private practice. He had large ideas and great energy and the character of a leader. His manner was severe, perhaps even rigid, sometimes actually high-handed, but he was also generous, warm-hearted and sensitive. Apparently Miss Szold was as impressed by Bluestone as the others were, and they agreed that he would leave with his wife in early spring, and Miss Szold would go with them.

It was no easy matter, this picking up and going off to Palestine again. She felt it was insane to leave Rachel, that she was condemning herself to learn about Rachel's death from a distance of 7,000 miles. But she had a ferocious sense of duty, and Hadassah was her duty. Measuring one against the other, the dying sister and the hospital across the seas, she told herself there was no way to decide. Merely having to decide was a form of torture.

Certainly she had not been comfortable in America the past three years, even apart from the family's tragedies. Hadassah and Keren Hayesod were at each other's throats half the time, and it was always Miss Szold who was called on to make peace. She hated Zionist infighting just as she hated politics. Someone once said of Miss Szold, "You know, politically she was at home in any man's bed," meaning she never knew or cared what a person's politics were. It was true. She considered politics a ridiculous business and a distraction from real work. Weizmann repeatedly asked her to join the "government," the Zionist Executive, and she repeatedly refused because of her dislike of politics.

Moreover Hadassah itself changed. The breathless insecurity of the early years, when it was possible to speak of equipping a rescue ship with the savings from trolley fares, had given way to bourgeois prosperity. There were elegant fashion shows and luncheons through which Miss Szold sat like a lump, a showpiece, uncomfortable about her clothing and dreading the moment when speeches began and she would have to exude a vague sort of hot air known as inspiration.

In Palestine there was pioneering, the sense of creation. Even the Arab question was wholly fascinating to her. "There is above all the Jewish people itself—a wonderful people and a nasty people." So she returned to Palestine, not with Dr. Bluestone, but a few days afterward, eating her heart out about Rachel every inch of the way.

What would she see when she got there? Change was the only constant in Palestine. Her last visit had shown her a country bustling with vitality and thousands of immigrants pouring in, mostly from Poland. The Jewish population had risen to 121,000 out of some 800,000. The Hebrew University in Jerusalem was officially open, with Dr. Magnes as its first president. In Government House, Sir Herbert Samuel, unmourned by the Yishuv, who never forgave what was considered his appeasement of the Arabs, had been replaced by an elderly soldier, Field Marshal Lord Plumer. The Yishuv expected little of Plumer, an ultra-British conservative, no intellectual and most unimpressive in appearance; at sixty-eight he had surely come to the Holy Land for a two-year tour of duty in exotic surroundings to be followed by an honorable retirement. One Zionist newspaper dismissed him as a "God-fearing, churchgoing, perfect old gentleman."

Within weeks of her arrival Miss Szold set off with Dr. Bluestone for Tel Aviv in an open auto, clanking and groaning on the road that snaked its way down the Judean hills. From time to time she called a halt when a particular flower or weed caught her eye. Climbing down, plucking the flower, bringing it back to the car, she never failed to inform Dr. Bluestone of its Latin name.

He had little sympathy with these interruptions; he felt she was being didactic.

It was an uncomfortable trip for him altogether. Miss Szold's conversation was impersonal and stiff, and he found it a chore to talk to her, a strain to sit beside her in uneasy silence. Her bearing puzzled him. She struck him as a person who took a tragic view of life, who wanted others to know she bore her great burdens meekly and humbly, but so far as he could tell the burdens were self-imposed.

And why was a woman who chose to dedicate her life to the charitable care of the sick so emotionally flat, so cold? Years later a friend of hers suggested that Miss Szold had been awed by him, but he could not agree. How could anyone be awed by him? His Yemenite orderly was not awed by him, and Miss Szold was a person of importance, a woman who would one day have her place in history. She was cold, he decided, because she had been born that way.

One of the reasons for the trip to Tel Aviv was to inspect the hospital, a miserable affair housed in five separate makeshift buildings. But before they reached the hospital they stopped on the outskirts of the town and walked toward a series of encampments where thousands of new immigrants lived in primitive huts on the bare fields. Because these fields were used for their sewage and garbage disposal they were a massive breeding ground for typhoid.

As the Americans drew nearer they saw the people themselves, young men and women and many little children. No one seemed to have any occupation, although there were garden plots in front of most of the huts, where vegetables were planted. Inside one of the huts Miss Szold caught sight of flies swarming around a single open toilet. How often was it cleaned? Rarely, from its appearance, and just as rarely disinfected. She was told it served 150 families.

A group of women who stood about in the mud street went up to Miss Szold and Bluestone and took them to a one-room hut occupied by a woman in bed and her husband, who paced the floor with a baby of five months in his arms. What seemed to be millions of flies encrusted the ceiling and walls. They learned the woman had had typhoid for eight days.

Bluestone told the woman there was not a single vacant bed in the Tel Aviv hospital, but he promised to vacate one the next morning; in an aside to Miss Szold, he confessed that he could only secure the bed by dismissing another typhoid victim whose condition was somewhat improved, though once at large, she would be a danger to all who surrounded her. But the husband and neighbors were not satisfied. They demanded to know what would become of the baby when the mother was taken to the hospital. Bluestone looked helpless and hopeless.

If the journey to Tel Aviv had been stiff and uncomfortable, the journey back was grim. Everything Miss Szold had heard since her return to Jerusalem was confirmed by the sordidness of the hut settlements. The boom of 1925 was a bubble; nothing was left of it but broken hopes and deserted buildings in the towns. Unemployment, hunger and disease stalked the country, and typhoid would be epidemic within weeks.

Both Bluestone and Miss Szold were weighed down by the peculiarly American guilt that writhes before the sight of squalor and human suffering. But it was especially painful for Miss Szold, who had been an active Zionist for more than a quarter century. She believed in the Jewish homeland with all her heart. Certainly the Jewish homeland must be peopled by Jews; certainly she wanted to see their number increase. But the national home was an insecure and volatile enterprise, and some of the Jews who came there faced more serious dangers than those they left behind. To many Zionists this was a price they were more than willing to pay, but Miss Szold was not so single-minded. All her life she had been troubled by a mind that saw the many-sidedness of things, and again and again in the years that followed she would blame herself for the dangers to which, as a working Zionist, she exposed others by bringing them to Palestine.

Nothing much had been done for the thousands of newcomers; little was being done for them even now. For Jewish Palestine was on the brink of depression, with faith in the Zionist venture approaching the lowest ebb since the Balfour Declaration.

As for Dr. Bluestone, she felt he already regretted having come.

At the Hôtel de France the director's office was warmed by a potbellied stove into which Yussef, the Yemenite orderly, shoved crumpled newspaper, bits of wood and a few chunks of hard coal. Then he poured a quart bottle of kerosene on the whole and lit a match to it. Bluestone gasped. Suppose the building caught fire? Yussef told him there had never been a fire in Jerusalem, and Bluestone subsided. In that city of golden stone it was certainly true.

His perception of life in Jersualem was that everything there contradicted the laws of the rest of the world.

The Yishuv's new department of health, Vaad Habriut, was not a nonpartisan agency but a tool of labor. So powerful was the hold of labor that no janitor, nurse or physician could be fired without the assent of a committee of janitors, nurses or physicians. And no decision could be reached by a committee until all agreed; it was a consensus method brought from eastern Europe. Much was brought from eastern Europe.

When an employee came to his superior with a complaint against another, the practice was for the superior to run back and forth between the two until some sort of adjustment was reached. In this way everyone saved face and the dispute was kept "at home," out of the reach of Gentile or British ears. And this too came from eastern Europe. But Bluestone, who came from America, did what Americans did. He brought complainer and complained-against together, heard them both out and decided on the spot. To the east European mind that was unacceptable. The east European mind was what all the Americans discussed among themselves, and all agreed it was devious, impenetrable to logic, and fascinating.

One day Bluestone learned that a midwife at the Tel Aviv hospital had incipient pulmonary tuberculosis, a source of mortal danger to newborn infants. He instructed the hospital to discharge her immediately. Tel Aviv refused. Presently a little parade of committee representatives arrived in Bluestone's office to tell him they did not necessarily disagree with the idea of a discharge, but they insisted on a court of arbitration. It was a matter of *prinzip* with them, a word that was frequently heard in Palestine. The point was argued before the potbellied stove for hours without result, for Bluestone saw no need for a court of arbitration. Pulmonary TB was beyond arbitration.

A general Histadrut committee descended on him and spent many more hours in discussion. Bluestone turned his back on them and went to the Zionist Executive, where he pleaded with Colonel Kisch to settle the matter. Kisch sent an arbitrator to Tel Aviv; the man returned to tell Bluestone, "You are free to do as you think best." All this time the midwife continued her work among the newborn infants.

One morning a Histadrut official came into Bluestone's office, where he was warmly received. The official looked amazed. "But why," said Bluestone. "I never held this business against you personally."

And the official, flinging his arms out wide, cried, "That too is a form of argument! How can you fire this woman?"

"At two this afternoon I want her out of the hospital," Bluestone retorted, "or I will report the case to the Mandate's Department of Health and they will deal with it."

The Histadrut man sucked in his breath. "Oh no. No Jew would ever do such a thing. . . ."

Bluestone assured him he would, and to avoid that ultimate degradation the woman was quickly dismissed. *Davar*, the Labor newspaper, greeted the act with angry headlines: "Once again America has treated us like natives!" *Davar* had been conducting a running feud with Dr. Bluestone, whom they criticized and insulted at every turn as the representative of Hadassah and American capitalism, and his employees read it all; they could hardly help reading it, for the price of *Davar* was deducted from their wages.

Miss Szold believed she had made no mistake in choosing Bluestone. "He is an excellent administrator and a human being of fine fiber." He was noble, he was tactful, he was truly kind-hearted, she told her family, but she never said a word of it to him. Something in his bearing put her on her guard, stiffened her defenses and paralyzed her sense of humor. In his presence she simply congealed, so that he never saw the playfulness, the sweetness that Dushkin and Seligsberg saw; he could hardly believe it existed. But when they talked about labor, the Histadrut, *Davar* and the committees—Miss Szold called them "soviets"—they were fellow Americans and partners in suffering.

There was, however, a fundamental difference between them, and from the day of her arrival in Jerusalem it had troubled Miss Szold. She saw that Dr. Bluestone looked at his tasks from a purely professional point of view, "and if Zionist politics stand in the way of professional achievement, so much the worse for Zionist politics."

She believed that sound medical practice and Zionism were not irreconcilable. But if and when they were, "I personally am not interested in medical work in Palestine." For she was first of all a Zionist. She had been drawn to the medical work by way of Zionism. Bluestone was a physician and public health worker first and last. This clash of priorities occurred over and over again in their dealings with each other.

On every other question he and she agreed. And when the measures he proposed in public health or in sanitation were frustrated by the Zionist Executive because there was too little money to go around and what there was went into more Zionistic schemes, Miss Szold would run across the street to argue with Colonel Kisch. At other times she would call a meeting with one of the committees and try to explain what was good medical practice. More often than not she came back defeated. "She tore herself apart," Bluestone recalled, "trying to reconcile what was irreconcilable."

He suffered from a pervasive sense of disillusion with Zionist politics. The Vaad Habriut, the so-called department of health, had the power to block him at every turn. The Zionist Commission, even Chaim Weizmann in London, insisted most urgently that he hire a particular elderly physician because he had once made such an excellent Zionist speech. The Kupat Holim, antagonist and archrival of Hadassah, owed them money and not only wanted to borrow more but proclaimed their right to borrow more; with it they would build a hospital of their own while Bluestone struggled to balance his budget with shrinking funds.

He could not ignore the fact that the HMO was an extraordinary accomplishment, that if some of the doctors were mediocre or worse they were the best available in that barren land. But he had come to build, to realize visions, and the Jews of Palestine were all builders, all visionaries. It was a community of experts. One fitted oneself into their rhythms or left. Bluestone hung on hopefully.

That June, Miss Szold stayed home for a week or so, confined to bed with her first Palestinian disease. Papataccie, or sand-fly fever, brought intense pain in the back, head, eyes and limbs and a general malaise that prevented any more active work than reading. She went through *The Forsyte Saga* from beginning to end, and Norman Douglas's *South Wind.* For the privilege of reading Galsworthy she felt she would always be grateful to the sand fly, the most delicate, mercurial and fairylike insect imaginable. She wondered how a man felt who had achieved such a masterpiece. "Some of the pages were so beautiful that my soul ached." But she was puzzled by the sequel, the second half of *The Forsyte Saga,* set in modern times, where there were paragraphs upon paragraphs whose language hardly seemed to be English. "I don't know what the phrases mean, either because they are the jargon of modern science or modern art in the slang of the modern drawing room," and *South Wind* was utterly beyond her. There was hardly a page in it she understood fully, and she was left with the uneasy awareness that she did not belong to the generation that read or wrote such books.

As for *Women in Love,* her opinion was not what Adele had hoped for. She felt that Lawrence was a good stylist, but "I cannot accept all of his philosophy even when I understand it."

For Adele and Toby Seltzer the works of D. H. Lawrence had proved a dangerous enthusiasm. Several years earlier three of the books Seltzer published, including Lawrence's *Women in Love,* had been seized by the New York Society for the Suppression of Vice. Seltzer stood trial and was vindicated, and Adele rejoiced, especially because sales of the book boomed with the publicity. When the Lawrences came to America and she and Toby stayed with them in Taos, New Mexico, again Adele rejoiced, calling the visit "the crown and apex of my whole existence." But Toby was not really a businessman. Somehow he could not handle the financial side of publishing, and his relations with Lawrence began to suffer. When he was arrested again for publishing "Casanova's Homecoming," by Arthur Schnitzler, he felt unequal to a second fight and withdrew the book. He was tired and sick and heavily in debt.

Adele drove herself to pay back all his creditors, feeling she was stuck for the rest of her life with makeshifts and shabby clothes and slavery for Mrs. Schiff. For a while she took very seriously the prospect of opening a tearoom, but in her heart of hearts she cherished a plan for going to live in Communist Russia, where no one was as rich as Mrs. Schiff.

Henrietta ached for her. The family was always on her mind, and their news was rarely cheerful: Rachel no better, Rachel's husband, Joe, either sick himself or climbing out of a sickbed to earn money for her medical care. Bertha had five children to educate and no money. The Szolds simply lacked the trick of making money, Adele said.

That summer Miss Szold received the telegram she had been dreading ever since she had left America in March. Rachel was dying; unless she came back immediately there was no hope of seeing her alive.

All the way home she drugged herself with books and slept as many hours as she could to keep from thinking about Rachel. She got to Baltimore late at night, went to her room to read the mail that was waiting for her and learned that Dr. Bluestone wanted to resign.

The next day she saw Rachel. The first sight of her chilled the blood, and Henrietta struggled to keep her face calm, to control the rising sense of guilt—it seemed wicked to have left her all these months. Bertha and Adele came and went, Joe was close to hysteria, and they clung to one another, saying very little. No one saw any point in pretending now, for minute by minute Rachel was slipping away.

She died in September. It would be harder than ever for Henrietta to return to Jerusalem, for the irrational suspicion that things might somehow have gone otherwise if she had remained all along at her sister's side refused to disappear. From then on she would never escape the belief that Palestine had wedged itself between her and the rest of the family and the fault was her own. She had chosen Palestine.

Miss Szold went back to Jerusalem in January of 1927 to find what looked like the failure of the Zionist adventure. The township of Tel Aviv was bankrupt. There were terrifying stories of suffering, even of nakedness. Unemployment among the Yishuv had risen to 8,000. Every Zionist organization in Jewish Palestine except the HMO was in debt to the hilt, the sum of their indebtedness adding up to seven figures in pounds, and in the Zionist offices telephones and electricity were regularly turned off for nonpayment. There was little immigration and much emigration.

One day in March she watched the Purim carnival pour through the streets of Jerusalem, children in masks and homemade costumes, bearded, side-locked Hasidim in dark suits with dark hats on their curly dark heads, singing, dancing, clattering with little wooden noisemakers. From time to time she caught a glimpse of faces behind the masks; pinched, pale, the eyes feverishly bright, they were the faces of people who were literally starved.

22

Thirty years had passed since Herzl first called the Zionists of the world to a congress in Basel and bullied them into rented evening dress. Since then Herzl had died, a World War had come and gone and in its aftermath the Jewish people were given their homeland, an outcome Herzl himself believed it might take fifty years to attain. They had built schools and hospitals and agricultural settlements and an all-Jewish town named Tel Aviv. Hebrew was spoken by a generation whose children knew no other language. There were factories, shops, businesses as well as acres of oranges and tomatoes, a Jewish life in Zion that was not the polished monarchy Herzl envisioned, but a life at once more vulgar and more idealistic, for it was rooted in the socialist and egalitarian aspirations of eastern European Jewry.

So the dream that was not Herzl's but was inspired by Herzl had taken flesh, yet the Zionists who met in Basel in 1927 were more despondent than at any previous congress. The Zionist adventure had never before seemed beyond reach, even when it was a figment of Herzl's theatrical imagination, for when there is no hope it is possible to hope for everything. They had something now, a small family business, so to speak, but it was doomed to bankruptcy. In Palestine when David Ben-Gurion appeared in public he was greeted by shouts of "Leader, give us bread!" Emigration from Palestine was almost twice as great as immigration; the chalutzim were considered failures, for they required endless financial support from the Zionist Executive. Left was pitted against right, and it was a rare optimist who came to Basel with the conviction that the Zionist movement could recover in the foreseeable future.

The fifteenth congress addressed itself to the economic crisis by adopting many measures of which Brandeis himself would approve. They resolved to run the Yishuv along normal business lines, preference in immigration to be given to those with independent means, "socialist experimentation" to be discontinued, the kibbutzim to prove they could stand on their own or suffer the consequences.

But the aspect of the Basel congress that would concern Miss Szold most directly was not the move toward a business management so much as the Zionist Executive that would carry it out. Until then the Executive had been a coalition; now Weizmann proposed a commission form of government, composed of members not bound by any party program. In place of the usual five-or six-member cabinet he asked for a group of three, each member to

hold two portfolios. Their task would be to say no to all demands for expenditure
not covered by anticipated income.

Weizmann's three candidates were the British lawyer Harry Sacher, Colonel
Frederick Kisch and a Dutchman, S. A. van Vriesland. The left had no affection
for Sacher and was bitterly opposed to van Vriesland as an unvarnished reaction-
ary, but now there were outcries against van Vriesland from the right. He
had recently married, his wife a divorcée whose first marriage had been dissolved
by Dutch law but not by Jewish religious law. The Orthodox party suddenly
announced they would not accept him, and the congress was deadlocked for
days. Weizmann then turned to Miss Szold. Would she serve as the third
member of the business executive?

She fought against it. She told him she was not fitted by age, temperament,
knowledge or experience to serve with the "government" and had been saying
so for the past four years.

Labor didn't like her, yet they had confidence in her; the Orthodox Mizrachi
were not satisfied with her religious philosophy but considered her only half
bad. If she entered the triumvirate both agreed to accept it. Moreover the
Americans of the Brandeis faction, above all her respected friend Judge Julian
Mack, told her it was imperative for them to have someone on the Executive
they could trust to carry out the tremendous retrenchments they demanded
as a price for their support of Weizmann. Whom could they more readily
trust than the frugal, hard-working, conscientious Miss Szold?

Feeling badgered and bludgeoned, she gave way. During an all-night session
on the fourteenth day of the congress, the ticket of Sacher, Kisch and Szold
was presented; at seven in the morning it was voted in. "And I received congratu-
lations!" she wrote to her family. "As a matter of fact what is happening to
me is that I am losing my soul." Kisch, the chairman of the Executive, was
to be charged with immigration and the political department, Sacher with
colonization and labor, Miss Szold with education and health, the term of
office for each being two years. American delegates assured her she would have
their fullest support. Sympathy, understanding, above all money were promised
her in profusion.

To mark the solemnity of the occasion the entire party went to the hotel
balcony and arranged themselves for a formal portrait, Miss Szold seated in
front with Eder and Weizmann, whose broad, dark Russian faces radiated power
and resolve, Kisch and Sacher standing behind, both young, well-tailored, relaxed
and somewhat equine. Miss Szold wore a large hat jammed on her head from
which gray hair escaped wispily at the sides. She stared past the camera without
expression. Had she accepted her fate, found consolation in the importance

of her role as the first female member of the Executive, the first American since 1921? Did she see the future as an invigorating challenge? There was nothing in her face to suggest it.

Yet a number of Americans in Palestine were convinced that Miss Szold's reluctance was only half the story, Dr. Bluestone among them. He believed she had wanted all along to be part of the "government," and when she had refused before it had been with the hope of being dragged in against her will. Certainly it was something she had done for years, allowing herself to be pushed into work she both feared because she believed she was inadequate and wanted because her instincts told her it was the right direction. And the right direction this time may well have been away from America, that alien presence resented by the Yishuv, and toward the mainstream of Palestinian life.

Then she left for New York. She did a good deal of earnest speech making there, often in the same dark velvet dress with its collar of good lace. One of her speeches, calling for a restricted and balanced budget, was described by *Davar* as "a dagger struck into the raw flesh of the Yishuv." She knew the kind of opposition that awaited her. She knew also that she was entering a new stage of her life as a Zionist. From now on she would look at Hadassah, the HMO and American Zionism with different eyes. In crossing the street she would be leaving the American side. "Pray for me," she told her friend Emanuel Neumann, "say Mass for my American soul."

She was frightened. However much she may have wanted to be part of the shadow government, her dislike of Zionist politics was unfeigned. She begged Adele to come with her, but Adele, who felt an almost paralyzing sense of pity for her sister, was held to America by Toby and debts. She thought of Henrietta as a thoroughbred setting out to live in the jungle. "My love again, dear, dear sister of mine," Adele wrote in her letter of farewell, "don't let the wild beasts eat you up. Come back before they do."

Miss Szold consoled herself with the promise of her niece, Harriet Levin, to come to Jerusalem to live with her for a year or so. They might even find an apartment together so she need not continue to live as a guest of Sophia Berger.

On November 30 she was welcomed back to Palestine by *Davar* with the announcement that she was totally unfit to head the department of education. She stopped in to see Dr. Bluestone at the Hôtel de France—to the despair of labor and the Weizmann forces, he was still there, for he had been persuaded by Hadassah to stay on—and again her reception was chilly. Bluestone felt she was turning her back on those ideals of American medical practice she had once shared with him; she was choosing, more clearly than ever before, Zionism over public health. Then she went across Tancred Lane to the offices of the Zionist Executive.

To Hadassah she was still founding mother, first president and chief source of inspiration, but their relationship changed with that walk across the street. She was to become less a person to the Hadassah leaders, more an icon of infinite value for publicity purposes. This is not to say there was any trace of hypocrisy in their publicity when they described her as their beloved leader, which they did repeatedly. But they loved her the way saints are loved, formally and at a distance.

Although she was charged with two portfolios, health and education, Miss Szold left the health affairs of the Yishuv in Hadassah's hands for the time being, mostly because her other portfolio demanded immediate attention. The school system of the Yishuv had been stopped cold for weeks, due to an enormous budget cut at the 1927 congress; it was only now beginning to thaw out and, very sluggishly, to operate.

She saw the effects of the cut in the form of a telegram from Haifa that lay on her desk: "It is impossible for us to maintain order among the teachers who are hungry for bread. We are discontinuing our work because we haven't the strength to continue it." Whenever she glanced at that telegram she asked herself: Did the Americans know, when they pushed her into this, what she would actually have to do? Did they know, when they promised sympathy, support, above all money, how much was needed? And if they knew, where was it? Why must she refuse the schoolteachers their chalk and books, even their pitiful salaries, which started at about $500 a year?

She began to study the Education Code, and again she felt betrayed, for she had never suspected that the schools of the Yishuv were built on such flimsy foundations. The Education Code had been created by the Zionist Commission when the British mandate began in somewhat the same spirit that a system of private education might be created in another country. There was a little support from the British government; the rest came from international funds or local fees. Jewish schools were subject to British regulation, as private schools would naturally be, but the Yishuv always felt it neither wanted nor needed British help. The Jews were the People of the Book. They knew more about education than anyone.

What Miss Szold saw was a school system at once disorganized and archaic, modeled on earlier European systems to such an extent that whole segments were walled off from real life in Palestine. And it was poisoned by political jealousies, a mirror image of the three main political streams that cut across the life of the Yishuv, for there were three separate school systems.

Town children were educated either at Orthodox schools run by Mizrachi or at the nonreligious schools of the centrist party, the General Zionists. Children of the agricultural settlements were educated by Labor Zionism. Each system resisted unification as they would have resisted a threat to their existence; each was a training ground for future party members, each bred up children to whom the children of the other two were unknown, unsavory, unacceptable. Where there was hardly money enough to do one thing well, almost everything had to be done two or three or even more times. There were four teachers' seminaries, one for Labor, one for General Zionism and two for Mizrachi, coeducation being unthinkable to the Orthodox. Their combined enrollment was 500; a single teachers' seminary could have educated all 500 together.

High schools were private, expensive, reserved for the privileged few. On the elementary level eight years of education were offered but never compulsory, and the dropout rate, especially among the children of the poor, was alarming. Except for the schools of the kibbutzim, which were models of child-centered, progressive education, although miserably poor and housed in huts, schooling was rigid. The curriculum of the General Zionists had been copied from a prewar Prussian system, while that of the Mizrachi was almost exclusively religious, with every attempt to expand the secular material furiously rejected.

The school day seemed unconscionably long. The school buildings were chiefly Arab houses, disreputable and decrepit. No money had been set aside in the budget for new buildings and none for repair of existing buildings. There were no vocational schools, no continuation schools, essentially no college-trained teachers.

Perhaps it was not so surprising after all, this Education Code and what it revealed about Jewish Palestine. Ever since her return with Dr. Bluestone a year and a half earlier, Miss Szold had been mulling over the changes she had found and measuring them against the hopes of that first, heady year when Sir Herbert Samuel appeared like a second Nehemiah. What was it but a failure, or at best "a business mismanaged"? And why should the school system be otherwise?

By the end of December she told Rose Jacobs of Hadassah that not even her own terrified imagination had been somber enough; her first four weeks on the Executive seemed like four years, a long, unbroken line of events, discussions, perplexities, enigmas, intermingled with her rebellious refusal to accept her fate.

With her colleagues on the Executive, Miss Szold's relations were amiable but impersonal. Those two hearty British gentlemen, Harry Sacher and Frederick Kisch, scarcely knew what to make of her, although they treated her from start to finish with exquisite courtesy. She was something of an exotic to them, a maiden lady a full generation older, puritanical in habit and manner, solemn, compulsively hard working, and so very very small. They were both large men.

Sacher and Kisch appreciated Miss Szold's efforts to learn all about their portfolios. It seemed to them a sort of praiseworthy eccentricity—certainly they made no attempt to learn about health or education—but since both men were away from Palestine on Zionist affairs for weeks and months at a time, while Miss Szold hardly budged during her entire term of office, she often had to attend to their duties as well as her own. The eccentricity had a practical side.

They worked well together; there were no hidden undercurrents of dislike, jealousy or personal animosity. There were no political squabbles, since Miss Szold never talked politics if she could help it, and Sacher was unable to recall a single political discussion during their two years together. "She would have liked to believe that in a world inhabited solely by men of good will and pursuing noble purposes by the purest methods, political difficulties would vanish. But that cannot be called a [political] philosophy. . . . It was an emotion, and indeed a refusal to face unpleasant realities."

Weizmann's feelings about her were rather different. Weizmann had hand-picked the triumvirate and was to support his choice against volleys of criticism in 1928 and again in 1929; but he did not care for Miss Szold. One can only guess at the reasons. It may have been her didactic manner, her self-righteous-ness; in the company of so impressive a man she could hardly have been at her best. Whatever the reasons, he valued Miss Szold for her American contacts but did not like her. In the words of one Palestinian writer, "Weizmann couldn't smell her."

With Field Marshal Lord Plumer, the High Commissioner who replaced Samuel, Miss Szold was a personal success. They were almost exactly the same age; both were religious without religiosity, formed by the humane liberalism of the nineteenth century, and both were genuinely high-minded.

The Yishuv soon found itself mistaken in its early estimation of Plumer, the little man with the receding chin, bushy mustache and monocle who looked like a caricature of the bumbling British army officer. In fact he was confident, precise, conscientious, intent as no high commissioner before or since on "equal-ity of obligation" to Zionists and Arabs alike. There was also a streak of Christian humility in a man whose first official action was to go with his wife to the Anglican cathedral in Jerusalem to pray. Personal pomp and pomposity repelled him. He went about the Old City during his leisure hours without escort or guard, wearing his dark blue suit, stiff collar and bowler hat and carrying a tightly furled umbrella, a remarkable sight in those serpentine alleys.

One of Miss Szold's earliest successes with the Plumer administration had to do with the support of Jewish education. She approached them with the proposal that they increase their contribution to Jews and Arabs alike, no ploy on her part, but the expression of a heartfelt belief with which Plumer was intensely sympathetic. She won from him the first substantial sum for Jewish education, and he was to work hand in glove with Miss Szold on a number of projects, always with a sense of mutual appreciation.

It is an unfortunate truth that women, however much they may believe in a cause, often believe in it even more powerfully after men have been persuaded of its rightness. That this was true of Hadassah's leaders became dramatically apparent in early 1928.

For months before their 1927 convention, Hadassah headquarters had smoldered with talk of rebellion against the ZOA. Under Lipsky's regime the ZOA spent extravagant sums for propaganda, their bookkeeping was erratic, they lived from crisis to crisis, borrowing at the last moment to avert the crisis they should have insured against months before. Hadassah, on the other hand, always operated according to the methods of a prudent housewife, every dollar they raised for Palestine going straight to Palestine without deduction for overhead, which came out of dues. Hadassah borrowed no money they could not repay in the immediate future.

The 1927 convention had ended in a compromise between Hadassah and the Lipsky forces. This compromise was largely engineered by Miss Szold, anxious as always to avoid a rupture that might damage the movement, and by Hadassah's new president, Irma Lindheim. Miss Szold thoroughly liked and admired her; she was young, attractive, combative, possessed of an almost reckless desire to act on conviction. All this Louis Lipsky knew. The Brandeis men had been out of power since 1921, and ever since Lipsky had feared an uprising from the Brandeis camp. Lindheim was a Brandeisist; his fears were therefore in no way allayed by the 1927 compromise.

Among the Brandeis men the flare-up in Hadassah was seen as a signal. There was growing discontent with the Lipsky regime, not only among Hadassah women but throughout the ZOA membership at large. The following winter leaders of the Brandeis faction held a series of secret meetings in Washington and plotted the overthrow of the Lipsky regime.

The agendas of these meetings were immediately conveyed to Hadassah's leaders, for many were married to Brandeis men, as was Irma Lindheim. They felt stronger now, more sure of themselves. This time they would not compromise. Unless there was a change of administration within the ZOA, Lindheim wrote to Miss Szold, "Palestine can no longer depend upon America as its chief support." The moment had come, and she was ready for it.

In the spring of 1928, Rabbi Stephen Wise and Irma Lindheim resigned from the United Palestine Appeal, an agency created by the ZOA. Lindheim's resignation took place in the full light of a press conference and was amply covered by the *New York Times*, which called it the revolt of Hadassah against the regime of Louis Lipsky of the ZOA.

Lipsky informed the general membership of Hadassah that Mrs. Lindheim had betrayed the spirit of Henrietta Szold: "What was formerly a Jewish woman's movement—auxiliary, complementary, aiding and comforting the main stem of the movement—became an organization animated by the sense of women's rights. Like all other women's movements of this sort, it represented resistance to the domination of men, which resistance was turned into a demand for equality which, as soon as it was attained, became a desire to dominate and control." Miss Szold would never have done that, he said. Miss Szold was womanly.

In the summer of 1928, as Hadassah's annual convention approached, Lindheim reconsidered her promise to Miss Szold to run for a second term. Her husband had died; the events of the past few months had left her played out and disillusioned and fearful of breaking down. Her doctor advised a trip to Europe, and Lindheim agreed but decided reluctantly to stand for reelection all the same. Then she left, intending only a vacation abroad. In reality it was the start of a long journey whose end was a kibbutz on the northern borders of Palestine, for Lindheim was to become one of the few leaders of American Zionism to make a lifelong home in Zion.

The events that followed at Hadassah's 1928 convention and the ZOA convention directly after it showed Lipsky at his most theatrical. Indeed from Hadassah's point of view he looked positively villainous, although in fact he was doing nothing more malicious than fighting for his own beliefs with whatever weapons came to hand. And these beliefs were honestly held; no one, not even Lindheim or Brandeis, could accuse Lipsky of financial dishonesty arising from a desire to line his own pockets. A miserable bookkeeper, he was nevertheless a loyal Zionist who wanted only to stay in power.

He was also an admirer of the Yiddish language and Yiddish theater and literature, so it was entirely natural for Lipsky to assume the mantle of high drama, both pathetic and noble, in appealing to an audience peculiarly receptive to such a tradition. At one point he entered the packed convention hall unannounced, igniting a ten-minute demonstration of acclaim among his Hadassah followers so raucous that Hadassah's vice president had to clear the room of everyone but delegates and reporters. He came, Lipsky declared, to make peace. Then he unleashed a tirade against the national board and Lindheim.

Lindheim, already in Europe, had taken the precaution of putting in the hands of a board member a touching letter that reduced the audience to tears and assured her reelection as president. But in the ZOA convention that followed, Lipsky unsheathed another dramatic weapon the women were helpless to counter. They were still comparatively ignorant of parliamentary procedure, which Lipsky and his faction had mastered. Five thousand Hadassah members were disenfranchised through a technicality and Hadassah's delegation reduced in number by more than 100.

Miss Szold sent a message from Jerusalem to the 1928 convention, as she did every year when she could not be present, and its tone was conciliatory: "The danger now is that, striving with each other in the large Jewish camp of America, you may lose yourselves for Palestine. . . . Leave off trying to determine who is right, who wrong. An army of builders is needed." Her words were only too true, for American pledges were $200,000 in arrears. She felt abandoned in Jerusalem, pushed onto the Executive by American promises and left there as a hostage while schoolteachers went hungry and Hadassah and the ZOA carried on their feud.

Her message had no effect. On the floors of past conventions lifelong friendships had been shattered, men had wept, one speaker had lost his voice because he talked too much, and then whispered hoarsely from the platform that he had given his voice for Palestine—thunderous applause and sobs among the audience. So Palestine was often overlooked in the excitement of fighting about Palestine.

At this convention the Brandeis men were armed with righteous indignation but little else. They had no plan, no leaders willing to serve, only their indignation, which was not enough. Because of the lost Hadassah votes and the waffling of the leaders, once again Louis Lipsky was reelected.

Yet his regime had come to an all but formal end. After the convention the ZOA entered upon a period of chaos, their membership declining by 1929 to 18,000. A year later a "historic peace" was concluded within American Zionist forces, Brandeisists joining with Lipsky-Weizmann followers in a coalition administration. Hadassah leaders achieved the full representation they had fought for and to which their numbers entitled them; by 1933 they were an essentially autonomous body.

Never again would they be exhorted to attend to their womanly duties and leave politics to the men. As membership in the ZOA declined, Hadassah membership rose toward 27,000 in 1932. From then on the most powerful voice in American Zionism would be Hadassah's. Even Louis Lipsky admitted it in time. He became an admirer and supporter; the women considered him a friend. Hadassah was in a position to forget the past and be magnanimous.

On the Fourth of July, 1927, the little colony of Americans in Jerusalem celebrated with a baseball game. It was a sport entirely unknown to Palestine or the British, and Dr. Magnes and Dr. Bluestone, who captained the two teams, had had to conduct a house-to-house canvass in order to scrape up eighteen players. The result was an ill-assorted lot including two rabbis, an HMO dentist, the American secretary of Ronald Storrs, and Louis Ehrlich, the husband of Miss Szold's secretary Emma; there was one female player, a Mrs. le Bouvier, and as umpire, the ancient Dr. Romain Butin of the Catholic University in Washington, complete with clerical collar. According to William Schack, an art critic who played first base under Bluestone, no one was in any sort of condition except the captains, Magnes being in especially admirable shape, tall and straight and fast on his feet at the age of fifty.

The day itself was sunny and hot, almost tropical, with an occasional breeze that fluttered the stars and stripes. At the very moment when Dr. Butin called "Play ball!" a squadron of splendidly mounted Arabs fanned out over the rise above the field, their horses' hooves clattering on the matted rocks. The Americans had phoned the police to warn them about an assembly of possibly edgy baseball fans and the Arab horsemen had been sent to keep order, but the only fans were a handful of wives and friends clutching American pop bottles. The game proved a personal triumph for Magnes, who hit a double, a triple and a homer, stole second, third and home and out of delicate consideration for the feelings of the younger players managed to strike out once. His team won by an unrecorded score, perhaps 26 to 5.

For some years afterward the Fourth of July baseball game was a regular feature of Jerusalem life. In the summer of 1928, Harriet Levin, who had joined the Berger-Szold household, spent the long evenings after work at batting practice while her aunt was glued to her desk.

For Miss Szold, Harriet's arrival meant that at long last there was "someone of my own blood" in Palestine, that she was no longer an odd fragment of humanity but a woman with a family, with forebears and descendants; she was more like other people now. Otherwise nothing had changed. She still felt betrayed by her American friends and frustrated as a member of the Executive, three English-speaking outsiders among the Yishuv whose job was not spending money.

Dr. Bluestone had resigned, this time unalterably. "I am sorry for Hadassah," she wrote when she heard about it. "I am sorry for my friends in America, and I am also not a little sorry for myself. Sweetness seems to have gone out of life for me." A distinct note of self-pity pervaded her letters during this period, and she was aware of it, accused herself of it, yet it seemed inescapable. In her misery she fought with Sophia; what they fought about is unclear. Perhaps it was the constant presence of the man Sophia loved and would soon marry, an abrasive, opinionated man; perhaps there was no reason beyond the petty irritation of daily life. She cherished old friends, many of them far more difficult to get on with than Sophia, so it is a measure of Miss Szold's unhappiness during the years on the Executive that Sophia, whom she used to speak of with love and pride, became someone to resent and to resent doubly because she was generous.

For some time the two women had been living in a new house expressly built for Sophia near the Damascus Gate. Its interior was cool, shadowy and spacious, with high ceilings and floors of brilliant glazed tile, the walls hung with Bokharan and Persian embroideries. Sophia entertained for Miss Szold; every important visitor from America must see Miss Szold and be seen by her, and the capable, sociable Miss Berger put on long, loose robes of pale yellow, a gold Arab circlet on her head, and gave them luncheon or tea while Miss Szold sat like a boarder in someone else's home. It had been endurable so long as their friendship endured, but that was shattered now. Yet where could she go? Harriet worked and was too tired for housekeeping; Miss Szold worked all day and much of the night. So she was pinned down at home as well as at work: "I fall a victim to comfort and despise myself, for all companionship between Sophia and myself has ceased. It's sad and ugly."

She felt alone, exposed, an object of pity, and could not bring herself to describe her feelings even to her sisters. She had left them to fulfill a duty that was at the same time a high honor, and when it turned to bitterness she hid from them. But she had no one else, and the misery gushed out on paper almost against her will. "What *am* I to do?" she implored them. "Is this the meaning of old age?"

She was living an Ibsen drama, she said. "Everything, everything, in my personal relations, in my Zionist relations, has been just as hard as I feared it would be," and "the worst of all disharmonies is that I can't get away from self-pity." When her term of office was up she might well be through with Zionism forever, not because she despaired of Palestine, but because it was spoiled for her now. Surely Zionism was supposed to bring the Jews together, but she saw no such thing. She saw only the falling away of old friends, of the very people whose loyalty had made the movement sacred to her.

But the months on the Executive had longer-lasting effects than this wave of self-pity. Her temper was made worse by it, which she deeply regretted. At the same time a certain hardening process, a toughening of the character perhaps necessary for the survival of an aging woman in an alien world, took place during the same period. Once Miss Szold was certain she was right, she became immovable. According to her friend, the philosopher and educator Ernst Simon, both Miss Szold and Magnes were "this type of fighting democrats who become psychological dictators." And Reuben Katznelson of the HMO had much the same impression. Miss Szold would make a conclusion for a committee, then say, "Now we proceed." Her conclusions were never easily reached; she came to them by a long, slow process of introspection after which she had no intention of allowing the "soviets" to wear her down or talk her out of what she believed to be rational. One was high-handed in Palestine or one was ground under.

Nevertheless the teachers came to accept and even love her. In spite of her uncertain Hebrew, her alliance with bourgeois America and her heavy hand, they saw that she was harder on herself than on anyone else, the first to arrive each morning, the last to leave at night.

Theirs was the earliest, most tentative beginning of a personal response, not to the American from Hadassah, but to the woman. Miss Szold was still a stranger to the Yishuv, and outside the doors of her office was perceived as such, but within the school system and especially among the young there was a growing awareness that she was on their side, their champion vis-à-vis the establishment. She helped form a teachers' organization and acted as its chairman; she got an educational journal under way; she saw the problems of the teachers as one who had been a teacher herself and the problems of the youngest among them as one who had been young, uncertain of her vocation, conscious of the vast gap between desire and performance. She was modest, she was simple and it touched them.

And in the summer of 1928 she prepared for a Berlin meeting of the Zionist General Council, to which she would bring an extensive plan for educational reform: modification of the tri-partite system, a more sophisticated teacher-training program, vocational schools in the towns and continuation schools for the army of little dropouts who so often became semiliterate shoeshine boys or petty thieves. Louis Lipsky would be there, coming straight from the smoke-filled rooms of the ZOA convention. She did not look forward to meeting him or to meeting Weizmann, who seemed to hold her personally responsible for the failure of American pledges. He had pulled her onto the Executive not because he had any great faith in her executive ability but because the Mack-Brandeis people trusted her. She was a trade-off against American money. When the money failed to come because the Americans wasted their energies on internecine struggles, he felt the fault was hers.

In Berlin every one of her educational reforms was rejected. Even today the public schools of Israel are split into two systems, religious and nonreligious, and the same split cuts across adult life, sometimes erupting into violence. The entire meeting left a sour taste in her mouth.

Her absence from Jerusalem had been only a matter of weeks, but when she came back she saw the country with fresh eyes, noting on every hand the signs of increasing prosperity. It had the curious effect of depressing her spirits or perhaps making even more clear how depressed she had been for months. She told Bertha: "The situation in the country is improving steadily. I don't like my present life."

Although it was hardly possible to speak of normalcy in a land as abnormal as Jewish Palestine, it seemed that something like normalcy had indeed arrived with the end of 1928. University buildings rose on Mount Scopus, a hydroelectric plant produced light and power from the River Jordan, agricultural settlements numbered 100 and the Jewish population had increased to more than 150,000. The Arabs were increasing as well, both by multiplication and by continuous immigration from neighboring countries; they were close to 1 million now. Yet the percentage of Jews to Arabs had risen steadily since the start of the decade. December 1928 brought a rush of fresh optimism.

In that month the Zionist General Council met in Berlin to vote on Weizmann's Jewish Agency, a partnership of Zionist and non-Zionist business-men in the running of the Yishuv. The Americans were against it, including Miss Szold, and the right-wing followers of Vladimir Jabotinsky were against it, but the final vote was 39 to 5 in favor, and the news swept through the Yishuv like the first rains of spring. There was a quickening, an invigorating awareness that not only Zionists but Jews everywhere in the world were ready to join hands and build with them. People called it the Pact of Glory. The next international congress would give it formal ratification.

Lord Plumer's peaceful reign had come to an end; he had left during the course of the summer at his own request. The disturbances of the early twenties were all but forgotten, partly because of Plumer's impressive, authorita-tive personality, partly because of the recent depression, which assured the Arabs they had nothing to fear from Zionism, for it was not going to take over Palestine after all. Therefore when Plumer was approached by Whitehall on the subject of economy he agreed to a drastic cut in military expenditures. British armed forces consisted now of a single RAF squadron and two companies of armored cars, the gendarmerie having been disbanded.

Colonel Kisch believed the new arrangements were dangerous, for the imperturbable and even-handed Plumer was not likely to be replaced by a man of similar abilities. A friend of Magnes's, an Arab named Musa Alami, who served as junior crown council, was also uneasy. He felt there were dangerous fires beneath the surface.

So did Magnes. Since 1926 he had been the moving spirit behind a little group called Brit Shalom, the Covenant of Peace, whose purpose was to promote a binationalist state at once Jewish and Arab. It seemed to Magnes and his friends that while the Zionist leaders were eager to reach accommodation with the Arabs, their efforts were half-hearted, that there was more lip service than

concrete action. The Yishuv disapproved of Brit Shalom largely because it was
made up of people with names like Arthur, Wolfgang and Hans. German
Jews, in Europe or America, continued to look down on eastern Europeans as
they had in Baltimore forty years earlier. In Palestine, where east Europeans
were the majority, they paid the Germans back with an icy dislike.

Brit Shalom was very small, a handful, no more. Edwin Samuel, Sir Herbert's
son, who was now in government service, admonished them not to publish
their numbers because people would laugh. As for Miss Szold, although she
never took the mission of Brit Shalom as seriously as Magnes did, she considered
herself a platonic sympathizer. "She certainly realized that politics and ethics
are not identical," Ernst Simon recalled, "but she thought that politics that
does not reckon at all with the ethical element is in the long run bad politics."

So Lord Plumer was gone, much of the British military were gone and
the Bluestones had returned to America. In New York, Dr. Bluestone was to
become director of Montefiore Hospital, in which post he served for the next
twenty-three years of a distinguished medical career, working even longer as
chairman of the Medical Reference Board of Hadassah and the Hebrew University, a trusted friend of each of Hadassah's presidents. But he never returned
to Palestine, not even for a brief visit in his long and active life. And it was
not clear who would replace him now.

Miss Szold had chosen a young immigrant ophthalmologist named Chaim
Yassky, who was designated temporary director along with Reuben Katznelson;
she hoped Hadassah would make Yassky's appointment permanent, but they
were holding out for an American. Moreover the national board still refused
to surrender their tight control over every detail of the HMO's administration.
Miss Szold told them that while it had been possible ten or twelve years ago
to ram a system from without down the throats of the Yishuv, that time was
long past. "Here in Palestine an organic life is being developed. You and I
may not like some of its manifestations. As a matter of fact I confess to you
that some of its manifestations have aroused my indignation and destroyed
my nerves. But for better or worse, that is the organic life that is being developed
by Zionists here who are bone of the bone and flesh of the flesh of our ideal."

To her repeated requests that they appoint Dr. Yassky on a permanent
basis she got no response. She seemed to get no response to any of her letters
to Hadassah.

She was growing old, she reflected. Not simply older, but old, and with
each year she saw herself becoming more and more like Sophie in feature,
mentality and character. Sophie was a woman who knew the one best way to
do a thing and declined to let others do it their way. Sophie went into another
woman's kitchen and without invitation showed her how to make matzoh

dumplings, because only she could do it really well. Sophie was impatient.

During that summer of 1929 Miss Szold sat in her office at the Executive talking to Harry Friedenwald, who had come to Jerusalem for a long visit. Brilliant sunshine spattered the rough stone floor, birds sang outside, and the two veterans talked about Baltimore and childhood, about Zionism and its failure in America, about the Jewish Agency. It seemed to Friedenwald that she was clear-sighted, sound in judgment, a woman of great integrity who was far too good for the politics of Palestine.

She said she was going to Zurich for the Zionist congress, and after that she would go back to America forever. The problems of Palestine were beyond her strength.

23

In the summer of 1929 notables from all over the world descended on Zurich to take part in the formal creation of the Jewish Agency, Sholem Asch, Albert Einstein, Leon Blum, Louis Marshall, Felix Warburg, Sir Herbert Samuel, and Lord Melchett among them. It was a congress like no other before or since, expansive, hopeful, glittering, yet deeply shadowed by a series of ominous events in the Holy Land.

The Agency was Weizmann's interpretation of Article 4 of the Mandate, which provided that "an appropriate Jewish agency" join with the Mandatory government in running the affairs of the national homeland. The Zionist Organization itself had served until now as the appropriate agency through the Zionist Executive.

The Mandate further provided that the Zionist organization was to "secure the cooperation of all Jews who are willing to assist in the establishment of the Jewish National Home." It was Weizmann's intention to bring these abstractions to life, partly in order to defuse the antagonism of non-Zionist Jews, partly to broaden the base of support for the national home, mostly to gain access to non-Zionist fortunes. For this goal, which he had been pursuing since 1921, continued to elude him. Non-Zionist Jews had given tremendous sums to Jewish philanthropy of every sort everywhere in the world, sums great enough to have created a homeland in Palestine several times over. Even the money spent by the non-Zionist Jews of Germany on their own social services would have been sufficient to transform the Holy Land. But after six years of unremitting labor Weizmann had succeeded in establishing a partnership with them.

The Agency pact was signed on August 11, 1929. Within months American Jewish fortunes were to crumble under the impact of the Great Depression. Anti-Semitism would become respectable in Germany, and Haj Amin, the Mufti, would watch, admire and take instruction from the leaders of the Nazi party.

Meanwhile all the usual business of a congress proceeded: the reports, the mudslinging, the attacks on the Executive and its works. Under pressure Miss Szold agreed to stand for election to the next Zionist Executive, which was not to be a triumvirate but a larger body and a most peculiar one in that its role as the government of the Yishuv would be taken over some months later by the Jewish Agency Executive, not yet elected. Yet the Zionist Executive would continue to exist side by side with the Agency Executive, although it would be far less important, concerned chiefly with fund raising and propaganda.

It was unclear what role Miss Szold would play in the new and oversized Zionist Executive, to which she was duly elected. She was not even sure she was wanted on it, for the Orthodox Mizrachi seemed to resent her presence there and were avid to take over her education portfolio.

But no one gave more than half-hearted attention to events in Zurich. People moved through the festive rooms of the congress hotel, women in evening dress, men in top hat and black tie, under the gaze of Herzl's portrait flanked by huge blue-and-white Zionist flags, in the full awareness that the history of Zionism was out of their hands that summer. They scoured the daily bulletins distributed at the congress for news of Palestine and met one another in the corridors with questioning eyes.

When Miss Szold had left Jerusalem for Zurich, she told an American friend not to visit the Holy Land that month. It would be too dangerous, she said. All the leaders would be gone, there was a distinct possibility of Arab riots, and the new High Commissioner could not be trusted. Now, day by day the news that reached Zurich suggested that if violence erupted it would be on an unprecedented scale.

In Jerusalem a mild dispute over a portable bedroom screen, placed before the Western Wall during Yom Kippur services to separate men from women, had taken on frightening implications. The removal of the screen by British police at the most solemn portion of the service had given rise to accusations of anti-Semitism. There were further complications of a religious nature, tangled and intricate and freighted with passion, as all religious disputes in the Holy Land inevitably were. At one point the Mufti launched a wave of propaganda stating that the Jews planned to lay hands on all Moslem holy places.

By summer the screen was forgotten and the focus of emotion fixed on the Western Wall itself, that remnant of the ancient temple that is to both religious and nonreligious Jews the most sacred spot in their sacred land. Delegates to the congress heard that the Mufti was inciting Arab mobs. Colonel Kisch and several others went from Zurich to London to warn the Colonial Office that there must be special precautions taken at the Wall on Tisha b'Ab, the holy day that mourns the destruction of the temple.

On Tisha b'Ab, August 15, British authorities unwisely granted permission to several hundred young Jews for a march on the Wall. They were Revisionists, members of a right-wing party newly founded by Jabotinsky, who believed in immediate and massive Jewish settlement on both sides of the River Jordan. They held a demonstration, taking oaths to defend the Wall at all costs. The next day was Friday, and masses of Arabs flowed into Jerusalem to attend Sabbath services at the Mosque of Omar. They staged a counterdemonstration.

The air was hot and still. With each passing moment it seemed that it could grow no hotter, yet one had only to hold out a naked arm to feel the heat increase. On August 17 a Jewish boy kicked a football into an Arab garden and ran in to claim it and in the brawl that followed was stabbed to death by an Arab. His funeral became a Zionist demonstration; on the following Thursday and Friday great hordes of Arab *fellahin* streamed into Jerusalem clutching knives and clubs.

An American correspondent, Vincent Sheean, who had come to Palestine expecting to write pro-Zionist articles for *The New Palestine*, found himself sending home news dispatches about the civil unrest instead; it should be noted that by now Sheean had decided he had no pro-Zionist statements to make, for to his amazement he found himself more sympathetic with the Arab cause than with that of the Jews. "The situation here is awful," Sheean wrote on August 23. "Every day I expect the worst." Later that day he learned the Mufti was about to address crowds around the city walls, and "We walked up the narrow street, through excited or terrified groups of people, to the Damascus Gate. There we found ourselves in the midst of a mob of country Arabs, who seemed to be in a frenzy of excitement." The chief of police had observed that the Arabs were armed with clubs and knives and gave orders that the crowd be disarmed, which proved too difficult as well as provocative, according to evidence he gave later before the British commission of inquiry. The chief then went to the Mufti and asked why the crowd were carrying clubs and was told that recent events had made them afraid of the Jews. There was no need to worry, the Mufti added, with his air of elfin innocence.

> The houses on the other side of the mob, opposite us, belonged to a group of Georgian Jews. . . . The attention of the crowd was directed towards them. In front of the Jewish houses were ranged six policemen, armed only with short truncheons. The mob gathered with incredible speed—it could

not have taken more than two or three minutes for them to get dense in front of us. The long yells that filled the air were enough to curdle one's blood. . . . The fellahin were flourishing sticks, clubs and knives and . . . they rushed on regardless of the efforts to stop them. Some rushed under the horses' bellies, others squirmed through between the inadequate six; in another moment we heard smashing and a long scream. There was nothing we could do but run, which we did—up the hill towards the Italian Hospital, where there were British police. We found a half dozen bewildered young fellows up there who . . . had firearms. We told them what had happened, and *one* of them set off towards the Georgian houses. . . . Where we stood, in the area at the top of the hill, a mob of Jews in all stages of terror, fury and despair were assembled. They were held back by some of their own people, but a short time before one of them had thrown a grenade at some of the Arabs coming up the hill, and had killed two.

Edwin Samuel, at the government offices just outside the Damascus Gate, heard a faint, distant shouting "like the ominous buzz of bees," and when he went to the balcony saw Arab crowds running toward the Damascus Gate while others came running out of it attacking Jewish passers-by at random; in the garish sunlight Samuel caught the flash of daggers. He saw that some Jews took refuge in nearby Arab houses; later he learned that most of them were saved, but others were attacked indoors and killed.

In the days that followed Hadassah's hospital became a nerve center linked to Hadassah clinics all over the country, for all communication had broken down and newspapers were stopped by the British. Since Chaim Yassky was in Zurich, Reuben Katznelson and his wife had taken charge of the Rothschild Hospital. They had sensed what was coming, and fifty extra surgical beds were ready a week before the riots began. The new Straus Health Center, opened only four weeks earlier, housed and fed refugees. Many homeless people were fed by the Hadassah school lunch program, babies cared for at its infant welfare stations. Telegrams from abroad begging for news of relatives were directed to Hadassah. Medical bulletins were issued, not by the Department of Health, but by Hadassah.

When Colonel Kisch visited the Rothschild Hospital he met old Jewish women with stab wounds all over their bodies.

And Vincent Sheean

made my first acquaintance with a peculiar thing we may call the pogrom heritage. . . . The moment the Jews felt themselves under attack, their lives in danger and their future insecure, they assumed that the world was in league against them—that all persons who did not happen to be Jewish were their enemies . . . it took the form of a strange, complete despair. In its simplest form it was the conviction that a Jew had no friend but God. . . .

I saw one Jewish acquaintance who seemed downright heroic during those days. His name was George Hyman, and he was a secretary to Dr. Magnes. . . . He was a young American of a studious habit of mind. . . . When the outbreak came, Hyman started to work at once. He obtained a rifle and a special constable's brassard, and, armed with these badges of authority, began to move the American Jews in his neighborhood down the hill to the consulate. He made trip after trip over dangerous roads for two days and brought many people to safety. I doubt if he could have used his rifle if it had been necessary, for he was not what might be called a military sort of man. But his friends and neighbors were for the most part older than himself, and even less military; he did his best for them. When I saw him at the consulate he was exhausted, nervous, upset, his voice trembled and broke when he tried to speak; his slim young figure looked as if it would crumple at any moment. And yet he went on until he had seen every one of his people down from their exposed and unguarded position on the hill.

I admired Hyman's behavior more than that of anybody else I saw in Jerusalem during those days. And yet, when I tried to talk to him, I saw the same incomprehensible glaze cover his eyes—the expression that said: "You are not a Jew; I am a Jew; therefore you are my enemy and I am afraid of you."

Because of the economies of the Plumer regime there were fewer than 300 British police, among them many Arabs who refused to fight fellow Arabs. When Zionist authorities asked for permission to arm young men in the settlements it was refused; the British counted instead on reinforcements from their garrison in Egypt. They took three days to arrive, and during those three days the flames leaped across the country. In Hebron, where an ancient community of some 700 souls centered around a Talmudic college, Arab mobs on August 24 murdered and dismembered sixty adults and children. A physician who went to Hebron in the wake of the riot found he could barely operate because of the continual need to vomit. The little Hadassah clinic had been ripped apart, test tubes smashed, walls torn down, every floor battered.

In the little town of Safed, the northern home of Jewish mystics and the Kabbala, twenty people were murdered and more than a hundred houses destroyed. In all the small towns Hadassah's was the only medical service— an American tourist, a Hadassah member returning in September to Pittsburgh, reported that someone in Haifa told her, "If Hadassah had done nothing else in the land during its years here, this one week of its activities would be worth all the money it has spent."

In the course of the entire conflagration, 133 Jews were murdered by Arabs, and 116 Arabs died, almost all at the hands of British police. So rapid had been the spread of bloody violence it was hard not to see incitement and well-laid plans. Indeed the first proclamation of Sir John Chancellor, the new High Commissioner, who returned from London at the time of the Safed outbreak, assumed incitement; but his later statements wobbled, apologized and eventually outraged the Yishuv. Vincent Sheean's verdict was that from start to finish "the Jews were restricting themselves (except in isolated incidents) to self-defense, and that the attacks were for the most part attacks of Arab mobs upon Jews." He laid all blame at the door of the British, the inadequacy of their police force, the heavy reliance on Moslem police. Nonetheless Haj Amin, the Mufti, captivated Sheean as he had captivated wiser and more experienced men. Sheean found him "an extremely level-headed, deliberate man, mild-mannered and thoughtful . . . also a humane man . . . his influence in the actual crisis had been used on the side of peace."

In the wake of the 1929 riots many Zionist leaders, Weizmann, Ben Gurion and the brilliant young theoretician and orator Chaim Arlosoroff among them, looked inward as well as outward for an explanation of the tragedy that had been visited on them. There was a good deal of heart searching and some serious efforts to reach out toward the Arabs.

Miss Szold wanted to return to Palestine after the Zurich congress. However Weizmann told her she would be more useful in America, so she set off for America. Although she had no expectation of being useful there she submitted as always to Zionist discipline.

In New York she paid a visit to Felix Warburg, a non-Zionist banker and philanthropist, who was now chairman of the Jewish Agency Council and the recognized leader of American Jewry. Bald, with a great mustache, large dark eyes, dark eyebrows and a massive jaw, he had the genial, princely charm of one who has always been rich but also the condescension to those who were not. It was Warburg's belief that the Zionists had made a mess of Palestine, and he could hardly wait for the non-Zionists of the Agency to get their efficient hands on it.

His conversation with Miss Szold suggested she ought to be in Palestine, not in America. He went so far as to read her a copy of a letter he had sent to Weizmann stating that if Miss Szold did not return to Palestine immediately someone else would take her place on the Zionist Executive.

Miss Szold retorted that she was an elected member of the Executive. She had duties, rights and privileges, and they could not be abrogated at his whim.

Then she set off for Palestine and on the way stopped in London to see Weizmann. He told her Warburg thought that in view of the planned reorganization (the transfer of authority from Zionist Executive to Jewish Agency Executive) she might as well resign at once. She would surely not be elected to the Agency Executive. Furthermore, Weizmann continued, Mr. Warburg was irritated with her for having left America before the fund-raising campaign with which she was supposed to help was under way. He was also irritated because she had come to London without permission.

Miss Szold told herself she was not hurt by this series of insults. She was not hurt, she repeated in a letter to Warburg. Why should she be hurt? She was merely puzzled over his having said nothing to her about resignation when she was there with him. "I hope it was not out of consideration for me that you refrained from telling me what was in your mind. In matters of public concern, I assure you, I can be as objective with reference to my person as though I were a thing. . . ."

But she was not a thing. She had been shunted from London to America, then at the end of two months from America to Palestine; told to resign from an office to which she had been elected; made to feel superfluous, and the wounds bled. Since no one would accuse her to her face—of being too old, or insufficiently trained for health or education, or too much a Zionist, or whatever else Warburg had against her—she had no way to defend herself beyond the quiet struggle to hold on to the shreds of her dignity. By denying she was in pain. Denying it to Weizmann, the seductive intellectual who saw through people and ideals and stripped them to their skeletons. Denying it to Warburg, who was powerful and patronizing. Denying it above all to herself, as she denied fear and the knowledge of evil and whatever else was ugly.

The two-month visit to America had another unhappy aspect: her relations with Hadassah. They were almost all strangers now. The high-minded women with whom she had joined the People's Council for Democracy and Peace in 1917 were scattered and had been replaced by others whose lives and personal concerns were worlds removed from her own. During the course of the American visit several of them urged her to write an autobiography, all sorts of people being sent to plead with her to that end. Miss Szold was mortified. She felt Hadassah had "put its hand into my soul," that there was a "liberty taken with my inners," as if all the well-dressed women with children and husbands and houses and cars and weekly visits to the hairdresser threatened to expose her shapeless life in which there was no husband, no children, no home, not even a room with her own furniture in it. Not even a bookshelf to hold her own books. She had nothing and she was nothing—Warburg had all but told her so. And Hadassah, for purposes of propaganda, dared to ask that she reveal herself to the world. The pain of it lingered for months.

On her return to Jerusalem she found a letter from Warburg attempting to soothe the wounds he had inflicted. Perhaps, he said, he had been more brutally frank than was otherwise his habit; he hadn't precisely demanded Miss Szold's resignation, only told Weizmann to get as many resignations from his Executive as he could.

If he had written no more Miss Szold might have been assuaged, but Warburg proceeded: "I think I told you in the friendliest spirit when you were here, if you should decide to devote the next three years to writing the history which you have been asked to compile [of Baron Maurice de Hirsch] Mr. Berkson can attend to the duties of the Educational Department without further sacrifice of your health and nerves in Palestine. I also stated, I think, that in the field of health somebody must be found who can mold the innumerable institutions of different value into some sort of a federation. . . ."

Miss Szold read the letter to mean, "Damn the Zionists, and get thee to a home for genteel old ladies!" She felt she could never go back to America now; it was poisoned for her by Warburg's opinion.

There was a sense of waiting, that spring in Jerusalem, a sense of suspended animation; she was busy because it was impossible not to be busy in Palestine, but she was not overridingly busy, her role on the Agency still undetermined, and the Zionist Executive marked time until the Agency replaced it. Since Harriet had returned to America, and since the break with Sophia Berger was not yet healed (it healed in time, although the old intimacy was lost forever), Miss Szold moved herself and her possessions to a new home, a modest kosher establishment called the Eden Hotel, where she lived in a single room.

It was at the Eden Hotel that she picked up a newspaper one morning to learn that the waiting was over. Elections to the Executive of the Jewish Agency were completed, and she was not one of the elect. This rejection of Miss Szold, this casting off—for it was nothing else—was politically motivated and politically intended. But Miss Szold did not feel it politically; she felt it as personal and total. She could not pretend this time, could not deny. She was rejected and felt rejected, in the newspapers and before all the world. The wounds would ache for months, and she would not even try to conceal them. "I shall sit down," she told her sisters, "and decide what to do next, and the next thing, whatever it may be, will be a life decision. Funny, isn't it? To stand at the crossways at my age—to be 'unemployed' for the first time in seventy years. . . ."

There was a spurt of amazement at the news both in Palestine and America, followed by a welling up of sympathy and indignation. Protest telegrams poured in to Weizmann. *Davar* spoke of her "rich experience" and covered itself with apologies for the cold welcome it had given her when she first came to the Executive. The teachers, the political parties—all but the Orthodox Mizrachi, which kept a stony silence—passed resolutions. "It is absolutely embarrassing. Whenever I appear, the opportunity is taken to show me distinguished honor and respect, and to denounce what happened in London," she told her sisters. And even to convey to them the fullness of this outpouring "really violates my modesty. The whole country . . . is up in arms." It was the first time she had ever been made to feel the Yishuv cared whether she came or went. She decided to lie low for a while and give Weizmann every chance to reinstate her.

She waited in vain. She sat in her bedroom at the Eden Hotel surrounded by baggage and boxes. She had never owned a wardrobe-chest in all her years in Palestine, living out of her wardrobe trunk instead because she believed she was always on the verge of going "home." Now she was being pressured to go home, for she felt she had no choice but to resign from her anomalous position on the Zionist Executive and leave, but where was home? Balancing the return to America against the staying on in Palestine, the "Warburg incident," as she called it, against the sisters, nephews and nieces, she felt more than ever like a bit of flotsam, a fragment, rootless and unwanted. One day she was certain she would stay on in Palestine forever; the next she could hardly bear the idea of growing old and dying there, out of sight of the only people in the world who loved her.

The very thinking jarred loose the sinews that bound her to America, and they vibrated; when they vibrated they hurt. "After all," she wrote to her sisters, "what part do I play in your lives when I am in America? It appears that ten years of wandering away from home have loosened bonds . . . [but] because these things have been shaking me, I have been not a little homesick lately."

That same month the British released their position paper based on the findings of a commission of inquiry that followed the 1929 riots. This so-called Passfield White Paper struck at the heart of the Yishuv. From now on both immigration and land purchase would be severely restricted. The tone of the paper was patronizing, even hostile. Weizmann saw it as a betrayal of every British promise and resigned as president of the World Zionist Organization. There was turmoil within the Agency, in America, in London, throughout the Yishuv.

To Miss Szold the Passfield White Paper came as a thunderbolt. Pacifist though she was, and a stickler for legality, she wrote to friends in Haganah, the semilegal Jewish self-defense force, to offer solidarity in their resistance: "I cannot bear arms, but my home is open to anything you want to leave."

In London the surviving members of the coalition that had issued the Balfour Declaration united in opposition to the Passfield White Paper, and the Labor government faced a powerful combination: world Jewry, the political opportunists of the opposition and all those men of goodwill who hated to see the Balfour Declaration dishonored. Within four months the Prime Minister presented Weizmann with a letter that modified the position of the White Paper.

For the next few years Palestine was to live in uneasy peace. Hunger and unemployment stalked America and much of Europe, but in the Jewish homeland Jews and Arabs were comparatively prosperous; Sir John Chancellor retired and was replaced by a new, more sympathetic High Commissioner, General Sir Arthur Wauchope. The riots had brought about one significant change through the acknowledged leadership of Haj Amin, the Mufti. According to the journalist Christopher Sykes, who was to meet the Mufti and converse with him in Persian in the mid-thirties:

> He was interested in religion. Though a man of great slyness and skill in argument he did not make the common mistake of sophisticated leaders by giving his followers a complex programme. He gave them one of the utmost simplicity: Down with the infidel! In Palestine, as in most Moslem countries, there was no great anti-Jewish feeling, and an Arab could be anti-Zionist without indulging further enmity to Jews. Under the Mufti's influence this was all changed. The enemy was the Jewish people. To be a Jew was in itself an offence. Arab nationalists adopted anti-Semitism on the coarsest European model. The Mufti also put an end to cooperation with the Administration as a feature of Arab nationalism. . . . He taught his followers to regard the British as an infidel tyranny in alliance with other infidels against Islam. He had the advantage of holding his beliefs in complete sincerity.

The waffling of the Labor government that issued and then modified the White Paper served a useful purpose in giving to each side the feeling they had achieved something: the Arabs had achieved a massacre, followed by the White Paper, an assurance that their national aspirations were appreciated by the Mandatory; the Zionists had achieved the virtual reversal of the White Paper and thereby an implied assurance that the Balfour Declaration remained the policy of the Mandatory, although its interpretation was more limited than they used to hope. Nevertheless in the opening years of the new decade distrust of the British solidified, growing sharper and more outspoken, and Jabotinsky's militaristic followers became a conspicuous part of Jewish life in Palestine.

In the room at the Eden Hotel, Miss Szold read a letter from Adele describing the birds that had lodged in her chimney. It tugged at all her senses, always so quiveringly alert to natural beauty, reminding her of what she was missing at home and how little time there was left to enjoy it. Soon the trees would be turning color in the parks and forests near Baltimore. She loved those autumnal trees. She longed for fresh corn and tart apples and the Negro spirituals that always moved her to tears.

Group after group came to her with suggestions for work that needed her, but she could not decide. She stayed on in limbo, having resigned from the Zionist Executive; she waited, as she had so often waited before, for someone else to make a decision. In October, when Hadassah invited her to New York to discuss the establishment of a Hadassah representation in Palestine, she was puzzled, unsure why the matter required a trans-Atlantic voyage, but she went.

No sooner had the ship docked in New York than she learned the reason for Hadassah's invitation: a surprise celebration of her seventieth birthday. Someone had arranged for a *New York Times* photographer to record the moment she disembarked. Miss Szold stiffened with anger—"How dare you subject me to this!"—and then, as the Hadassah women who came to greet her looked at one another with dismay, she disappeared into her cabin. She returned moments later, having carefully combed her hair and rearranged her dress for the benefit of the camera.

She submitted to the celebration as gracefully as she could. Hadassah had attained a membership of 37,000, and if Miss Szold was still estranged from them, it was impossible not to proud of their size, their influence, the multiplicity and intricacy of their undertakings. So much had grown from so little. Great sums of money were raised at the luncheons, teas and dinners that Hadassah staged in connection with the birthday, great quantities of inspiration dispensed by Miss Szold herself.

The family celebrated privately. Adele had bought a Ford, the first car ever owned by a member of the Szold clan. Henrietta thought when she saw it: "That Ford is a stunner!" More than anything she wanted a trip, no matter where, in Adele's Ford, and the sisters finally escaped from Hadassah's official festivities to the Shenandoah Valley, the apple country, and across to the Atlantic coast. Adele drove fast, and Henrietta loved being driven fast.

Yet she was haunted by the belief that Zionism was dead in America. Even the young people, with whom she felt so much more sympathetic than the middle-aged, seemed to go about their Zionist duties with their hands and feet rather than their hearts. The rounds of desultory speech making, the "being inspirational," depressed her; the fulsome praise seemed depersonalizing, for she felt the woman they described was not herself. It was as if nobody knew her.

America had changed beyond recall—something aside from the depression. There was a garishness, a stridency. Radios blared, and most of what they blared was jazz. Skinny girls with dresses that ended above their knees and circles of rouge on their cheeks smoked in public and drank too much and used slang and worse. Gangsters were heroes. She had no place in such a world.

At seventy Miss Szold was much thinner than she used to be, and more attractive. In a strange way she had grown into her features, so that people who knew her only in old age believed she must once have been quite lovely. She walked as briskly as ever, sometimes slowing her pace to accommodate some "older" person a few years younger than she was. The serene old age she used to dream about still eluded her, for she was restless, full of yearnings that had to do with Palestine, yet tied hand and foot by inertia. Palestine had rejected her. Unless it reached out to bring her back she would remain in America giving inspirational speeches until she died of it.

VI

JERUSALEM: A MOTHER OF MANY CHILDREN

24

In March of 1931, Miss Szold was called back to Palestine to do a piece of work she wanted to do and felt capable of doing. There was no pushing and shoving this time, no anguished protestations of inadequacy, although she spent many weeks thinking it over and after deciding to go insisted she was not exuberantly happy with the decision. This was merely habit. She was seventy years old, and she was needed on the other side of the world, the only place she really wanted to be. She sailed in early May, and after eighteen days at sea in two different ships was back in her room at the Eden Hotel.

At her last sight of it, it had been simply a hotel bedroom, a single room with a single bed, an ugly Morris chair and a washstand as blatant as a naked light bulb. When people came to visit she had been compelled to receive them downstairs in the public salon. Now the little room had undergone certain changes at the hands of friends. A coverlet was thrown over the bed and some cushions added, which made it a studio couch; a screen concealed the washstand so that she could rinse out her stockings and underwear at night and hang them up and the world would never know. For ten dollars she had a bookcase made and filled it with the books she had brought from America. She asked for an extension phone, and it appeared one day, which gave her the courage to think about a portable stove.

These modest alterations gave her the greatest pleasure; she felt positively smug about them. From her windows she looked out at the Old City as well as the growing new Jerusalem, built of a pale golden native stone. No other material could be used, according to a decree by Ronald Storrs, who had loved the city no matter what its inhabitants thought of him. On the deep window sills she placed the plants that she watered every day in a solemn ritual; two plants were as good as a garden to her. What was best about the new arrangement was that she need not run downstairs to the public salon when visitors came.

And people did come to the Eden Hotel to see her. First of all, her return had a "messianic" quality, according to her own account. Some friends had traveled all the way from Jerusalem to Jaffa to meet her when she disembarked; others crowded into the hotel room as soon as she reached it. There had been a steady stream of callers ever since and by now there were so many plants and flowers she could hardly turn around.

People seemed to wait about on the street in order to wish her *Shabbat Shalom* when she walked to synagogue Saturday mornings. Friends and acquaintances came for tea Saturday afternoons. "Everyone" dropped in, tourists from America, nurses from the Rothschild Hospital. "It was the most interesting afternoon when one went to see her," a nurse recalled. "She spoke of literature, of anything under the sun, and with such understanding—and she was a very charming hostess, she'd go out of her way to make you comfortable, you felt uncomfortable because of it."

The first beginnings of Miss Szold as a public property appeared with this return in the spring of 1931. As the decade wore on she became aware that one of the tourist guides who waited at the railroad station was in the habit of informing visitors that he would show them where Miss Szold lived, he would show them Miss Szold herself, she was one of the musts on every American tourist's itinerary. The waiter at the hotel spoke freely to visitors about her eating habits; very precise, he said, she takes no more on her plate than she can finish, when she asks for four prunes she never means five. Her departure for work each morning on the bus that left the Jaffa Road at 7:45 became a daily feature of Jerusalem life. There was the gnomelike little woman of seventy wearing gloves, carrying a heavy briefcase, who would not take a taxi or auto when she could take a bus. Never earlier than 7:45, never later, although the buses ran often.

She was widely known and would become in time a national heroine, but she remained an alien. Hanging on news from home, she was pathetically grateful when Bertha forwarded the letters Adele wrote to the Baltimore family. "There isn't much in them," Adele observed. To Bertha, Henrietta wrote, "She doesn't realize that she herself is in them." Friday afternoons she wrote to her sisters. By the time the shofar sounded the hour of sunset the letter was finished and sealed; she did no writing and no work until sunset on Saturday. And the weekly letters carried across the ocean her repeated longing for someone of her own blood.

"Miss Szold never was a part of that country—and I say that dogmatically and positively. Never. She was a stranger in a strange land. She would like not to have been but she was." A woman who worked with her in the early thirties is speaking now: "She wasn't at home with the people. I don't care who tells you that she was. . . . She spoke Hebrew but never with ease, *never*

with ease. . . . She had surrounded herself with the things that were home—
home meaning America. She was quite a bit of a botanist but tending all
these little plants was to remind her, always to remind her." Miss Szold said
much the same to Bertha and Adele; she was leading a life of isolation, she
told them, in spite of all her contacts in the country. Nothing, nothing could
bring back the old times. It was Lombard Street that filled her eye and heart.

Her energy was only slightly diminished, her ascetic regime hardly at all.
She still rose early and spent an hour or so at gymnastics followed by a Hebrew
lesson. Although she no longer arrived at the office before anyone else, no
longer stayed on when the others were gone, she worked at home until midnight
or after. And she took naps. She lay down for a nap in the afternoon and
napped during work as well, light dozes of which she was perfectly aware,
convinced that the secret of her amazing energy was this gift of half sleep
from which she sprang to attention at crucial moments. "I can remember
meetings where she was, her head was dangling away and she looked as if she
was out," a young protégée recalled. "And so they started trying to pass something that she had been disapproving of—and boy, that arm came out, her
fist came down on the table, she was wide awake."

What brought her back to Palestine was her election to the seven-member
Executive of the Vaad Leumi, the National Assembly of the Jews of Palestine.
She was to help in the transfer of health and education services from the
hands of the international Zionist organization to the communities of the Yishuv.
It was what Miss Szold had believed in for years, that the Yishuv, and not
the Zionists of Europe or America or anywhere else, ought to take responsibility
for its own ongoing life. The money would come from local taxes as soon as
the communities were well enough organized to levy taxes. No one knew when
that would be.

Only after she got there did she realize the Vaad Leumi also intended
to set up a central social service bureau as a clearinghouse for hundreds of
charitable organizations. Miss Szold seized the moment. She decided to create
something more extensive than a clearinghouse, nothing less than a full-fledged
system of modern social services, planned, run and paid for by the Yishuv.

She had already helped in the initial stages of the transfer of health services,
a task made less difficult by the splendid organizational powers of Hadassah.
They were pulling out of countrywide hospital work and turning all their energies
toward partnership with the Hebrew University and a teaching hospital. For
the vision of Hadassah's Medical Unit as the health department of Jewish
Palestine belonged to the past. Instead, Kupat Holim of the Labor Zionists
was to become the chief source of health care for the Yishuv, a semiofficial
national health service whose institutions provided medical services for 65 per-

cent of the nation's population in 1978. But Hadassah set the standard in the beginning, a fact of which they are justly proud, and the research and teaching hospital would perform a similar service on a more sophisticated scale. Hadassah's early philosophy that health care be made available to Arabs as well as Jews created another enduring model. The Emir Abdullah, later king of Jordan and grandfather of the present king, was hospitalized at Hadassah's hospital during World War II, as was a prince of Saudi Arabia. Throughout the troubled history of the modern state ordinary citizens of neighboring Moslem countries and those of the "administered" territories within Israel have been treated, generously and sometimes at great expense, in Jewish hospitals, a practice that was Hadassah's gift to the Yishuv.

The transfer of health care was under way. The transfer of the schools would be completed in a shorter time, and in this too Miss Szold would continue to help. But she made the Central Social Service Bureau her main task. It would serve as the opening wedge in the long and labored process of creating a system of modern social work, against intense opposition from the Yishuv and its leaders, and without money.

Meanwhile it was necessary to catch up on the new realities of Palestine, to listen to what people were talking about. She went out to dinner and listened, hearing on every hand anti-British sentiments that dismayed her. Not that she disagreed—she was often among the first to level specific accusations against the government—but she had an abiding belief in British justice and British honor, and it was the tone of this talk she disliked. It was carping, discontented, destructive.

The Arabs lost faith in Great Britain during the same period, but for other reasons: under the Mufti's tutelage the English were their enemies as well as the Jews. The combined effect of these attitudes among the two peoples they governed was damaging to the morale of British civil servants in Palestine. No longer was the Holy Land the crown of a colonial career; it was only a place to serve one's time, isolated from Jew and Arab alike, and escape as soon as possible. In such a climate of disillusion and cynicism young people turned increasingly toward Jabotinsky's Revisionist party.

Miss Szold, who never enjoyed political talk in any case, found consolation in the state of the economy. Palestine had hardly suffered from the worldwide depression; there had been a great spurt of activity in building and in the purchase of land for orange growing. The fact that immigration was almost at a standstill contributed to the state of peace with the Arabs, a sullen, heavy-hearted truce that was nevertheless welcome after the tragic fires of 1929. All in all it was not an inauspicious time to start the task with which Miss Szold was concerned: shoving the Yishuv from dependence into adulthood.

There was of course no money; this she had been prepared for. The Yishuv had never before taxed itself; it already paid taxes, however light, to the British, and without governmental powers the Vaad Leumi could not squeeze taxes out of a reluctant population. But in the matter of social services Miss Szold faced what was perhaps worse than a lack of money: a complex of negative attitudes deeply entrenched among both sections of the community, the new Zionists who had come to redeem the land with blood and sweat and the old Yishuv, pious and stubborn in equal proportion.

Since the late twenties the new Yishuv of the Labor Zionists had outnumbered the old. In the early thirties Labor Zionism became the dominant factor in the life of the Yishuv and Histadrut the largest employer of labor in the country, providing its members with an extraordinary range of social and cultural services: libraries, publishing houses, a traveling theater, sports clubs, agricultural schools, as well as insurance, full medical coverage, old age and disability benefits. The Histadrut was and is an institution unique in the world.

But the rest of the community, those outside the labor force, were not particularly their concern. There were sick or aged or widowed city dwellers reduced to begging. There were the insane, and a single institution for the insane in the entire country. There were children born retarded or defective, in whom the Yishuv took no more interest than did the British.

Ben-Gurion said in 1927: "The question is not that there are so many unemployed and no bread. I don't believe in improving the situation by philanthropy. . . . The danger is that society will become degenerated." To the Jews of the new Yishuv, whatever Miss Szold had in mind would inevitably lower the level of morality and hold back the creative powers. They wanted no part of it.

The old Yishuv, on the other hand, believed in charity; over the years an extraordinary network of benevolent societies had grown up, active, manifold, utterly disorganized and in general "a matter of hysteria," as Miss Szold observed. Some 400 worthy institutions took the form of burial societies, societies for ritual slaughtering, foundations for study, soup kitchens, orphanages, societies collecting dowries for penniless brides, the whole forming a tangled, chaotic and redundant network whose goals were antique and unrelated to the modern world. The old Yishuv saw no need to change. They preferred their charity spontaneous and disorganized. Miss Szold and her social service bureau were, above all, a threat to their independence; they did not want to account to anyone for their methods or their funds.

But Miss Szold was resolved to organize social work along modern lines, with or without money, with or without approval. She knew quite well what her shortcomings were: no training whatever, almost total ignorance of the field. Nevertheless she hired a secretary, a young man named Chaim Japhet, and moved into an office at the Vaad Leumi. Japhet rather expected to work in a little cubicle of his own, but she told him they would share one room because she wanted to listen to his Hebrew, which was excellent.

For many months after that, Japhet recalled, "She decided not to do anything until she will learn what is social work—what contains those two words, social welfare. How? Any man who arrived from Germany, the Netherlands, America—volunteers or professionals—we had talks with them. Then she got addresses from social services all over the world and wrote to them for pamphlets." She wrote to New York, to Berlin, Vienna, to Bertha, Alice Seligsberg and the U.S. Children's Bureau, requesting whatever material was free because there was no money, not even for books. "Then she prepared her plan . . . the plan is like a guide, how to do, what to do, even after ten years."

This plan was submitted to the Vaad Leumi in the summer of 1931 and accepted, presumably because it would cost them nothing, the costs to be borne by each individual community once the communities had revenues; and since this was in the future it need not trouble anyone for the time being.

The plan itself was based on the institution of family case work, an American specialty familiar to some European nations, especially Germany, but unheard of in Palestine. And since family case work required a staff of professionals, there must be a school for social work. Professionals needed libraries; there was not one book on the subject in Hebrew. Professionals also required a larger corps of volunteers; the country had volunteer do-gooders in profusion, and they must be kept, for they would assure that social work retained what to Miss Szold was infinitely precious: the "spiritual" quality in social service. But the volunteers must be trained; they must learn modern methods of fund raising, a united drive in place of piecemeal solicitation, and they must get over their unfortunate tendency to weep, so that the objects of their philanthropy were not always bathed in sentimental tears. There were other aspects to this plan of Miss Szold's, which was a remarkably extensive and clear-headed creation on the part of an aged amateur working under the certain knowledge that she would not be taken seriously.

But there was still no money. Miss Szold was well aware that one of the reasons she had been elected to the Vaad Leumi was her ability to draw money out of America. And the other members of the Vaad Leumi accepted her plan with this in mind: if it had to be, perhaps America would help pay for it.

Early in 1932 the money appeared in the shape of a gift from the Palestine Endowment Fund, a charitable enterprise set up by Justice Brandeis and Judge

Mack, one of the many forms in which the Mack-Brandeis faction continued their service to the Holy Land. The gift was small, just enough to start three little social service centers in the three main cities, each under the leadership of a professional. Those three professionals were the entire supply of trained social workers in the country.

The plan she had outlined to the Vaad Leumi, the systems under which the urban centers were organized, first in the cities, then in the towns and villages, and all that grew from them—a school for social work, countrywide social work conferences—remained essentially intact until the birth of the state in 1948. Most of it still exists thirty years later.

While Miss Szold and her Department of Social Welfare struggled for a place in the sun, a woman in Berlin—small, fierce, dark-eyed, a rebbitzin, musician and writer named Recha Freier—suddenly felt what she called "the push of reality." A recent convert to Zionism, until now her Zionism had been dreamy, planless, untied to any organization, barely even expressed. It had consisted only of a vision that all the Jewish youth of Germany might somehow be transported to Palestine. Suddenly she knew "that it must be, that it will be and that I will perform it."

The dramatic turn of phrase was typical of Recha Freier. A friend once said of her:

> She seemed utterly disorganized and full of unbelievably impractical ideas. Although she was a mother . . . I am not sure whether she could have fried an egg or made tea. If she did it she might have kept her hat on, even her overcoat—and it would most likely be a man's coat. . . . Since she thought and lived on a plane of practical impossibilities, she actually carried things out which no practical person could have achieved.

One day in early 1932 a group of adolescent boys came to Recha Freier's home. She was unsure why they came to her in particular, only that they were thin, excited, with gloom and despair on their pale faces. They had been sacked from their jobs because they were Jews. This was a year before the Hitler regime came to power, but it was a time of economic depression in which the long-standing disease of German anti-Semitism festered close to the surface.

The boys were looking for a way out, perhaps a chance to work in the coal mines of western Germany. Could Mrs. Freier help? At that moment "the utter senselessness of Jewish life in the Diaspora stood palpably before my eyes." She visited the Jewish Labor Exchange in Berlin the next day; the director assured her that as soon as the economy straightened out the boys would find work again and told her to let matters take their course meanwhile. "The way that director shrugged his shoulders made me shudder."

One night a very simple and clear idea occurred to her. The boys must go to Palestine, to the workers' agricultural settlements, where they would get a training for life on the land. "I was sure that this idea could be realized, for it was absolutely true and it was timely."

She turned to German Zionist leaders, but they were for the most part apathetic; their Zionism struck her as theoretical rather than practical, but she was in no way deterred. Once having determined on a course of action, whether a creative act or an act of charity, Recha Freier held to it, sometimes outfacing the very object of her charity. "My mother has gone to extreme lengths sometimes, and upset our entire family—which by the way she's done very often and does very often—by supporting individual children in whom we think she's really wasting her time and effort," Shalhevet Freier recalled many years later. "If she has a feeling about something she will immediately do something about it. She just will not waste her time."

She spoke next to a group of young people, mostly of east European origin, at a Zionist elementary school in East Berlin. They were excited, enthusiastic; they came to her home next day begging to be allowed to "register" for Palestine. The Zionist organization in Germany began to take notice. Mrs. Freier was told they were prepared to accept her plan, "providing that the Vaad Leumi . . . in Palestine established a satisfactory body to supervise arrangements for settling the children . . . and provided they accepted responsibility for financial matters." It was therefore suggested she get in touch with the director of the Social Service Bureau in Jerusalem, Henrietta Szold.

At this time Miss Szold was immersed in two specific tasks: the organization of the three social welfare centers in the three cities, and something quite new that fell to her lot without warning. She had become an honorary juvenile probation officer for the British.

The Mandate government in Palestine had no lack of good will toward Jewish social service projects, but it had no money. The Colonial Office in London provided none for such purposes, just as they refused to sink into the educational system enough to pay for compulsory education for Arabs and Jews; it was not necessary for "natives." And there were some 10,000 Jewish children in Palestine who got no education at all; thousands more left school after a few years to become bootblacks, paper boys, errand runners.

Most of these children belonged to the growing communities of so-called Oriental Jews, those who came from neighboring Moslem countries or North Africa. There they had lived in the Middle Ages; in Palestine they found themselves defeated by the modern world. Men who had ruled huge families with traditional authority discovered they had no salable skills. They became tyrants and child beaters. Faithful to tradition, they put their daughters out to work as servants at the age of ten and married them off at twelve or thirteen. Their sons went briefly to schools that were not attuned to them. The charities of the old Yishuv made no provision for playgrounds, children's libraries, vocational schools, nor did the new Yishuv take any interest in the children of the unemployable. The British ignored them except when they broke the law.

But early in 1932 the British appointed a probation officer, the retired headmaster of an Episcopal boys' school, well bred and well intentioned but entirely ignorant about Jews, Palestine and probation work. Miss Szold had the lucky idea of putting herself in touch with him and offering to collaborate. The offer was eagerly taken up.

Now she plunged into a new world of children's courts, police stations and the schools, homes and work places of delinquent boys. She visited Oriental Jews who had left Persia, Georgia, Iraq, Yemen and Kurdistan to crowd into the cellars of the Old City, eight, nine, ten family members in one room. The brightest and most adventurous boys were those who escaped at the age of ten or eleven, and Miss Szold found them playing dice and cards for hours on end in hallways and alleys or haunting the movie houses. They were nimble, canny, undersized.

When the law caught up with them they were sent back to their parents or to foster homes or to the country's only institution for troubled youth, a prison-reformatory at Tul Karm.

Miss Szold went to Tul Karm one day with Zipporah Bloch, the social worker in charge of Jerusalem. A lunch had been prepared for them, unfortunately not kosher, so the two women ate only bread. Then the Arab director described his methods to Miss Szold, British methods that relied on flogging. The word itself was not used; according to British custom one referred to "strokes." "I try to give them the strokes myself," he told her, "so they won't be too hard." But the number of strokes for each type of offense was beyond his control, defined by British statute. She learned that the Jewish boys were mostly sentenced for petty crimes such as thieving, while among the Arabs were a number of murderers. Little boys who had watched their fathers beat and torment their mothers vowed one day to put a stop to it. The boys grew bigger; the day came when they were big enough to protect their mothers; a bitter fight between father and son sometimes ended in a death. These boys were often the natural leaders of the reformatory inmates, for they were the oldest. They had determination and a primitive sense of justice.

When they left, Miss Szold told Miss Bloch that the director made a good impression but as for Tul Karm itself, it was bad, very bad, not for the

Jewish children alone, but for all of them. Nothing was done to prepare them for life.

She blamed the British, she blamed the Jews, she felt on all sides the tremendous gulf between what must be done and what could be done. Her probation work revealed to her a division in the Yishuv even more disturbing than those that stemmed from politics. There were Western Jews who got the jobs and educations and ran the Yishuv, and there were Oriental Jews, imprisoned by their own ignorance and cultural patterns. Not only was this division terrible in itself; what was more painful to her was that nobody cared. It could go on forever. They could become two nations of Jews in the one land.

In the course of 1932 Miss Szold had a letter from Recha Freier, placing before her the plan for German youth to come to Palestine and settle on the kibbutzim, to work and learn in an atmosphere free of the anti-Semitism that poisoned Germany. Could Miss Szold and the Vaad Leumi assume financial responsibility? Would Miss Szold get immigration certificates?

The plan seemed outrageous to her. Certainly it was based on complete ignorance of life in Palestine. Ten thousand children of the Yishuv had never gone to school, yet a rebbitzin in Berlin proposed that German children leave their excellent and varied schools and the web of modern social services for which the German Jewish community was world famous to be educated by the Yishuv. She would be depriving the children already in her care to accommodate the newcomers, many the offspring of comfortable bourgeois families. Let the rich Jews of Germany care for their own.

Moreover the German youth were to come without their parents, which seemed heartless to Miss Szold. If they longed for Palestine, they must persuade their families to settle there. Why not? Immigration had picked up somewhat in the first half of 1932, but it was still slow. Let them come, let them all come, but together.

She had no sympathy with any part of this plan and told Recha Freier so in the bluntest terms.

Recha Freier had already been in touch with a representative of the Histadrut, who had given her the names of several kibbutzim that were prepared to accept groups of young Germans, including Kibbutz Ain Harod, one of the largest. But without Miss Szold's approval they would not act. It was Miss Szold who must apply to the British for immigration certificates.

At this point, in June 1932, Mrs. Freier learned of the possibility of sending a few German youngsters to the Ben Shemen Children's Village, an institution supported by German Jews for the benefit of the children of east European Jewry. Ben Shemen was able to offer immigration certificates on its own. It was not a kibbutz, the number of boys involved would be minute, their parents most reluctant, but to Recha Freier it was a start. In order to guarantee their maintenance for two years a friend of hers pawned some jewelry, a Jewish department store owner helped collect equipment, a charitable organization paid fares. All was done with the knowledge of the parents but without their full consent; at the last moment, the parents signed. The handful of boys and their families came to the Berlin railway station on Wednesday, October 12, 1932, to find crowds of young people from the Zionist youth groups waiting on the platform singing Hebrew songs. "The platform seemed to tremble under my feet," Mrs. Freier recalled. "The work had begun; no one could interfere with it any more. . . . Cheering broke out as the train left. The parents wept."

Zionist youth groups like these were to play a distinctive part in the events that followed. Superficially they resembled Boy Scouts in England or America, but in those countries the leaders were adults. The Zionist youth of Germany were led by people only a little older than themselves, and their origins were not Zionist, not even Jewish, but German, for they sprang directly from the German *Wandervogel* bands. A *Wandervogel* is literally a migratory bird, a bird of passage. The name is no more romantic than the *Wandervogel* bands themselves.

Since the first decade of the century, the children of middle-class German families had felt a need for a world of their own, a world apart from that of their rigid and materialistic elders. For there seemed to be no role for the young in Kaiser Wilhelm's Germany. It was their business to keep out of the way until they were grown. Fashions were the fashions of middle age. Literature spoke the language of middle age. Youth was only middle age incomplete. Young Germany withdrew as a result and looked backwards toward a more beautiful past, toward medieval romance and, further still, to Teutonic legend and myth.

They wanted to live in the simplest style on close and intimate terms with nature, to be free, spontaneous, natural. They formed little bands that wandered over their beloved countryside in the costumes of huntsmen-farmers, singing folk songs. They became splendid choral singers, splendid walkers. They believed they were growing closer to the "people," although they had nothing to do with the people beyond sleeping in the haystacks of farmers whose lands they rambled across.

The most powerful binding force of the *Wandervogel* bands was the group itself. Success was measured by loyalty to the group and ability to dissolve the individual ego within the group. They had no dealings with adults if they could help it. Throughout was a pervasive air of youth worship, a pure and heady and romantic adoration of the fresh and ideal.

Jewish youth had belonged to the *Wandervogel* from the beginning, although not in great numbers. Some bands began to limit the numbers; Jews
were "one-sided," it was said, too intellectual, too intense, descriptions that
were on the whole accurate. Some Jews stayed on in those groups that refused
to allow anti-Semitism; others began to feel the need for an organization of
their own. So powerful was the mystique of the group that they hardly felt
they were succumbing to anti-Semitic pressure, only to the desire to be among
their own kind.

In 1912 the Jewish Blau Weiss was formed, retaining all the trappings
and strivings of the *Wandervogel.* Indeed they were simply another *Wandervogel*
band and only vaguely Zionist; other groups sprang up in their wake, but all
remained *Wandervogel* bands. When a Zionist youth group in the course of
its ramblings met one of the long-established groups, they exchanged greetings
as equals. *"Shalom,"* cried the Zionists. *"Heil!"* called the Gentiles in response.
And in their beginnings the Jews turned to Zionism the same way their Gentile
fellows had turned to chivalry and Teutonic myth. They were retrieving a
purer, more idealistic past and rejecting the world of their parents.

But it was necessary to learn about that past. Most came from homes
where religion was only a formality and Zionism an exotic business of interest
only to Slavs. Of life in modern Palestine they knew nothing. The Zionist
youth groups therefore set about recreating their origins, learning Hebrew, conducting romantic studies of chalutz life, all very visionary. Those who actually
went to Palestine had the advantage of a brief training period on the farms
of the Hechalutz, an organization of young pioneers in Poland and Germany
that gave bourgeois youth the chance to milk cows and shovel dung.

But they were only a handful. Even among the Zionist youth groups very
few were prepared to exchange the comforts of Germany for that distant and
barren place.

25

In the autumn of 1932, German immigrants came to Palestine in increasing
numbers, as did immigrants from Poland. Both countries had suddenly grown
uncomfortable for Jews.

Recha Freier planned a trip to Jerusalem the following spring to raise
money for the children who were to go to Kibbutz Ain Harod when their

immigration certificates came through. Since she had first been compelled to postpone the Ain Harod group, there had been significant changes in the German situation. For one thing, she realized that if the massive youth migration she dreamed of was ever to become a reality she could no longer work alone; there must be an organization. It must be composed of the only people committed to Zionism and the young: the groups of German Zionist youth.

With the leaders of these various organizations Mrs. Freier formed a committee called the Jüdische Jugendhilfe, the Aid to Jewish Youth. The date of the first constitutional session of the Jugendhilfe was January 30, 1933. As the committee left its meeting place, they turned and entered the avenue Unter den Linden, where they saw a torchlight procession. Hitler had formed a cabinet at the request of President Hindenburg and on that day took office.

In the spring, during a three-week period in April and May, the racial laws that aimed at "cleansing the civil service" of Germany were declared. Teachers, university professors, scientists, including some of Nobel rank, and social workers by the hundreds were suddenly without work, without a future. The effect of the new dispensation on the Jews of Germany was strange, for they were Germans heart and soul, lovers of German culture and language who believed that all that was best in Western civilization was rooted in Germany. Many were half convinced the Nazis must somehow be right, that the cause of German anti-Semitism lay with the thousands of Jews from eastern Europe, people of an alien and inferior culture who had flocked to their country after the war, as well as with the Zionists and their obsession about Palestine.

Others, however, suspected that the time had come to leave, perhaps for only a few years during which the Nazi regime would blow over. Some headed for Palestine. To that pioneering land they brought money and expensive clothing, hats, overcoats, gloves, neckties. Whatever they had to say was said with precision, at length and with much formality. There was a word for these German Jews, *Yekke*, whose origin is uncertain; perhaps it refers to jackets, which they invariably wore. The Yishuv wore no jackets and owned no ties, and except for a few old Sephardic families, had no money; and it found the Germans insufferable.

But they were Jews after all. A danger to the Jews of one country was a danger to all; and the Jews of Germany had been charitable. They had dispensed their money and their social services, if never their friendship, to the eastern European Jews when they had appeared on their soil. The realization grew that what was happening in Germany was the first test of the Jewish homeland: Were they prepared to receive their injured brothers? Solidarity, guilt, fellow feeling and above all the desire to show that the homeland stood ready to meet the hour of need moved the Jews of Palestine.

That spring Chaim Arlosoroff, the political officer of the Jewish Agency, traveled to Berlin to meet Zionist officials and see what measures could be taken for the emigration of German Jews to Palestine. One scheme involved an agreement with the Nazis that would allow Jews to transfer to Palestine goods to the value of 5,000 pounds, so that they might enter as "capitalists," a category with generous quotas. Because Arlosoroff was keenly interested in the fate of the young, he visited Recha Freier's office to discuss her Jugendhilfe, but Mrs. Freier was in Palestine at the time. Nevertheless he published his views on the transfer of youth. Some 600 to 700 might be lodged at small expense in the kibbutzim; boarding schools and children's villages like Ben Shemen could be multiplied by ten; altogether the Yishuv ought to find room for 2,000 or 3,000.

The purpose of this transfer was not to remove the children from physical danger; there was no physical danger. But there was a noxious cloud of anti-Semitism in Germany, in the schools, the newspapers, on the radio, and its effects would linger for decades after the Nazis themselves had disappeared, a matter of two years, three at the most. The children must be taken out of Germany because their self-respect, their belief in themselves as Jews and people, would shrivel there.

One day Miss Szold had a visitor at her office in the Vaad Leumi. It was her first face-to-face meeting with Recha Freier and a strained, nervous affair for both. Mrs. Freier described the structure of the Jugendhilfe, the composition of the group that waited to leave for Ain Harod, the enthusiasm of the kibbutzniks of Ain Harod, the desire of the Histadrut to begin this youth migration, for which certificates were necessary. And Miss Szold repeated her reasons for refusing certificates: the needs of Oriental children in Palestine were far greater and more pressing than those of bourgeois children in Germany. The schools of the Yishuv were inadequate for those who were there already. She was a social worker, she said. She knew the texture of Palestinian life from the inside. She was certain German children were better off at home among their families.

Mrs. Freier replied that she didn't come from social work. She didn't understand social work. She understood Germany, the needs of the German Jewish youngster. But social work—she was in quite another world. There the discussion ended. Mrs. Freier came away from the interview with the conviction that Miss Szold was rigid, unfeeling and determined to ride roughshod over all who opposed her.

Now the newspapers were full of Chaim Arlosoroff's return from Berlin. Banner headlines in the Revisionist press attacked his negotiations there—aimed at persuading the Hitler regime to allow some Jews to transfer property to

Palestine—as doing business with the Nazis. Arlosoroff was young, highly gifted, Russian-born but German by education and like Weizmann a strong believer in Great Britain and Arab-Jewish rapprochement. His views were centrist and moderate. As the political officer of the Jewish Agency he was the natural enemy of the Revisionists. The growing power of those brown-shirted youths and their resemblance to Mussolini's blackshirts had been striking features of the 1931 Zionist congress, where every fourth delegate had been a Revisionist.

Arlosoroff joined his wife at a Tel Aviv hotel. They took a walk on a deserted beach one Friday evening, where they met two strangers. Before the eyes of his wife Arlosoroff was shot to death by one of them. Then the strangers fled.

The consequences of this crime were strange, baffling, infinitely disturbing. Histadrut leaders claimed Arlosoroff had been killed by Revisionists; the right maintained it was not a political murder at all. Most of the Yishuv took the former view, Miss Szold among them.

A Jew had been murdered by a Jew. A Jewish crime was being concealed by Jews. All the visions she had brought with her to the Holy Land—the dream of the revival of Jewish law reinterpreted to fit the modern world, the dream of prophetic Judaism uniting and revitalizing the Semitic peoples of the Middle East—had been hidden away in the corners of her mind, dimmed treasures she hardly dared show to anyone. Instead she had found consolation in what the Yishuv did well. The farmlands were green and radiant, the young pioneers glorious, their interest in life almost painful in its intensity. Now this. This wretched murder of a brilliant young man and the lies that followed. It erased everything else. It shook her in a way no disappointment in Zionism had yet done. It was all anyone in her circle talked about, the only topic she could write home about. She believed "the Jewish ethic has disappeared from our scene. . . . Today it is a week since the tragedy occurred. It seems a year."

And when Miss Szold was asked to take charge of Arlosoroff's plan to bring German children to Palestine she accepted, although it was hardly different from the scheme of Recha Freier, whom she had twice refused with vehemence. In August she wrote to the Mandate's immigration department asking for 500 certificates during the six-month period from September 1933 to April 1934 for German children, to be aged fourteen through seventeen, who would live in kibbutzim and private homes. At the end of two years, unlike any previous category of students, they would remain in the country, in effect becoming immigrants beyond and above the immigration quota. There was reason to believe government would look with favor on her request, for the present High Commissioner, Sir Arthur Wauchope, had visited Ben Shemen at Arlosoroff's invitation, heard his plan and been convinced of its rightness.

Miss Szold was not convinced, and the reasons for her about-face were never clearly stated but rather implied in her letters home. Arlosoroff's murder weighed on her, a hideous blot that could only be lightened if his work were carried on after him. Moreover it seemed that German children were already coming to Palestine without their families. The total legal immigration in 1932 had been 9,500; in 1933 there were 30,000. That summer such an influx of refugees jammed Tel Aviv that whole families slept on the beach for want of rooms, and the illegals, who were not numerous in spite of Arab claims, included hundreds of youngsters on their own. Therefore the work of this new committee would not pull German children away from their families; it would provide a legal and constructive way of doing what the young people were doing in any case.

Yet she was skeptical of it and distrusted it, seeing flaws of which no one else seemed to be aware. For example many of the children who would be coming from Germany had Orthodox backgrounds, but there was only one Orthodox kibbutz in the entire country, all others being resolutely, devoutly atheist. Had this been made clear to German parents? She doubted it; she doubted they had any accurate picture of Palestine and believed few of them would send their children if they knew the truth.

That autumn Miss Szold attended a conference on German Jewry in London and entirely by accident overheard a conversation that clinched her worst fears about the business. Mrs. Weizmann and two distinguished English Zionists were discussing the youth transfer, apparently without knowing Miss Szold could hear them, and the entire tone of their conversation was somehow light-hearted, as if sending German children into Palestine were no more complicated than packing them off to boarding school. One had only to assemble the young people in Berlin and ship them to the Yishuv, where all would become happy farmers and laborers. They were eager for it. Everyone said they were.

Miss Szold was shocked. The women were ignorant of religious and political realities, even of human realities. It occurred to her that German Zionist leaders might be equally ignorant, and she went at once to an official of the London office and told him: "I heard such and such a conversation. I am afraid this thing is going to be pretty messy." Did he think she ought to go to Berlin and sound out the Jugendhilfe? He encouraged it.

Miss Szold bought a ticket for Germany that day and left the following morning.

What was most striking about this new Berlin were the posters. In hotels, restaurants, office buildings, around pillars in the street and across the windows

of the Jewish shops, printed posters were flung up: "The Jews of the World
Want to Destroy Germany. German People—Resist! Don't Buy From Jews!"

Meanwhile ordinary Germans came and went. Housewives in their little
hats and lightweight coats carried string bags with their groceries sticking out;
men in caps and heavy work jackets or the pinch-waisted overcoats of the
fashionable returned from work with newspapers under their arms. They stopped
to look at the posters on the pillars, they said nothing, they walked on. How
well-behaved they were. How polite, how orderly. They spoke so quietly, these
Germans, their choice of language always excellent and refined. At Miss Szold's
hotel the chambermaids, the porters, even the little errand boys were models
of good behavior. In perfect order they assembled one morning in the hotel
lobby, everybody, including the bootblacks. There they were made to stand
at attention while the radio broadcast an address of Hitler's. First some Beethoven music, beautifully played. Then the high-pitched voice of Hitler. He began
a tirade against those who were fleeing the country—the Jews, the socialists,
the liberals, the pacifists—and he paused between phrases. And in those pauses
the great audience in the hall where he spoke shrieked out in unison, "The
Jews, the Jews!"

What did they feel, these well-behaved and ordinary people who stood
in the lobby around her? She could not tell and dared not ask.

Miss Szold presented herself at the offices of the Jugendhilfe. They had
been reorganized the previous summer and were now part of a new organization,
the Arbeitsgemeinschaft für Kinder und Jugendaliyah; in Palestine it would
be known as Youth Aliyah, a simple and inspired choice. Here she learned
that her suspicions in London had been right. Even at the heart of German
Zionism no one seemed to realize that the children they were ready to pack
off to Palestine with two years' worth of financial guarantees might or might
not adjust to Palestine, to the heat, for example, to the primitive atmosphere.
Some would get sick or injure themselves or otherwise prove incapable of hard
work on the farms. Did they even begin to suspect what life was like on those
kibbutzim, how rigorous, how exhausting? Chalutzim who came from eastern
Europe were often broken by it, and many went to live in the cities or left
Palestine altogether. Who would care for the failures, physical or mental, among
these children? And with what funds? And what was being done to minimize
failure by learning more about Palestine and the kibbutzim, by inspecting individual kibbutzim to see how one differed from another, which were primitive,
which more advanced? She had prepared a series of exhaustive questionnaires
and sent them ahead to the Jugendhilfe, but they paid no attention to her
questionnaires. They knew little about Palestine and made no attempt to learn
more. Nor did they see any reason to coordinate their actions; like so many

individuals, each of the various youth groups carried on its own dealings with kibbutzim and other institutions of the Yishuv. Miss Szold decided they were very young, very sincere and in their methods totally chaotic.

The time had come to discuss with them the education of the German children in Palestine, to determine who would teach them in what sort of schools, and what they would learn in two years that would transform them from Berliners to Hebrew-speaking chalutzim.

Unfortunately histories of Youth Aliyah suffer from an almost total lack of records for the early months. What is known is that when Miss Szold arrived in Berlin there was no precise plan for the education of the Youth Aliyah children. They would go to the kibbutzim, yes, but the kibbutzim had only elementary schools. Yet when the first Youth Aliyah group reached Palestine in February of the following year their system of education was known, agreed upon, its spirit and letter clear to both partners. Its broad outlines have remained essentially unchanged for the duration of Youth Aliyah, which still exists today.

Apparently the educational scheme was composed by Miss Szold and the Jugendhilfe together during that week in Berlin. It was an amazing vision, amazing as an ad hoc creation, hardly less so if it had been mulled over and revised for months. Perhaps no more powerful tool has ever been devised for the passage of a band of young people from one culture to another.

They themselves were to be their own transformers, the shapers of their future selves. Within the framework of collective life on the agricultural kibbutz, a self-contained, democratic entity fitted to the needs of Zionism and Zion, decision making was to begin and end with the children's group. And the origin of this system was the German Zionist youth movement, the child of that bird of passage the *Wandervogel* band, for Miss Szold grasped its value and saw the uses to which it could be put.

Each of the existing Zionist youth groups was to assemble its candidates for emigration and send them to a Hechalutz preparation camp for six weeks of training. Throughout this period their character as a group would be preserved. Socialist, centrist, Mizrachi, whatever, their stay in the camp would serve to weld them into a tighter unit. Like the *Wandervogel*, they were to be first, last and always a self-governing group.

The training period would have another purpose. At the end of their six weeks an executive committee of the young people must decide which of them was fit to go to Palestine. Those who were judged unfit might stay and try again.

As the next step, bands of about fifty immigrant boys and girls and their leaders, men or women in their early twenties, would travel to Palestine and settle on a kibbutz with political values identical to those of the youth group they had belonged to at home. The youth leader would remain with them for the next two years, which were to be years of secondary education. The leader, who would serve as their chief academic teacher, would live with them in the part of the kibbutz constructed for their use. The kibbutzniks would act as teachers in the agricultural life and would begin the moment the young people arrived. They were to be working members of the kibbutz from the start. There would be no long road to adulthood and middle age; they would enter the world of work when they entered their two years' schooling. When the two years were done, the group, which had made all its own decisions until then, would decide where and how they meant to settle on the land. The role of the youth leader was never to act as authority, but as an educational resource and intermediary with the kibbutz and the world beyond.

The schooling Miss Szold planned with the Jugendhilfe was to consist of two portions: a four-hour morning spent in farm labor among the barns, chicken runs, workshops and fields of the kibbutz; and a four-hour afternoon in which they would study Hebrew, Jewish history and literature, the geography of Palestine and such subjects as grew out of their morning's work—botany, physics, chemistry. Another important feature would be periodic exploration of the countryside with their leader. As the *Wandervogel* had rambled across a beloved land, so would they.

It must be noted that the *Wandervogel* ideal had become considerably diluted by the time Miss Szold reached Berlin; with the advent of Hitler, Zionism grew suddenly popular in Germany, and many who joined the Zionist youth groups brought with them the wounds of an anti-Semitic and authoritarian society. But among the youth leaders and the older members of the movement the vision remained, and it was from them that Miss Szold received and transmuted it, finding in the group mystique, the worship of youth and the concensus method of reaching decision an echo of the rebellious young idealists who had come to Palestine in the second and third waves of immigration. They had built the kibbutzim that were now to receive Hitler's rejects.

When she returned to Jerusalem she learned that Arthur Ruppin, chief of the Jewish Agency's newly created German Bureau, had named her director of a Youth Aliyah bureau that was to be attached to the larger body. He told her she was the only figure in Palestine capable of dealing with all political parties, as the leader of Youth Aliyah must. She was the only nonpolitical person of stature in the country.

Miss Szold refused, angrily and emphatically. Her doubts about Youth Aliyah were in no way diminished. She had been willing to help until now, reluctantly willing to head a committee. Committees came and went, their leaders with them; they became absorbed into other committees. A bureau attached to the Jewish Agency that ran the Yishuv had overtones of permanence, and she had no intention of taking on a task that might last for several years. She was in fact poised for another departure to America. Once again she would try to make a place for herself there, perhaps in Baltimore; she told people she meant to sit on Bertha's front porch in a rocking chair and crack Indian nuts.

But Ruppin said, "Either with you, or not at all."

Years before she had written to a friend: "I should have had children—many children." Now it seemed she had been led, step by random step, toward vicarious motherhood at the age of seventy-three. She had objected at every stage of the journey and objected still, but she could not refuse Ruppin's ultimatum. It was her duty, and it was right for her.

Miraculously so. She would be working from then on with young people from Germany, from the very culture that represented her own childhood, and with the kibbutzniks as well, whom she admired as the truest expression of the Zionist ideal. The scheme could not have been more right for Miss Szold if she had thought of it herself. But she had not thought of it herself, and she saw fresh objections even now. While she was in Europe there had been an outbreak of Arab violence directed against the new tide of German immigration. She would be bringing children to a land that awaited a bloody reckoning.

The Youth Aliyah bureau Miss Szold now headed was a very small undertaking with limited ambitions and no funds of its own, not even an office. The entire staff—Miss Szold and her secretary, Emma Ehrlich—used a little room in the Jewish Agency where a single filing cabinet held all the papers related to the German children. But to Miss Szold it was a large and awesome task. "I do all connected with it in fear and trembling." It was also amazingly dull. She called it superior clerical work.

And although she claimed this was a disappointment—that the youth migration should have throbbed with life and vitality, whereas so far it was nothing to her but so many papers and piles of details—in her letters to Adele, Henrietta confessed that she needed it, depended on it as a drug. For the world had become incomprehensible to her. "I can't understand the stabilization of exchange, the good of purchasing gold, the value of raising the price level—nothing, nothing do I understand. I am befuddled by all I read," most of all by Germany, by Hitler.

When it was not Germany and the disintegration of its national character that grieved her, it was Palestine, where she saw the disintegration of all her ideals. A Revisionist accused of Arlosoroff's murder had been acquitted. He was to be tried twice and acquitted twice. No one was ever found guilty of the murder of Arlosoroff.

But the tone of Henrietta's letters to Adele during this period and through-out the thirties suggests it was more than history that left her with the sense of understanding nothing. Old as she was, "in a certain sense I have not stopped growing . . . my inner world, perhaps it is my world of feeling, of instinct, expands." Even in her eighties she was to be aware of this continuing inner growth, occasionally distressing because it was so different from the serene and changeless old age she used to expect, more often enriching, as if some small portion of the youth she never had had finally been granted her.

In youth and maturity she had lived behind fortifications built up to protect a fragile self-esteem from the batterings of life. In her seventies the inner being seemed to peer out, wary, yet buoyed up by the knowledge that she had survived so far. Perhaps the world beyond the fortress was not so dangerous after all; perhaps emotions were less threatening than she used to think.

That autumn the request she had made to the government for 500 youth certificates was largely granted, in the form of 350 certificates for young people between the ages of fifteen and seventeen in a category known as "B iii": students whose total support was guaranteed. In the months that followed Miss Szold attended to the details that preceded the children's arrival—barracks were to be built as temporary housing, followed by concrete houses; schools had to be built. She made periodic forays to Ain Harod and Rodges, the two kibbutzim that were to receive the first children, struggling through the mud to spur on the construction workers or inspect their progress. At the same time much of her energy was devoted to a running battle with Berlin.

They were slovenly about paper work. They sent her certificates of immigra-tion partially or inaccurately filled out. The British Immigration Department, however, demanded perfect accuracy, each certificate to include all details of background, precise guarantees of financial support, health information attested to by a doctor and a dentist, mental and moral fitness. Miss Szold hated to think how the government would respond to incomplete forms. She responded by hurling them back from her desk to the Arbeitsgemeinschaft. Moreover Berlin continued to correspond with individual settlements—these children could go here, that group of children there—although the Berlin people had never visited any of the settlements. She was the head of the movement. She wanted each of those decisions made by herself. She flew from despair to rage, freely communicated to her coworkers abroad.

On February 19, 1934, Miss Szold set out for Haifa to meet the first Youth Aliyah group. It was a miserable day with darkly shrouded skies, blasting wind and hard rain. The ship had tried to drop anchor off Jaffa the day before, but when high seas made it impossible they came instead to the new port of Haifa. There the young people and their *madrich*, their youth leader, disem-barked, all handsomely dressed in clothes such as the Yishuv had never seen before, sturdy, well-made corduroys for boys and girls alike, the clothing in which people of leisure visited the countryside. The wharf was cluttered with their bicycles, rucksacks, mandolins, cellos, even flagpoles. These luxuries were added to an ample supply of basic equipment ordered by Miss Szold: blankets, sheets, undergarments, work shoes, trousers, shirts. The children were greeted individually by Miss Szold, who knew each name; she saw them through customs and a lengthy medical examination, followed by brief reunions with grandparents or other relatives who had arrived months before. Then they were herded across the new wharf to the workingmen's kitchen facing Haifa Bay. Seated with Miss Szold at a long table where they waited to be fed, the children burst spontaneously into Hebrew song, the gift of their Hechalutz training. From that moment they were papers and statistics no longer; the German youth became as truly her own as the troubled outcasts of the Palestinian towns.

After dinner Miss Szold, the *madrich* and the children headed for the railway station. The train bore them through the Emek Jezreel and toward the luxurious green of Harod Valley, still battered by rain, hail and winds that howled throughout the next four days. When at last they reached Ain Harod, with its palms and palmettos and great stretches of glowing lawn, they were greeted by the entire kibbutz, who had planned a welcome that seemed to Miss Szold a miracle of delicacy and tact.

The newcomers were shown to their barracks, where rooms were assigned; they were led to the storeroom to stow their belongings, and the route to the storeroom was so laid out that they saw on the way every aspect of life on kibbutz: workshops, stables, incubators, all the mysteries of agriculture the kibbutzniks were to teach the young people. And when the tour was over there was a more conventional welcome, music, singing, hora dancing, speech making. Miss Szold found it solemn and joyous, "a religious poem." She would have liked to stay on in Ain Harod for a month.

But she had only two days. Part of the time she hovered about the quarters of the newcomers checking on screens, mosquito netting, showers and toilets. She was most particular about the toilets, flushing them one after the other to make sure they worked. Then she inspected the barracks, where the newcomers had already put up their posters and photographs and stored their books.

The books were of course German books. Even in the first two days they took on a potent significance, for they represented a past that the children must throw off. Some seemed vaguely ashamed of it already, as if they meant to become Hebrew speakers and Palestinians in a single leap. This could be damaging, partly because the past can never be destroyed without doing damage to the self, partly because it was in itself so precious. To Miss Szold it embodied all the serenity of her early childhood, the books in her father's library, the

16. Judah Magnes

17. Louis Lipsky

18. Lloyd George addressing a British Zionist Federation dinner in London, 1931. Weizmann is at his left.

19. Miss Szold with Weizmann, Eder, Van Vriesland, and her two fellow members of the Triumvirate

20. New York's Mayor La Guardia presents Miss Szold with a key to the city in 1936: "If I, the child of immigrants, am today Mayor of New York... it is because of you."

21. In her "demure gown, cut ... so that no more skin showed than can be covered by the fourth part of an American lady's handkerchief"

22. Tending her plants on the balcony of her room at the Eden Hotel

23. The celebration at kibbutz Kiryat at which Miss Szold was presented with a cake inscribed "To Our Mother," as Recha Frier watched

24. Instructing a Youth Aliyah member in a Keren Hayesod settlement

25. Talking with a soldier

26. Miss Szold and Emma Ehrlich share a joke

27. Miss Szold and Hans Beyth confer with kibbutz officials.

28. Querying the Teheran children

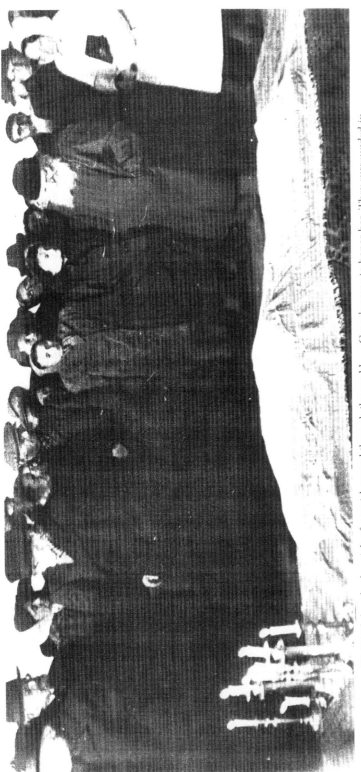

29. "With her death a sigh of anguish passed through the world. . . . Crowds came to honor her. They surrounded in silence her minute body . . . covered with a light blue cloth adorned with Hebrew verses, and at her head candles for the departed were placed in silver Sabbath candlesticks."

letters written to aunts, cousins, grandmother in old German script as her mother watched and corrected. She could not let these children abandon that past.

She spoke to them about it in German. Her German was the language of Schiller and Goethe, a museum piece. As Chanoch Rinott, the *madrich*, recalled later: "We brought with us Kafka; I had in my group two or three very intelligent, intellectual kids—existentialists," sophisticated young minds to whom her formal and antique speech might have been amusing. It was not. "There was this empathy, this understanding. I accepted her as a mother figure very willingly; there was very much of a natural authority built into her composed of age, appearance, prestige," and for the children it was the same. She told them not to throw away their books from home, to treasure their German heritage; there was no need to forget or be ashamed. They remembered her words; they remembered the woman herself. It was commonly said by this group and each of those that followed, "But you see, Miss Szold took a particular interest in us, in our group. More than the others, she was interested in us."

This drama of the youth group's first arrival, the meeting at the wharf in Haifa, the journey to the kibbutz, the welcome, the physical presence of Miss Szold with all its implications of home and Germany, was to be repeated over and over during the next few years. And the drama that followed it, of which Miss Szold heard reports at her desk in Jerusalem during the ensuing months—tension between newcomers and kibbutzniks, tension among the members of the youth group itself, tension within each adolescent—was also to be repeated with each fresh arrival. In the case of later groups Miss Szold was prepared, but the earliest intimations of sexual problems at Ain Harod took her by surprise; indeed she heard of them only from abroad. She hardly knew how to react, for her first and last encounter with sexuality had occurred almost thirty years ago, it had taught her little, and she had had no reason to return to the subject since.

Now sex was there again, at Ain Harod. It reared its disturbing head that spring at a time when Miss Szold was desperate for some way of raising money for the German youth. Americans were interested, especially Hadassah. Freed of their obligations to the hospitals and clinics, which were now in the hands of the Yishuv, Hadassah leaders were looking for a new project. But rumors had arisen that the young people of Ain Harod were living in barracks where the sexes were intermingled.

Not true, Miss Szold pointed out. What was true, and she was certainly aware of it, was that the "elders" of the kibbutz, people in their thirties now, were believers in sexual freedom, a subject they took with the utmost seriousness.

Once they married or formed permanent attachments they were monogamous for the duration; but their philosophy was well known, and now that German boys and girls were being settled in the kibbutzim descriptions of freewheeling sex appeared in German-Jewish publications.

She redoubled her efforts to solve the question of placement for religious youth, for their parents and sponsoring organizations would be the first to react to the rumors. And she was by no means untroubled herself; a girl at Ain Harod was discovered to be pregnant and brought before Miss Szold with her future husband. To Miss Szold it was an intricate matter involving Jugend-hilfe funds—who would care for the two of them, where would they go, what was their future—and she plowed ahead in close consultation with the Ain Harod leaders. Together she believed they had handled the matter with the "finest modern pedagogic attitude towards life and youth." But one of her young secretaries saw the pregnant girl after her release from Miss Szold's lecture, dissolved in tears because she had been cut off forever from Ain Harod. The kibbutz, her parents, even the Jugendhilfe urged that she be allowed to stay, not with the youth group, but as part of the kibbutz. Miss Szold refused: "Their act has excluded them. . . . I am not even referring the point to . . . superior authority, for I cannot in this case submit my judgment even to a superior authority." One of her reasons was the fear of damaging propaganda. Another, so the secretary believed, was that "to Miss Szold it was a sin."

She knew her limitations all the same. She hired an experienced social worker whose responsibility it would be to visit the youth groups from time to time and consult with them over sexual problems; she instructed another to make unannounced visits of inspection; she looked about for someone of her own generation, some expert on sex among the German refugees who could advise not only the young people but herself. For the rest, she trusted the youth leaders and kibbutzniks, whose devotion seemed to her almost religious. Then she put the matter into one of the neatly compartmentalized bureau drawers of her mind.

Miss Szold did not work only for Youth Aliyah. Her Youth Aliyah projects were supposed to be sandwiched in among the work she was properly concerned with, the Department of Social Welfare, the unloved, the much neglected. The racial laws in Germany served one useful purpose in that they brought to the Yishuv trained professionals in many fields. One of them was a formidably talented woman named Siddy Wronsky.

In Germany, Wronsky had been a lecturer and writer on social work of national stature. She was now fifty years old, with a little money of her own, and she put herself at Miss Szold's disposal. She agreed, in fact, to help with the long-cherished plan for a school of social work. She would be the first teacher, for a time the only teacher, and the director.

Miss Szold's next step was to find a student. She came across a young Canadian woman in her early twenties named Sylva Gelber, whom she offered a small stipend, a "scholarship," thus persuading her to become the student body. Later Gelber was joined by three or four others, all somewhat dubious about this small and fragile undertaking. "Her intentions were of the very best," Gelber recalls, "but Siddy Wronsky spoke dreadful English, I spoke dreadful German, two of the other students were native Hebrew speakers and Dr. Wronsky knew no Hebrew. So how she taught us I can't quite figure out, but Miss Szold had established this school; it was her dream child." They learned political science, psychology, pedagogy, social work, the history of social work, methods of social case work and practical case work all in one year.

Once each week the professional social work staff of Jerusalem met with Miss Szold to talk over cases. In winter they drank hot tea while Miss Szold had hot water; in summer they drank iced tea and Miss Szold had nothing at all. They found her difficult to work with, tactless, confronting, grudging with praise, but they respected and in several cases loved her. The progress of social work was satisfying on several fronts, thanks to the Germans. There were clinics in a number of small towns now as well as the three major cities, and a country-wide conference of professionals and volunteers in 1934 brought forth a total of sixty, who "sat through three perfectly unsentimental, ungushing sessions," as Miss Szold noted.

In April 1934 the Ahavah orphanage emigrated from Germany to Palestine. Again Miss Szold journeyed to the Haifa wharf to meet them and then climbed in the bus that took them on the winding road "higher and higher until we saw below the sea of city lights and the harbor studded with illuminated vessels. . . . The children . . . were beside themselves with joy." Three little houses on Mount Carmel had been rented by the directors of the orphanage to receive them, and in one of them they were given supper. A former housekeeper of Ahavah who had settled in Palestine prepared and served the supper. The whole was such a charming picture of homecoming in a strange land that Miss Szold was hardly less moved by it than were the children.

And yet—this occurred repeatedly in her Youth Aliyah dealings—the comfort of the Ahavah children, paid for by German and other Jews, caused her a poignant jealousy. "The other side was revealed yesterday in so ghastly a way that I haven't been able to reconcile myself to living." A gang of eight young Jewish pickpockets had been arrested in Jerusalem, a similar gang was arrested in Tel Aviv, and the police claimed to be so outraged that they were railroading the boys to the British reformatory at Tul Karm, "in which society will confirm their infirmities."

For the thousands of street children there were no single beds with or
without mosquito netting, no indoor toilets, no devoted *madrich*. No one cared
what they ate or if they ate. They were a submerged and forgotten race.

An outrageous scheme stirred in her brain. She saw a gang of adolescents
from the back alleys of Jerusalem brought to a kibbutz, not a big, well-established
settlement like Ain Harod, but a newer one, small and primitive, where daily
life was a struggle. There they would be exposed to the idealism of the kibbutzniks, fed on good plain food, educated by a *madrich* familiar with their background who would hike with them over the countryside and teach them Zionism
by teaching them the shape and texture of Zion; they would learn self-govern-
ment; they would become bound to the land and one another. Who would
pay for it? Probably no one. But once this scheme was formed in her mind
she knew she must bring it to life, for she felt its rightness in her bones.

In this she was almost alone. A year or so later she hired a young social
worker to investigate living conditions among Oriental Jews; his survey of 1,000
families was the first systematic attempt to learn about their lives. The Yishuv
had other matters to attend to, and the Zionists of America preferred not to
know the seamier side of Jewish life in Palestine. By 1978 the Jews of Oriental
origin accounted for half the population of Israel, and were still the have-nots;
their incidence of criminality and illiteracy was higher, their average income
markedly lower than that of the "Western" half. Miss Szold saw the future
only too clearly.

In the 1930s juvenile delinquency in the towns of the Yishuv was on
the rise for reasons to which she was peculiarly sensitive. More than hunger
and parental neglect, the young suffered from a growing suspicion that the
world no longer made sense. It was a suspicion that tainted Europe and America
as well. In the States the settled certainties of the period before the war had
been replaced by Hoovervilles and bread lines; in Italy and Germany people
turned to the black magic that was Fascism; even in England it held a distinct
appeal. Palestinian life in the twenties had been hard, but it made sense because
the Yishuv was building a homeland. Now the goals and the ideals behind
them were dimmed, muddled. Young lives were damaged by it—the suicide
rate among Jewish adolescents rose sharply in the early thirties—and Miss Szold
was haunted by it.

That spring a little crowd of Revisionist boys and girls smashed all the
windows of the new Vaad Leumi building with heavy stones. At a fair in Tel
Aviv demonstrations between two political parties grew into a small riot, with
over 100 wounded, "and along with all of this," Miss Szold wrote home, there
was the "constant thrum-thrum of the Arlosoroff murder trial dragging its slow
length along." In June, "I feel like screaming at the top of my voice all the

time, I can't bear to set foot in Tel Aviv, the hundred per cent Jewish city, the hundred per cent garish. . . . Am I old and cynical and hopeless? . . . The German children's work gives me satisfaction until suddenly I realize that I am bringing them into a community that no longer is connected in my mind with anything reminiscent of Messianism. However, they all go to the country districts, and after all there one finds idealism."

The truth was that Miss Szold in her seventies had become two people, one an old woman yearning for home and family, dismayed by life in the 1930s, encased in everlasting loneliness and longing for the serenity of old age. Only in serving the children did she catch a glimpse of it. And at the same time she was a shrewd and toughened veteran. For whom Youth Aliyah was a noble and beautiful movement but also a legitimate way of bringing immigrants into the country above the immigration quota. Who dealt with the British honestly because it was her nature but also because she wanted their trust for the sake of these same immigrants. Whose relations with the Agency, the Vaad Leumi and the Jugendhilfe were hard-driving and, when she could get away with it, high-handed.

Especially with the Jugendhilfe, whom she bullied mercilessly by threats of resignation. Her colleagues in Palestine wrote time and again to Berlin that if Miss Szold were to resign, Youth Aliyah might come to a dead stop. They had no choice, therefore, but to make their peace with her. She wanted centralization—all communication between Palestine and Germany to go through her hands—and what she wanted, she got.

Her . . . at the offices of the Vaad Leumi was considerably expanded; by the mid-thirties there were some twenty people working in the social service department, all of whom felt the pressure of Miss Szold's frustrations. "People grumbled," one young social worker recalled. "They were afraid, some of them; I would hear her scream, you could hear her everywhere. Anything that wasn't perfect made her impatient. Yet the concern for the child—or whoever—was absolutely genuine." Throughout those years of pioneering work in the social services, Miss Szold's usual expression was one of resentment compounded by hatred for the bureaucracy and the need to submit to bureaucracy. Submission was a habit with her, as a woman and as a well-disciplined Zionist, but the lifelong habit of taking orders was no longer enough to mask her dislike of it.

On the Vaad Leumi there was little love lost between Miss Szold and her colleagues. Both the measures she proposed and the woman herself seemed alien to them, while her opinion of her fellow members was that intellectually and socially they were living in the Middle Ages. One observer recalled that in the early thirties the Vaad Leumi referred to Miss Szold "as 'the old girl' with something like contempt, certainly with dislike." Their resistance only sharpened her stubborn determination to get what she wanted, and before her onslaughts the Vaad Leumi often fell back, threw up its hands and let the old girl have her way.

She felt more diffident in her relations with the hard-boiled politicos of the Jewish Agency. Youth Aliyah represented only a tiny part of the great flood of immigration from Germany and Poland; with the larger immigration Miss Szold had no connection except through her distant link to the Agency. Now the British, both in Palestine and London, sympathized sufficiently with the German Jews to overlook illegal immigration and to allow a massive legal immigration in 1933. But German Jews were not eager to come, nor was the Yishuv especially fond of them. Therefore the Agency used this leniency mainly to bring in Jews from Poland. They arrived in boatloads singing Zionist hymns and wept with emotion when they set foot on the sacred soil. They walked down the streets of Tel Aviv and Jerusalem dazed with happiness, savoring each step, for there was no one who pushed them aside. Many brought brides they had married only in order to foil the immigration laws and whom they intended to divorce as soon as possible, so two immigrants would arrive on a single certificate. Rabbis in eastern Europe and Palestine connived in this procedure as a patriotic duty.

Miss Szold believed it was cynical and unworthy of a great people. Within Youth Aliyah there were no evasions. In December of 1934 she began to suspect German parents were "resorting to our youth certificates as a device to bring their children over on account of their own unfortunate situation or for other reasons and have no intention of permitting them to remain with the groups to which they were assigned." They would be taken to live with relatives in the towns, to earn money for the support of their families. Miss Szold felt that such candidates must, in the future, be refused. The Agency might evade and connive in order to rescue Polish Jews from squalor and humiliation and "the anti-Semitism of things" and laugh her down when she objected to the procedure. It was not in her nature to do the same for her children.

By the spring of 1935 it was clear that Youth Aliyah needed a staff and an office of its own. It had become a Frankenstein to Miss Szold, a splendid and awesome creation that nevertheless sapped her energy and time; she lived at a furious pace, at a run, "gasping, hoping against hope that if I sleep less I'll catch up to myself." She never did. At the end of April she was still wearing her winter clothing. One day in Jerusalem a high wind picked her off her feet, tore away her umbrella, threw her to the ground and tumbled her over and over. She scrambled back up, rescued her possessions and ran on again. There was no time to rest.

Partly it was her own fault. She insisted on seeing and supervising all the business of the office. She insisted on hearing everyone who came to her door and wanted to talk, including beggars; the secretaries were instructed that nobody should be turned away.

A Hebrew secretary, a German secretary and in time several others were hired, all young women and most of them married, as was Emma Ehrlich. They were hard workers and remarkably pretty; people used to joke about it, calling them the American beauties, although only Emma was American. Into this enclave of females a man was about the enter, a German sent by the Jugendhilfe as their representative in financial matters, and Miss Szold braced herself to receive a stranger, a sharer of authority.

What she did not know was that Hans Beyth was also reluctant. He was something of a rare bird, a German-Jewish banker who had been a Zionist since his teens. "On the one side he had all these friends, these chalutzim, and on the other side he had also Aryan friends, and all the high society life of Berlin in the years after the war when everyone started to make money," according to the woman he later married. Beyth was glad of a chance to come to Palestine but would have preferred to stay in banking, to lead the sort of life he had before. He was in his early thirties, adventurous, unattached, and decided he would work for Miss Szold and her no doubt excellent youth movement for a time and afterward go on to something else.

Hans Beyth arrived in May and reported to Youth Aliyah and Miss Szold, who had been installed in a new and larger office around the corner from the Agency, a small stone house with a garden in front and honeysuckle vines draped over the gate. Miss Szold saw a tall, broad, Nordic-looking figure, handsome and handsomely dressed, which might have put her off at first except that his manner was warm and direct. She sensed the presence of a kind, affectionate man, someone who would not judge.

What Hans Beyth saw was a woman, very authoritative, very old, but a woman somehow in need of protection. "He was an artist to handle people, and especially women," someone had observed.

That summer Miss Szold and her new colleague set out on a grand tour of all the youth settlements, for she would have to deliver a report on the movement at the Zionist congress in Lucerne. She knew the route by heart. Twice a week she visited youth settlements, a few at a time, usually with the feeling that she was leaving behind her a world of arrogance and intrigue and entering a land of noble beings. The difference now was that Hans Beyth sat beside her in the car, attentive to every word she said. When the car stopped he helped her out; when they walked across rocks he held her arm in a firm grip, almost lifting her along, his head bent down to listen while she spoke.

Even on kibbutz, life was of course far from perfect. She never failed to inspect the toilets and showers, and some were neglected. It made her "boil." There was a disorderliness, a certain indefinable lack of harmony and simple good manners. No one cared about appearances; it was life on the most primitive level. Was she right to bring half-grown boys and girls into such surroundings?

She climbed into the car for the drive to the next settlement, staring thoughtfully out the window, full of doubts. The next settlement and the next after that held their own problems, their own neglected plumbing, their own leggy adolescents in odd cotton caps with the brims turned every which way, who put before her an accumulation of crises large and small, personal, social, vocational. She thrived on this. She believed absolutely that Youth Aliyah depended on her welcoming the children when they arrived and visiting them regularly in their new homes—sensing, seeing, talking, listening.

There were young people who wanted to leave, to live in the cities. There were cases of mental disturbance, even psychosis. There were some who simply did not fit, perhaps through no fault of their own; they endangered the group as a whole and alternatives had to be found, although there was no money for alternatives. Some felt that after all they were not meant for life on the land. This one wanted to study; that one wanted to paint; many expressed a desire for vocational training. A girl whose mother was a dentist begged to be allowed to help the dentist who served the kibbutz. Some boys were drawn to carpentry, some girls to nursing. She heard them all out but had no solutions to offer; they and their parents had been told in Berlin that Youth Aliyah meant agricultural training and nothing else. They must adjust. Later, when there were more Youth Aliyah children and many more individuals, it was Miss Szold who tried to adjust, to find special training for the special child, but some of her colleagues felt she was always rather resistant.

There were moments during the trip when it seemed clear to her that the movement had failed, that the children's groups were splitting apart; whatever they came to Palestine for, it was not Zionism and farming. At other times she simply looked at them, at their youth, their health, their numbers, and felt triumphant. She herself had brought them there; she had given them to the Yishuv. Photographs of the period show her smiling into the sun from under a curious black hat, holding her purse by the straps and surrounded by long-legged, sunburned boys and girls in rumpled shorts and open-necked shirts, smiling back.

As August approached, the outlines of her progress through Europe became clear. First she would go to Lucerne and the Zionist congress, from there briefly to Amsterdam, then for a month to Berlin to confer with the German partners, followed by a twelve-day vacation in Vienna with relatives. Emma

Ehrlich would be with her throughout. In Lucerne she would meet her old friend Rose Jacobs, now president of Hadassah, and Tamar de Sola Pool, who was president of the New York chapter. This was something to look forward to, whereas the formal sessions of the congress would be an ordeal for Miss Szold, who hated the long-winded pompous speeches, the personal animosities. Her own speech on Youth Aliyah was only partly written when she got a letter from Recha Freier reminding her among other matters of how Youth Aliyah had begun: not with the appointment of Henrietta Szold as head of a branch of the Jewish Agency, but with the first group that was sent to Ben Shemen by Recha Freier. The tone of the letter was that of someone with a grievance. Miss Szold thanked her and promised to incorporate the material in her congress report. All her public speeches from that day on included the acknowledgment, in ever more emphatic terms, of Mrs. Freier's original inspiration. Some people thought Miss Szold's repeated acknowledgments had a mechanical quality. In any case for Recha Freier the grievance remained; it rankled, it festered, it caused a real and piercing pain.

In Lucerne she found the true business of a Zionist congress already under way in lobbies, hotel rooms and sidewalk cafes, where delegates hammered out agreements that might appear later as formal pronouncements. Newspapers were devoured, for the press caught news before it was news. Much of Miss Szold's own business with Rose Jacobs and Tamar de Sola Pool was conducted during long walks along the flowery banks of Lake Lucerne. They told her Hadassah leaders were interested in supporting Youth Aliyah. She said Hadassah ought to stick with the new research hospital and leave Youth Aliyah to the Europeans. Mrs. Pool said she was convinced Hadassah could raise $100,000 for Youth Aliyah in two years. Miss Szold retorted that she didn't believe it.

Of course they needed that money most desperately, but what they did not need, she said, was the firm managerial hand from New York running Youth Aliyah in Palestine. Suppose Hadassah's board agreed to the drive; she wanted it clearly understood that she would "brook no interference from America or from Hadassah representatives in Palestine or Germany." No policy making, no directives, only money this time. Rose Jacobs nodded. She was still undecided, she said. There were other projects Hadassah might like to back instead or in addition. She would go on to Palestine after the congress and see for herself.

Now the public sessions began. And it was in the full light of international publicity that Miss Szold was presented one morning by Chaim Weizmann, in a charming speech, to a packed hall. Mention was made of her forthcoming seventy-fifth birthday. Miss Szold stood up. The audience stood up en masse. The hall was filled with applause. She launched into her prepared report, beginning with "a word of thanks especially to the initiator of this movement, Mrs.

Recha Freier. It was she who had this brilliant idea and made it a reality."
She included an appeal to the religious groups to create kibbutzim for Orthodox
children. She praised the kibbutzniks, described the schooling of the newcomers,
the alacrity with which they learned Hebrew; she insisted on the need for
money. The British government would supply certificates; it was up to worldwide
Jewry to supply the money, for this was more than an act of rescue, it was
"the return of the father to the children, and of the children to the father."
She sat down to what the protocols of the congress described as "continued
thunderous applause."

She was followed by Weizmann, who announced that a new settlement
was to be created in the Negev by a group of young Germans and named in
her honor. This was not a complete surprise, for a delegation had come to
her some days before with the news; she had been reluctant then and was
paralyzed now; her heart began pumping so hard she could barely hear the
rest of Weizmann's words: "Miss Szold—we have given you some flowers to
show that even Zionists sometimes find roses in their paths," and a great armful
of red roses was presented to her.

Rose Jacobs went on to Palestine, Miss Szold and Emma to Amsterdam,
where they attended the first Youth Aliyah Conference, at which representatives
of all the organizations that supported the movement voted to extend it to
countries beyond Germany, first of all to Poland. But for Miss Szold this conference was an interlude, a blur. As soon as it was finished she hurried to Berlin
for a month-long stay.

The train that took her there approached the border just as the loudspeaker
blared out the news of the Nuremberg Laws: German citizenship was to be
confined to Aryan persons, non-Aryans within Germany were to be subjects
rather than citizens; sexual relationships, marital or otherwise, between Jews
and Germans were forbidden; German women under the age of forty-five were
not to be employed as servants in Jewish homes. As they crossed the border
Miss Szold whispered to Emma, "This is the land of Schiller and Goethe."

26

When Miss Szold and Emma stepped off the train in Berlin they were met
by a little crowd of young people from the Jugendhilfe who told them that
all sorts of preparations had been made for the visit: dinners, meetings, speeches.

In spite of the blow that had fallen, the Nuremberg Laws, the schedule would be kept to the letter.

That evening the Jews of Berlin welcomed Miss Szold at a meeting of some 100 people, the leaders of various Jewish organizations. Their principle speaker was a man named Julius Seligsohn, who had been in America more than fifty years earlier. He recalled a celebration by the Jews of Philadelphia to mark the hundredth birthday of the philosopher Moses Mendelssohn, with the chief address delivered by a Rabbi Benjamin Szold. Mr. Seligsohn quoted from Szold's address; he analyzed the way in which it showed a love of German literature, of German language, of the German people themselves, with whom Rabbi Szold was so deeply identified.

The implication was that in this way his daughter had been prepared to take up work for the German immigrants, especially German youth. She was shaken by the speech. She remembered her father's Philadelphia address, and it was strange to hear it quoted now, strange and wonderful that someone else should bring it back across more than half a century. She felt embarrassed, amazed and full of pride.

Everywhere she went in Berlin she was received with something like homage; she described it in great detail to her sisters, apologizing at length for dwelling on such matters. It had nothing to do with her as a person, she said, everything to do with her speaking German, with her coming from the world "outside" to concern herself with the fate of beleaguered fellow Jews. "The remainder of the exaggerated praise is ascribable to the excited state of Jewish feeling in Germany. But you had a right to know what happened to me. I had to write about myself."

There were moments of exaltation, when the dignity of the German Jews embraced and uplifted her; at other times she moved through an atmosphere made thick with "*the* nasty black thing . . . one cannot escape from it. The whole of life is permeated with it." It was the hatred of Germany for its Jews. The Jews themselves loved Germany and thought of themselves as German through and through, yet those they loved cast them off.

One evening Miss Szold was taken to a meeting with some Youth Aliyah parents. She expected a dozen or so seated around a table, with whom it would be possible to carry on an intimate conversation. Instead she found herself in a large hall where some 700 or 800 waited. She began her speech: the daily life of the Youth Aliyah children, their work on kibbutz, their studies, their trips through the countryside.

In the hope of assuring these parents that they were not forgotten by their children, she said she had letters day after day from young people who begged to know when they might bring over their mothers and fathers: "Will you let me, Miss Szold, go out of the kibbutz, back to the city, in order that I may earn money, and I am hard-hearted and my answer is, it will be a long time before you can bring your parents here and I cannot let you go out into the city where you would learn nothing, earn a pittance and not be adjusted to the land to which we have brought you. . . . After two years you may begin to think of rescuing your parents." During the last sentences she heard noises from the street, the sounds of marching storm troopers returning from a meeting. She heard them chant, "Death to the Jew!" Without a pause she finished her speech and called for questions from the parents.

Their questions were very specific. No one wanted to know about Zionism or Palestine or Youth Aliyah. Each of them wanted to ask about a particular child. Many had photographs that they held up. How was the broken leg, the poor study habits, the dental problems of the boy or girl in the picture? . . .

Jugendhilfe leaders took her through the countryside to visit the preparation camps, past village after village where the Jews of Berlin had to send bread and milk because the Nazis had forbidden the sale of food to Jews and children were starving. "With my own eyes, as I passed through villages, one after the other . . . I saw huge signs stretched across the main road with the legend: 'Jews not wanted!' . . . or 'Girls and women, the Jews are your corrupters!' "

She conferred day after day with the leaders over technical matters that could only be thrashed out in person, among them the problem of the preparation camps. Harassed by the secret police in a perpetual game of cat and mouse, it seemed clear they could no longer continue in Germany but would have to be transferred to Holland, France, England, Scandinavia; arrangements were already under way. Another problem was the children of junior high school age, cut off from all schooling, adrift in Berlin. Many had been sent from the villages, where Jewish life was being strangled. Something must be done for those children, perhaps a boarding school with a Zionist theme.

It was during those meetings that the Berlin leaders came to know Miss Szold, to see the woman behind the martinet. Eva Stern, chief of the Arbeitsgemeinschaft, wondered if the truth about Germany was really sinking in; she sensed an idealism that might never come to terms with the existence of evil, as well as a sense of honor that could make it impossible to cheat and deceive in a time when lives might depend on it. Moreover the American woman would go back to Palestine where Palestine itself would protect her from the realities of Jewish life in Germany. The letters of the Berlin office would continue to be written under the fear of censorship. Refugees from Germany would have stories to tell, but Miss Szold would discount those stories as exaggerations or isolated incidents.

Eva Stern was young, as were most of the German leaders of Youth Aliyah;

the head of the Jugendhilfe was just past twenty. They sensed the future in a very terrible way. The man who became principal of the Jugendhilfe boarding school had a child come to him one day from one of the villages who told him both his parents had been gunned down by the Nazis. Forever after the principal remembered it was that moment when he first caught the smell of death. And Eva Stern was right about Miss Szold. She lacked the capacity to imagine horrors; she saw only that the Jews of Germany lived "in a stirring time, at once depressing and elevating." They accepted with heart-rending dignity their terrible fate, which was, she believed, that all the young would leave and the old would stay on in their thousands, silent and proud and sad among the joyful Germans.

By the end of October Miss Szold was back in Jerusalem in time to read accounts of a pitched battle between Hadassah and the ZOA. Each organization wanted the right to act as sole American agency for Youth Aliyah fund raising. Hadassah won, for they were bigger, stronger, better organized and convinced the task was uniquely suited to their membership. They decided to launch their opening drive by inviting Miss Szold to New York for a celebration of her seventy-fifth birthday.

However Hadassah's purpose in inviting her was not confined to Youth Aliyah. The salvaging of German children was to be used as a bridge to the German Jews of America. For the creation of the Jewish Agency had been a failure in one respect: the Agency lost its non-Zionist supporters in time and became increasingly a Zionist body. Hadassah wanted to convert the German-American Jews to Zionism in order that their fortunes might be used for the upbuilding of the homeland. More than that, they hoped to enlist the influential Yahudim who could make a difference in American foreign policy. One day there would be a Jewish state in Palestine, and on that day they wanted America to be its friend.

So Miss Szold, Hadassah's most potent propaganda weapon, left Palestine in early December and landed in Baltimore. There she had the pleasure of a long and private reunion with her sisters, with Bertha's children, with friends, old, old friends, white-haired women she had gone to school with. Harry Friedenwald was there, and at a party in her honor he summoned back all the warmth and simplicity of Lombard Street, the harmonious childhood that so often filled her mind and heart in Palestine until she wondered if the world had ever been as radiantly safe as it was in her memories; yet it must have been, for Harry Friedenwald had the same memories.

From there she went to New York. She had been warned that she was to have her birthday in public, to "be a fake great woman." Hadassah conventions were always harrowing for Miss Szold, who had a powerful fear of being caught before a huge convention audience wearing her old gray sweater. They were all so well turned out nowadays. The depression made no difference, apparently. Age made no difference. Yet for all her addiction to worn, outmoded clothing, Miss Szold was also aware that she was slimmer than she used to be and some of her Hadassah acquaintances were not. "How is Zip?" she used to ask visitors in Jerusalem. "Fat?"

She traveled by ship to Hoboken, arriving late at night. Rose Jacobs and several Hadassah women were there to meet her in the cold and wet, along with reporters and newsreel cameramen. She was filmed and recorded right on the dock: "I come on behalf of German Jewish children," she told the newsreel cameras, "who are leaving their homes and coming to Palestine to be educated."

The words were very carefully chosen, as were all Miss Szold's public words in America. The German children were leaving their homes. Precisely why was never described, nor was the atmosphere in Berlin and the villages where food could not be sold to Jews. No marching storm troopers appeared in her American speeches, no placards demanding Jewish deaths. She said nothing about the Jugendhilfe. Above all she mentioned no one by name, because in Germany the work of Youth Aliyah depended from start to finish on the Nazis. So far they had allowed Jugendhilfe officials to leave the country on fund-raising tours and to return, carrying their passports and special papers that guaranteed freedom of movement; once the Nazis decided these officials or their friends were spreading propaganda damaging to the regime, then passports, papers, the children themselves would be forfeit. So Miss Szold spoke to the newsreel cameras only about Palestine and the young people who were coming to learn farming, to live the pioneer life. "And then her picture was shown on the movie news," a Hadassah leader remembers, "and there she was with her wonderful eyes, her wonderful voice, coming over for two full minutes."

Soon after Miss Szold's arrival, Tamar de Sola Pool told her at breakfast, " 'Miss Szold, you're going to be received by Mayor La Guardia.' . . . She sprang to her feet and flew like a torpedo to the other side of the room and looked at me angrily." But she agreed. She even agreed to have her hair done at a beauty parlor for the first time in her life, although when someone suggested lipstick she clapped both hands across her mouth. In a new hat and a coat that was not new but adequate, she was driven by Zip Szold to New York's City Hall, preceded by an escort of police cars that tore through red lights, a fast and noisy ride. Once Zip turned to see how Miss Szold was taking it and saw a look of delight. The mayor, half Italian, half Jew, was hardly taller than Miss Szold, and photographers caught them laughing into each other's eyes while Rabbi Stephen Wise, a giant, hunched down. La Guardia presented her with the keys to the city in a graceful speech: "If I, the child of immigrant parents, am today Mayor of New York . . . it is because of you. Half a century ago you initiated that instrument of American democracy, the night school for the immigrant." The newsreel cameras caught it all.

A breakfast meeting was held in the home of Mrs. Felix Warburg, who had agreed to serve as first honorary chairman of Youth Aliyah. People came to it from all over the country. Miss Szold had even gone to Franklin Simon and bought a new dress, but Mrs. Warburg, an imperious woman, announced that they must have short speeches and Miss Szold could speak only ten minutes.

Miss Szold had reason to be especially sensitive to the vagaries of Mrs. Warburg, whose husband had caused her so much pain a few years earlier. Her sister Adele had also suffered as the social secretary of Mrs. Jacob Schiff, Frieda Warburg's mother. Furthermore Miss Szold had come all the way from Palestine, and she had on a new dress. Ten minutes, she said, would not suffice.

Rose Jacobs ran back and forth between the two opposing forces and worked it up to twenty minutes. The speech began with the customary homage to Recha Freier: "How did this whole system originate? It originated in the mind and heart of a woman with lustrous eyes and most attractive features and manner, a God-created propagandist, Recha Freier." It seemed that Mrs. Freier grew more appealing year by year, at least in the speeches of Henrietta Szold.

Once she was back in Jerusalem the uncomfortable aspects of the public birthday evaporated, and she remembered it only as a homecoming to Hadassah. After years of division she "belonged" to them again. It was more than belonging, for the great organization that had grown from such small beginnings was prepared to join hands with her across the globe and work for a cause she had come to love as she loved no other project in her life.

But the reunion with her sisters left her hungry for more; her days were full to overflowing, she told them, yet she longed for something she could only struggle to express. It was not appreciation, not precisely; it was blood sympathy. There was no one in Jerusalem to whom she could pour out her heart.

Certainly there were friends, not intimates, but a small circle of friends, and well-wishers in amazing number. More than 1,000 birthday letters were piled on her desk, every last one of which she would answer herself. Within the Youth Aliyah office she was among a band of acolytes whose lives were at her disposal. Their feelings for her were at once tender and clear-eyed. "As she grew older she became more beautiful, I'm convinced of it," one of the secretaries recalled. "The wisdom showed out of her eyes somehow. She loved me in the end, I know she did, although she was cool at first. She was suspicious, she was suspicious of any stranger; it took years until she trusted someone."

Night after night Hans Beyth and Emma came home with her to work at the Eden Hotel until midnight or later, and when Emma went abroad for two years another secretary took her place. No matter how late they had worked the night before, Miss Szold expected to see the entire staff in the office at eight. Even after some of the secretaries had babies, "Nobody could say my child is ill, or I can't. There was no reason," one woman remembered. They accepted it, although their husbands were less accepting. Sometimes a husband came to the hotel to wait downstairs for his wife, and Miss Szold would shift uneasily in her chair, bang on the desk and say, "I don't like husbands!"—a joke that was not a joke. Emma soothed her with words, Hans Beyth by putting his large hand over her own. He massaged the back of her neck when she had headaches, traveled with her twice each week to the youth camps, protected and comforted her and forgot that Youth Aliyah was supposed to be only a stopping place for him.

As for Emma, she adored Miss Szold the way a nun adores a mother superior. She stationed herself between Miss Szold and the other secretaries like a protective barrier, for which they often resented her. That Emma Ehrlich, a beautiful, dark-haired young American with no particular education, no interest in intellectual affairs, no striking characteristics beyond her fantastic devotion, should attach herself to a woman of Miss Szold's stature was not surprising. But that Miss Szold should attach herself to Emma was a source of amazement to all who knew them.

For Emma had become her closest companion. They walked down the street absorbed in each other's conversation. Sometimes Miss Szold amused Emma with imitations of dignitaries in the Agency or mimicked someone they passed on the street and the two of them laughed so hard they had to stop walking. Whenever Miss Szold went to parties Emma went with her as aide-de-camp. Indeed Miss Szold rarely went anywhere without Emma. People wondered what it was Emma gave her.

Miss Szold wanted to be loved, but she was not easy to love. And apparently Emma, out of her own needs, offered love that was close to veneration. They became in time extremely dependent on each other; in Miss Szold's eyes Emma could do no wrong. Emma was brave, intelligent, honest, indispensable, as Alice Seligsberg used to be, or Julia Dushkin. And unlike those other adoring friends Emma was a junior partner in the enterprise that had begun to enrich Miss Szold's life to the point where she sometimes wondered if she was not actually happy.

Early that year the first youth group faced its "graduation." They were adults now, ready to enter the labor force at eighteen. Some would join relatives; others would go to work in the cities; most would remain on the land. They were leaving Ain Harod at a difficult time, for a sense of feverish unrest gripped the country. It was to blaze into open war within months, Arab guerrillas against the British army.

Throughout the northern uplands, groups were graduating that spring, and Miss Szold attended all the ceremonies as the honored guest, the mother of Youth Aliyah. But spring brought other ceremonies, Nebi Musa, Easter, Passover, with their ominous undertones. In 1936 the outer world had drawn dangerously close to Palestine. There were Italian troops in Ethiopia, British warships in the eastern Mediterranean. Axis Italy began broadcasts in Arabic, and many of the young Arab intellectuals were forming Fascist parties of their own.

The British had allowed a legal immigration of 60,000 during 1935 alone, roughly equal to the Jewish population of the country when the Mandate was declared, and they had overlooked the illegal immigration of a few thousand more. By 1937 the Yishuv would number close to 400,000, over a quarter of the country's population. Now the Arabs demanded an end to Jewish immigration, an end to land sales to Jews. What they wanted and hoped the Axis would win for them was an end to the Mandate, to British rule in the Middle East, to British pride and British power. They wanted to see England utterly crushed, and they wanted their country back.

During this period David Ben-Gurion, political officer of the Jewish Agency, met secretly and often with moderate Arab leaders at the urging of Dr. Magnes. But nothing came of it, through no fault of Ben-Gurion or the men with whom he conferred. The time for counsels of moderation had apparently slipped away.

That spring there were scattered atrocities of which Jews and Jewish property were the victims. Then the isolated incidents took on the appearance of guerrilla warfare, with troops that included mercenaries from the neighboring Arab countries, a war directed not only against the British but against those moderate Arab leaders who remained loyal to the British. In a sense it had become a revolt of the Arab young against age and authority and established order, but the theme was always Zionism and the Jews.

In the opening weeks of the outbreak the Jewish Agency acted swiftly and with uncommon wisdom, proclaiming a policy of *havlagah*, self-restraint. There were to be no armed operations by Jews against the rebels. Self-defense was permitted, nothing more. This decision was highly unpopular among Haganah and the young kibbutzniks, but they submitted to it. At a time when the world was threatened by a new barbarism the Jews of Palestine joined together in an extraordinary display of moral strength.

Because the earliest outbreaks took place in Jaffa, thousands of refugees camped in tents in nearby Tel Aviv while their houses were gutted and burned. Refugees from Hebron and other towns fled to Jerusalem, living in synagogues and private homes. Miss Szold had the satisfaction of seeing her social service centers and the workers she had trained rise like disciplined troops to meet the emergency; food, clothing, housing and health care provided for 9,000 in Tel Aviv alone.

The country was in flames. Five British battalions were brought in from Egypt, then three more, yet the area of attack widened day by day. From Ain Harod Miss Szold learned that 500 orange trees had been destroyed. At Mishmar HaEmek, "the beautiful woodland, the pride of the settlement, has been set fire to eight times. The other night the match was applied to ten different places . . . the other day 150 olive trees of seven years' growth were cut down—in this treeless country!" The kibbutzniks planted by day to replace what was destroyed by night; at the end of May the eighth incendiary fire in Mishmar blasted 20,000 trees.

She mourned for the settlers. She sympathized with the High Commissioner when she was not outraged by his lack of righteous indignation. She antagonized some of her friends with her concern for the Arab *fellahin*, who were certainly starving, their shops shut down, their villages lifeless, those who refused to take part in the strike terrorized by guerrillas. She was sealed up in Jerusalem, cut off from the youth groups by the no-man's land of the hill country, uncomfortable with her friends and isolated by the curfew. Three times each week she went to bed at two and rose at five; on the other days she had four or five hours' sleep, including naps. "All the rest of the time, all my waking hours, I am strenuously at work. I never, never relax. . . . I am inhuman!" About her last request for 450 immigration certificates, including 50 for Polish children, she heard nothing. The government wrapped itself in impenetrable silence.

By summer she had resolved to travel again, although there were still daily battles in the hill country. The Tel Aviv refugee camps were breaking up as the exiles from Jaffa were absorbed into other towns, and she had been asked to supervise the massive liquidation. Very early one morning Miss Szold took a bus for Tel Aviv, one of three, accompanied by an armored car bristling with fully armed British troops, a signaling device and a machine gun. She sat in the front; opposite her and next to the driver was another British soldier with a rifle across his lap, very young and very dignified, his face rosy and flushed. Except for a single Arab the passengers were all familiar types to her, ordinary Jews going quietly about their ordinary business, as unconcerned as if they were not entering a battle zone. To Miss Szold the soldiers and their guns were humiliating; above all she hated the thought of being protected by a slip of a boy.

The bus set off; at the slightest jolt, cry or whistle on the road the passengers stirred in their seats. They were not unconcerned after all; they were frightened. As she was. Several times the British soldier called out, "Now the danger is past." He had a half-Irish accent.

She looked out the window at the hills, sensing the presence of machine guns. Suppose they were fired on? She wondered about it for several minutes, then pictured herself holding her large purse before her eyes as a shield. To protect her face or to keep from seeing? She smiled. She liked the British soldier, liked her fellow passengers, especially their pretense of unconcern. Amid the knifings, stabbings, beatings and random murders, "the Jews go right on." Fifty-five had died so far; the number of Arab deaths was incomparably greater but unknown, for there was no record of them. British troops engaged them in the same hills the bus was passing through, but when they were routed they carried their dead away with them, not from sentiment but to avoid identification. Other Arabs died at Arab hands. It was sickening. She wondered if things would be different "after"; everyone thought in terms of before the war, after the war. She wondered whether something would be learned from so much death.

Convoy travel was unbearably slow; she would be making the trip twice a week for a while, and she did not like the idea of so many hours cut out of the short life that remained to her. She decided there was no point in being safe. She would travel without a convoy from then on.

On her return to Jerusalem she ran into a big crowd, a funeral. Whose? She was told that a professor of Arabic at the Hebrew University had been sitting at his desk at home when a dumdum bullet shot through his iron shutters, tearing off the back of his head. As he fell the Arabic manuscript he had been working on floated to the floor. Miss Szold remembered him as the mildest man, a lover of Arab culture, a firm believer in Arab-Jewish rapprochement. There was sporadic shooting the rest of the day.

Arab outbreaks in Palestine traditionally brought in their wake British commissions of inquiry. That summer it was announced that one more commission, distinguished by the prefix "royal," would come from England and sit in Jerusalem to hear evidence about the causes of the unrest; it would compose a ponderous report and return to England, after which another commission would use the report to recommend specific action, a long, dignified, expensive process usually as useful as a Gilbert and Sullivan operetta. Miss Szold felt she could tell them all they wanted to know without their ever stirring from their English hearths: the riots were due to "an understandable Arab opposition springing from a nationalism akin to the Jewish brand, and an unintelligible English policy which might have been formulated, we think, so as to do justice to Jew and Arab." Like her friends she blamed the British for having done nothing to bring Jew and Arab together. Unlike most of them she blamed the Jews as well, who kept aloof from the Arabs socially and in business. They had helped to make of Palestine two airtight compartments.

About a month after the news of the Royal Commission she heard, unofficially, that her request for 450 youth certificates would be refused. She asked for an interview with the High Commissioner and found him almost immovable but not entirely so. His personal feelings were mixed, and it was hard to deny Miss Szold. He finally granted 100 certificates on condition that no more requests be made until after the Royal Commission's report and the action taken on it. An indefinite period, she concluded, for the action might be to end immigration altogether.

She wrote immediately to Hadassah saying there would be no more certificates for an indefinite period. In the meanwhile, why not use American funds to place Palestinian children in kibbutz schools? "Lord knows how badly they need it!" From time to time bands of young people from the Oriental community approached her, anxious to know why the German children were given everything while they had nothing. After all, the kibbutz schools, built for Youth Aliyah children, were designed to make foreigners into Palestinians, to make city children into farmers. And here they were, city children who longed for an education, yet somehow they were shut out. Why? She had no answer, except that the Youth Aliyah children were supported by foreign money. Now some of that money was piling up in America. She had a fierce desire to get her hands on it and tell the young people that someone did care after all, that their fate was important to the Jews of the world. What she could not say was the truth: the Jews of the world did not know they existed and preferred not to know because it would spoil their picture of Palestine.

In mid-November 1936, the Royal Commission came and seated itself in the ballroom of Jerusalem's Palace Hotel to examine the causes of the Arab war. There began a series of sixty-six sessions at which some forty Jewish witnesses, including most of the leaders of the future state of Israel, gave testimony and were cross-examined. Cables from Hadassah implored Miss Szold to use her time on the witness stand to beg for certificates for German children. As for the Palestinian children, the project was out of the question.

Miss Szold was called to the Palace Hotel near the end of the sessions. Awed by the Royal Commission, her testimony was nervous, defensive, at one point almost absurdly awkward. She found no opportunity to bring up Youth

Aliyah and left the hearing with a sense of personal failure.

The Commission went home, but the Yishuv was not yet free of it. During the months ahead they were to live suspended in an atmosphere thick with speculation and rumor. All immigration waited. The German youth groups waited, expectant and full of hope. The Polish children waited less hopefully, for they had had nothing so far but promises.

27

Miss Szold was at Ben Shemen when she heard the decision of the Royal Commission. Three or four hundred people gathered in the dining room, enveloped in thick silence, while the report was broadcast first in English, then Hebrew, then Arabic. In contrast to the work of past and future commissions, this one went straight to the core of the dilemma that was Mandate Palestine. It was impossible, they said. Justice could not be done in that small country to two peoples with contradictory aspirations. The solution was to make of the small country one smaller Jewish state, the rest to be joined to the kingdom of Trans-Jordan. Jerusalem would remain under perpetual mandate.

Among the Yishuv the news was received with high excitement as the first step toward nationhood. It was in this light that Weizmann perceived it. Small as the territory was—Miss Szold called it a "toy state"—it would be their own, with all the trappings of sovereignty, and surely in time the territory could be enlarged. But Americans, including Hadassah, were not impressed; they objected to the size, to the loss of Jerusalem, the Hebrew University, the Hadassah hospital, and Miss Szold opposed it for totally different reasons. To partition Palestine would be to kill forever the dream of brotherhood between Arab and Jew; without it Zionism had no meaning for her.

She composed a speech to be delivered at the 1937 Zionist congress in Zurich:

> The British Government failed, also we failed; and unless we snatch our last opportunity to retrieve ourselves we shall stand before the tribunal of history as failures. . . . What I see before us if we accept the Judenstaat of the Royal Commission is a repetition of the past. We entered the land by means of the sword, the Judenstaat of the Royal Commission will compel us to keep the sword in our hands day after day, year after year. . . . I am not pleading for justice to the Arabs alone, I am pleading for justice to ourselves, to our principles, the sacred principles for which our martyrs gave their blood.

But at the congress she heard Rabbi David de Sola Pool hissed and booed for statements like her own. At the Agency Council immediately afterward Magnes delivered a fervent plea for fresh negotiations with the Arabs, in the hopes of an undivided Palestine, and was almost howled down. Although the congress rejected the partition plan of the Royal Commission, it was willing to consider other partition schemes with more generous boundaries. Miss Szold put aside her own speech undelivered.

She wrote to Magnes some weeks later:

> I cannot stand up against the official action, because I can protest against it only with my instinctive feelings. . . . I bump up against my intellectual limitations. . . . I am a moral coward in view of my intellectual limitations. Suppose I were, with a word of mine, to destroy such good as may, after all, be tucked away in the folds of the negotiations I abhor and do not understand! In other words, I cannot follow your example—standing calm and unassailable before a [jeering] audience, with only one voice demanding that you be listened to. There's my confession and my torture.

It was not the first time she had choked back her instinctive feelings out of the fear that others were somehow wiser, and it was not the first time she envied people like Magnes the courage to speak their personal truths right or wrong. But she was learning—growing and learning even at seventy-seven—and the day would come when she would stand beside Magnes and say what she believed.

Before the end of the congress, Miss Szold made a brief trip to Berlin. Tamar de Sola Pool saw her off on the train looking brisk and energetic. Mrs. Pool was at the station three days later when Miss Szold returned to Zurich transformed into an old woman, shrunken into herself. "I was in Germany, and saw what I saw, and heard what I heard. . . . I was on the spot only forty-eight hours. Into that short time those whom I met packed more bitterness than I knew could possess a human being and yet let him live."

Although on their last visit Miss Szold and Emma had stayed with a family of rich and cultivated Berlin Jews, this time they went to a hotel, for it was unwise to compromise people, either by living with them or talking to them or even asking the time. There were other changes. In order to hold an informal meeting, two Jews would enter a house; when they left two others went in. Some people put a pillow over the telephone because they believed the Gestapo had a way of listening to them through the telephone even when it was not in use.

They were afraid. Furtive, scarred, in the grip of a strange passivity. Unlike the small-town Jews, they were not shot or beaten up, and some of their neighbors even continued to greet them. But the heart had gone out of Berlin Jewry. To Miss Szold they looked like living corpses capable of no emotion but fear. And they were increasingly reluctant to send their children to Palestine; they had lost interest in Palestine. The Youth Aliyah fund-raising office was to close down at the end of the year because of that lack of interest. Sensing some great catastrophe, shapeless and unimaginable, the Jews of Berlin clutched their children to them.

But when the Nazi government imposed a huge collective fine on the Jewish community one year later, the money appeared in no time, and it was a sum that could have transformed Jewish Palestine. Blind, encased within a protective membrane of their own making, they ignored even America, where the quota for German immigrants went unfilled until 1938.

So the Jugendhilfe had called for Miss Szold, hoping her presence would invigorate at least the Zionist community. A hall had been rented. The parents of children with certificates were to meet her there, as well as parents with children already in Palestine and those whose children wanted to go. When the parents came, they crowded around Miss Szold shouting questions, holding out photographs; many expressed their happiness that their children were safe in Palestine, but some had brought petitions and thrust them at her. Suddenly a wave of emotion washed over her, as if all the sensations of the past thirty-six hours—the furtiveness, the passivity, the vision of Germany as a prison in which the Jews would rot—flew at her in a single moment. It took the form of an unaccountable fear; she was afraid of being torn to pieces.

In February of 1938 Miss Szold sailed back to Palestine after a trip to New York for Hadassah's jubilee convention. She was returning to a country under martial law. Two Arab clans battled for leadership of Arab Palestine, and guerrilla warfare threatened to destroy the economy as it ravaged the trees. The Mufti had fled in disguise, eventually making his way to Europe, where he lived as a guest of Hitler.

A new High Commissioner tried to restore order, and Jerusalem bristled with entanglements of barbed wire in streets empty of all but steel-helmeted British troops. For several days the Old City was entirely in the hands of Arabs, and in the countryside pitched battles between guerrillas and the military were so commonplace that the oldest Youth Aliyah children took their turn standing guard on kibbutz.

Although at this stage of the guerrilla war most casualties were Arab, the Yishuv suffered from a terrible sense of abandonment, as if every man's hand was against it, abroad and at home. Surely Great Britain was against it. In the coming World War the Jews would have no choice of sides, but the

Arabs would have to be lured away from the Fascists if England were to maintain
her hold in the Middle East. And there were 200 million Moslems beyond
Palestine, in Egypt, India and other countries, whose goodwill England must
earn. All this the Jews understood. England would abandon them to court
the Arabs, and when England abandoned the Jews of Palestine, it would inevitably close off the country to the Jews of Germany, Poland and the other
European nations already infected by the virus of the new anti-Semitism. Every
illegal immigrant became a triumph in this race against time.

On March 10, the government announced the new immigration schedule
for the period April through September 1938. There would be nothing in the
labor schedule. In the student category immigration was to be unrestricted.
"We could hardly believe our senses. . . . Unrestricted!" Miss Szold cried.
One day later Nazi Germany marched into Austria.

The Yishuv was so stunned by the news that it almost ignored the Jewish
aspect, for the Nazis had burst the boundaries of Germany, and no one tried
to stop them. They could go anywhere, everywhere. The rest of Europe was
either paralyzed by fear or already crypto-Nazi. Miss Szold consoled herself
with her certificates. "If we collect enough money we can empty Germany,
the old Reich, and the Province of the East, of all young people under seventeen." Enough money meant enough in the bank in Palestine to cover the
two years' keep of every child; without this guarantee no child could enter.

There was another barrier: the youth movement in Austria could not func-
tion as it had in Germany. Austrian Jews were unprepared for Hitler and disorganized as a community. While the Germans had a multitude of social services
and the resources of the richest Jewry in Europe, the Austrians had neither,
nor did they have a vigorous Zionist organization. Certainly there was no time
to prepare one now. The process of deterioration that had reduced the Jews
of Germany to their present status over several years was telescoped in Austria
to weeks, and far more brutally.

There was no Youth Aliyah organization in Austria, only eight Zionist
youth groups in constant struggle for supremacy. If the children of Austria
were to be rescued, someone must go to Vienna and set up an office. Miss
Szold prepared to go, but three days after the Anschluss she had a cable from
London begging her to abandon the trip. Zionist officials in Vienna sent word
that a Nazi functionary named Eichmann, who dealt with Jews and Zionists
in Austria, had given

> definite warnings on specific matters. One such matter was any visit by you
> to Austria. You are definitely warned by Eichmann not to attempt to set
> foot in Austria. You were mentioned by name by him. Furthermore: you are
> begged by Dr. Loewenherz [an officer of the Zionist organization in Vienna]
> to heed this warning. . . . At the moment Mrs. Loewenherz is kept as hostage.

Miss Szold stayed in Palestine, and it was months before the head of the Jugendhilfe was allowed to enter Vienna.

One day Hans Beyth met a friend on the street in Jerusalem covered from top to toe with blood, not his own blood, he explained. In a taxi riding from Jaffa to Jerusalem he had been stoned and shot at and the woman beside him seriously wounded. The woman herself was a newly arrived refugee from Austria who had lived for months with several others on a raft in the Danube because the Nazis would not let them land in Austria or take refuge in neighboring countries.

To what am I bringing these children, Miss Szold asked herself when she heard the story. To blood lust, savagery, hatred, to training in the use of arms, she replied.

The same Eichmann who would not allow her into Austria appeared in the Berlin office of the Jugendhilfe. He approached Eva Stern with the question, "Why don't you send many more of these children to Palestine?" She told him the British would not allow children in unless there was money for their keep, "So we collect first the money." And that was a slow process, for there was no Zionist money left in Germany and everything had to be collected abroad. "But when you leave Germany," he said, "you spread stories about us." "No," she said, "We do not spread stories."

"He shouted at me; he said you have to cease with your work; he wanted my passport but I didn't give it to him." She wrote immediately to Miss Szold saying her office must be transferred to England.

Miss Szold agreed. But first she wanted Eva to visit Poland and organize there for youth migration; a small number had come so far, but for all the pressure to get Jewish children out of the squalid ghettos of Poland, the movement had been dogged by bad luck, and the Polish Jews still had no Youth Aliyah.

Eva went, although reluctantly, and in Warsaw a Youth Aliyah office was opened. And in October 1938, when 28,000 Polish Jews living in Germany were expelled to the area between Germany and Poland, dumped into a wasteland without food or shelter, this new Youth Aliyah office sent a representative to keep the Zionist youth groups together, housed, fed, still training themselves for Palestine. For Youth Aliyah had become more than a Zionist movement. To the children waiting in preparation camps in Germany or Austria, to the children in no-man's land who might never reach Palestine, it was a framework that kept them self-respecting and human. It was their philosophy and their lifeline.

In London, Eva Stern opened an office for fund raising and propaganda; the Jugendhilfe and a small Arbeitsgemeinschaft crew remained in Berlin. The former was staffed by a succession of young people replacing those leaders who went on to Palestine; the last director of the Jugendhilfe was to die before a firing squad because he refused to hand over children for deportation. The last director of the Berlin Arbeitsgemeinschaft would be sent to Auschwitz with her assistant; they had had many opportunities to leave the country but had chosen to remain, as did Recha Freier, who somehow avoided Eichmann's close attention. Her eldest son had left Germany for England, her two younger sons and their father followed later, but Mrs. Freier stayed on with her youngest child and the Jugendhilfe.

No sooner was Eva Stern established in London than Hadassah urged her to attend a conference on refugees that would take place that summer in Evian, France. At the invitation of President Roosevelt, representatives of thirty-two governments were to discuss the thousands of stateless and homeless Jews whose numbers increased each month. In Romania the government announced that one half their Jews must leave; whether they emigrated or drowned in the Black Sea was entirely their own choice. In Hungary a bill was introduced into parliament specifying that 300,000 Jews were to lose their jobs within the next few years. In Poland it was the declared policy of successive governments to make their 3 million Jews so miserable they would have to emigrate. Those Polish Jews living in Germany who were expelled to the German-Polish border were naturally rejected by the Poles. There were even Jews living on the high seas, for three ships had left Hamburg that year carrying hundreds to Latin America, where they had not been permitted to land, and they had shuttled back and forth to Europe, to Palestine, with their human cargo, whose humanity no one was willing to recognize.

But the Evian conference was hedged about by a number of preconditions set up by the British, one of them being that Palestine must not be allowed a representative, since Palestine could not take in refugees. Another was that no Jewish organizations were to speak at Evian. Eva could see no point in going; therefore Hadassah turned to Miss Szold. Perhaps they could have the rulings changed; perhaps Miss Szold would attend as their representative.

But Miss Szold was fighting other battles in Jerusalem. Although the government had announced unrestricted immigration for students, that was not what it meant. What it meant was not clear, not even to the government, whose interpretation changed week by week. Much was implied rather than stated; her intimate contacts with immigration officials suggested that the British could not be pushed beyond a certain point. Whatever else changed, it seemed they intended to control both numbers and country of origin. German children, yes; Austrian children, yes. But for Poland and Romania and Czechoslovakia, caution must be observed. She believed they would not accept more than 1,000 for the six-month period.

Explaining the veiled and vacillating intentions of the government to America and to the Agency was no easy matter. To Hadassah she wrote, somewhat cryptically, "We have had reason to realize that warnings given us by our friends are well founded." But for the first time the Jewish Agency was showing a close interest in the details of the Youth Aliyah bureau with its permission for "unrestricted" immigration, and she was unable to convince the Agency men that the warnings, elusive and unwritten, were nevertheless authentic and substantial. Miss Szold felt the Agency breathing down her neck. They wanted her to exert pressure; she believed she would endanger everything she had built so far by doing so. And she intended to defend the future of her bureau against the Agency themselves if need be. Relations between them had always been strained. She was used to it. A little more could make no difference.

By June, Hadassah had given up on Evian, for it was clear that no change would be made in the ruling that Palestine might not send a representative to the conference on refugees. All mention of Palestine as a possible haven was to be forbidden. "Do you wonder that . . . we view the Evian Conference with distrust?" Miss Szold wrote to her sisters. "It was a fine gesture. Doubtless Roosevelt was honest in his intentions. . . . No country is going to open its doors to receive the unwanted."

But Miss Szold was wrong about Evian. There was one country willing to open its doors to the unwanted, and its name was the Dominican Republic. Among the thirty-two representatives who spoke in the most humane and sympathetic terms of the condition of the refugees, none had been empowered to take any action except for the Dominican Republic. Hardly larger than Palestine, it offered to receive 100,000 Jews from Germany and Austria, provided only that they work on the land. There was some response to this offer; America then agreed to take in 30,000 a year, and Great Britain the same. But for the millions whose countries expressed a desire to be rid of them the conference solved nothing. As Christopher Sykes observed, "If only half a dozen of the thirty-one states . . . had had the courage, imagination or sense of responsibility to follow the example of the Dominican Republic, then, in theory at least, Hitler's victims would have been saved, and in practice many more saved than in fact were."

The failure of Evian surprised nobody in Palestine and certainly not the Jewish Agency. It only confirmed their belief that Jews were not wanted anywhere on earth except in what was supposed to be their homeland. The English, who ruled the homeland, were for the moment refusing all adult immigration. Therefore the Agency continued to pressure Miss Szold, who had access to "unlimited" certificates. She was under pressure from Poland, Romania, Czechoslovakia and Hungary. There was continued pressure from Hadassah for more vigorous publicity. They wanted German children brought to America to present their case to the public; they suggested sponsors for individual children, the sponsors encouraged to correspond, to send gifts. Miss Szold refused outright; no child was to be made to feel grateful, for gratitude curdled the soul. So the summer of 1938 was spent under siege. Everyone competed for certificates, for money, "yet the room blazes with flames and the foundations rock as in the moment of an earthquake," and it was not the time for competition. Her staff was drawn even more closely together by it. Hans Beyth had become essentially an equal partner in the work, and the secretaries, some of whom had relatives in Germany or Austria they were desperately trying to rescue, drowned their personal concerns in work, as did Miss Szold. She was as lonely as ever, and from time to time she told her friends, "I don't want to die in this place."

When she was very angry—and her temper was worse than ever those days—she would lash out as if at the room itself and demand: "What am I doing here? What for!" She should have been attending to her father's papers, she would say. Why was she there, of all places in the world? Everyone would rush to soothe her then.

When Hans Beyth married he kept it a secret from Miss Szold until the actual day of the wedding. Afterward his wife learned she would have to share him with Miss Szold. Two days each week they still visited the youth groups, "And you see my husband didn't like to take me when he went away with her. He would always say he has to look out for Miss Szold, and if I am with them she will be . . . she doesn't feel so well. She could have said, 'Take your wife with you if you are two days in the whole week away,' but she never said it." Hans Beyth was with Miss Szold in Tiberias when his first child was born: "I think there she felt a little bit guilty that he was not at home."

In the course of that summer Miss Szold's extraordinary body let out a cry for help: dizzy spells, a fluttering heartbeat, difficulty in breathing. At the Hadassah hospital she learned she had angina and must rest; for two weeks she rested in a private sanatorium, after which she was told to work only six hours a day. Later on, perhaps by autumn, she could work a normal day of twelve hours, no more.

One of the secretaries, Lotte Steigbügl, came to read to her during this period of enforced idleness. They sat together in the room at the Eden Hotel, which was full of the scent of flowers, dead flowers, for Miss Szold could never bear to throw a flower away. Sometimes their smell was almost painfully beautiful to her: "The air of my room is fragrant with the perfume of orange blossoms. I wonder how orange trees stand it." The books that were read aloud were often German books that Miss Szold and Lotte both loved, but there were business letters, reports and bulletins from the office staff as well, so that the two women in the flowery room, the elderly invalid and the young refugee, moved back and forth from the Germany of Schiller to Germany of 1938. One evening Lotte read from a collection of writings by Youth Aliyah children, horror stories, accounts of their experiences in Europe. Halfway through she stopped because she was weeping and could not see the page. Then she said to Miss Szold, "You know something? I'd like to spit at a Nazi!"

Miss Szold looked up at her, astonished. "How can you say such a thing?" She had not wept, although she was moved by the horror stories, and she could not understand why a well-bred German girl wanted to spit at anyone, even a Nazi. Nevertheless she had her own fantasies about the Nazis. Neville Chamberlain was in Munich to confer with Hitler, and what Miss Szold saw in her mind's eye was "Hitler across Chamberlain's knees, with Chamberlain swinging a rattan down on the bully." A week later she wrote: "From time to time I find myself indulging in bloody desires. If one could only lay Hitler and ten or twelve of his sadistic associates across one's knees and administer painful, even gory punishment, and thus save millions of lives. . . ." Please excuse me, she added, for using such strong language.

In the autumn she was back at work on a normal basis. It was the autumn of Cristallnacht, a sudden and terrible outbreak against the Jews of Germany and their property in which more than 800 Jewish shops were destroyed, over 100 synagogues burned, 20,000 Jewish citizens rounded up and arrested. In England, parliament debated the report of the Woodhead Commission, a successor to the Royal Commission, and this second version of a partitioned Palestine left the Jews with 400 square miles and no sizable town but Tel Aviv, a solution not even the English could have taken seriously.

Jewish life in Germany reached a turning point with Cristallnacht. Until then violence had been rare and isolated; now the Jews of Germany were virtual outlaws, money, power, entrenched position incapable of protecting them. It was in this climate—a fire storm let loose in Germany, the offer by Britain of a Jewish state the size of Hong Kong—that the Executive of the World Zionist Organization met in London. They cabled Miss Szold that she must announce in the Palestinian papers that 5,000 German children were to be brought to Palestine. They would be brought by the Vaad Leumi, they would be children of all ages, and they would go to foster homes.

Miss Szold disapproved—more than disapproved. She could hardly bear to lend her name to such a scheme. These 5,000 were to be part of a group twice that size that would be brought in during the following year. She opposed it "hand and foot and I opposed it because I sensed that it had been conceived for political purposes." In this she was certainly right; Zionist leaders intended the adoption scheme as a form of emotional blackmail against the rigidity of Great Britain, a way of calling the world's attention to the desperate homelessness of Jews.

Miss Szold objected to the use of children for political purposes, although she did place the announcement in the papers. She felt certain the government would never approve 10,000 certificates, and she wondered who would supply the astronomic funds needed for this mass adoption. As for so many children being absorbed by the Yishuv, it would be a staggering process, with the search for adoptive parents, the necessary negotiations with natural parents. She had never liked the idea of foster homes, and when the natural parents were alive she liked it even less.

But Eva wrote from London that her German friends were panicking. Everyone realized they must leave, although it meant forfeiting whatever they owned. No one knew where to go. Some were lucky enough to get to America. For others the only possibilities seemed to be Peru, Honduras, Bolivia and China. Several had visas for China, a country they could not even picture. But those German Jews who had heard of the child adoption scheme had such great hopes for it that Miss Szold felt her heart contract. There were after all a few institutions in the Yishuv already taking in a few children from thirteen to fifteen along Youth Aliyah lines; she felt these should be expanded. They would be the answer, not the wild adoption scheme so unfamiliar to the government.

She refused to take the chairmanship of the movement but agreed to put all the resources of Youth Aliyah at its command. The government, meanwhile, did nothing. And without certificates the plan, wise or unwise, was only a plan. Throughout the Yishuv a passionate desire to receive the children expressed itself in a multitude of ways, including a touching letter addressed to Queen Elizabeth. Five hundred children's certificates were granted the following year with the stipulation that only those whose blood relatives requested them would be accepted. Of these 500, about half had emigrated elsewhere by then or otherwise disappeared. Miss Szold's skepticism proved right. All along she had believed that the Children's Aliyah, as it had come to be called, was politically motivated and therefore tainted, as well as impractical. She saw several hundred children as a distinct possibility, 10,000 not. But neither her original skepticism nor her being right in the event endeared her to her colleagues at the Agency or in the Vaad Leumi. In succeeding years the Children's Aliyah was absorbed into Youth Aliyah.

Throughout this period Miss Szold's correspondence was full of the tension between her own cautious approach and the more sweeping views of the Agency

and Hadassah themselves. She was aware—and she pointed it out frequently—
that government policy fluctuated wildly, but she was absolutely certain they
would never succumb to pressure and public demonstrations whose purpose
was less the rescue of children than getting the government to expand all
immigration. The government would respond only to practical measures, to a
building program of schools that met their standards, to money in the bank.
"It doesn't mean salvation for our young people if we stick them into underdevel-
oped [settlements], undeveloped not only because they haven't the school and
dormitory facilities, but undeveloped also agriculturally, most of them supporting
themselves with the extremest difficulty by hiring themselves out for outside
work, day-labor."

From Poland during the same period came the urgent demand that out
of those certificates she had in hand a substantial number go to them. She
chose to ignore the demand and save the certificate for Germany. "One has
to ask which is the more important: to rescue Jewish youth from Germany,
or to create a never-to-be-rectified bitterness," Miss Szold summed it up for
Eva. "I take the liberty to respond to the question: to create this bitterness."
Another unpopular decision concerned teenagers from Romania. Two small
groups of Romanian youth had been placed in schools before Miss Szold learned
that their passports were almost all forged and many were overage, one girl
nearly twenty-one. The young people themselves were not to blame, apparently;
they were under the impression that Youth Aliyah had no objection to forged
papers. But Miss Szold was indignant, embarrassed. Lies had been told, and
the government might be punitive as a result. She believed the movement
was now absolved of all promises to the Jews of Romania.

But to her colleagues at the Agency objections to overage Romanian youth
were simply sanctimonious quibbles; the young people were now in Palestine,
and nothing else mattered. As for Poland, Miss Szold, in their opinion, knew
nothing about its miseries; she was a minimalist with respect to Poland, just
as she was about the Children's Aliyah. And she began to wonder herself;
through all the months of paper battles, she wondered if they were right and
she was the victim of her own psychological makeup.

The question remained, and is heard even today, whether Miss Szold was
truly a "minimalist," with the connotation "obstructionist," and what resulted
if she was. Of her temperament there can be no doubt: she was hypercautious,
meticulous and politically naïve. Eva Stern was convinced Miss Szold never
understood what the Nazis were doing because it was not in her to understand.
Certainly her fantasies of spanking Hitler suggest Eva was right. And at the
same time she did understand Palestine, the present and future needs of all
its people, especially the outsiders, far better than most of her contemporaries.

But it seems beyond dispute that she was mistaken in the belief that it would not mean salvation for the German children to be stuck into undeveloped settlements. In the matter of the Polish Jews she was again mistaken because she failed to foresee the German invasion of Poland.

Nevertheless—and it is a most important nevertheless—the Children's Aliyah was not a failure because Miss Szold refused to believe in it. On the contrary, that generous scheme was launched by the simple expedient of finding others to take charge of it. That it did not work was due to bureaucracy and the British. Yes, Miss Szold was a minimalist. But an obstructionist? She could always be bypassed and worked around. Among her closest colleagues and collaborators, especially Hans Beyth and the financial manager, Georg Landauer, it was a frequent practice to bypass Miss Szold's rigidities. She was almost certainly aware of it.

And what she chose to do out of her belief that it was right to do, she did superbly. She had two sets of standards, one for herself, one for everyone else. Thousands of children entered the country illegally while Miss Szold was getting other thousands in in accordance with the law. She accepted "illegals" into Youth Aliyah when there was room for them. If she failed to understand Hitler, if she put too much faith in the British during the years just ahead, she was in no way unique. Within the Agency there were many who did the same, for those were cruel and tragic times.

For six months or more she had been trying to sever herself from the Social Service Bureau, which meant finding a successor. There was still no successor, but she felt she must leave all the same, abandoning eight years of work into unknown hands because she simply lacked the strength to continue. The social services had grown considerably since the mid-thirties, but the demands on them at a time of economic depression and vast illegal immigration were staggering. Shiploads of illegals arrived each night on Greek vessels from Austria and Czechoslovakia, 2,400 during December alone. After a voyage of four to six weeks they slipped overboard in the dark, to swim ashore as signal lights from government airplanes raked the coastline. Those who were caught were sent back to Europe, for the British were haunted by fears of Nazi spies among the refugees.

The great tide of illegals fueled the hatred of the Arabs and hardened the British. Eventually Gestapo agents took a hand in it, supplying visas and exit permits, both invalid, to desperate Jews whom they jammed into "the little death ships" of the German Danube Steamship line, vermin-infested, ancient, overloaded and underfueled. For political reasons the Agency could not deal with them as it dealt with legal immigrants, therefore their care fell entirely on the Social Service Bureau. But Miss Szold had to make a choice, and she had no hesitation in choosing Youth Aliyah—because she loved it, because she believed, probably with reason, that it could not continue without her, and because it tied her past to the future. It made her whole.

The movement was changing; it was far more complex now. Some of the preparation camps in Austria and Germany continued, but a new network was created in Holland, Denmark, Sweden, England. London was in direct contact with all, ready at a moment's notice to send its representatives everywhere, including no-man's land. And London was in constant touch with Miss Szold, whose vision of Youth Aliyah never changed. She was not so much rescuing children from something as for something: a new life in which they would be part of a heroic undertaking.

Letters from America were full of family picnics, trips to the country, the smoothly running lives of people protected by an ocean from any threat of war. Bertha and Adele had been writing for months about a long visit to Palestine in the spring; it was something Henrietta could hardly bear to contemplate in case nothing came of it. In mid-March Hitler invaded Czechoslovakia, and the war that had moved closer at Munich came closer still, but the sisters were resolved to have their visit, and just before Passover Bertha and Adele arrived. In her joy at having them with her, Henrietta tried to put out of her mind the initial shock at the sight of Adele. She looked ghastly: thin, without appetite, her skin broken out in dark red hives. She suffered from enteritis. Still, they were together; they could revel in endless reminiscences of Lombard Street and the beautiful past.

Within weeks of the sisters' arrival, the government issued another White Paper, which destroyed for all time whatever fragile hopes remained of a Jewish homeland under British protection. The findings of the Royal Commission had been rejected by both Arabs and Jews. The findings of the Woodhead Commission and their offer of a minuscule state had also been rejected, and a conference of Jews and Arabs had therefore been called in London. Because the Arabs refused to sit in the same room with the Jews, two conferences had taken place. There could be no meeting of minds between opponents so deeply divided. The British had therefore announced they would impose a settlement, and this White Paper contained it: Jewish immigration was to be limited to 75,000 in the next five years. There would be no partition. Palestine would become neither a Jewish nor an Arab state but rather, at the end of ten years, a Palestinian state in which control over immigration was to rest with the majority. Since the majority would be Arab, Jewish immigration would cease.

Jews throughout the world responded to the White Paper with a deep and bitter sense of betrayal; the homeland was being sacrificed as Ethiopia and Czechoslovakia had been sacrificed. The strong had abandoned the weak for the sake of Arab friendship and Arab oil in the face of a world war in which both were seen as indispensable, but the pain of abandonment at a time when the nations of Europe turned their Jews out of doors like criminal strangers was in no way assuaged by an understanding of Britain's global position.

For Miss Szold and her sisters, the ugliness of world affairs was, for a brief moment, eclipsed by the interest of their reunion. Adele and Bertha went with Henrietta to the four crowded rooms of the Youth Aliyah office to meet the people she worked with. Bertha, with her ready laughter and easy, motherly manner, was everyone's favorite. Adele was something of a puzzle; quizzical, thoughtful, she looked them all over and kept her opinions to herself. In Jerusalem she saw that her sister was a woman of importance; the stream of people that came and went from her office ranged from bearded rabbis to Hashomer Hatzair of the farthest left. They came with complaints or requests, financial, ideological; they came to do battle, and Henrietta gave as good as she got.

The sisters visited the kibbutzim and saw the other side of Youth Aliyah. In one kibbutz they stood before a large dining hall on a sweeping lawn bordered with bushes; in the background soared an avenue of magnificently tall trees. Only a few years ago, Henrietta told her sisters, it had looked like a mining camp. Children poured out of the long, low buildings to see Miss Szold. She knew all those who had been sick or troubled by name, for accounts of their progress came to her office week by week, even followed her on her travels through Europe. What was most extraordinary was her reaction to these children; she was warmed by them, she opened up, she danced, sang and played with them. People who found her stiff-necked and rigid exclaimed when they saw it. Yes, she enjoyed the children, they said. It was hard to believe, but when she danced with them she was full of grace and loveliness. Even the pediatrician Helena Kagan said: "I could not do what she did—to play with them like that. I gave my life to these children, but I could not play with them."

So spring and summer revealed to the skeptical Adele the richness of Henrietta's creations in Palestine, and it should have been a beautiful visit. Yet it was not. Over all hung a shadow they never spoke about. Adele was sick, and it was obviously more than enteritis, but not speaking became a habit they were unable to break. Somehow Henrietta could not take command. Bertha followed her lead, and Adele stoically refused to complain. She had a form of amoebic dysentery the doctors could not control, but she never told her sisters. She did announce she would leave in August; after she went with them to the Zionist congress in Geneva she would go home.

But as it happened Adele was compelled to stay on for several months, and her wretched health was almost forgotten. Bertha got out of bed one morning and collapsed within an hour. The night before she had been her blooming, good-natured self, but now she seemed to be slipping away into another world. Henrietta wrote a hurried account to Bertha's family in Baltimore: "For several days we were dazed—there seemed no hope. Since then she has been recovering, though very very slowly." The doctor came every other day; a nurse was with her constantly. Henrietta hurried back from her office when she could, consumed by fears she revealed to nobody. Her letters to Hadassah leaders in Geneva rarely referred to the personal crisis.

Throughout her sisters' visit she had attended to all the duties of her office, including voluminous correspondence with Hadassah, whose demands for "representation" in Youth Aliyah had become importunate. She had planned to meet the leaders in Geneva and discuss their demands face to face, probably without the slightest intention of giving in. It was not until 1943 that Hadassah had a hand in the governance of Youth Aliyah. And now everyone was in Geneva except Miss Szold.

Everyone was still in Geneva when Hitler announced his pact with Stalin on August 22. Teenaged representatives of the Polish youth movement met in the bleak dawn of the final day of the congress to say their farewells to the others; each was determined to rush back to Warsaw before the German invasion of Poland. Circumstances had brought them to Switzerland and safety; at all costs they must make their way back to their comrades in the Warsaw ghetto. Leaders of the Jugendhilfe fled to Berlin with the same intensity of resolve—to escape the safety of Geneva, to return to mortal danger and their comrades.

What Miss Szold did was take refuge in her office, where she composed a plan for a Youth Aliyah constitution, a very orderly constitution full of rules for organizational procedure, as if she could build a protective barrier around Youth Aliyah, shutting out all evil and disorder. She sent it off to Hadassah. Two days later Poland was invaded, and England and Germany were at war.

28

In London, Eva Stern lived through those last days of August at the nerve center of Youth Aliyah, close to the continent and in direct contact with British authorities, without whom nothing could be done. There were telephone calls to Berlin, Prague, Vienna, sometimes several a day. On August 25 she learned that British authorities would no longer be responsible for the entry into England of Youth Aliyah transports. Since there were thirty-one children in Germany awaiting departure to England, she took it on herself to phone Berlin, telling them to ignore official notices and rush the children out of the country.

The next day Germany mobilized, requisitioned its railways and closed the German-Dutch border. It seemed impossible to hope that Jewish children could travel through Germany at such a time. Nevertheless, Berlin telephoned to say they were ready to try. Holland, they said, would allow the children to enter and cross the country if London could guarantee their admission into England. With the help of German Jews in England the guarantee was obtained. The next morning Berlin telephoned again; the children would leave on Wednesday, August 30, and Dutch friends, non-Jews, would shepherd them across Holland.

Meanwhile 400 children were stranded in Trieste because the Mediterranean was closed to shipping; places in Yugoslavia were found for them, if only money could be guaranteed for their keep. Children in Prague were sent to the homes of Danish farmers. Children in Berlin were accepted by Norway and Sweden. At times the London office was in touch with eight countries at once.

On Wednesday, August 30, Berlin telephoned to say the transport was leaving for Holland, then England, at nine that night, and the leader would wire Eva Stern from every stop. She did not know it, but this was to be her last direct contact with her coworkers in Germany.

On Thursday Stern and her staff waited, hour by hour, for the wires from the transport leader, remaining in the office until midnight without word. When a telephone call from Harwich, Friday morning, announced the German children had arrived, they could hardly believe it. They set out immediately for Harwich. But that day London was a city in turmoil, for the evacuation had begun of close to a million children, their mothers and teachers, and warnings were posted that no one else could count on rail or bus accommodations. By a stroke of luck Stern and her party were able to squeeze into a train leaving for Harwich at ten. At Harwich they learned Germany had started its attack on Poland.

They found the leader of the children's transport standing with a newspaper clutched in his hand, staring at it in a misery of horror and disbelief. Only two days before, he had left Berlin with a return ticket by plane, having said a casual goodby to his old mother, who was all alone in Berlin now. But the children were safe. They were in a playground at the moment, and Eva Stern went up to greet them, calling, *"Shalom."* *"Shalom,"* they replied; they seemed wonderfully cheerful among the swings and slides and climbing bars. With Eva they took the train to Euston Station in London, and from there went to Gwrych Castle in North Wales, which had been lent to the movement by Lord Dundonald for the use of Orthodox Youth Aliyah.

There were still 300 children holding Youth Aliyah certificates within Germany. What could be done for them? And if, as seemed likely, nothing at all could be done, how were Eva and her staff to accept this new reality? The first thing she did was fire off cables to Miss Szold, to Hadassah and to South Africa, informing them: REMAINING LONDON CONTINUING WORK.

On September 7, Eva received a letter from Denmark with news she could not believe. Forty-seven German certificate holders had reached Denmark one day *after* the outbreak of war. The rest of the 300 were expected to follow.

The letter from Denmark enclosed another from a twenty-three-year-old Jugendhilfe worker, one of those who had rushed back to Berlin from Geneva: "The tension has grown until we feel that we must soon explode. It is only natural, for all day we have to show a smiling face to those who are left. . . . But at night when we are in bed it all comes over us like a sudden shock and we want to weep." They were in almost daily contact with the children in the training camps. Although the balance of the 300 would leave within days, the young leaders themselves would remain.

So German authorities were prepared to allow Jewish children out; and the British were prepared to issue certificates within certain limits. That summer they presented Miss Szold with 1,000 beyond the regular schedule. The task of the London partners was to move as many as possible out of the training camps in neutral countries and into Palestine so their places could be taken by children from Germany. But all customary routes were blocked; children in Austria and Czechoslovakia as well as Germany had to be moved across closed frontiers in countries where all public transport was mobilized for war. Yet somehow it was done, somehow routes were created, loopholes found and the children hurried through them. Although Mediterranean fares had doubled, money was found as well as ships, and every single young person to whom a certificate was awarded in the summer of 1939 eventually reached the Holy Land.

In Palestine the outbreak of war caused economic crisis. Prices rose, food was hoarded; with the disruption of trade in the Mediterranean the building industry came to a halt, the citrus industry declined, and for the next two years unemployment was epidemic. In their relations with the British the Jews found themselves in an impossible position, for, as the White Paper of 1939 made clear, the British were now the enemies of Zionism. At the same time they were the enemies of the Jewish enemy, Nazi Germany. This paradox was expressed in the slogan developed by Ben Gurion to define the Yishuv's position during the war: "We shall fight with Great Britain in this war as if there was no White Paper, and we shall fight the White Paper as if there was no war." More than 26,000 Palestinian Jews eventually joined the army, navy or air force of Great Britain.

To Miss Szold this meant that Youth Aliyah graduates, even some of the older Youth Aliyah students, would be eager to bear arms. They would ask her advice, and she did not know how to answer them. Her own life had taken on a mechanized quality. She worked, but the output seemed pitifully small. The cables that crossed her desk were thrilling and sometimes terrifying. Within the country there were 3,354 children under her care. Another 700 would arrive during the next two years; the children were coming out of Germany, and it was a miracle, just as Eva said. All this was true, and still her life was stale, mechanized.

The entire period that had begun with her sisters' arrival at Passover had been haunted by a sense of mortality; now that Bertha was almost well they could see once again that Adele was seriously ill and had been all along. Adele wrote to her husband: "You are my home, Toby. I come to roost and rest with you." She sailed in late November entirely alone, and in Jerusalem Bertha and Henrietta could speak of nothing but Adele and her health. "The long interval between mails is torture," Henrietta wrote, but even when they came Adele's replies told her little.

In December, Bertha and Henrietta celebrated their joint birthday, Henrietta's seventy-ninth. Gifts and messages came from all over the world, and from the children of Youth Aliyah there were plants, flowers, seedlings and seeds, albums of photographs, hand-made jackets and scarves, woodwork, metalwork. In the office the staff held a special celebration that was traditional with them for Miss Szold's birthdays. All the desks were moved together to the center of the room and on the massed desk tops a great mound of presents was built. There were playlets and poems in a lighthearted mood, but for Miss Szold the birthday was deeply shadowed by Bertha's forthcoming departure and her fears about Adele.

Soon she would be alone. She should have been hardened, but she was not. She was very old now. Bertha, who was so much younger, had been close to death, and Adele was certainly in danger of death. Perhaps for the first time Miss Szold faced the possibility that both sisters might die and leave her alone in the world, absolutely alone and forgotten by death among all those people who knew nothing about her.

Bertha left Palestine in February of 1940, and because her letters took months to arrive, there was an interval when all Miss Szold could do was launch long letters of her own without hope of an answer. She had moved from the Eden Hotel to a boardinghouse, the Pension Romm, where she felt deserted; the sensation was like a bodily pain. She begged for reassuring news of Adele, but before there were any letters in reply, a cable came to Hans Beyth at the Youth Aliyah office informing him that Adele was dead.

He went from one staff member to the other asking who should break the news to Miss Szold, and how, and at what time. Should she be sitting down when she heard it? Should there be others in the room? What measures ought to be taken in advance in case she was overcome by shock and grief? He did not want to tell her himself, but neither could he feel certain anyone else would do it with the same sympathetic delicacy, for they were all in a state of panic. Miss Szold was seventy-nine, and they could not tell what such a wound might do to her.

In the end Hans Beyth brought the message. He told her as gently as he could; she took it with amazing calm. He came out and informed the others. They could hardly believe him. Finally someone said it must have been because she was so deeply religious. No other explanation seemed possible. Resigned to the will of God, she had stoically accepted her loss.

But Miss Szold accepted nothing. It was not calm, serenity, resignation, but her terrible fear of showing weakness, of revealing herself.

Inside, she was tormented and full of guilt. She blamed herself, always herself. Yet she came and went and worked and dealt with scores of people and problems from behind a smooth facade. The Youth Aliyah staff watched and marveled, and some suspected this was a woman with a very cold heart. "I am so alone. There is no one who really and truly knows me," she mourned. Loneliness pressed in on her, guilt weighed her down. She should have seen, she should have known. Did Adele speak of her at the end? Did Adele forgive her? What had Adele really thought of her in her private heart? Over and over the inner spirit seethed and the surface remained so calm, so controlled.

One of the Hebrew secretaries, a chalutz who had been a master mason, used to work in her room with her during the evenings. He deeply admired Miss Szold, and from the moment he had come to Youth Aliyah he had fallen into the habit of observing her. "You see the way she had of looking at me, the way of talking to me—I would say it was some light around her, in her eyes; not usual, not as others. . . . You see she was as an old woman very, very esthetic. She was looking at me if I was sitting opposite her to see what kind of tie, how I'm dressed. And she used to say: yes, I must go to the dressmaker. . . . I didn't understand how she did not marry twice or three or four times."

Now he saw something else: "She had something inside her soul, a kind of tragedy. Sometimes when we were sitting one opposite the other she became so sad. So sad, I could say the sadness of the whole world came on her shoulders, and her head sank. But in the moment she saw that I see it, so suddenly she changed. 'Yes?' she said. 'So what are we doing now? So what is about this child, and what about this institution, and where are we going tomorrow, and what did you arrange about this problem?' and so on. 'There is no depression here and not a sign of weakness,' she seemed to say."

He never connected the sadness of the whole world with loneliness. Months had passed since the death of her sister, the death she accepted with such religious calm, and he had no way of knowing that her letters to Bertha were still anguished, that the loneliness was untouched by all those people who admired and respected Miss Szold.

This inner realm of loneliness and loss was embedded in a world of larger discontents that did nothing to relieve it, for the Yishuv bristled with anger and bitterness and frequent violent demonstrations against the 1939 White Paper limiting immigration. All immigration had ceased with the declaration of war, and when it was resumed early in the year illegal immigration started up again in full force. The government promised to subtract the number of these illegals from the total legal allotment.

Nevertheless Miss Szold's relations with the government continued to be sympathetic. She got 1,600 certificates for the period April to September 1940. She was living now on cables from London, shutting her ears to the radio because it was full of Hitler's conquests and the crumbling of the Western democracies. During the miserable spring and summer of 1940, when each of Hitler's dazzling victories cut the Jewish heart like knives, she saw the countries of refuge, with their precious network of preparation camps, engulfed, Denmark and Norway in April, the Low Countries two months later. Individual children who fled from Belgium were caught that summer in the fall of France. The government agreed to issue certificates to children trapped in Holland, Belgium and Denmark only on condition that they did not travel through enemy-held territory. Yet how was this to be done? What route was possible for children in England? Long distance travel by air was in its infancy and hopelessly expensive, even if planes could be found to transport nonmilitary cargo to the Middle East.

Early that year a voice was heard from among the thousands of Polish Jews who had been expelled from Germany to no-man's land, a voice from Lithuania, where some fifty Youth Aliyah children waited in misery, cold, hungry and tormented by vermin. Their *madrich*, a young German named Daniel Gelbart, had been allowed to enter Poland with his charges, but when war broke out they had fled toward the Lithuanian frontier on foot, walking more than 200 miles night and day over roads splintered with wood and glass. Many were shoeless. The towns they passed were in flames, their feet festered. There was no food and no life anywhere, only death beating down from the skies. They learned later that the roads they had chosen coincided precisely with the German route of attack.

From the Lithuanian frontier they had made their way by rail to the old Jewish city of Vilna, where they resumed Youth Aliyah training and sent a cable to London, a cry for rescue. They longed for word of their parents, for bread, for blankets, for news of Palestine, for certificates. "Almost every comrade is bitten by the same depression," Gelbart wrote in a letter that followed the cable. "I am not able to get at the roots of this general weakness . . . it weighs on me like a stone." As it happened Youth Aliyah in London had been holding their certificates since the eve of war, after which all contact with the Jews of no-man's land had been lost. Hadassah sent money, London sent encouragement, but the children remained in Lithuania because there was no clear route to Palestine.

"We talk war all the time, we read war, we eat war, we work war," Miss Szold wrote to America, "especially those who are in Youth Aliyah, wondering all the time whether the route that was open yesterday remains open today." She felt old, played out, useless. She had fallen and wrenched a leg muscle, and for weeks she was confined to bed, made wretched by the knowledge that her fragile body could play her false at any moment and leave her a burden on others. When Passover came she was still in bed, and Hans Beyth, Sylva Gelber and a few others brought a seder to her room; they all sang Negro spirituals afterward.

American citizens were leaving Palestine, urged by their government to return home while it was still possible, and for a while she thought she had better join them. Rose Jacobs had come to organize Hadassah's emergency council, a group of American workers headed by Magnes and empowered to act for Hadassah now that quick communication was impossible. The first meeting of the council was held in Miss Szold's room at the pension, and some of her friends hoped she would go back to America when Mrs. Jacobs did. One day she realized she was not going to go. "I made my choice twenty years ago," she said.

Italy had entered the war in June, Tel Aviv and Haifa were under bombardment by Italian planes for a time, and there were a number of civilian deaths. Jerusalem took nightly blackout precautions. Social workers prepared the urban centers against invasion, and although Miss Szold had left the social service bureau, little of their work was done without consulting her. In the countryside the kibbutzim built bomb shelters and held air-raid drills. Among the youth groups, the strains of war showed in unexpected ways. Recent arrivals had been traumatized by Hitler, and many of the children were joyless, passive. There was little comradeship and much aggression. She cast about for ways to adjust the machinery of Youth Aliyah to the pressures of war, creating a system of sex education for *madrichim* and conferences of *madrichim* and psychologists that tackled the questions of youth and anti-Semitism, youth and military service.

But Youth Aliyah was a movement of rescue, and no one was being rescued. From April through September 1940 not a single child entered the country, only the cables, constructing escape routes, abandoning escape routes. For a while it was thought the children in England could travel around the Cape of Good Hope, through waters infested by mines and submarines, across India and Iran. But they would have to pass through Iraq, and Iraq refused transit visas. Leave the children in England, where they are safe for the moment, Miss Szold told London. Meanwhile negotiations were started with Russia and Turkey in the hope of opening a northern route. Russia immediately agreed, but for months the Turkish government stalled.

It was early November when Miss Szold heard the triumphant news that Turkish transit visas had been granted for 733 candidates, the only qualification being that they must pass through in groups of fifty. The first group set out from Denmark, headed for Sweden, Finland, Russia, the Black Sea, Turkey and Syria on its way to Palestine; others would leave Romania, Yugoslavia, Bulgaria and Lithuania, the latter with Daniel Gelbart. But many weeks before the first fifty arrived, a large contingent of Youth Aliyah children entered Palestine. Fleeing from death and destruction, their entry was marked by death and destruction.

For ten days a ship had been anchored in Haifa Harbor, holding 2,000 refugee adults and children, most of them illegals. All were refused permission to land. They had come on three separate ships and had been removed from the ships and placed aboard the S.S. *Patria,* which would take them to Mauritius to wait out the war. England no longer returned illegals to Europe and Hitler. Neither would they allow them into Palestine, nor would they say what their fate would be when the war was over.

The entire Jewish population of Haifa came down to the harbor to watch preparations for the *Patria's* departure. Some stood for hours at a time with binoculars, scanning the faces of passengers in the hope of finding among them one particular face. Youth Aliyah children read the passenger list; some found the names of their parents, and wrote to Miss Szold, imploring her to get them off the ship. Delegation after delegation pleaded in vain for release of the 2,000. But there were seventy-seven certificated children on board the *Patria*. Whatever else could or could not be done for the rest of them, Miss Szold believed she had a right to those seventy-seven.

She was granted an interview with the chief secretary of the immigration department, in the course of which she was most cordially refused. She came out of the interview in her usual state of composure, but back in the Youth Aliyah office she banged her fist on the table and screamed at everyone in sight.

Six days went by, during which preparations for the removal of the *Patria* to Mauritius continued, and the Jews of Haifa watched. On the seventh day the *Patria* exploded. Then, very slowly, it turned on its side. The passengers were either spilled out or jumped out.

Now the watchers on shore saw bodies and portions of arms and legs floating in the water. Planes circled overhead; little tugboats plied the littered waters retrieving corpses with fishhooks. Some people swam ashore. Some were found trapped inside the ship. In all, 240 died in the *Patria* disaster.

Nothing was proven, nothing was definitely known, but it was felt that the explosion had been a bungled act of sabotage, as indeed it proved to be, an attempt on the part of Haganah to disable the ship's engines and pressure the government into letting the refugees ashore. When Miss Szold learned there were five of her children among the dead her sorrow was tinged by the deepest anger against the British who had kept them aboard, against the saboteurs whose miscalculation had cost so many lives. But the government bowed to events and allowed the survivors ashore. They were sent to the detention camp at Athlit and would be released in good time.

A month later Miss Szold was eighty years old. The Yishuv celebrated for a week, and the birthday itself was declared a national holiday for all Youth Aliyah children. Delegates came from every youth group to Ben Shemen to honor her. There were extremely dry and dignified addresses by Agency colleagues and a lyrical speech by a girl of sixteen with the face of a medieval saint. There were young people from the graduated youth groups, of whom many were now married and parents. There was a long walk through the garden, radiant with flowers after the November rains, and much music and gift giving.

In the evening everyone gathered in the dining hall, festooned with greenery; hundreds of young people sat on chairs facing a platform, and at the front, on a row of low stools, sat the littlest children and Miss Szold, also on a low stool. It was Hanukkah, the festival of lights that is also a festival of liberation, and the speeches recalled the refugees on the open seas or in prison camps who must celebrate the holiday in darkness. Then Miss Szold was sum-

moned to the platform to light the first Hanukkah candle. Even standing on
tiptoe she could not reach it. A tall young man sprang to her side and guided
her hand until between them the candle was lit. Then the choir began the
traditional Hanukkah songs.

29

During those first years of war Palestine was like a vacuum chamber sealed
off from the world. Terrible things took place elsewhere, but within the country
there was a deadness. Both legal and illegal immigration were slight. No tourists
came. Even the Arabs were quiet, and the Yishuv turned in on itself, grasping
every local event and squeezing from it the last drops of interest and excitement.
The first group of fifty children from the transit camps was such an event.

The thousands who preceded them had come from Germany or Austria,
and in their eyes were reflections of hatred. Some were little Fascists. Some
hated themselves and could hardly believe the country they had come to really
wanted them. Now Miss Szold met fifty young people who had spent a year
in Denmark among Christian farmers.

They arrived in two separate groups headed for two different kibbutzim.
And the first words of each group when they were welcomed by their hosts
were, "How many cows have you?"

They were sturdy, well-dressed, well-fed and bursting with vigor. Miss
Szold questioned them closely. What were the farmers like with whom they
had lived? Cultivated people, she was told; each house had a library including
scientific and historical books. Where did they go to school? In the high schools,
with the Danish children. How did they get along with their host families? It
was marvelous, they said. They had such beautiful manners, such nice eating
habits. They talked with the children all the time about Zionism and its objec-
tives.

About Zionism? What did they know about Zionism? she asked. Nothing,
and the children had explained it all. The farmers argued with them. Why
must they go to Palestine, they were asked. Weren't they receiving good care
in Denmark? Hadn't they been shown every kindness and consideration?

Her heart expanded as she listened; they were sitting in the dining hall
of Mishmar HaEmek, the kibbutz where Irma Lindheim had come to settle,
and she saw how eager the children were to begin their new lives, how vital

and full of hope. But within months their stay in Denmark would pass into the limbo of forgotten things, and that was not right. She told the *madrich* they must be encouraged to write about their reminiscences, for they were an important bit of history. There *was* goodness and decency in this world that had no room in it for Jews. People must remember that.

She did not say this to the children, however. What she told them was that the Danish farmers had taken them in out of humanitarian motives; and where had they learned humanitarianism? From the Old Testament, which enjoins kindness to the stranger. It was as if she feared, even now when they were safe in Mishmar, that their Zionism might melt away. Perhaps she was also a little jealous of the Danes.

But of all the arrivals that excited the Yishuv during the airless, lifeless year of 1941, none was so electrifying as that of Recha Freier.

She left Germany because her usefulness was at an end. Having incurred the enmity of Eichmann and of certain Jewish leaders, there was nothing more she could accomplish there. With her eleven-year-old daughter she put herself in the hands of professional smugglers and was led across the Yugoslavian border into Zagreb; then she sent the smugglers to Vienna, where a group of children waited. These children were brought in over the course of several months while winter came, the mountain passes froze and the route outside grew increasingly uncertain, for the German conquest of Yugoslavia was expected at any moment.

The children were distributed among private families by night, and in the daytime met at an improvised Youth Aliyah school set up by Mrs. Freier. Illegal immigrants hidden throughout the surrounding area gathered at the school, "for they felt less forsaken in the neighborhood of the children." From the British consulate she got visas for Palestine; from the Jewish Agency office in Istanbul she was able to get ninety certificates, and on the day the Germans entered Yugoslavia Recha Freier, her daughter and ninety of the children left for Belgrade, Greece and Palestine. One of the boys they took with them had contracted polio in Zagreb and was hospitalized for a time. Mrs. Freier refused to leave him behind even though the safety of the entire group might be compromised if he could not keep up. They would carry him—on their backs if need be.

It was a daring and heroic operation, Recha Freier's journey from inside the Reich to Yugoslavia to Jerusalem, and perhaps no part of it was more daring than the waiting for months until all the children were gathered in. Now the Yishuv took stock of the woman who had done these things, and what they saw was someone far from heroic in appearance. Recha Freier was very small, as small as Miss Szold; she was cultivated, musical, poetic; she had a low, breathy voice and a tendency to shift abruptly from one mood to another. Living with her son Shalhevet, who had left his father with the younger boys in England, she took stock of the Yishuv.

She would of course continue her work for Youth Aliyah, which meant dealing with Henrietta Szold, who was said to be highly incensed over Freier's recklessness in endangering ninety souls for a single child.

Soon after her arrival Recha Freier attended a meeting of Youth Aliyah leaders; Miss Szold was sick and unable to come, but everyone else of importance was there. As they seated themselves at the long conference table Mrs. Freier chose a chair that was conspicuously placed, the chair in which Miss Szold always sat. Then she took over the meeting like a high wind, all force and direction, sweeping the others along with her without a pause for minutes, rules or orderly procedure. She was sitting in Miss Szold's chair, but no one could have been more unlike Miss Szold.

That evening Ernst Simon, a professor of education at the Hebrew University and attached to Youth Aliyah, had a phone call from one of his graduate students, who had also been present. The student had decided the subject of his dissertation: Classicism versus Romanticism in Youth Aliyah, or Henrietta Szold versus Recha Freier.

The day came when Mrs. Freier got in touch with Miss Szold and a meeting was arranged, during which Mrs. Freier meant to claim her rightful place in the organization she had brought to life. Apparently she hoped for a position of substantial importance in the Jerusalem office, yet the structure of the bureau was such that there was only one important place. Perhaps Mrs. Freier was unaware of that. Perhaps, as her son Shalhevet believed, she still felt it was rightly hers.

The meeting was brief. Miss Szold made an offer of a sort of interim position in which Mrs. Freier would get to know the work in Palestine. She would be supported by the bureau meanwhile, and after that—well, after that they would see. Without another word Mrs. Freier stood up and left.

Miss Szold was hurt. "We believe that you have no basis to take such a position towards us and to refuse our proposition," she wrote, but she would have been hurt no matter what Recha Freier had said or done. Her very existence in Jerusalem was a source of pain, a reminder that the title Mother of Youth Aliyah had another claimant.

Everyone took sides. Almost everyone agreed Recha Freier could not be made the chief executive of Youth Aliyah, for there wasn't an organizational bone in her body. And it was an intricate organization. To the Yishuv at large Miss Szold was the kind old woman who traveled all the way to Haifa in every sort of weather to meet the incoming children and it was touching that she did so, but hardly necessary. However she did far more. She negotiated deftly and honestly with the government, with all political parties, with the Agency and the kibbutzim. She considered the fate of each child her personal responsibility, encouraged them to write to her and answered every letter herself, at length, out of the fullness of the heart. She was often able to squeeze extravagant sums out of Hadassah for a particular child in need of costly medical care, which was possible only because Hadassah trusted her judgment and her compulsive honesty.

But she could never have generated the romantic vision that was Youth Aliyah, just as Mrs. Freier could not have run the complex structure it became. The Yishuv knew and acknowledged that. All the same Mrs. Freier inspired compassion. Not pity—she was too strong to be pitied—but there was something painfully moving in her situation. "There are two sides to Youth Aliyah," she wrote, "the one of light, the other of darkness. . . . I was fated to live and work on the other side, in darkness, affliction and suffering."

For a brief moment Mrs. Freier saw that her opponent was not an overlord but a human woman whose life had its own dark places. A celebration was held at the kibbutz Kiryat Anavim, in the Judean hills some five or six miles from Jerusalem, an oasis of green in an austere landscape. Miss Szold, Mrs. Freier and others were invited. They sat around a table in the dining hall, and at the center of the table was a cake with a frosted inscription, "To Our Mother."

The woman sitting beside Miss Szold cut up the cake and put on Miss Szold's plate the piece that held the word "Mother." Miss Szold devoured it. "Yes, she took that piece and devoured it," one guest recalled. "You know she was a very delicate lady, she did not usually devour things. There was everything in that scene—there was most of all her shame, as it were, that she was not a mother. Mrs. Freier had four children of her own . . . and Miss Szold who was not a mother at all, she ate up that cake." Recha Freier watched and understood and felt a shortlived compassion.

A short story was published in Palestine entitled "The Judgment of Solomon," in which two mothers—one the biological mother, the other the adoptive mother—fought for the love of one child. The natural mother was anguished, for she had given up her child only in order to save his life, while the adoptive mother was cool, kind, rich and secure and would never surrender the boy she had saved and come to love. Everyone in the Yishuv recognized the natural mother as Mrs. Freier, the other as Miss Szold. The child was Youth Aliyah.

In the 1950s Recha Freier published an account of her work in Germany for the Jugendhilfe "because she wanted to place on record the way she saw things, and she was asked not to do this as long as Miss Szold was alive, in order not to drive nails into Miss Szold's coffin," Shalhevet recalls. And she wrote and continues to write letters to Hadassah explaining her role in the development of Youth Aliyah, letters full of pride and suffering that move the women greatly. But whatever concrete offers they make, such as naming a building in her honor, she refuses. The wound is too deep for remedy.

From the time Mrs. Freier came to the Yishuv, Miss Szold had partisans who felt that Recha Freier was untruthful, undependable, jealous and a trouble maker. The antagonism is alive to this day.

In the spring of 1941 Youth Aliyah moved in a new direction, inward to encompass the children of the Palestinian slums. The earlier Nazi policy of allowing Jews to escape if they could had come to an end. Now Germany and German-held territories were closed to emigration. Two million Jewish children were sealed within Europe.

With the help of an office of the Jewish Agency in Istanbul, a trickle of refugees still made their way across Turkey to Palestine; others were snatched from the Balkan states by the extraordinary ingenuity of an Agency diplomat with headquarters in Geneva who shifted children from one endangered haven to another until the fortunate could be placed on trains or ships for the Holy Land. But the stream of Youth Aliyah was running dry, and there were empty beds and schoolrooms on the kibbutzim. Although Hadassah was still extremely dubious of Miss Szold's plans for the children of the Palestinian towns, in early 1941 they sent her a sum of money for that purpose. Miss Szold did what she always did: before action there must be thought, research, planning. Her young colleagues of Youth Aliyah were amazed and disappointed, for they had expected to see busloads of Oriental children moving from the Old City into the empty places on the kibbutzim. Instead they saw long lists of reference material compiled for psychologists, conferences, discussions, planning, investigation. Miss Szold had already settled thousands of children from foreign countries. What was the need for research on those who were already within Palestine?

Nevertheless she drew up plans for small beginnings that would also work for thousands. Sixty children were to be selected out of a larger group sent to preparation camps. There must be equal numbers of boys and girls, no easy matter to sell to the parents in the Old City, who traditionally kept girls at home. There must be a special curriculum, and there must be partnership with youth groups of German origin, for it was her greatest hope that the two halves of the Yishuv, Oriental and Western, might be knitted together. Therefore the sixty who were chosen would be divided into three groups and sent to three settlements of Youth Aliyah graduates. The "children," in effect, would educate the "grandchildren."

Chanoch Rinott, the *madrich* who had come with the Ein Harod group in 1934, was with Miss Szold when the first Oriental youngsters entered their kibbutz. He looked them over and saw surly little street Arabs, Yemenite, Kurd, Georgian, Moroccan. They alarmed him, for they were unfamiliar types in whom he searched for some semblance of the familiar. He said to Miss Szold, "Would you tell me—what do you make of these children—how do you understand them?

She looked back; it was a particular look she had, almost aggressive. "What do I make of them—how do I approach them? They are children!"

It took him a long time to understand what she meant, and in the end he decided she was telling him not to make categories, not to label any child Moroccan, Georgian, Yemenite, introverted, clever, rebellious. "She found out—and she lived it—what children have in common. Not what makes them different. She expressed the basic human presence of the child."

The Town to Village experiment, as it was called, grew from the first sixty to encompass hundreds and eventually thousands of children. Today it is the main work of Youth Aliyah. Here is Chanoch Rinott on the present role of the movement:

> If you look into the recent publications in this country about what is the right approach to these Oriental kids, you will find Youth Aliyah was the first to live it, to face it—to try to tackle it. You'll find here many hundreds, possibly more than hundreds, of teachers, educators, who will tell you, "my main school was Youth Aliyah." There's no question about it. I was later in the Ministry of Education as Director-General. I met there many madrichim as well as Youth Aliyah graduates who moved into teaching, and their underlying principles were made first in Youth Aliyah. And in a most intensive way, because if you *lived* with these kids, you knew them very much more intimately than a teacher who comes from another community, sometimes travels to the school, to the immigrant community. Youth Aliyah by its very nature had an insight into the sociological world of the immigrant.

Even when the first Oriental children went to their first kibbutzim they did little to fill the hundreds of empty places. Miss Szold wondered if the movement could also include the children of Syrian and Yemenite refugees who streamed into British Aden. She turned to the children of the illegals who had come ashore by night with their parents while the lights of British patrols played on them, and some 750 were eventually drawn in. She went to immigration officials and implored them to release sixty children interned with adults from the S.S. *Dorian* after six months at sea. The barbed-wire slum that was the Athlit detention camp was no place for children, but the government could not be moved.

In the matter of forged documents—older children holding the certificates of younger ones or the entrance of Youth Aliyah children who had come through enemy-occupied lands against British regulations—she remained adamant. What Hans Beyth or her other colleagues did was their affair. When emissaries from the Agency begged her to use her personal influence with the government to make this or that irregular exception she always refused. Just as she refused to use influence to save her Austrian relations. For this she was much criticized, as she was for her attitude toward military service.

There was tremendous pressure for young people to join the British forces, and Miss Szold suspected part of the pressure came from a desire to train Jewish soldiers for future battles against the British, the Arabs or both. This she could not approve. Her entire mind-set went against the spirit of the times. "War has now come near to us in Palestine," she wrote. "There are Jews who believe that if this fortress is captured today by our enemy, the whole Jewish people would be so injured by the loss that it could not recover. My personal faith is otherwise."

Early in 1941 the Vaad Leumi accepted a plan Miss Szold had been working on for the past five years for a semigovernmental children's bureau. It was to be funded initially by money that would be her gift to the Yishuv, some $70,000 given her over the course of years by Hadassah. The purpose of the bureau would be to insure that all Jewish children in Palestine, rich and poor, Oriental and Western, would have the same claims on the Yishuv.

With the best will in the world the Yishuv was to prove itself unready for the children's bureau. Today it is a social service agency that does good works, but it is not what Miss Szold had envisioned.

Her father's papers, bound and placed in a specially constructed steel case, were presented to the Hebrew University during that same period. Now she faced what were surely her last years on earth with folded hands. She had a shroud made and kept it in her bedroom closet. She called Emma to her room one day and told her she wanted to be buried in that shroud on the Mount of Olives. She had grown old in harness; she would die in harness. If there was any difference now it was that she worried less about "catching up," and she was somewhat more impervious to the opinions of others. The temper she had always hoped to conquer still gave her no peace. "I have always thought that with growing old I would become more rational, less bound to lose my temper," she told Ernst Simon, "and *nothing* happens. All ages are difficult. Do you think eighty-one is an easy age?"

For some weeks that winter Miss Szold was very ill. Half the Yishuv was down with flu during an almost historic snowfall, and she lay in bed writing long letters to Bertha, who was going through the family treasures and getting rid of things. Was the little red Hungarian pitcher among them? she asked, and the black embroidered dress front she and Rachel together had made for Mama? Was there a scrapbook in which all her Shulamith articles had been pasted? She had been reading *Gone With the Wind,* and finding it "homey— the language and atmosphere. Partly it transports me into the days of my contract with the Misses Adams." That was a lost world, all its innocence and purity beyond recall. America had joined the war, and "it's a pity that the last refuge of one's soul is gone."

She recovered in time to learn that the government would allow the entry of fifty illegal children from the S.S. *Struma,* a vile and ancient cattle ship carrying some 800 passengers from the Balkans, that had lain at anchor off Istanbul for the past two months. The Turks would not allow them ashore without visas for Palestine. The government had refused visas but finally agreed to accept fifty children. Before their transfer could be completed Turkish authorities ordered the boat away from their shores, and it was towed into the Black Sea, where it exploded and sank. The cause of the explosion remains unknown. There was one survivor.

A terrible outcry went up throughout the Yishuv. The explosion of the *Struma* was seen as an attempt at mass suicide, the result of desperation because the British refused visas, and all the resentment aroused first by the White Paper, then by the tragic sinking of the *Patria,* boiled over into implacable hatred. Hadassah cabled Miss Szold: APPALLED STRUMA DISASTER CABLE IMMEDIATELY IF CHILDREN PREVIOUSLY REMOVED. She kept this cable in her portfolio for three weeks before she could bring herself to reply.

In June of 1942, when Tobruk, in North Africa, was captured by Germans and more than 20,000 British soldiers taken prisoner, the question uppermost in the minds of the Yishuv was whether the British had enough reserves to hold off a German invasion of Egypt and Palestine. There were many who even doubted British willingness to defend Palestine. It was a common practice during this period for Jews to carry cyanide pellets; Weizmann and his wife were never without them. Friends implored Miss Szold to leave the country, but she shrugged it off. The Nazis in North Africa were unreal to her, as perhaps all the Nazis had always been.

On the other hand she saw the signs of a new terrorism within the Yishuv; ugly and motiveless, it was a violence of the absurd, protesting the White Paper but aimed at fellow Jews, Jewish institutions, Jewish banks. The Agency hesitated to condemn it in public, afraid of revealing division within Zionist ranks. To Miss Szold, who abhorred all forms of violence, this hesitation was the worst cowardice. The Jews would survive Hitler—she had no doubt whatever on that score—but how they would survive, what would be the state of their souls, the strength of the ethical ties that bound them to one another, to their prophetic past and the world at large, were more troubling questions.

For some time now she had been part of an informal group that had grown out of the disbanded Brit Shalom. Magnes's belief that Arab nationalism was healthy and desirable, and that some Arab leaders would surely be open to friendly gestures from sympathetic Zionist leaders, remained very much alive. Former members of Brit Shalom continued to meet as friends with common interests. The core of this group were Magnes, Ernst Simon, Miss Szold and Martin Buber.

Buber was a pacifist, a mystic, a believer in the mission of the Jewish people to unite Oriental boundlessness with the European intellectual tradition. East European Zionists found him fuzzy and irrelevant, but to Jewish students from central Europe his romantic and antiintellectual idealism was magnetic. He had come to Palestine in 1938 and taught at the Hebrew University, a dark-eyed, copiously bearded figure in his early sixties, usually withdrawn from political life.

This group of friends sat for hours in Simon's high-ceilinged study, where every wall was lined with books, the tables littered with journals, newspapers and manuscripts in half a dozen languages. There was not much else in the room but a desk, the tables, some uncomfortable chairs and a threadbare carpet. But the air was rich with the talk of virtuoso talkers. Everyone talked except Miss Szold, who preferred to listen; she felt humble in this company, conscious of the distance between their academic degrees and attainments and her own stunted education. But she did not feel defensive, because these were men who knew and accepted her; and her high-minded, almost disembodied concern for the ethical development of the Jews was perfectly understood here.

Both Buber and Magnes had a tendency to orate; Buber in particular had a penchant for the intricate and darkly mysterious phrase. To Ernst Simon it was the style of a prophet and therefore somewhat unsuitable. There were no more prophets, as he sometimes pointed out, and they had no followers. They were officers without an army.

Until the spring of 1942 the descendants of Brit Shalom exchanged prophetic philosophy and conversation, sharing a strong revulsion at the violence they saw emerging on every side, the violence of Jews against the English as well as rarer but more disturbing eruptions within the Yishuv. But that spring they began a series of regular meetings in Magnes's house. The subject of their discussions was a visit by Ben-Gurion, chairman of the Agency Executive, to America. Ben-Gurion's purpose was to create American support for the transformation of Palestine into a Jewish state or commonwealth.

Magnes believed such a program would lead inevitably to war with the Arabs. He also believed the Zionist establishment had by no means exhausted all paths to Arab-Jewish rapprochement and pointed to the undeniable fact that Arabs and Jews were closer now than at any time under the Mandate. The war had drawn them together. Although nothing had changed politically, on a personal and practical level much had changed.

Therefore the little circle of friends made a decision that seemed unremarkable at the time. They called a meeting in Jerusalem of some 100 believers in binationalism and Arab-Jewish rapprochement, the purpose of the meeting being to plan an organization they would call Ihud, "union." Magnes was elected president, and Miss Szold and Buber were among the five members of the presidential board. Ihud was conceived simply as a discussion group, a debating society. They would explore ideas, they would join with other binationalist groups, including Hashomer Hatzair. They would criticize the policies of the Zionist leadership and publish a Zionist periodical.

This was August 1942, a time when rumors of Nazi slaughterhouses in Poland and Russia were beginning to reach the Yishuv, where they were dismissed as hysteria, the imaginings of shattered minds. American Jews had been electrified by Ben-Gurion's plan for a Jewish state not in some distant era but as soon as the war ended. Millions of European Jews, uprooted from their native lands, would come to beat on the doors of Palestine, and only if the Yishuv held the reins of government would they be allowed to enter. The British White Paper, as it now stood, would turn all but a handful away. Hadassah embraced Ben-Gurion's policy with a whole heart, as did the ZOA, but even non-Zionist Jews were persuaded. They were ashamed of their government's refusal to house the exiled Jews of Europe. By supporting a state both financially and with whatever influence they could bring to bear on U.S. policies, they would atone for the sins of those who governed them.

No word of Ben-Gurion's success in New York reached the Yishuv for months, and at the time of the Ihud meeting neither Miss Szold nor Magnes had the faintest idea that Hadassah was wholly committed to statehood. More than committed, they were "hysterical" on the subject, as one leader recalled. But descriptions of Ihud flew to New York, where they were described as a group of rebels extending a hand to the Arabs, making promises and creating policies, all of which were shaped by the vision of an Arab-Jewish entity, a Semitic federation, no Jewish majority, no Arab majority, but binationalism. No stand on immigration had yet been decided by Ihud, for they had not yet held a second meeting, but whatever position they took, the Americans assumed it would be minimalist, obstructionist, hateful.

The Jewish press and the *New York Times* were full of Ihud. There arose a humming, as of many voices, denouncing Magnes, demanding his removal from the presidency of the Hebrew University. And wasn't he also connected with Hadassah through their emergency council? Shouldn't he be removed from that as well? As for Miss Szold, the founder and heroine of Hadassah, what did the women mean to do about her? Surely they would denounce her along with Magnes, the ZOA and the Jewish press observed; surely they would make a public statement so that the world and the U.S. State Department might see that Miss Szold did not speak for the Jews and Zionists of America.

Hadassah sent her a cable requesting "fullest exposition aims and plans." Miss Szold replied in a long air-mail letter that the aim of Ihud was solely to shape public opinion; it had no intention of speaking or acting as the representative of the Jewish people, and she was amazed that judgment of Ihud had been passed before the organization was even properly born.

This letter reached New York on the eve of the ZOA-Hadassah annual convention at the Pennsylvania Hotel. A friend of Magnes's, an American physician from Palestine, hurried to the convention and sent back reports that captured some of the heat of those autumn days when the leaders of American Zionism met for the first time to vote on the proposal of a Jewish state: "I landed here in the middle of the storm concerning Ihud. The fires of wrath were stoked diligently by Ben-Gurion, and the sheep followed the shepherd." The word "traitors" was abundantly used.

There were lengthy and anguished discussions and much pain. On November 5, Dr. Magnes's medical friend wrote to him, "For a while it looked as though Hadassah would split wide open, but an open breach was prevented and now they are licking their wounds." A compromise had been reached.

Ihud was neither damned nor condoned. Hadassah and the ZOA came out jointly in support of Ben-Gurion's program and indicated that all other plans were unacceptable to them. No names were named; no violent denunciations followed. Even to reach that moderate position had required all the stubbornness of which Hadassah's president, Tamar Pool, was capable.

But the implications were there, and Miss Szold was deeply hurt by those implications to the point where she almost resigned from Hadassah. To this day there are Hadassah leaders who turn pale when they remember the 1942 convention.

In Palestine the reaction to Ihud was immediate and virulent: Magnes, Szold, Simon and Buber were publicly reviled. A newspaper headline proclaimed, HER OLD AGE SHAMES HER YOUTH! referring to Miss Szold and the young people of Youth Aliyah. "Authoritative personages" demanded that Szold and Magnes be expelled from the Zionist organization as the destroyers of Zionism. When Ben-Gurion returned to Palestine he referred "in strong, not to say abusive language to Ihud in every one of his numerous public addresses," Miss Szold noted.

Magnes got the most and the worst of it, so much so that Haganah provided him with a bodyguard against his will. He had never been loved by the Yishuv, for he was too distant, too elegant, too righteous. Miss Szold, on the other hand, was a national monument, the old woman who met the ships. Many people decided she had been led astray by Magnes. Others saw in her the same qualities Magnes had. To some of the Agency men she was a minimalist. To many she was still an alien; her personality was rigid and sanctimonious; she talked too much and too long. A politically open-minded writer described one reaction to that personality: "She was a preacher, you know. She took the floor; I've seen people coming out—I remember the scene, coming out— a sharp intake of breath, then, 'Oh my goodness, for hours she talked. . . .' She would say words of great wisdom; she was self-righteous."

In the face of these attacks Miss Szold never altered her resolve to stand by Magnes and Ihud; and in none of her letters to Bertha or her exchanges with Hadassah was there any hint of self-conscious doubt or distrust of her intuition. In 1937 she had kept silent because she had feared the establishment was wiser; in 1942 she ignored them, not because they were less wise, but because she was very old. She had completed her life's work and she could finally afford the luxury of telling what to her was the truth.

The visions of Ihud were impractical. There was not a single Arab leader of substance prepared to take the same steps forward, and several who dared to make gestures of conciliation in the years immediately after the war were assassinated by fellow Arabs. But the lack of response was unimportant to Miss Szold. She was not responsible for the actions of the Arabs, only for her own.

Throughout the early autumn months of 1942 the stories brought by Polish refugees hovered over the Yishuv like a distant cloud that one could see if one looked for it but that one could also fail to see. This cloud, as of the smoke rising from many ovens, grew denser and more difficult to ignore with each week, yet it remained unseen except out of the corner of the eye. Meanwhile there was a fresh influx of visitors from Poland, not to the Yishuv, but to a Polish Red Cross camp just outside of Teheran, in Iran.

Remnants of the Polish army, followed by thousands of refugee adults and children, straggled into the camp on the southern shores of the Caspian Sea, 14,000 in all. Many were Jews. Their journey had begun shortly after the fall of Warsaw, when vast numbers of Poles were deported to Siberia to work in the forests and labor camps. When work grew scarce they wandered south, walking by day and night from village to village, scrabbling for food, eating grass, dogs, the pits of discarded fruits. Thousands died of hunger or malnutrition. Now the survivors of three years' wandering were limping into Teheran. A Jewish Agency official visited the encampment and reported to Miss Szold: there were thousands of Jews and hundreds of children, including infants, many separated from parents who had abandoned them or had simply dropped to the frozen ground one day and implored them to go on alone. The older children carried the little ones, clung to them, refused even in the Red Cross camp to be separated from them. All were wild looking, filthy and covered with sores.

Subsequent cables told her there were 600 children, certainly the vanguard of thousands more. Miss Szold's first act was an urgent appeal to the chief immigration officer for 800 certificates. "Quick action is required," she said, "principally for the reason that unless these children are removed they will be scattered to a number of countries bordering on Persia under the aegis of non-Jewish organizations." Lost to the Yishuv, lost to Jewry.

While she waited for word about the certificates and word from Hadassah about money and further word from the teachers, nurses and social workers sent to the encampment, Miss Szold sifted through her own feelings and admitted she was frightened. These children were all ages, while Youth Aliyah was equipped chiefly for children fifteen through seventeen. Because they were all ages, many would have to be supported, not for two years, but for ten or more. And they were bruised, not only physically but psychologically. For the most part, Youth Aliyah children had been carefully screened, and even then there were some thirty cases of schizophrenia among those selected before the war, for which the movement bore the cost. It was not part of their contract but part of Miss Szold's contract with herself: she became their mother, and she could no more abandon a psychotic child than could his own mother.

All the same she decided Youth Aliyah must accept every one, always provided they got certificates. The sick, the defective, the infants—at whatever cost the movement must enlarge and evolve to make room for all. This too was frightening, for Miss Szold had already realized that Youth Aliyah was centralized only too well. She had told Hadassah a few years earlier that she was not the dictator of Youth Aliyah, but now she was "constrained to admit that. . . . I was vested with almost autocratic powers." She herself sought those powers, although she does not seem to have recognized it.

But there it was. In the face of this new and daunting task it was necessary for all to consider that she might break under the strain, and if she did there would be disruption, if not annihilation, of the movement. She believed Hans Beyth should be made her successor, but so far nothing had been done about it.

Toward the end of September the government announced a grant of 800 certificates. Money and diplomacy must be relied on to do the rest, to move the children into Palestine. They could be brought south to Baghdad, then across Iraq, but Iraq refused to let them through even in sealed trains, nor would they be permitted to fly over Iraqi air space, for it was against their principles as a Moslem country to encourage Jewish immigration to Palestine. The refugees could go north to Turkey, then cross from Damascus, but Turkey also refused. A Hadassah leader in Washington with State Department connections called on the Turkish ambassador without result. She called on companies with major oil interests in Iraq, again without result.

The children remained in Teheran, where they were safe, clothed and fed, where their running had come to an end and homes were promised them. But they had survived so far only by putting the past out of their minds, and on Yom Kippur, the Day of Atonement, the past invaded the children's camp in the form of sudden hysterical weeping. It must have started with only a few, but it spread among hundreds "We cried for our lost childhood," one girl remembered, "and for our mothers and fathers. And when we thought we had cried ourselves out, another awful truth hit us all at once—we children had deserted our fathers and mothers to save our own lives. And then we discovered we still had more tears to shed."

Miss Szold used this period of waiting to plan. The children must come at first to the detention camp at Athlit, the barren, ugly government quarantine station she despised. Although she wanted them out of Athlit as soon as possible, they could not be sent to permanent homes directly from quarantine. They were fragile; they needed rest and feeding, and in any case the choosing of a permanent home for a particular child was not to be done quickly, especially with the younger ones. Therefore she decided they must go to temporary centers all over the country for a period of five or six weeks, and doctors, psychiatrists, teachers and social workers must go with them, not only to attend to their present needs but to unearth the past. The choice of permanent homes, kibbutzim or other institutions, depended upon that past and most of all on the religious affiliations of the parents. Children over the age of fourteen would be allowed to speak for themselves, but the younger ones must go to settlements or institutions their parents would have chosen for them.

Since most Polish Jews were Orthodox, those temporary camps would be conducted according to Orthodox practice, and the youth leaders would be able to observe the children during daily prayer and keep notes of their observations. From those notes, pieced together with whatever the children remembered, the religious practices of their vanished homes would be conjured up and the new homes selected accordingly. It seemed simple enough, a departure from Youth Aliyah practice and an expensive and time-consuming procedure, but essentially simple. Nothing about the Teheran children proved to be simple, however. Nothing turned out according to expectation, least of all the religious question.

30

The cloud that the Yishuv had refused to notice had grown fat and black and billowed out to cover the skies. A cable from Weizmann and Stephen Wise in America confirmed the rumors of Nazi slaughterhouses and mass exterminations. Two million were already dead. The Jewish Agency responded with a cable to the ZOA, begging them to ask the Red Cross to intervene, President Roosevelt to intervene: "Broadcast condemnations by leading American publicists might influence Nazis." Appeals were sent to the Pope. While neither the Pope nor Roosevelt wished to see the Jewry of eastern Europe gassed or burned to death, neither were they prepared to take active measures to prevent it, or for that matter even comparatively passive measures. Like Churchill, Roosevelt took refuge in the statement that the quickest way to save the Jews was to win the war.

Therefore the Yishuv turned to the only ally left to them. On the first of December 1942 they began three days of ritual mourning. In Haifa the Zionist flag was flown at half mast, and black flags flew over all private and public buildings; in Tel Aviv rabbis carrying the Scrolls of the Law headed processions that formed at five different places and marched through the principal streets with thousands behind them. In Jerusalem distinguished rabbis stood shoulder to shoulder at the Wailing Wall with porters and workmen, reciting psalms from dawn to dusk. And in a Talmudic school in the Bokharan quarter a group of kabbalist students selected a special rabbinical court of three to pronounce the Anathema: the Scroll of the Law was opened, the ram's horn sounded; then the senior rabbi called down imprecations on Hitler and enumerated the crimes by which the Nazis had placed themselves irrevocably beyond the pale of mankind. The entire Nazi party was put under the curse pronounced by Moses against Amalek, by Joshua against Achan, by Elisha against his tormentors.

Now all the Jews of Palestine seemed to reach out to the Teheran children as the living remnant of sisters and brothers they had abandoned twenty, thirty years ago, when they themselves had walked out of the townlets of eastern Europe. Turning their faces toward a new life in a new land, they had replied to the heartbroken letters of their parents that there was a great work to be done in Palestine, that they were building not for themselves but for the Jews of the world. The memory of those they had left behind rose before them during the days of ritual mourning. They pictured the hideous deaths of aged parents, the families of eight, ten or twelve of whom they were the only certain survivors. The children would be their atonement. Everyone clamored for the children, labor groups, kibbutzim, individuals put in their request for such and such a number. Many of the children had relatives in Palestine, who now put themselves forward. There were others, such as parents separated from a child in Poland in the course of flight to Palestine, whose last remaining hope was that the child might be among this precious hoard, and they too put themselves in touch with Miss Szold. Still others, who had no hope at all, begged her only to let them know once and for all that their child was not among the Teheran children; let us know that he is dead, they implored her, and we can sit *shiva* and accept that he is gone.

These very human claims would be settled somehow, but Miss Szold was still unable to see her way out of the religious dilemma: "It promises to turn into a Kulturkampf. Can I enter the lists? I am not prepared to fight. My misfortune is my ability to see both sides even of the fundamental religious question." It was Miss Szold's opinion that every parentless child from Poland under the age of fourteen deserved an Orthodox upbringing unless there were clear indications otherwise; but there were two shades of Orthodoxy, one ultra, one not. There were no ultra-Orthodox rural settlements in Palestine. The nonreligious, meanwhile, began to feel she was favoring both religious parties over themselves, who had built Jewish Palestine.

Letters piled up on her desk from rabbis, from rabbi's wives, from South Africa, America and England. Rabbis descended on her, lectured her, warned her. She wrote a note to herself, a memorandum of a talk she meant to deliver to some of these religious leaders: "Warnings—you have no right to warn me."

The Religious Committee of Youth Aliyah finally suggested she divide the children fifty-fifty between religious and nonreligious institutions, which she refused to do. To Miss Szold such a matter was not amenable to arithmetic.

As for money, Hadassah was eager to assume full responsibility. And in December 1942 it was Hadassah that secured safe passage for the Teheran children through the good offices of the British embassy in Washington. The first group of 700 set out by train to a Persian Gulf port, where they embarked for Karachi; they would be transferred to an empty British troopship that would bring them to Suez, in all a seven weeks' journey. Their exact time of arrival in Suez was not to be known; Hans Beyth would be summoned there at a moment's notice to escort them home.

This news electrified the Yishuv, and among the leaders of the Jewish Agency it had the same effect as on the population at large: excitement mingled with guilt and nostalgia further exacerbated by political passion. Agency leaders had never before shown much interest in Youth Aliyah affairs. They considered German and Austrian children the proper business of Miss Szold, but Polish children, the children of the vanished townlets, were another matter. What did Miss Szold know about Polish children? She had dealt for the most part with carefully selected, healthy, disciplined youth from Germany and Austria, who came to her fifty or so at a time. Now it was a question of many hundreds at once and a great army of thousands to follow, for the full extent of the European tragedy had not yet been enacted; only in 1944, when the extermination camps fell into Allied hands, did the vision of an army of survivors vanish. Of 3 million Polish Jews, all but 100,000 were to die by the end of the war.

Miss Szold wrote to Bertha, wondering why she was not considered competent to deal with Polish children when she had already brought in 200 or 300 from Poland "and not a dog stuck out its tongue." She wrote to Hadassah, explaining that much of the opposition to herself was surely due to Ihud. Although she was deeply wounded by the Agency's attitude, although a sense of rejection permeated her letters to Hadassah on the subject, she said nothing to them about her feelings. It was always her belief that she was not entitled to feelings in such matters.

But she was reaching out to them for help all the same, letting them know she was hurt although she scarcely let herself know. Perhaps elements of political strategy were involved. Perhaps she had turned to Hadassah and revealed her feelings indirectly to Hadassah, in the knowledge that they would defend her as she would never defend herself.

At all events Hadassah went into a state of exalted shock. Cables and letters flew from New York to the Jewish Agency, and not from Hadassah leaders alone. The Weizmanns were in America at the time. Vera Weizmann cabled. Chaim Weizmann cabled jointly with Moshe Shertok. The national board cabled, and Mrs. Pool also wrote directly to Miss Szold.

In effect the Weizmanns, Shertok and Pool informed the Agency that American women would trust their money unquestioningly to Miss Szold. A committee of Agency men was another matter entirely.

On February 10, 1943, Hans Beyth was summoned to Suez and instructed by the government to keep all his movements secret, above all not to telephone the date of the children's arrival in Palestine. Emma therefore wrote out a

code, which he tore into bits and hid in his shoes so he could phone his wife
with an innocent message containing the date of their arrival. Then he left
for Ludd and the train to Suez.

The atmosphere in the Youth Aliyah office became rapturous, dreamlike.
In an air of holiday people moved about with childish smiles on their faces.
The weather was warm, birds sang from the trees and rooftops, the rosebush
at the gate quivered with spring, and Miss Szold collected promises of socks,
skullcaps and great stores of food without telling whom they were for. Whenever
anyone asked for Hans Beyth she said he was home with flu.

On February 15 the coded message arrived by phone: the children would
reach Athlit in two or three days. Once they were within the borders of Palestine,
traveling north by train, the secret was out, and everyone knew "the children,"
the objects of so much yearning, had come at last. When Miss Szold and
Emma arrived at the Haifa railway station the morning the train was due,
they found the platform jammed with men, women, journalists, photographers
and crowds of schoolchildren carrying armfuls of wildflowers, packets of chocolates, oranges. Toward noon they saw the train pull in with hundreds of little
hands waving small blue-and-white flags through the open windows.

At the sight of it the crowd on the platform burst into "Hatikvah," the
Zionist anthem. The train doors opened and the refugees poured out, the
children jumping quickly to the ground. They wore a strange assortment of
clothing, many of the boys in military sweaters and helmets given them by
the British army in India. The people on the platform called out the names
of townlets in Poland, and some of the newcomers called back. They began
to surge toward one another. A father saw a son he thought to be dead. A
boy of fifteen walked up to his mother and shook her hand quite stiffly, then
held out a bottle of perfume he had somehow, somewhere, bought for her in
the course of his journey. A four-year-old orphan who had neither a relative
nor a friend in the entire world began to weep. A girl on the platform recognized
a boy who had lived next door to her in Poland and asked after his parents,
and he too began to weep, for he had seen them murdered by Nazis. A brother
and sister, aged ten and eight, whose parents died of typhus in the Teheran
camp wept with them. A contagion of weeping swept the crowd. A schoolteacher
led his pupils in songs of the chalutzim. The newcomers and the welcomers
joined them, but the four-year-old boy was too young to know the songs.

Children and adults were taken by bus to the detention center at Athlit
for the initial sorting out; the children then left for eleven preparation centers
where they would stay six weeks. In their progress through the country they
were met by singing and outstretched hands throwing flowers and food through
the train windows. The offices of the national institutions were emptied; work

came to a standstill everywhere. The people who crowded to the train stations came in carts, on horseback, most of all on foot. The route to the preparation centers was marked with posters and placards calling to them, "Blessed be the newcomers to the land of our fathers," and everyone sang out that special word, *Moledet,* which means fatherland, not only the people of the Yishuv but English soldiers and policemen and American military personnel. On a street in Jerusalem packed with ecstatically happy masses an engineer from Oklahoma called, *"Moledet,* children, *Moledet,"* without any idea what the word meant. There were Arabs in the crowds with little sacks of oranges who said nothing about the fatherland but blessed the children: "May Allah be with you, you are now the children of all mankind. . . ."

Miss Szold went home to bed; she had bronchitis that threatened to become pneumonia. She had a day nurse, a night nurse and a fever. But she intended to climb out of bed when the time came for the interview sessions; over 700 children were to be interviewed one by one with care and discretion in the presence of representatives of the chief religious and nonreligious groupings— the Agency committee. Thanks to Hadassah's influence Miss Szold was to have the final word. She remained the head of Youth Aliyah, but it was directly attached to the Agency now, and she had six unwelcome colleagues.

And the children themselves? A sister and brother recall their first meal in the preparation camp:

> We were sixty little savages. . . . Our eyes fairly popped at the abundance of food on the table—piles of fresh bread, as much as we wanted, more than anyone of us could possibly have eaten. We just stood and stared at the tables, and each of us had the same thought—it must be some sort of a trick, a hoax. . . . At first we were suspicious of everyone around us.

There were periods of terrible loneliness and exhaustion:

> It was as if all the years in which I hadn't dared to give in had caught up with me at last. At fourteen I'd seen people dying and dead around me without ever being afraid for myself. Here in Palestine at seventeen I found myself getting panicky at the slightest headache or scratch. . . . In Siberia I'd worked eighteen hours each day without any time off. In the kibbutz I was pretending to be sick all the time.

They were homesick not for the immediate past but for the distant past of the *shtetl,* the townlets, with their rich warm atmosphere of Jewish life. The *madrichim* wanted them to be strong, wholesomely free of doubts and conflicts and sad memories; the *madrichim* had no use for that rich, warm *shtetl* life, which meant to them the old, dead confining past. In the end the children swallowed down their nightmares "and taught ourselves to stifle our fears and guilt feelings. For years many of us went around with a kind of amnesia."

In one thing they held out against the *madrichim* and all other authorities; the older children would not relinquish their younger sisters, brothers, cousins. At no cost would they allow them themselves to be separated when the selections were made. So they stated now; so they would tell Miss Szold when the day came.

It came in April. Since the children had been scattered to almost a dozen temporary camps, they were brought to several urban centers, and Miss Szold left her sickbed to interview them at the centers. She was still weak, for her illness had bordered on pneumonia, and she felt sorry for herself. She was sorry for Hans Beyth, who was also sick. She was sorry for the children because people would not leave them alone; the public had to be forcibly kept away from the temporary camps. But most of all she was sorry for herself. She had taken on a task that was proving too much for her, yet she resented every attempt by others to share in it.

Children whose temporary camps were in the north were brought to an orphanage in Haifa, a new and modern building whose dining hall ran the length and breadth of the first floor. The residents had been sent away so that the dining hall could be used for the interviews. Trees shadowed the windows, but children of the neighborhood peered through them, and a few even ran inside, eager for a share in the excitement.

Miss Szold sat at a long table with Hans Beyth and the six members of the Agency committee, the nonreligious in their open-necked shirts, the religious in dark hats, dark suits, with earlocks and spreading beards. When the war was over many of the rescued children would be voting adults, and each faction wanted those votes.

The children came in a few at a time. They saw the table—a high court for their future, a high court of placement—as a frightening sight. Yet the children, in their way, were almost frightening to Miss Szold. How hard they looked, how suspicious. In the faces of the little street Arabs she had searched for and found the universal qualities of childhood, but the faces of the Teheran children were different. When she looked into their eyes they were opaque. Flint.

Two children enter, a boy of ten whose name is Selig and his sister, Gisia, perhaps fourteen. The girl pushes the little one in front of her as they approach the high court. The boy sees Miss Szold, puts up his hand and says to her, *Shalom*. Gisia says the same: *Shalom*.

Miss Szold replies in Yiddish or, rather, tries to. She speaks elegant antique German, but although Yiddish resembles German, being the fifteenth-century form of the language, it is not the same. In what she takes to be Yiddish Miss Szold says, Here is a chair, and points.

Selig says: What?

Now the word "what" is not so much a question as a sort of magic spoken to gain time, to figure out what the questioner really wants. It is an instrument of survival; no matter what is said to you, your first response must be "What?" The what, of course, is in Yiddish.

The man from the labor movement now says in Yiddish: Be seated.

And the ultra-Orthodox leader says, also in Yiddish: Please, sit. Already there is a sense of competition in the air, even kindness has become an instrument of competition.

So the two children file down along the table, passing all the members of the high court, and they sit.

Miss Szold, in Yiddish-German: How old are you, Gisia?

Gisia: What?

Miss Szold repeats the question. Gisia answers in Polish and Yiddish mixed together: Last year I finished thirteen.

Miss Szold asks: To what school did you go?

Now it's getting hotter, because she may say she went to a religious school or she may say she went to no school at all.

But Gisia only says: What?

Miss Szold, baffled: What what?

Gisia: To a public school. She knows quite well what the question is. And she knows quite well, even frightened out of her wits, that she is running the show.

And Miss Szold, who grasps this immediately, says to the group, She understands what I say—why all these whats?

But the word Gisia had used for public elementary school means a general nonreligious school, and the others see this. Gisia sees that they see it. Before any further questions can be put, she says: I want to be in Mimek Hamishmar. Meaning Mishmar HaEmek, the far left, nonreligious kibbutz.

Hans Beyth, very fatherly but in choice German, for he is as ignorant of Yiddish as Miss Szold: We will discuss it later. We want the best for you. Right now it is impossible to make decisions.

Gisia, in Yiddish, firmly and loudly: But I have already decided.

Hans Beyth, still the good father: We must discuss it. You know only one place, we know many places, we must decide for you.

Gisia: I'll go only to Mishmar, this we have already decided. Her gesture includes Selig, who has been silent throughout. And with us will go Moishe and Gittle, Yentle and fifteen other comrades.

There is a long pause during which the members of the high court do not look at one another.

Then Miss Szold addresses Selig: Did your father go to synagogue?

Selig: What?

Miss Szold repeats the question.

Selig: I don't understand anything, I can't remember whether my father went to synagogue.

Miss Szold, again: Did he go to synagogue, your father?

Selig: Not on the Sabbath, not on the Sabbath night. His voice has grown lower, however, and he is not meeting her eyes.

Miss Szold, gently: Your father, was he religious?

Selig: What? Then, after a moment, in a whisper: Yes, he was a devout Jew.

For Miss Szold the first hundred children were no easier to question than the first dozen; the most patient observation failed to reveal the child in them. There was no humor, no innocence, no mischief, certainly no gratitude. The children who had eluded death eluded her. Girls who had protected the lives of several younger ones at the risk of their own, not once but over and over again, complained now because the clothes they were given had mends; many resisted the idea of going to kibbutzim because they were told they would learn to work, to farm. They did not want to work. They wanted the years of childhood that had been snatched away from them.

The one quality that redeemed them in Miss Szold's eyes was the fierce protectiveness of the older for the younger. There were many Gisias who had constituted themselves the heads of "families," one or two siblings and several they referred to as cousins, who were really companions picked up on the way. They would not be separated from the younger children. Just as Gisia held on to Selig, watched him, pushed him before her when she came and went in the course of the interview, so did she hold herself responsible for his future. Where she went, he must go. The high court assured her he would be well taken care of even apart from her. Hans Beyth, always the good father, said that Palestine was a little place. It was not Siberia, and they would see each other often. The older girls refused so fiercely that Miss Szold felt her eyes sting, her throat choke up with the intensity of their protectiveness.

But that was the heart of the problem. In the course of the interviews she learned that some 80 percent of the children had come from religious homes. The agreement was that while those over fourteen could choose for themselves, those who were younger must go to religious settlements and institutions if the parental home had been religious. Yet all the autonomous older girls refused flatly, emphatically. No persuasion could induce them to change, although Miss Szold went so far as to tell them she considered it their duty to give up their own ambitions for the sake of the younger children, for the sake of the dead parents' hopes and wishes. The girls were adamant. For in Poland only boys were pious and nothing was expected of the Jewish daughter, she need not learn Torah or anything else. During their wanderings the girls had discovered a world in which boys and girls were equal, and they intended to enter that world along with the younger children. The religious members of the high court believed the children should be separated nevertheless, but to Miss Szold, the final authority, there was something inviolable about such attachments. They brought to her mind deathbed promises; who knew or dared to discover the reasons behind them? Besides, she believed only police action could keep the younger children from running away to rejoin the older.

The interviews came to an end. Miss Szold had been unable to attend several sessions because the respiratory ailment persisted and it was literally impossible for her to get out of bed; Hans Beyth had to go in her place. Next she took the stenographic records of the interviews, the earlier reports of *madrichim* and doctors and psychologists and the recommendations of her fellow members of the high court and began the final stage, the final decision making, which resulted in ninety-three appeals from religious bodies and a storm of cables arriving daily from abroad.

The chief rabbi considered it his sacred duty to arouse the Orthodox Jewish world against Miss Szold, and throughout these final stages—the ninety-three appeals discussed, adjusted, whittled down, then fresh appeals made from the fresh decisions—cables and letters from America, South Africa and England accused her of destroying traditional Judaism, the yeshivas, the Torah itself.

While the children had been in the preparation camps, Orthodox representatives had visited them, cajoling, threatening, insisting they ask for placement in Orthodox institutions. At the same time, however, some of the *madrichim* placed in the camps had been cruelly insensitive to the religious practices of some of the children. To Miss Szold it was clear that both sides saw the children as pawns. Now she heard that Orthodox leaders in London were talking about a separate Youth Aliyah.

She wondered if the movement could survive this new threat from the religious party, if she herself could survive:

> Where were they when the work of building began, and where were they when the youth immigration began? They appeared on the scene late and unprepared, yet with maximal demands. The neglect of generations is a heavy sin that cannot be atoned for in a single generation, and at the hands of one old, weak woman. . . . I can bear no more.

The battle over the Teheran children seemed to sum up her perceptions of her twenty-three years in Palestine, seen in their darkest light as a woman old, weak, sick and emotionally battered might well see them. It was a battle involving only Jews, and for her the problems of Jewish Palestine were the problems of Jews to which the British, the source of power and often of misused power, were nevertheless peripheral. As were the Arabs. Except for their leaders they had never been the enemy in her eyes. What was wrong with Jewish Palestine began and ended with the Jews, with their selfishness, their squabbling among themselves, their division into Oriental and Western, religious and nonreligious, with the abandonment by religious leaders of their spiritual mission in order to take on political missions.

Her family, the Jews of Palestine, kept her at arm's length, admiring her in the abstract while responding to her scoldings with the reminder that she did not belong. To the religious she was an enemy disguised as a rabbi's daughter. To the nonreligious she was still an outsider, and the Teheran business only underscored it. Leaders of the Jewish Agency, the establishment, saw her as a partner of Magnes, that traitor to Zionism, inadequate to the task of handling Polish children and kept in power only by the insistence of Hadassah, meaning American dollars. Even to Hadassah she felt she was an icon rather than a woman.

She was heartsick over it. Emma Ehrlich said later that the respiratory illness that killed Miss Szold began with those interviews and never receded, because of the suffering that followed.

Most of the children arriving now came as had the Teheran children, part of the backwash of great streams of refugees pouring through southeastern Europe. All had to be interviewed, evaluated, observed. Hundreds of thousands would follow when the war was over, and Miss Szold wanted them to have a welcome marked by comfort and grace; she made elaborate, costly plans for a reception center including dormitories, a library, a natural science museum, and sent them to Hadassah. Hadassah sent money in honor of the tenth anniversary of Youth Aliyah. Miss Szold thanked them and asked for more.

Some weeks later she found herself in the Hadassah hospital with dysentery and gout. She did not like being hospitalized; she did not like taking up a bed when others needed it more, and the thought of Youth Aliyah groups arriving at Haifa when she could not welcome them was galling to her.

By June she was well enough to work half time. Children were arriving from camps in an area called Trans-Dniestria, a part of the Ukraine to which Romania's Fascist government had shipped 185,000 Jews in 1941 and 1942.

One hundred thousand had perished there, burned to death or stripped naked
in the subzero cold and shot to death. But in early 1943 the first awareness
of a coming Allied victory closed down the camps, and parentless children
wandered out among the survivors. Eight thousand drifted through Romania,
3,000 of them dying of hunger or sickness in the course of a year. Four thousand
were gathered into an orphanage and cared for by an underground organization
of Romanian women. Another 1,000 still wandered from village to village
scrounging for food. Although most of the Trans-Dniestrian survivors were
ignored by Allied governments, who shuffled papers and made sympathetic
pronouncements but provided neither visas nor money, one gesture was made.
Half a dozen relief agencies removed 600 children from the orphanage in Bucha-
rest and sent them in groups to Palestine, to Miss Szold and Hans Beyth at
Athlit.

They were fragile, hollow-eyed, emaciated ghosts. When Miss Szold saw
the first of them she wrote to Bertha: "The misfortune that has overtaken
our people is alas of one color, one tone, one meaning. The elements are always
the same: starvation, exposure, flight, horrible scenes of cruelty, separation of
families, bloody spectacles, wandering in the woods, hiding in cellars, and for
a few, escape."

Two million Jews had died at Nazi hands so far, as Miss Szold and the
Yishuv learned in November of 1942; the millions remaining alive were dying
now in camps far worse than any Miss Szold could imagine, because their
sole purpose was swift, efficient extermination. But she still believed a great
mass of Polish Jewry would enter the Yishuv when the war was over, with
many thousands from other European countries, and Youth Aliyah must be
ready for them. They must plan, she told Norman Bentwich; nothing should
be done rashly or superficially, for there was no hurry. Ten thousand children
had already been rescued by Youth Aliyah with patience and method and the
determination that no one child should become lost in the mass.

Then the hot weather began, and doctors at the Hadassah hospital begged
her to move into the nurses' residence on Mount Scopus. The principal, her
old friend Shulamit Cantor, said there were two extra rooms she could have;
she would be displacing nobody. Nevertheless Miss Szold resisted, for she felt
she was being lured into an old ladies' home. Mount Scopus was far from
the center of things, and she would be unable to work half days. She was not
sick, after all. She had made certain arrangements with Emma in case of her
death, but nobody imagined for a moment that she was sick. When another
group of children arrived, largely from Romania, and the doctors forbade her
to make the journey to Haifa, she took it almost as an insult. But Joe Jastrow
had died that spring, and Thomas Seltzer, Adele's husband, was dead, and

Miss Szold, who was certainly not sick or even feeble, made out her will. Nothing was wrong with her except eighty-three years.

By July it was apparent that she had pneumonia. She went into the hospital, and Magnes and the British military got her the first penicillin used by a civilian in Palestine. For a while she seemed to recover, moving out of the hospital and into the two-room suite in the nurses' home, where she walked up and down on the verandah every day for exercise, exactly 100 steps. She had many visitors, and they usually brought chocolates.

Yes, she was better. The doctors were not entirely convinced, but she could tell she was better. "I am still lapped in kindness," she wrote to Bertha, but "I don't want sympathy and thought and care and consideration, I want to work!" Emma was with her every day. The Youth Aliyah staff came to see her not only on business but for the pleasure of it; important people came and people who were nobody, the student nurses at the hospital, and Lord Gort, the new High Commissioner, whom she insisted on meeting fully dressed in the hall downstairs. One nurse came every morning especially to brush Miss Szold's hair.

By December, Dr. Magnes began making notes of his daily visits, which were sent to Hadassah, describing Miss Szold's health and spirits. These accounts conveyed a sense of awe, as if Magnes hoped to capture the progress of a great soul moving toward death:

> This morning I visited Miss Szold again. . . . She wanted to have from me the text of the telegrams I had sent to Hadassah in order that she might know what her sister Bertha had heard about her. I said that the text itself could really be of no importance to her, and that we had telegraphed just what the doctors had suggested. She said that she would have a long, long road to travel, and would she have the strength to travel it? . . . She asked about the Hungarian children, and I told her that there were prospects of many thousands being saved. . . . She asked if there had been any meetings of the Hadassah Emergency Council. I said that there had been one on vocational training. . . . She said, "Why must I be so dependent upon everyone?"

Another day, pointing to the student nurse: "Did I have to bring this girl here from Germany so that she might wait on me?"

There were attacks of breathlessness, nightmares in which her sisters and her family deserted her, long intervals when her mind cleared and she was hungry for every detail of "business," and finally the pneumonia itself succumbed to treatment. The pneumonia was gone, but Miss Szold had been exhausted by it, unable to eat, unable to fight. "Do you realize what a struggle I am having. . . . It is very hard. Can you imagine how hard?" she asked him once.

On December 27 she was told Weizmann wanted to visit her. She did not want to see him, she said, not while she was weak, sick, dependent on others. That must have been one of the hardest parts of her illness: not only being dependent but being an object of pity. Exposed, pitied, an object—she had fought against it all her life and fought while she was losing her life. But Magnes and Shulamit Cantor persuaded her together. Weizmann was on his way to a Zionist meeting in London, they said. He hoped to carry a message from Miss Szold. So she agreed.

Magnes brought Weizmann to the bedroom and waited outside in the sitting room; the two men had been estranged for many years. The door between the two rooms was open, and Magnes could tell that Miss Szold spoke with great difficulty.

Her first words to Weizmann were, "The attitude of the Yishuv towards England is very bad." He agreed, for it was still his hope that the Jewish state might be born under the protection of England and in the ripeness of time. But she had more to say, for Miss Szold had seen Magnes in the waiting room, and she asked the nurse to call him in. When he came and stood by her bed she took his hand and at the same time took Dr. Weizmann's hand. It gave her great joy, she said, to see the two of them together.

When they walked out some ten or fifteen minutes later both men were moved by their reunion; they stopped in the hallway downstairs and repeated her words, and Magnes wrote them down. "We must never quarrel," Weizmann added, and Magnes said, "No, that seems to be an injunction from on high."

One day in February, Magnes saw that the storm was over; Miss Szold was resting calmly, her breathing easier, her face less anxious, but her life was ebbing slowly away. The doctor said something might happen at any minute, or it might wait until morning. There were hurried conferences with doctors and nurses over the possibility of releasing a statement to the press or radio at that point. In those conferences nobody used the word "death," only "happening," "event." The general opinion was: "In view of what we were expecting during the night, why excite the outlying places when in the morning they would know something definite."

It was now about 7:30 in the evening. Within minutes Miss Szold's breathing became slower and more fitful. Her pulse was difficult to find. Several people gathered around the bed. "Two, three, four times at long intervals a slight breath in the throat, and then that stopped," Magnes wrote. "She was gone. I took her hand for the last time."

The news spread quickly. People began to come, and the funeral was planned according to Emma's recollections of what Miss Szold wanted, although Emma herself was beginning to show signs of the long months of suffering. Someone suggested the body be taken to the large hall of the Hadassah hospital, but Mrs. Cantor said: "No. This is her home and this is where she died." It was therefore agreed that her body lie in the hall of the nurses' school. The next morning Emma and some of the nurses carried her down the stairs and placed her on a low platform that had been put in the middle of the room.

Now the narrative is taken up by the Hebrew secretary of Youth Aliyah, the man who was first a chalutz, then a master mason, finally a worker for Miss Szold:

> With her death a sigh of anguish passed through the world, the hearts of parents and children were filled with sorrow. Because that vitality came to an end, that vitality of a tree with roots.
>
> Crowds flowed to the assembly hall in the nurses' residence bearing her name on Mount Scopus. They came to honor her. They surrounded in silence her minute body, like that of a young girl . . . covered with a light blue cloth adorned with Hebrew verses, and at her head candles for the departed were placed in silver Sabbath candlesticks. They came from all walks of life, young and old, whispering prayers, reading psalms, crying, silent, they looked at the small body which housed a great spirit. Most orphaned were the children of Youth Aliyah and its graduates, they came and went and were lost, confused.
>
> . . . A girl stood in a corner as if nailed to the spot, her body immobile and tears streaming from her eyes.

Recha Freier came and watched by the body for hours.

The day of the funeral was cold, snowy, with dark skies and gusts of wind. Thousands came to follow the funeral procession from Scopus to the Mount of Olives; they came from all over the Yishuv, from the towns and villages and the farthest settlements. A boy from among the Teheran children recited the kaddish.

One of the social workers, Sylvia Gelber, watched the body, wrapped in the white shroud Miss Szold had kept folded in her closet for several years, as it was lowered into the wet earth. According to the custom of Jerusalem there was no coffin, only the winding sheet. The members of the burial society then jumped into the grave to pack the earth around the body, brisk, businesslike, stomping with their boots. The woman who was watching shivered, feeling the cold and wet as if they pressed against her own body.

Then the earth covered her up.

AFTERWARDS

Hans Beyth died only two years after Miss Szold. He had gone to welcome a group of children newly released from the Cyprus detention camps where the British had placed them to wait out the war. Riding in a convoy toward Jerusalem, up the Judean hills past hostile Arab villages, with Golda Meir and two Agency members in a car behind, they were fired on. Beyth stood up to return the fire and was killed.

Judah Magnes made a hurried trip to America in early 1948 to plead for United Nations trusteeship over Palestine rather than statehood. But when the state of Israel came into being in May of that year, he told his son, "Do you think that in my heart I am not glad too that there is a state? I just did not think it was to be." He died within months.

Bertha Szold Levin died in 1958. Among her children, grandchildren and great-grandchildren certain traits crop up from time to time that remind the family powerfully of Aunt Henrietta.

Louis Ginzberg died in 1953. His widow lives in New York in her own apartment, and at the age of ninety spends her summers in Maine fishing for bass and perch. Her son, Eli, a sociologist, economist and writer of worldwide reputation, is married to the former Ruth Szold, Robert and Zip's daughter.

Recha Freier lives in Jerusalem not far from her daughter and grandchildren. Eva Stern-Michaelis also lives in Jerusalem, as does Helena Kagan, still in the Arab house where Miss Szold came to stay in 1920. Emma Ehrlich lives close to the Central Zionist Archives and devotes much of her time to work on the letters and papers of Miss Szold.

Youth Aliyah still lives in Israel. There are 270 facilities, kibbutzim, youth villages and youth centers, training some 16,000 Youth Aliyah children today. Thousands of Israeli-born youngsters benefit from the "internal aliyah" that grew from Miss Szold's town to village experiment. In all nearly 155,000 young people from eighty lands have passed through Youth Aliyah since its inception, and their contributions to agriculture, industry, education, the arts and the defense forces are nationally recognized.

The women of Hadassah number 360,000—the largest Zionist organization in the world. They have sent more than $70 million to Youth Aliyah since 1935 and a little less than $500 million to Palestine and Israel to meet the needs of manifold projects from 1922 to 1977. The Hadassah-Hebrew University Medical Center at Ein Karem in Jerusalem, the expanded facilities on Mount Scopus, the Henrietta Szold School of Nursing, are only the most conspicuous of their undertakings. They have a volunteer representative in Washington and are invited to U.S. State Department briefings; they are an accredited observer to the U.S. Mission to the United Nations.

All this stems directly from the handful of women who met with Miss Szold in 1912 to sit in one another's parlors and watch stereopticon slides.

Appendix: Organizations and Other Terms

aliyah: immigration.

AZMU: American Zionist Medical Unit, sometimes called the Unit; a medical relief mission sent to Palestine in June 1918 by the Zionists of America and organized by Hadassah.

Bilu, Biluim: first pioneers to go to Palestine after the Russian pogroms of 1881.

Brit Shalom: Covenant of Peace, a Jewish association in Palestine advocating Arab-Jewish rapprochement, from 1925 to 1933.

chalutzim: agricultural pioneers of Jewish Palestine; singular, chalutz.

FAZ: Federation of American Zionists, founded 1898. The first nation-wide Zionist organization in America.

Haganah: semilegal Jewish self-defense force.

Histadrut: General Federation of Jewish Labor; affiliated labor unions of Jewish Palestine, founded 1920.

HMO: Hadassah Medical Organization; after 1921 this term was used for the AZMU.

Ihud: Union, a Zionist discussion group advocating bi-nationalism and Arab-Jewish rapprochement, founded 1942.

Jewish Agency: a body created in 1929 uniting Zionist and non-Zionist Jews throughout the world for the upbuilding of Palestine; often called the Agency.

JPS: Jewish Publication Society of America, founded in Philadelphia in 1888.

the Joint: American Jewish Joint Distribution Committee, founded 1914 to serve as over-all distribution agency for funds collected by American Jewish groups for overseas relief.

Keren Hayesod: foundation fund for colonizing work in the Jewish homeland, established 1920 by the World Zionist Organization, a bone of contention

321

between American Zionists of the Brandeis faction and adherents of Chaim Weizmann.

kibbutz: collective agricultural settlement in Palestine; plural, kibbutzim.

Kupat Holim: health care system of the Histadrut.

Mizrachi: Orthodox Zionist organization.

PC: In America, during World War I, the Provisional Executive Committee for General Zionist affairs, an interim substitute for the Executive of the World Zionist Organization, then dispersed by war.

UPA: United Palestine Appeal, established 1925 by the Zionist Organization of America as a fund-raising organization for Palestine.

Vaad Leumi: National Assembly of the Jews of Palestine.

World Zionist Organization: founded 1897, composed of Zionist societies throughout the world whose delegates meet annually at the Zionist congress.

Yahudim: German-American Jews.

Yishuv: Jewish community of Palestine.

Youth Aliyah: organization that rescued Jewish children from Nazi-endangered countries during World War II, in Berlin called the Jugendhilfe; its fund-raising arm in Berlin and later in London was the Arbeitsgemeinschaft für Kinder und Jugendaliyah.

ZOA: Zionist Organization of America, formed in 1917 as successor to the FAZ.

Zionist Commission: from 1918 to 1921, a body formed at the request of Great Britain to act as its link to the Jews of Palestine.

Zionist Executive: after 1921 replaced the Zionist Commission; acted as shadow government of the Yishuv and was effectively replaced in 1929 by the Jewish Agency Executive.

Notes

The chief source of Henrietta Szold material is the Henrietta Szold Archive of the Central Zionist Archives, Jerusalem. It is divided into two sections: a collection of personal letters, chronologically arranged; and material related to her public life and work, arranged according to correspondent or subject. In the notes that follow, the source of material from the second category, public life and work, is indicated by the initials CZA followed by the folder number. Material from the personal file is not noted, except for the occasional citation whose origin might be unclear; in that case the designation CZA N file is used, preceded by the date of the letter.

Material from the files and Henrietta Szold Archive of Hadassah in New York includes speeches of Miss Szold's, her "Familiar Letters from Palestine," back issues of the *Hadassah Bulletin* and *Hadassah Newsletter*, reports, pamphlets and a history of Youth Aliyah. For this material the designation Hadassah is used. The family scrapbooks and personal letters of Alexandra Lee Levin of Baltimore are indicated by the initials ALL. Microfilm of Szold diaries in the American Jewish Archives in Cincinnati is designated AJA, followed by the code number of the microfilm reel. Ginzberg-Szold correspondence in the library of the Jewish Theological Seminary is cited with the abbreviation JTS. Archives of the American Jewish Joint Distribution Committee are referred to as Joint Archives.

I. BALTIMORE

Descriptions of Rabbi and Mrs. Szold and of Henrietta's girlhood come largely from an unpublished memoir written by Adele Szold Seltzer and found in the Hadassah Szold Archives; from Alexandra Lee Levin's *The Szolds of Lombard Street* (Philadelphia, 1960); and from a number of articles published in the *Hadassah Newsletter*, especially "Rooms in Our House," by Bertha Szold Levin, December 1945. Marvin Lowenthal's *Henrietta Szold, Life and Letters* (New York, 1942) was written after several interviews with Miss Szold. Rose Zeitlin's *Henrietta Szold: Record of a Life* (New York, 1952) had the cooperation of Bertha Szold Levin. For biographical background on Theodor Herzl I have relied on Desmond Stewart's *Herzl, Artist and Politician* (Garden City,

N.Y., 1974), Amos Elon's *Herzl* (New York, 1975) and Walter Laqueur's *A History of Zionism* (New York, 1972).

Page

6   A friend of his Breslau days: CZA N file, September 26, 1841.

7   "The Schaars can have no pleasure": Levin, *Szolds*, p. 381.

7   "Henrietta speaks daily of the dear Grandmother": Ibid., p. 40.

9   in America a father of daughters: Sophie Szold to Miriam Schaar, May 30, 1869, ALL.

13   Henrietta's letter to her parents: CZA N file, undated. Translated by Marianne Klein and Laureen Nussbaum.

14   "Be like your father": Levin, *Szolds*, pp. 109–110.

15   "It is the living": Lowenthal, *Henrietta Szold*, p. 14.

16   two blazing columns: *Jewish Messenger*, July 1878.

17   A small number of American rabbis: Moshe Davis, *The Emergence of Conservative Judaism* (Philadelphia, 1963), p. 186.

17   The acquaintance of a pleasant Gentile family: Zeitlin, *Henrietta Szold: Record of a Life*, p. 240.

18   "The little ones will be homesick": Salomon Beutum to Sophie Szold, August 19, 1881, ALL.

19   "Remember how angry she made you": Alexandra Lee Levin, *Vision: A Biography of Harry Friedenwald* (Philadelphia, 1964), p. 116.

21   and now it was seeping into America: *New York Times*, May 13, 1887.

21   Discussions in Rabbi Szold's study: Henrietta Szold, "Early Zionist Days in Baltimore," *Maccabean*, June–July 1917, pp. 265–266.

22   Ten years earlier Rabbi Szold had written: Irving Fineman, *Woman of Valor* (New York, 1961) pp. 97–99.

23   "Zionism converted me to itself": Lowenthal, *Henrietta Szold*, p. 53.

23   HS invited to give a talk: Conversation with Marvin Lowenthal, December 29, 1935, Hadassah.

24 ff.   For beginnings of the Russian Night School, see Alexandra Lee Levin, "Henrietta Szold and the Russian Immigrant School," *Maryland Historical Magazine* 57, no. 1 (March 1962): 1–15; Benjamin Hartogensis, "The Russian Night School of Baltimore," *American Jewish Historical Society Magazine* (1928), pp. 225–229.

25   A student at the night school remembered: Boris D. Bogen, *Born a Jew* (New York, 1930), p. 45.

26   Rabbi Szold's sixtieth birthday: Levin, *Vision*, p. 124.

26   an amateur and a humbug: Conversation with Lowenthal, December 29, 1935, Hadassah.

26   HS called the leading Jewish essayist in America: by the *London Jewish Chronicle*, cited in Alexandra Lee Levin, "Henrietta Szold and the Jewish Publication Society," *JPS Bookmark*, June 1961.

27 f.   On Southern women's clubs, see Ann Firor Scott, *The Southern Lady: From Pedestal to Politics, 1830–1930* (Chicago, 1970), pp. 150 ff.

28   tears blotted a postcard: Levin, *Szolds*, p. 229.

31   On the Zionist Association of Baltimore see Davis, *Emergence of Conservative Judaism*, pp. 268 and 272.

33 "I had the feeling": Conversation with Lowenthal, December 29, 1935, Hadassah.

34 "Henrietta, did you make absolutely": Levin, *Szolds*, p. 343.

34 "She was all there was of the Society": Louis Lipsky, "A Leader in Service," *Hadassah Newsletter*, December 1930, p. 5.

35 publication of Herzl's *Der Judenstaat:* Laqueur, *History of Zionism*, p. 84.

36 "formation of a Jewish state": Elon, *Herzl*, p. 227.

37 "He does not know the first thing about Jews": Ibid., p. 186.

38 "They possess an inner integrity": Ibid., p. 246.

38 "Black formal attire": Ibid., p. 237.

39 "little Russian Jew": *D. H. Lawrence, Letters to Thomas and Adele Seltzer,* ed. Gerald M. Lacy (Santa Barbara, Calif., 1976), p. 179.

40 On the tenth anniversary banquet of the JPS, see Levin, "Henrietta Szold and the Jewish Publication Society."

41 On HS nursing her father: HS to Louis Ginzberg, July 17, 1907, JTS.

41 f. On HS mourning her father: HS to Louis Ginzberg, August 10, 1907, JTS.

42 Mrs. Szold suggests that Henrietta edit her father's papers: Levin, *Szolds*, p. 366.

42 f. On the founding of the Jewish Theological Seminary, see Parzen, *Architects of Conservative Judaism* (New York: 1964); Davis, *Emergence of Conservative Judaism;* Eli Ginzberg, *Keeper of the Law: Louis Ginzberg* (Philadelphia, 1966).

43 "that wild man": Norman Bentwich, *Solomon Schechter: A Biography* (Philadelphia, 1938), p. 83.

43 "and then I realized": HS to Ginzberg, August 10, 1907, JTS.

44 HS's first meeting with Ginzberg: Fineman, *Woman of Valor*, p. 119.

II. NEW YORK: IN THE SEMINARY CIRCLE

Descriptions of Louis Ginzberg are based partly on Eli Ginzberg's *Keeper of the Law* and Herbert Parzen's *Architects of Conservative Judaism.* For the Conservative movement see Parzen and Ginzberg, as well as Davis, *Emergence of Conservative Judaism.* For Miss Szold's personal life, Fineman, *Woman of Valor*, and her diary, AJA 386G. For background on Palestine, Henrietta Szold, *Recent Jewish Progress in Palestine* (Philadelphia, 1915), and Chaim Weizmann, *Trial and Error* (New York, 1966).

Page

47 according to his son Eli: Interview with Eli Ginzberg, New York, 1974.

47 "there is no other Jewish religion": Bentwich, *Solomon Schechter*, p. 176.

48 "I left the room woefully deflated": *Louis Ginzberg Jubilee Volume* (New York, 1945), p. 2.

48 "the acme of the intellectual snob": Ginzberg interview.

49 "My father was a great admirer": Louis Ginzberg to HS, August 6, 1907, JTS.

49 "lewd life": AJA 386G, June 30, 1910.

49 "the ambitious start": Ginzberg, *Keeper of the Law*, p. 57.

Much of the material that follows, especially pp. 51–63 and 67–78, is based on Fineman, *Woman of Valor*, pp. 119–99, which in turn is based on a diary of Miss Szold's. This diary was made available to Fineman for his book, but was sent immediately afterward to the Central Zionist Archives, where it has been sealed at the request of the Levin family. The diary is devoted exclusively to

Miss Szold's relations with Ginzberg. Sources for other material in the section pp. 51–79 are separately noted.

52 "We had reached": Weizmann, *Trial and Error*, p. 93.

52 The Talmud is: Based on a discussion with Rabbi Maurice Pomerantz, Seattle, 1977.

53 "I am quite": LG to HS, October 10, 1904, JTS.

54 "I want . . . to assure you": this note is for some reason included with LG to HS correspondence, JTS; January 16, 1905.

56 "I have been sitting": Fineman, *Woman of Valor*, p. 135.

57 "my dear Miss Szold": LG to HS, July 1905, JTS.

58 "From the moment": LG to HS, September 1, 1905, JTS.

58 In the summer of 1905: Levin, *Vision*, p. 174.

59 "A young man looking full of youth": Zeitlin, *Henrietta Szold: Record of a Life*, p. 35.

61 A Jewish scholar: Harry Wolfson, quoted by Rabbi Louis Finkelstein in a speech delivered at the Rabbinical Assembly Convention, Grossinger's, New York, on May 9, 1973.

63 "There is absolutely nothing": LG to HS, May 16, 1907, JTS.

63 All this flying back and forth: interview with Louis Ginzberg's nephew, Rabbi Arthur Lagawier, Seattle, 1974.

63 "That the apple of their eye": Interview with Eli Ginzberg.

64 "The physician feared": LG to HS, June 21, 1907, JTS.

64 "Father lived": Ginzberg, *Keeper of the Law*, p. 121.

64 "I cannot yet realize": LG to HS, August 2, 1907, JTS.

64 "I cannot help thinking": LG to HS, August 6, 1907, JTS.

65 "Of course it was not": LG to HS, August 28, 1907, JTS.

65 "fantastic reverberations": Ginzberg interview.

66 "frightful nights": LG to HS, September 5, 1907, JTS.

66 "I am convinced": HS to LG, August 14, 1907, JTS.

66 "I know I cannot measure": HS to LG, August 13, 1907, JTS.

66 "When I wrote to you": HS to LG, July 24, 1907, JTS.

66 "Do you remember": HS to LG, August 18, 1907, JTS.

67 "There are only three": HS to LG, August 18, 1907, JTS.

69 "I would guess": Interview with Eli Ginzberg.

70 "The purpose of all the water": HS to LG, July 26, 1908, JTS.

70 "There has not yet been": HS to LG, August 14, 1908, JTS.

71 "One reason that I was able": Ginzberg, *Keeper of the Law*, p. 110.

71 "I'm not so sure": Interview with Adele Katzenstein Ginzberg, New York, 1974.

73 "Dear Fraulein Katzenstein": Ginzberg, *Keeper of the Law*, p. 128.

75 The record of the love story: This record becomes the diary on which Fineman bases his account.

76 "Should I take my name": Alexandra Lee Levin, *Dare to Be Different* (New York, 1972), p. 265.

77 "as a matter of truth": Ibid.

78 "earnest hope": Cyrus Adler to HS, July 14, 1909, Hadassah.

78 For Miss Szold's weight, a letter of September 7, 1908, CZA N file, mentions 161½.

78   Palestine population figures: Weizmann, *Trial and Error*, p. 125.

79   "I still feel bottled": AJA 386G. This diary is the chief source of pp. 79–100, and specific quotations are not noted hereafter.

84   a source of amazement: Arthur Ruppin, *Memoirs, Letters, Diaries* (London, 1971), p. 93.

86   confirm Arab suspicions: Laqueur, *History of Zionism*, p. 221.

89   Ruppin had contracted typhoid: Ruppin, *Memoirs*, p. 83.

89   In Jaffa an incident: HS interview with Marvin Lowenthal, December 29, 1935, Hadassah.

91   a dinner party: Levin, *Dare to Be Different*, p. 93.

91   Mrs. Ginzberg was troubled: Interview with Mrs. Ginzberg.

93   An account of the life of Aaron Aaronsohn can be found in Anita Engle, *The Nili Spies* (London, 1959).

94   "You are so earnest": Lowenthal, *Henrietta Szold*, p. 62.

99   Miss Szold inspected the bedrooms: Lowenthal's interview with HS.

III. NEW YORK: A SECOND LIFE

For the early history of Hadassah the best sources are: Isidore S. Meyer, ed., *Early History of Zionism in America* (New York, 1958); Extracts from the diaries of Mrs. B. A. Rosenblatt (Gertrude Goldsmith), concerning the early history of Hadassah for the years 1911–1914 (Haifa, 1934), mimeographed and available in Hadassah Archives; D. H. Miller, *A History of Hadassah, 1912–1935* (Ann Arbor, 1968), a detailed and reliable work; also a variety of articles in past issues of the *Hadassah Newsletter*. Marlin Levin's *Balm in Gilead: The Story of Hadassah* (New York, 1973) is a popular account of Hadassah's history. For events leading up to the Balfour Declaration, see Weizmann, *Trial and Error*, and Laqueur's authoritative *History of Zionism*. For material connected with Brandeis, see Melvin Urofsky, *American Zionism from Herzl to the Holocaust*, (Garden City, N.Y., 1975).

Page

104   "To his students": Finkelstein speech.

105   In her presence: See Meyer Weisgal, "A Tribute to Henrietta Szold," *Hadassah Magazine*, February 1973.

106   "The undersigned": Rosenblatt diaries, p. 2.

106   Ruskay quote: Interview with Sophia Ruskay, Seattle, 1974.

107   "The healing of the daughter of my people": today Hadassah uses as its motto "The healing of my people," a simplified translation of the same phrase.

108   "It became evident": Rosenblatt diaries, p. 9.

109   "Those two nurses": Interview with Dr. Arieh Feigenbaum, Haifa, 1974.

111   Rachel Landy letters of January 24 and February 17, 1915, to Hadassah: *Hadassah Bulletin* #11, 1915, Hadassah Archives.

111   Rose Kaplan reports to Hadassah: *Hadassah Bulletin* #19, 1916, Hadassah.

112   On Judge Julian Mack, see Harry Barnard, *The Forging of an American Jew: The Life of Judge Julian Mack* (New York: 1974).

112   Annuity arranged for HS: Lowenthal, *Henrietta Szold, Life and Letters*, p. 89.

114   "in practically all respects . . . a Brahmin": Urofsky, *American Zionism*.

115 Rabbi Wise a formidable womanizer: Helen Lawrenson, *Stranger at the Party: A Memoir* (New York, 1975), pp. 44–47.

115 "The highest Jewish ideals": Urofsky, *American Zionism*, p. 128.

117 "The mortality rate now": Joint Archives #124, January 18, 1917.

117 Helen Kagan wrote: September 25, 1917, CZA A125/26N.

118 For background of the People's Council, see H. C. Peterson and Gilbert C. Fite, *Opponents of War, 1917–1918* (Seattle, 1968), pp. 74–80.

118 "I cannot help feeling": Jacob DeHaas to HS, September 11, 1917, addendum, CZA A125/18N.

119 A long letter: Ibid., September 11, 1917, CZA A125/18N.

119 For a description of the meeting on September 23, see CZA A125/18N.

120 "To my great regret": HS to People's Council, October 13, 1917, CZA A125/18N.

121 "An almost feminine charm": Ronald Storrs, *The Memoirs of Sir Ronald Storrs* (New York, 1937), p. 439.

122 "It is a great cause": Weizmann, *Trial and Error*, p. 154.

122 Weizmann given carte blanche: Ibid., p. 173.

123 "England would have an effective barrier": Laqueur, *History of Zionism*, p. 183.

123 For months he had been urging Brandeis: Urofsky, *American Zionism*, pp. 205–206.

124 Balfour himself was not eager: Christopher Sykes, *Crossroads to Israel* (London, 1965), p. 8.

125 "Military authorities will allow entry": Joint Archives #124, January 12, 1918.

126 On the AZMU, see the pamphlet, "American Zionist Medical Unit" (Zionist Organization of America, 1919), and Levin, *Balm in Gilead*.

126 Contracts . . . "to minister to the needs of the people": AZMU folder, Hadassah, April 11, 1918.

127 AZMU departs in June 1918: Levin, *Balm in Gilead*, pp. 34–39.

127 Dr. Hirsch's withdrawal: Miller, *History of Hadassah*, p. 101.

128 De Haas's selection of personnel "irresponsible": Rubinow to HS, May 6, 1919, Hadassah.

128 Rubinow not a Zionist: I. M. Rubinow, "Henrietta Szold—An Appreciation," *Hadassah Newsletter*, December 1930.

129 Advice given to Dushkin: Alexander M. Dushkin, *Living Bridges: Memoirs of an Educator* (Jerusalem, 1975), p. 24.

129 "They respected her, but they knew": Interview with Alexander Dushkin, Jerusalem, 1975.

129 "I was a missionary": Dushkin interview.

129 for Emanuel Neumann, see his *In the Arena* (New York: 1976), p. 43.

130 "I arranged a citywide basketball tournament": Interview with Max Cohen, Brooklyn, 1974.

131 "The Zionist movement in Europe": Urofsky, *American Zionism*, p. 262.

131 f. On the attitude of the Russians toward the AZMU, see Rubinow's letters to HS in late 1919, Hadassah, and Urofsky, *American Zionism*, p. 268.

132 "filthy dirty": Miller, *History of Hadassah*, p. 251.

133 "On the other hand": Friedenwald to HS, March 5, 1919, Hadassah, HMO folder.

133 For Rubinow's letters, see Hadassah Archives, HMO files.
134 Brandeis had approached: Yonathan Shapiro, *Leadership of the American Zionist Organization, 1897–1930* (Urbana: 1971), p. 137; see also Urofsky, *American Zionism*, p. 267.
134 "She kissed me": Max Cohen interview.

IV. JERUSALEM: AT THE HÔTEL DE FRANCE

The account of the journey to Palestine and the first days there relies on Miss Szold's travel diary, AJA 386H. Her correspondence with Rubinow (Hadassah) and her letters home discuss the troubles of the Unit. The picture of Palestine comes from a variety of sources, especially Christopher Sykes's *Crossroads to Israel* (London, 1965); Albert Hyamson's *Palestine Under the Mandate* (London, 1965), and Storrs, *Memoirs*. Amos Elon's *The Israelis: Founders and Sons* (New York, 1971) provides a unique sense of the era. For American Zionism, see Urofsky, *American Zionism*; Miller, *History of Hadassah*, and Yonathan Shapiro's *Leadership of the American Zionist Organization*. Differences between the Weizmann and Brandeis factions are discussed at length on pp. 246–298 of Urofsky and in several sections of Shapiro. For Zionist history in general during this period, see Laqueur, *History of Zionism*.

Page

137 The Italian steamer: the travel diary AJA 386H furnishes much of the material from here to p. 152.
138 For an account of the 1920 riots, see Storrs, *Memoirs*, pp 346–347.
141 In 1920 the Yishuv: Laqueur, *Zionism*, p. 447; also Sykes, *Crossroads to Israel*, p. 25.
141 at the rate of about a thousand: according to Robert Szold, in Barnard, *Forging of an American Jew*, p. 264. For one-third who left, see Elon, *Israelis*, p. 136.
141 "They come in boat loads": Barnard, *Forging of an American Jew*, p. 264.
141 "I am certain": David Farrar, *The Warburgs: The Story of a Family* (New York, 1975), p. 103.
143 "We must raise a generation": Elon, *Israelis*, p. 137.
143 Zipporah Bentov: Irma Lindheim, *Parallel Quest* (New York, 1962), p. 440.
143 suicide: Elon, *Israelis*, p. 144.
144 "In the early days": Yosef Criden and Saadia Gelb, *The Kibbutz Experience: Dialogue in Kfar Blum* (New York, 1974), p. 129.
145 oil, only oil: See Sykes, *Crossroads*, p. 8 ff; also Jon Kimche, *There Could Have Been Peace* (New York, 1973), p. 63.
146 To one educated Arab: See Edward Atiyah, *An Arab Tells His Story* (London, 1946), p. 201 ff.
148 "steam tractor": Rubinow to HS, November 10, 1919, Hadassah, HMO folder.
149 Reuben Katznelson: Interview with Katznelson, Tel Aviv, 1975.
149 For this reason: Shapiro, *Leadership of the American Zionist Organization*, p. 143.
150 "made the statement privately": Rubinow to HS, November 29, 1919, Hadassah, HMO folder.
150 What Rubinow did not say: Several informants confirm the story of this relationship, including Dr. Rubinow's son, Raymond S. Rubinow of New York.

151 He was a westerner: Although born in Eastern Europe, Rubinow came to the United States at the age of eighteen; by his mid-forties he was thoroughly Americanized.

151 "They disregarded everything": Feigenbaum interview.

152 f. Storrs on Ussishkin: Storrs, *Memoirs*, p. 441.

154 "the ugliest woman": Interview with Leah Becker, Jerusalem, 1975.

154 "a mine of information": Interview with Jonathan Magnes, Jerusalem, 1975.

155 "As I stepped": Storrs, *Memoirs*, p. 354.

155 "Received": John Lord, *Duty, Honor, Empire: The Life and Times of Col. Richard Meinertzhagen* (New York: 1970), p. 372.

156 "to pare the nails": C. K. Ashbee, *Palestine Notebook* (New York: 1923), p. 273.

158 Kagan's view of Miss Szold: Interview with Helena Kagan, Jerusalem, 1974.

159 "More than one hundred": Translation of an undated letter signed by a Dr. Barouchine and forwarded by HS to the ZOA with a cover letter dated October 25, 1920, Hadassah, HMO folder.

159 One day that fall a young chalutz: Interview with Arieh Lifschutz, Jerusalem, 1975.

161 They had other ideas: Based partly on interviews with Shulamith Cantor, Jerusalem, 1974.

162 "Miss Szold had let it be known": Interview with Bathsheba Katznelson, Tel Aviv, 1975.

162 For the London Jahreskonferenz, see Urofsky, *American Zionism*, p. 272 ff.

163 membership in the ZOA: See Urofsky, *American Zionism*, p. 270.

165 Adele on Lawrence and marriage: Lawrence, Letters, pp. 175–177.

166 "I feel pretty sure I understand": Adele to HS, February 24, 1921, CZA N file.

168 For description of the Mufti, see Sykes, *Crossroads*, p. 159.

170 Miss Szold on the Arabs: "Familiar Letters from Palestine," #4, May 3, 1921, Hadassah.

171 Weizmann's visit to America: Weizmann, *Trial and Error*, p. 266; also Meyer Weisgal, *So Far* (New York, 1971), p. 59.

171 Brandeis people thought Weizmann's visit an insult: Barnard, *Forging of an American Jew*, p. 279.

173 Hadassah dispute over sending formal greeting to Weizmann: Miller, *History of Hadassah*, p. 122.

175 "a bomb is safer": Zeitlin, *Henrietta Szold: Record of a Life*, p. 109.

175 Miss Szold weeping: Both Max Cohen and Shulamith Cantor saw this.

179 f. Emma Gottheil to HS, December 12, 1922, CZA A125/32.

181 On infant care, see HS letter to Hadassah, "Familiar Letters from Palestine," #7, August 3, 1922, Hadassah.

182 "I seem to sow": Bentwich, *For Zion's Sake: A Biography of Judah L. Magnes* (Philadelphia, 1954), p. 126.

V. JERUSALEM: MISS SZOLD CROSSES THE STREET

This section relies on interviews and correspondence with Dr. Michael Bluestone; also Miller, *History of Hadassah;* Laqueur, *History of Zionism;* Urofsky, *American Zion-*

ism; Shapiro, *Leadership of the American Zionist Organization;* and Lindheim, *Parallel Quest.* Hyamson, *Palestine Under the Mandate,* and Sykes, *Crossroads to Israel,* provide background on Palestine. Discussion of the school system is based largely on Noach Nardi's *Zionism and Education in Palestine* (New York, 1934).

Page

185   "I know she loved us": Interview with Sara Levin Cooper, Baltimore, 1974.

185   Jastrow Levin's comments: Interview with Jastrow Levin, Baltimore, 1974.

185   "I wanted my children to know": Interview with Zip Szold, New York, 1974.

186   Dr. E. M. Bluestone: Interviews with him in Santa Monica, 1974, and New York, 1977.

188   Weizmann repeatedly asked her: CZA N file, September 15, 1927.

190   Yussef the Yemenite orderly: E. M. Bluestone, "The Humorous Side of Medical Life in Palestine," unpublished MS in Dr. Bluestone's possession, p. 2.

193   D. H. Lawrence and Seltzer trial: *Lawrence, Letters,* pp. 182–192.

196   Americans of the Brandeis faction: According to a personal communication from Sarah K. Stein (Mrs. Leonard Stein).

197   "a dagger struck": *Davar,* December 9, 1927.

197   "Pray for me": Neumann, *In the Arena,* p. 43.

197   Adele's letter to HS: November 18, 1927, CZA N file.

198   "It is impossible": Telegram from Haifa, December 13, 1927, CZA A125/23.

200   "She would have liked": Harry Sacher, *Zionist Portraits* (London, 1959), p. 97.

200   "Weizmann couldn't smell her": Interview in Jerusalem with a source who prefers to remain anonymous.

200   relations between Plumer and HS: Zeitlin, *Henrietta Szold: Record of a Life,* p. 77.

201   Hadassah's 1927 convention: *Hadassah Newsletter,* August 1927.

201   "Palestine can no longer": Lindheim to HS, April 10, 1928, Hadassah; folder Mrs. Norvin Lindheim 1927–1928.

202   *New York Times* article: *Times,* March 31, 1928, p. 7.

202   "What was formerly": Louis Lipsky, "What Will Hadassah Do?" *The New Palestine,* June 8, 1928, p. 593.

202 f.   raucous demonstration for Lipsky: Miller, *History of Hadassah,* p. 176.

203   "The danger now": HS message to the delegates to the convention of the ZOA at Pittsburgh, June 1928; Hadassah, folder Miss Szold's Convention Messages.

203 f.   Fourth of July baseball game: William Schack, "On the Horizon," *Commentary,* April 1949.

205   "this type of fighting democrats": Interview with Ernst Simon, Jerusalem, 1975.

206   "Now we proceed": Katznelson interview.

207   agricultural settlements numbered: Zeitlin, *Henrietta Szold: Record of a Life,* p. 111.

208   Edwin Samuel: Interview with Edwin Samuel, Jerusalem, 1975.

208   "She certainly realized": Simon interview.

208   "Here in Palestine": HS to the National Board of Hadassah, March 23, 1929, Hadassah, National Board file.

211   "The situation here": Vincent Sheean, *Personal History* (New York, 1940), p. 389.

211   "The houses on the other side": Ibid., pp. 389–90.

212   "like the ominous buzz of bees": Edwin Samuel, *A Lifetime in Jerusalem* (Jerusalem, 1970), p. 106.

212   "made my first acquaintance": Sheean, *Personal History*, p. 398–99.

213   A physician who went to Hebron: Interview with Chava Danziger Magnes, Jerusalem, 1975.

213   "If Hadassah had done nothing else": Levin, *Balm of Gilead*, p. 110.

214   "The Jews were restricting themselves": Sheean, *Personal History*, p. 401.

214   Sheean on Haj Amin: Ibid., p. 402.

214 f.   HS and Weizmann discuss Warburg's attitude: HS to Felix Warburg, December 23, 1929, Hadassah.

215 f.   Warburg attempts to soothe the wounds: Warburg to HS, January 10, 1930, Hadassah.

216   "rich experience": *Davar*, April 8, 1930.

217   "I cannot bear arms": Zeitlin, *Henrietta Szold: Record of a Life*, p. 118.

218   Sykes on the Mufti: Sykes, *Crossroads to Israel*, p. 155.

219   "How dare you subject me": Interview with Tamar de Sola Pool, New York, 1974.

VI. JERUSALEM: A MOTHER OF MANY CHILDREN

The history of Youth Aliyah can be found in two mimeographed pamphlets written at the request of Hadassah: Marian Greenberg's "Youth Aliyah under Henrietta Szold" (New York, 1960), and Zena Herman, "Henrietta Szold and Youth Aliyah" (Jerusalem, n.d., probably 1945). Both help to make this intricate history understandable. *Balm in Gilead* by Marlin Levin has anecdotal material on the movement. Norman Bentwich, *Jewish Youth Comes Home* (London, 1944), is useful. Two short pieces by Chanoch Rinott (Reinhold), a pamphlet, *Dynamics of Youth Aliyah Groups* (Jerusalem, 1953), and an article, "Major Trends in Jewish Youth Movements in Germany," *Yearbook of the Leo Baeck Institute* (London, 1974), provide insight into the philosophy and workings of Youth Aliyah. For the life and work of Recha Freier, see her *Let the Children Come: The Early History of Youth Aliyah* (London, 1961).

This section also relies on Akiva W. Deutsch, "The Development of Social Work as a Profession in the Jewish Community in Eretz, Israel" (Jerusalem, 1970), in Hebrew but with extensive English summary, and for developments in Palestine, Hyamson, *Palestine Under the Mandate;* Sykes, *Crossroads to Israel;* and Laqueur, *History of Zionism.*

Page

223   a decree by Ronald Storrs: See Storrs, *Memoirs*, pp. 326–332.

224   "It was the most interesting": Interview with Shulamith Cantor.

224   "Miss Szold never was a part": Interview with Sylva Gelber, London, 1974.

225   "I can remember": Gelber interview.

226   The Emir Abdullah: Levin, *Balm of Gilead*, p. 175.

227   "The question is not": Deutsch, "Development of Social Work," p. 42.

228   Japhet quotes: Interview with Chaim Japhet, Tel Aviv, 1975.

228   The plan itself: See *Social Service Bulletin* #12, July-September 1936, Hadassah; also "Social Service in Palestine," an unpublished paper by Henrietta Szold, 1932; Hadassah.

229 "the push of reality": Interview with Recha Freier, Jerusalem, 1975.

229 "She seemed utterly disorganized": Karl Stern, *Pillar of Fire* (New York, 1951), p. 66.

229 Freier and the group of adolescent boys: Freier, *Let the Children Come*, pp. 9 ff.

230 "My mother has gone": Interview with Shalhevet Freier, Tel Aviv, 1975.

230 HS as juvenile probation officer: HS to Mrs. Emanuel Borenstein, December 13, 1935, Hadassah.

231 the visit to Tul Karm: Interview with Zipporah Bloch, Jerusalem, 1974.

233 "The platform seemed": Freier, *Let the Children Come*, p. 17.

233 Since the first decade: For the history of the *Wandervogel*, see Walter Laqueur, *Young Germany*, (London: 1962).

235 The effect of the new dispensation: Freier, *Let the Children Come*, p. 22.

236 Mrs. Freier replied: Freier interview.

238 immigration figures: Sykes, *Crossroads to Israel*, p. 166.

238 HS overheard a conversation: Lowenthal interview with HS.

241 It must be noted: Interview with Hanoch Rinott (Reinhold), Jerusalem, 1975.

245 "We brought with us Kafka": Rinott interview.

245 But rumors had arisen: Exchange of letters in April and May 1934 between HS and a Dr. Prager of Haifa, CZA A125/98.

246 one of her young secretaries: Interview with Lotte Steigbügl, Haifa, 1975.

246 f. Description of the start of the social work school: Gelber and Chava Magnes interviews.

248 hired a young social worker: Interview with Carl Frankenstein, Jerusalem, 1975.

248 For the present status of Oriental Jews in Israel, see Ferdynand Zweig, *The Sword and the Harp* (London, 1969), pp. 115–24, and Alice and Roy Eckardt, *Encounter with Israel* (New York, 1970), pp. 85 ff; also *Jerusalem Post*, November 23, 1976, p. 11.

248 suicide rate: Noach Nardi, *Zionism and Education in Palestine* (New York, 1934), p. 71.

249 "People grumbled": Chava Magnes interview.

249 One observer recalled: Gelber interview.

250 preference in immigration to East European Jews: Sykes, *Crossroads to Israel*, p. 169 ff.

250 "resorting to our youth certificates": HS to Georg Josephthal in Berlin, December 20, 1934, CZA 125/94.

251 "On the one side": Interview with Lotte Beyth, Jerusalem, 1975.

253 "brook no interference": HS to Lola Hahn-Warburg, September 14, 1936, CZA A125/94.

253 f. HS at the Lucerne Congress: See *Protocol of the 19th Zionist Congress*, CZA, p. 182 ff.

255 f. For Miss Szold's speech, see CZA A125/83.

256 Eva Stern . . . wondered: A series of interviews with Eva Stern Michaelis, Jerusalem, 1975.

257 The man who became principal: Interview with Franz Ollendorff, Haifa, 1975.

257 a pitched battle: For a detailed account see Levin, *Balm of Gilead*, chap. 10.

257 ff. For HS visit to America: Interviews with Tamar de Sola Pool and Marian Greenberg, New York, 1975.

259   La Guardia's speech: Fineman, *Woman of Valor*, p. 379.

259   the . . . homage to Recha Freier: CZAA125/83.

259   "As she grew older": Lotte Steigbügl interview.

260   "Nobody could say": Lotte Beyth interview.

264   nervous, defensive: See "Proceedings of the Palestine Royal Commission, Thirty-fourth Meeting," CZA, especially p. 23.

265   "The British Government failed": CZA A125/30.

266   Miss Szold's letter to Magnes: October 10, 1937, CZA A125/30.

268   "definite warnings": CZA N file, April 13, 1938.

269   Eva Stern approached by Eichmann: Eva Stern Michaelis interviews.

270   For an account of the Evian conference, see Sykes, *Crossroads to Israel*, p. 222 ff.

271   To Hadassah she wrote: HS to Marian Greenberg, June 2, 1938, CZA S75/536.

272   When she was very angry: Shulamit Cantor interview.

272   Hans Beyth's marriage: Interview with Lotte Beyth.

274 f.   Miss Szold's correspondence with Hadassah: See particularly a series of letters in late 1938, CZA S75/770, and early 1939, CZA S75/771.

275   "One has to ask": HS to Stern, July 12, 1938, CZA A125/101.

276   Eventually Gestapo agents: Sykes, *Crossroads to Israel*, p. 264 ff.

278   "I could not do": Kagan interview.

279   Teenaged representatives: Marie Syrkin, *Blessed Is the Match* (New York, 1947), p. 194.

279 ff.   The account of Youth Aliyah's London headquarters during the first days of war comes from an unpublished diary kept by Eva Stern for the period August 25 to September 7.

282   More than 26,000 Palestinian Jews: According to a private communication from Michael Heymann of the Central Zionist Archives, who puts the figures at 26,000 to 30,000.

282   "You are my home, Toby": *D. H. Lawrence Letters*, p. 197.

283   News of Adele's death: Interview with Lotte Beyth.

283   "You see the way she had of looking at me": Arieh Lifshutz interview.

285   "Almost every comrade is bitten": "Flight from Grochow," a report by Bernard Gelbart, January 5, 1940, CZA A125/101, p. 3.

286   For ten days a ship: Arthur Koestler, *Promise and Fulfillment* (New York, 1949), pp. 60 ff.

287   the explosion had been a bungled act of sabotage: Sykes, *Crossroads*, pp. 269–270.

288   Now Miss Szold met: HS to Marian Greenberg, February 18, 1941, CZA A125/101.

289 f.   Recha Freier leaves Germany and travels to Palestine: See Freier, *Let the Children Come*, p. 64 ff.

289   the boy with polio: Steigbügl interview.

290   a meeting of Youth Aliyah leaders: Interviews with Simon and Rinott.

290   a meeting was arranged: Interview with Shalhevet Freier. For HS letter to Recha Freier, see April 27, 1941, CZA A125/85.

291   "There are two sides": Freier, *Let the Children Come*, p. 75.

291   Incident at Kiryat Anavim: Recha Freier interview.

291   A short story: "The Judgment of Solomon," by Yehuda Yaari, reprinted in Gerda
      Charles, ed., *Modern Jewish Stories* (Englewood Cliffs, N.J.: Prentice-Hall,
      1963).

291   Recha Freier published an account: *Let the Children Come.*

292 f. Chanoch Reinhold material: Rinott interview.

294   "War has now come near": Bentwich, *Jewish Youth Comes Home*, pp. 102–
      103.

295   a new terrorism: see Laqueur, *History of Zionism*, p. 377, and Sykes, *Crossroads
      to Israel*, p. 294.

296   Both Buber and Magnes: Simon interview.

297   For the formation of Ihud, see Bentwich, *For Zion's Sake*, p. 248 ff, and Susan
      Lee Hattis, *The Bi-National Idea in Palestine During Mandatory Times* (Tel Aviv,
      1970), p. 258 ff.

297   neither Miss Szols nor Magnes: According to a letter from HS to Rose Jacobs,
      June 7, 1943, CZA 125/35.

297   But descriptions of Ihud flew: See Maurice Perlzweig in October 16, 1942, issue
      of *Congress Weekly.*

298   Hadassah sent her a cable: According to a letter from HS to Tamar Pool, September
      6, 1942, CZA A125/151.

298   A friend of Magnes's: Dr. Jack Kligler. His running account of the ZOA-Hadassah
      conventions is found in CZA A125/152.

298   lengthy and anguished discussions: See Kligler's account; also an interview with
      Judith Epstein, New York, 1977.

298   Miss Szold was deeply hurt: According to Epstein.

298   In Palestine the reaction: HS to Tamar Pool, November 8, 1942, and January
      1, 1943, CZA A125/152.

298   A newspaper headline: HS to Bertha Levin, September 25, 1942, CZA N file.

299   A politically open-minded writer: Prefers to remain unnamed.

299   assassinated by fellow Arabs: Laqueur, *History of Zionism*, p. 267.

300   "Quick action": HS to the Commission for Immigration, September 1, 1942,
      CZA 125/104.

300   "not the dictator": HS to Hadassah, November 9, 1936, CZA S75/364.

300   "constrained to admit": HS to Tamar Pool, August 4, 1942, CZA A125/86.
      On January 8, 1942 Magnes wrote to Mrs. Pool, "Please do not be surprised if
      I say that there is no management committee of the Youth Aliyah . . . it is
      Miss Szold who is the Management Committee" (CZA A125/111).

301   "We cried for our lost childhood": Chasya Pincus, *Come from the Four Winds,*
      (New York: 1970), p. 85.

302   "Broadcast condemnations": Jewish Agency to ZOA, November 25, 1942, CZA
      A125/104.

302   three days of ritual mourning: *Palestine Post*, December 1–3, 1942.

303 f. Hadassah secures safe passage for Teheran children: Levin, *Balm of Gilead,*
      pp. 179–80.

306   reactions of Teheran children: Pincus, *Come from the Four Winds*, pp. 74 ff.

307   Two children enter: The interviews of Gisia and Selig are taken from an unpublished
      playlet written by Chanoch Rinott for Miss Szold's 83rd birthday, CZA A125/
      87.

311 f.   children from Trans-Dniestrian camps: Marian Greenberg, "Youth Aliyah under
         Henrietta Szold," pp. 86–88.
313 f.   Magnes's account of Miss Szold's last days: Judah Magnes, "Last Days," a
         diary sent to Hadassah, mimeographed, Hadassah.
315   "With her death a sigh": Arieh Lifshutz, *Henrietta Szold: The Educator of Youth
         Aliyah* (Jerusalem, 1955), p. 27.
315   Recha Freier came and watched: Recha Freier interview.

AFTERWARDS

Data on Youth Aliyah and Hadassah comes from recent Hadassah publicity and
from Judith Epstein.

Bibliography

BOOKS

Adler, Cyrus. *I Have Considered the Days.* Philadelphia: Jewish Publication Society of America, 1941.

Ashbee, C. R. *Palestine Notebook.* New York: Doubleday, Page, 1923.

Atiyah, Edward. *An Arab Tells His Story.* London: John Murray, 1946.

Barnard, Harry. *The Forging of an American Jew: The Life of Judge Julian Mack.* New York: Herzl Press, 1974.

Beirne, Francis F. *The Amiable Baltimoreans.* New York: E. P. Dutton, 1951.

Bentwich, Norman. *Jewish Youth Comes Home.* London: Victor Gollancz, 1944.

———. *My Seventy-Seven Years: An Account of My Life and Times.* Philadelphia: Jewish Publication Society of America, 1961.

———. *Solomon Schechter: A Biography.* Philadelphia: Jewish Publication Society of America, 1938.

———. *For Zion's Sake: A Biography of Judah L. Magnes.* Philadelphia: Jewish Publication Society of America, 1954.

Bentwich, Norman, and Bentwich, Helen. *Mandate Memories: 1918–1948.* New York: Schocken Books, 1965.

Bogen, Boris D. *Born a Jew.* New York: Macmillan Co., 1930.

Cohen, Aharon. *Israel and the Arab World.* New York: Funk & Wagnalls, 1970.

Criden, Yosef, and Gelb, Saadia. *The Kibbutz Experience: Dialogue in Kfar Blum.* New York: Herzl Press, 1974.

Davis, Moshe. *The Emergence of Conservative Judaism.* Philadelphia: Jewish Publication Society of America, 1963.

Dushkin, Alexander M. *Living Bridges: Memoirs of an Educator.* Jerusalem: Keter, 1975.

Eckardt, Alice, and Eckardt, Roy. *Encounter with Israel.* New York: Association Press, 1970.

Elon, Amos. *Herzl.* New York: Holt, Rinehart & Winston, 1975.

———. *The Israelis: Founders and Sons.* New York: Holt, Rinehart & Winston, 1971.

Engle, Anita. *The Nili Spies.* London: Hogarth Press, 1959.

Farrar, David. *The Warburgs: The Story of a Family.* New York: Stein & Day, 1975.

Fineman, Irving. *Woman of Valor.* New York: Simon & Schuster, 1961.

337

Freier, Recha. *Let the Children Come: The Early History of Youth Aliyah.* London: Weidenfeld & Nicolson, 1961.

Furlonge, Geoffrey. *Palestine is My Country: The Story of Musa Alami.* London: John Murray, 1969.

Ginzberg, Eli. *Keeper of the Law: Louis Ginzberg.* Philadelphia: Jewish Publication Society of America, 1966.

Grunberger, Richard. *The Twelve Year Reich.* New York: Holt, Rinehart & Winston, 1971.

Halperin, Samuel. *The Political World of American Zionism.* Detroit: Wayne State University Press, 1961.

Hattis, Susan Lee. *The Bi-National Idea in Palestine During Mandatory Times.* Tel Aviv: Shikmona, 1970.

Hyamson, Albert M. *Palestine Under the Mandate.* London: Methuen, 1950.

Jeffries, J. M. N. *Palestine: The Reality.* London: Longmans, Green, 1939.

Kimche, Jon. *There Could Have Been Peace.* New York: Dial Press, 1973.

Kisch, F. H. *Palestine Diary.* London: Victor Gollancz, 1938.

Koestler, Arthur. *Promise and Fulfillment.* New York: Macmillan, 1949.

Laqueur, Walter. *A History of Zionism.* New York: Holt, Rinehart & Winston, 1972.

———. *Young Germany.* London: Routledge & Kegan Paul, 1962.

Lawrence, D. H. *Letters to Thomas and Adele Seltzer.* Edited by Gerald M. Lacy. Santa Barbara, Calif.: Black Sparrow Press, 1976.

Lawrenson, Helen. *Stranger at the Party: A Memoir.* New York: Random House, 1975.

Learsi, Rufus. *The Jews in America: A History.* Cleveland: World Publishing, 1954.

Levin, Alexandra Lee. *Dare to Be Different: A Biography of Louis H. Levin of Baltimore, a Pioneer in Jewish Social Service.* New York: Bloch, 1972.

———. *The Szolds of Lombard Street: A Baltimore Family, 1859–1909.* Philadelphia: Jewish Publication Society of America, 1960.

———. *Vision: A Biography of Harry Friedenwald.* Philadelphia: Jewish Publication Society of America, 1964.

Levin, Marlin. *Balm in Gilead: The Story of Hadassah.* New York: Schocken Books, 1973.

Levinger, Elma Ehrlich. *Fighting Angel: The Story of Henrietta Szold.* New York: Behrman House, 1946.

Lindheim, Irma. *Parallel Quest.* New York: Thomas Yoseloff, 1962.

Louis Ginzberg Jubilee Volume. New York: American Academy for Jewish Research, 1945.

Lifschutz, Arieh. *Henrietta Szold: The Educator of Youth Aliyah.* Jerusalem: Jewish Agency in Israel, Division of Children and Youth, 1955.

Lord, John. *Duty, Honor, Empire: The Life and Times of Col. Richard Meinertzhagen.* New York: Random House, 1970.

Lowenthal, Marvin. *Henrietta Szold, Life and Letters.* New York: Viking Press, 1942.

Meinertzhagen, Richard. *Middle East Diary.* London: Cresset Press, 1959.

Meyer, Isidore S., ed. *Early History of Zionism in America.* New York: American Jewish Historical Society and Theodor Herzl Foundation, 1958.

Miller, D. H. *A History of Hadassah, 1912–1935.* Ph.D. thesis. Ann Arbor, Michigan: University Microfilms, 1968.

Morse, Arthur D. *While Six Million Died: A Chronicle of American Apathy.* New York: Random House, 1967.

Nardi, Noach. *Zionism and Education in Palestine.* New York: Teachers' College, Columbia University, 1934.

Neumann, Emanuel. *In the Arena.* New York: Herzl Press, 1976.

Parzen, Herbert. *Architects of Conservative Judaism.* New York: Jonathan David, 1964.

Peterson, H. C., and Fite, Gilbert C. *Opponents of War, 1917–1918.* Seattle: University of Washington Press, 1968.

Pincus, Chasya. *Come from the Four Winds.* New York: Herzl Press, 1970.

Rosenblatt, Bernard A. *Two Generations of Zionism: Historical Recollections of an American Zionist.* New York: Shengold, 1967.

Ruppin, Arthur. *Memoirs, Diaries, Letters.* London: Weidenfeld & Nicolson, 1971.

Sachar, Howard M. *The Emergence of the Middle East, 1914–1924.* New York: Alfred A. Knopf, 1969.

Sacher, Harry. *Zionist Portraits.* London: Anthony Blond, 1959.

Samuel, Edwin. *A Lifetime in Jerusalem.* Jerusalem: Israel Universities Press, 1970.

Scott, Ann Firor. *The Southern Lady: From Pedestal to Politics, 1830–1930.* Chicago: University of Chicago Press, 1970.

Shapiro, Yonathan. *Leadership of the American Zionist Organization, 1897–1930.* Urbana: University of Illinois Press, 1971.

Sheean, Vincent. *Personal History.* New York: Random House, 1940.

Stern, Karl. *Pillar of Fire.* New York: Harcourt Brace, 1951.

Stewart, Desmond. *Herzl, Artist and Politician.* Garden City, N.Y.: Doubleday, 1974.

Storrs, Ronald. *The Memoirs of Sir Ronald Storrs.* New York: G. P. Putnam's Sons, 1937.

Syrkin, Marie. *Blessed Is the Match.* New York: Alfred A. Knopf, 1947.

Sykes, Christopher. *Crossroads to Israel.* London: Collins, 1965.

Szold, Henrietta. *Recent Jewish Progress in Palestine.* Philadelphia: Jewish Publication Society of America, 1915.

Tsur, Jakob. *Sunrise in Zion.* London: Allen & Unwin, 1968.

Urofsky, Melvin. *American Zionism from Herzl to the Holocaust.* Garden City, N.Y.: Anchor Press/Doubleday, 1975.

———. *A Mind of One Piece: Brandeis and American Reform.* New York: Charles Scribner's Sons, 1971.

Wedgwood, Josiah C. *Memoirs of a Fighting Life.* London: Hutchinson & Co., 1941.

Weisgal, Meyer. *So Far.* New York: Random House, 1971.

Weizmann, Chaim. *Trial and Error.* New York: Schocken Books, 1966.

Zeitlin, Rose. *Henrietta Szold: Record of a Life.* New York: Dial Press, 1952.

Zweig, Ferdynand. *Israel: The Sword and the Harp.* London: Heinemann Educational, 1969.

ARTICLES, PAMPHLETS, AND UNPUBLISHED MATERIAL

American Zionist Medical Unit for Palestine. New York: Zionist Organization of America, 1919.

Deutsch, Akiva W. "The Development of Social Work as a Profession in the Jewish

Community in Eretz Israel." Jerusalem: Ph.D. thesis submitted to the Senate of Hebrew University, 1970.

Greenberg, Marian. "Youth Aliyah Under Henrietta Szold." Mimeographed. New York: Hadassah, 1960.

Halpern, Ben. "Brandeis' Way to Judaism." *Midstream,* October 1971.

Hartogensis, Benjamin H. "The Russian Night School of Baltimore." *American Jewish Historical Society Magazine,* 1928.

Herman, Zena. "Henrietta Szold and Youth Aliyah." Manuscript based on a collection of Henrietta Szold's letters for the period 1934–1944. Mimeographed, n.d., probably 1945. Central Zionist Archives, Jerusalem.

Kol, Moshe. *Youth Aliyah: Past, Present and Future.* Jerusalem: International Federation of Children's Communities, 1957.

Levin, Alexandra Lee. "Henrietta Szold and the Jewish Publication Society." Paper delivered at the 73rd Annual Meeting of the JPS. *JPS Bookmark,* June 1961.

———. "Henrietta Szold and the Russian Immigrant School." *Maryland Historical Magazine,* March 1962.

Lipsky, Louis. "What Will Hadassah Do?" *The New Palestine,* June 8, 1928.

Rinott, Chanoch. *Dynamics of Youth Aliyah Groups.* Jerusalem: Henrietta Szold Foundation for Youth and Child Welfare, 1953.

———. "Major Trends in Jewish Youth Movements in Germany." *Yearbook of the Leo Baeck Institute,* London: East-West Library, 1974.

Rosenblatt, Mrs. B. A. (Gertrude Goldsmith). Extracts from diaries concerning the early years of Hadassah for the years 1911–1914. Haifa, 1934. Mimeographed and available in Hadassah Archives.

Rubinow, I. M. "Henrietta Szold—An Appreciation," *Hadassah Newsletter,* December 1930.

Schack, William. "On the Horizon." *Commentary,* April 1949.

Straus-Mochenson, Nellie. *Our Palestine.* Tel Aviv: n.p., 1939.

Szold, Henrietta. "Early Zionist Days in Baltimore." *Maccabean,* June–July 1917.

Weisgal, Meyer. "A Tribute to Henrietta Szold." *Hadassah Magazine,* February 1973.

Index